Resurgent Voices in
Latin America

D1198691

Resurgent Voices in Latin America

INDIGENOUS PEOPLES, POLITICAL MOBILIZATION, AND RELIGIOUS CHANGE

EDITED BY
EDWARD L. CLEARY
TIMOTHY J. STEIGENGA

RUTGERS UNIVERSITY PRESS
New Brunswick, New Jersey, and London

LIBRARY OF CONGRESS CATALOGING-IN-PUBLICATION DATA

Resurgent voices in Latin America : indigenous peoples, political mobilization, and religious change / edited by Edward L. Cleary and Timothy J. Steigenga.
    p.   cm.
Includes bibliographical references and index.
ISBN 0-8135-3460-7 (hardcover : alk. paper) — ISBN 0-8135-3461-5 (pbk. : alk. paper)
    1. Religion and sociology—Latin America.   2. Religion and politics—Latin America.   3. Latin America—Religion.   I. Cleary, Edward L.   II. Steigenga, Timothy J., 1965–
    BL2540.R47 2004
    306.6'098—dc22

                                                                      2004000300

A British Cataloging-in-Publication record for this book is available
from the British Library

Manufactured in the United States of America

Contents

Acknowledgments

THREE YEARS of work on this book have engendered a number of debts to editors, readers, and contributors. Rutgers editors Kristi Long and David Myers made major contributions to encouraging the project and shaping the manuscript. We express our special gratitude to the reader of the proposal and manuscript, Manuel Vasquez, who provided invaluable insight and direction during both the initial stages of the project and the final editing of the text. Timothy Steigenga would also like to thank David Smilde, Jerónimo Camposeco, Rachel Corr, Dennis Smith, and Johanna Sharp for reading portions of the manuscript and providing comments to the authors. Edward Cleary was especially aided by discussions with Xavier Albó, Stephen Judd, Jeffrey Klaiber, Andrew Orta, and Samuel Escobar. The Wilkes Honor College of Florida Atlantic University and Providence College furnished essential support at various stages of research, travel, and manuscript preparation. Colleagues in Providence College's political science department were also generous in their support.

Pioneers, such as June Nash, Donna Van Cott, and Xavier Albó, and newcomers in scholarly research on indigenous movements assisted the authors in assessing the relations between indigenous activism and religion. We are especially indebted to the pastors, priests, indigenous leaders, and other individuals who have given of their time and efforts both in the struggle for indigenous rights in Latin American and in our attempts to understand that struggle.

This book is dedicated to Adaeze Norget and Lucy Steigenga, who were born, along with an initial draft of the manuscript, in December 2002.

*Resurgent Voices in
Latin America*

CHAPTER 1

Resurgent Voices

INDIANS, POLITICS, AND RELIGION
IN LATIN AMERICA

Edward L. Cleary and Timothy J. Steigenga

For the people in my village religion and politics were connected—they were basically the same thing. People became
most animated about issues relating to the festivals and the
church, and naturally political feelings would become involved. After all, we were used to these connections between
religion and politics, because traditional Mayan leaders served
both as religious and political authorities. Of course the nature of religious politics changed with the Pope, John Paul
XXIII, the whole church changed. For example, in Huehuetenango, the Maryknolls were the most influential. At first
their ideas were very North American, and they vehemently
opposed anything traditional. But after Vatican II, when the
Church began to change, they had some regrets about their
previous approach, and they became less interested in stop-
ping "pagan" practices. The important thing to understand is
that throughout this process, the people never completely
gave up their traditional beliefs, even if they had to practice
them in hiding.

—Jerónimo Camposeco

LATIN AMERICA is currently experiencing an indigenous
resurgence. From Mexico to the Andes, indigenous peoples have aggressively
stepped forward to demand their long-denied cultural, political, and economic
rights. The strength and depth of these movements first became publicly evident in the years leading up to the continent-wide celebration of the Fifth
Centenary of Spanish Conquest (1992). Latin America's indigenous groups
loudly protested the commemoration for downplaying the harm done to Indian peoples during the conquest. In the process, indigenous groups made

clear their demands for present-day changes in the political and economic arrangements of their countries.

The next ten years would witness the Zapatista rebellion in Chiapas, indigenous uprisings in Ecuador and Bolivia, and the growth of myriad national and transnational indigenous social movements and organizations. Indigenous peoples made an impact on national authorities like never before in the modern history of Latin America, toppling governments, demanding rights, and achieving significant positions in national representative assemblies. Although this resurgence appeared sudden and took most observers by surprise, the roots of indigenous mobilization are multiple and deep. Among those roots is the central focus of this study, the role of religion.

The common thread that runs through the contributions to this volume is that indigenous mobilization cannot be understood without a careful consideration of religious factors. While specific political openings and social and economic processes facilitated the indigenous resurgence, religious institutions, beliefs, and practices provided many of the resources, motivations, identities, and networks that nurtured the movement. In turn, indigenous religious practitioners have reshaped the religious field in Latin America.

AN INDIAN ACTIVIST'S STORY

Born in the late 1930s in the town of Jacaltenango, in Northwestern Guatemala, Jerónimo Camposeco viewed the interactions between religion and politics in Latin America from a perspective that spans generations, cultures, and borders. Jerónimo was raised in a Mayan Catholic household; his parents taught him both to follow Catholic teachings and to respect Mayan traditions. When he was born, his parents took care to ensure that the Mayan priests (Alcal Txah) were called to say prayers and burn *copal* (incense) both in his home and in the sacred places in the mountains. He was also taught to revere the Catholic saints and to participate in the many regional celebrations of patron saints.

When he was fifteen, Jerónimo convinced the Maryknoll priest in Jacaltenango to allow him to study at the seminary in Quezaltenango. Influenced by the teachings during his five years in the seminary and excited by the opportunity to work again with his own community, Jerónimo accepted a position as a teacher in a Maryknoll school in a village close to Jacaltenango. As Jerónimo explains, "The school was very strict in terms of Catholic doctrine and discipline, but we now attempted to instill respect for local traditions as well."

Years later, after completing his degree in education, Jerónimo took a position with the National Indigenous Institute in Guatemala City and began studies in anthropology at the University of San Carlos. He worked as an activist for indigenous causes, linking his work in Guatemala to other Native

American groups in North America and Mexico. His educational pursuit and his work with the institute were cut short, however, when he received death threats under Guatemala's military government in the early 1980s. He was forced to flee Guatemala with his wife and four children. Jerónimo's transnational connections with Guatemalan and North American indigenous organizations, forged during his years of work at the National Indigenous Institute, became a critical resource in his plight as a refugee and in the process of applying for political asylum in the United States. Now in his sixties, Jerónimo continues to work as an advocate for the Mayan immigrant community in South Florida.[1]

While Jerónimo's personal history is obviously unique, elements of his experiences reflect many of the larger processes examined in this study. Jerónimo is part of a generation of indigenous leaders in Latin America who gained access to educational and other resources through religious organizations. His political orientation was shaped, in part, by the changes going on within the Catholic Church. His experience as a teacher in a religious school, in turn, helped to shape the way a new generation of Mayans would practice their Catholicism. His work as an activist and an advocate for indigenous rights spans generations and national borders. As we examine the precipitant factors relating to indigenous mobilization in Latin America, Jerónimo's experience serves as a reference for the critical role of religion.

Before turning to the specific links between religion and indigenous activism in Latin America we should answer some prior questions. Who are the indigenous peoples of Latin America? Where they are located physically, socially, and economically? What is their present situation, and what are the demands they have brought to the attention of the governments of Latin America and the world?

LATIN AMERICA'S INDIGENOUS PEOPLES

Debates have flourished in academic and political circles for decades over the definition of "Indian." Social scientists in the 1960s and 1970s emphasized language and dress as major indicators of identity. Present-day social scientists and census-takers tend to use self-definition. Major exceptions exist, however. For example, in Peru's highlands almost all indigenous people are labeled (and call themselves) campesino (peasant). Thus, in Peru, the term "Indian" is reserved for the two hundred thousand or so indigenous people who live in the forest. So, too, the majority of Paraguayans are of Guaraní descent and speak that language, but only those who live in remote areas are considered *indios*. For practical purposes, we adopt a broader definition of indigenous peoples, one that encompasses elements of self-definition as distinct from dominant society, connections to precolonial society, and an interest in preserving elements and practices of ethnic identity.[2] Such a definition allows us to include a broad range of indigenous groups and transcends the particularities of national definitions that vary from state to state.

One way to describe the variety of indigenous groups in the Americas is through their geography and environment. Geography determines the ecological conditions that serve as the economic basis of life and culture for indigenous peoples. The ecological conditions of mountain and temperate or tropical lowland provided differences in natural resources that allowed for or inhibited vegetative or animal food sources for humans. Food-gathering established patterns of settled or nomadic life and served as a basis of culture and religion. Hence, neither Indian life in the Americas nor Indian religion can be understood without an understanding of the natural environment.[3]

In South America, anthropologists have found the greatest differences in environment and Indian culture between highland and lowland Indians. By far the larger numbers of Indians live in the mountains and their valleys. Here the cooler climate and somewhat greater ease in transportation provided the conditions for agricultural surplus and storage and communication between settlements. Economic surplus brought about economic classes, intellectual and ruling elites, leisure, and the conditions for a more sophisticated culture. Higher technologies and a measure of scientific achievement, as in astronomy and mathematics, followed.

The highland Indian groups inhabit the great Andean mountain range in western South America. The largest and best known groups are the Quechuas and the Aymaras. The much larger Quechua-language group is considered the main successor of the Inca people, an empire that extended hundreds of miles from Ecuador to northern Chile and Argentina. The Aymara can be found mostly in the Peruvian and Bolivian Altiplano, with a natural center occurring at Lake Titicaca. In a rough sense, they extend from Puno to La Paz, surrounded mostly by Quechua people.

The lowland peoples of South America are not as numerous and have greater language diversity than the highland groups. However, their contemporary political influence far exceeds their numbers. The lowlanders of the Andean countries mostly live in the Amazonian Basin, often on or near the great and small rivers that feed the Amazon River from the south and west. Indian peoples of southeastern Bolivia and Paraguay live in part of the Gran Chaco, a lowland area different from the Amazon region. Rough population estimates for these indigenous groups are 135,000 in Bolivia, 83,928 in Ecuador, 79,000 in Paraguay, and 242,120 in Peru.[4]

Within Middle America, both Guatemala and the Chiapas state of Mexico are areas where the great Mayan civilization flourished. Mayans were both highland and lowland peoples, with much greater numbers to be found in the highlands. The contemporary Mayan people have great language diversity. Some twenty-two major languages and some minor ones are spoken in Guatemala. A smaller number of Mayan languages are spoken in Chiapas. Cultural diversity there has been the cause of both conflict and adjustment as diverse Mayan refugees from Guatemala's civil war formed new settlements in the Chiapan forests.

Also located in Mesoamerica, Oaxaca has a varied terrain of mountains and flatlands, arid hills and humid seacoast. Oaxaca claims almost 20 percent of Mexico's Indian population, and almost 40 percent of the state's inhabitants speak an Indian language. The Zapotec, with 342,000 speakers, and the Mixtec, with 239,000, are among the largest indigenous groups in Mexico. Both language groups produced a refined culture that included writing and calendars. In all, some fourteen indigenous groups occupy separate or overlapping areas within Oaxaca.[5]

Today, estimates for the total number of indigenous people living in Latin America and the Caribbean generally fall between 35 and 40 million, making up from 8 to 10 percent of the total population of the region.[6] The cases included in this study focus on the Andean countries of Bolivia, Peru, and Ecuador and on the Guatemala-Mexico region because these areas account for the vast majority of Latin America's Indians. In Mexico, the indigenous number over 12 million, make up more than 14 percent of the population, and speak more than fifty different indigenous languages. In Guatemala, the primarily Mayan population is approximately 4 million, making up nearly 50 percent of the national population. Bolivia also has 4 million indigenous people, mostly Aymara or Quechua, making up more than 56 percent of its population. Peru and Ecuador round out Latin America's most indigenous countries, with 9 million (40 percent) and 3 million (29 percent), respectively.[7]

While indigenous people are increasingly distributed across urban and rural areas, the majority continue to work and live in areas dominated by rural agriculture. As such, regions with large indigenous populations tend to suffer from high poverty rates, low access to health, education, and social services, and ongoing conflicts relating to labor rights and land resources. Since the late 1960s, a combination of population growth, land consolidation, and civil unrest has fueled indigenous migration to urban areas and across national borders. As they move into major cities of Latin America (and the United States), indigenous people have become a major part of the labor force working in the formal and informal economies. From Mexico to Chile, the social and economic effects of structural adjustment in the 1980s and neoliberal economic policies in the 1990s left indigenous populations particularly vulnerable and less connected to their communities of origin.

Partly in response to these social and economic conditions and facilitated by political liberalization in the region, Latin America's indigenous peoples took part in a new wave of political mobilization and protest beginning in the 1980s. Grassroots indigenous organizations, international organizations, and religious and secular nongovernmental organizations raised questions of indigenous land rights, cultural rights, and social and economic rights. This volume explores the critical role that religious organizations, networks, beliefs, and practices played in the new wave of indigenous mobilization in Latin America. A brief review of the history of religion and politics in Latin America provides the necessary background for understanding the connections between these religious variables and indigenous mobilization.

RELIGION, POLITICS, AND THE INDIGENOUS

From the time of the establishment of the first colony on the Island of Hispaniola in 1493, Spaniards took over a rich, populous, and largely civilized empire, including all of the Mesoamerican and Andean cultural areas. Representatives of the Spanish crown made deals with existing elites, exploited indigenous rivalries, and obtained indigenous collaborators. Through a series of patronage agreements (known as *el patronato real*) the Vatican gained the commission to evangelize the inhabitants of the New World in exchange for giving the Spanish and Portuguese monarchies the rights to collect tithes and to appoint church officials.

Especially in the first century of colonization, church officials, priests, and influential laity lobbied colonial administrators and the crown directly over the treatment of the indigenous. Bartolomé de las Casas, a Dominican missionary bishop of Chiapas and Guatemala, Antonio de Valdivieso of Nicaragua, and Juan Zumárraga of Mexico City were all early defenders of the Indians in the face of colonial abuses.[8] These religious advocates eventually played a role in convincing the crown to enact of a measure of human rights for the Indians, in Las Leyes de las Indias. But in the end the Spanish system of landed estates, the *encomiendas,* prevailed and the majority of Indians suffered repressive labor conditions on the estates and in the mines. The encomiendas entrusted indigenous workers to a landholder, ostensibly for religious training. The landholder, in turn, was to provide food and housing for the indigenous worker. Because the supply of indigenous people appeared limitless, the *encomienderos* had little incentive to hold up their end of the bargain. Indians were often treated as less than human and left with barely enough basic foodstuffs and shelter for survival. Ultimately, exposure to European diseases, harsh conditions, and maltreatment led to a severe decline in the indigenous populations throughout Latin America. In some places more than 90 percent of the Indian population was wiped out.

In the end, the majority of the natives that the Spaniards and Portuguese encountered were converted to Christianity. Baptism, which was generally presumed by religious authorities to be a free and voluntary act, was the official rite of admission to the Catholic Church. However, the first archbishop of Lima, Jerónimo de Loaysa, noted that some missionaries acted imprudently and administered baptism without examining whether neophytes received it of their own free will. The question of how voluntary and complete conversion to Christianity was among the indigenous remains a matter of some debate.

In Europe, a brief doctrinal initiation (catechumenate) generally preceded reception into the Catholic Church. Neither in the Americas nor elsewhere outside of Europe was a lengthy period of training demanded. Instead the church embarked on doctrinal instruction of the peoples of Latin America mostly after baptism. Combined with a powerful attachment to native religious beliefs and practices, this lack of training laid the groundwork for the creation of a new form of Catholicism in most of Latin America, a folk or popular Catholicism that pooled elements of indigenous and Christian religion.

Syncretism and Popular Catholicism

From the time of the early missionaries many Indians practiced a synthesized form of Catholicism, combined with greater or lesser degrees of native religion. There was, and continues to be, a wide spectrum of religious practice, reaching from largely orthodox Christian practice in small towns, among those who read or write Spanish, to those who follow native religion with few Christian accretions. Approximately 10 percent of Latin America's indigenous people are orthodox Catholic in their beliefs and practices, while 10 percent are orthodox native practitioners.[9] The rest fall somewhere in between.

In many Indian communities the *costumbre,* or local ritual celebrations and practices (such as home altars and traditional native blessings) became the center of religious, social, and political life.[10] The organizations that grew up around and controlled worship were active religious brotherhoods. In some areas these were called *cofradías.* As Richard Wilson remarks, "Across Mesoamerica, the cofradía was the community institution that served for hundreds of years as a vessel for traditional Mayan beliefs and community values."[11] Cargo religion (religious rituals with sponsorship duties) continued in or ascended to a dominant position in Indian religious life in many communities of Latin America.

Events of the nineteenth century brought on a great scarcity of priests in Latin America, through wars against the Spanish, the exile of priests, and anticlerical governments. The ratio of priests to people greatly declined from about seven hundred laity per priest to several thousand per priest. In many remote areas there were no priests at all. Popular religion, nurtured at home and not in church, became the religion of most indigenous Latin Americans.[12] This kind of religion required low maintenance on the part of the organizational church, without much lay participation, except for participation in fiestas and processions.

Missionaries and the Push for Catholic Orthodoxy

During the late nineteenth and early twentieth century many Latin American countries passed legislation for the separation of church and state, allowing for at least a minimum of religious liberty and opening their countries to a diversity of religious groups. During this period, Spanish and Italian missionaries, many of whom had earlier seen their orders evicted from Latin American countries, began to make their way back into the region. A small number of Protestant missionaries also entered the region. But the major missionary push would come with the major changes in the international arena following World War II.

After World War II seminaries and convents in the United States, Canada, and Europe filled to overflowing with priests, brothers, and sisters. The Vatican issued a challenge to send 10 percent of these resources to Latin America. The target was almost reached, as country after country stocked up with foreign missionaries.[13] More than half of many Latin America countries' priests were foreign priests. These priests flowed into city and country parishes, generally with much greater resources than their national colleagues. Non-Catholic missionaries similarly fanned out to cities and rural areas. Many Indians experienced this encounter with foreign missionaries of the twentieth century as a cultural shock, similar to the first century and a half of interaction with Spanish and Portuguese missionaries.

When missionaries from the North Atlantic countries began creating parishes and missions in Latin America, they were initially appalled at the heterodoxy apparent in the indigenous practice of Christianity (which had come about, in part, due to the longstanding lack of clergy and religious schools).[14] To traditional indigenous religion, missionaries counter-posed orthodox Catholicism. Bishops, priests, and catechists began taking harder stands against traditional practices that seemed to them to have little to do with essential Christianity.[15] Dioceses began forbidding the celebration of Catholic masses within certain traditional celebrations. Some missionaries viewed traditional practices as contrary to a modern understanding of scripture. A few even went so far as to portray traditional practices as furthering *mestizo* political and economic control and the subordination of Indian peasants.

Changes in the Catholic Church: From Vatican II to Liberation Theology

An understanding of the critical religious changes that swept Latin America in the 1960s and 1970s is necessary in order to grasp the complex and contradictory relationship that subsequently evolved between religion and the indigenous. Changes within the institutional Catholic Church and the birth of liberation theology reshaped the Latin American religious and political landscape. Under the influence of missionaries and of internal reform initiated by Latin American bishops, the Catholic Church became renewed in a number of sectors. Millions of lay persons became active in the church and its social justice mission. Thousands of prayer and neighborhood improvement groups kept parishes busy. By the end of the millennium more than a million lay persons became catechists, providing a religious presence in almost every indigenous community. Seminary walls could not contain the number of students studying for the priesthood. Overall, the percentage of students studying for the priesthood increased 388 percent from 1972 to 2001, including a number from indigenous backgrounds.

These events were spurred and supported by major changes within the institutional Catholic Church. The general thrust of Vatican Council II (1962–1965) included two key factors that would affect Latin America: adaptation of a universal church to national and local cultures and awareness of the presence of God in other religions (as that of Latin America's indigenous). The Medellín Conference of Latin American Bishops (CELAM) in 1968 reinforced these trends,[16] emphasizing the "Latinamericanization" of the church.[17] Changes in attitude toward the indigenous became inevitable. Inculturation, the process of discerning where God is at work in a culture and articulating a theology sensitive to the local context, became the aim of church leaders and theologians. To summarize, CELAM changed its policy toward the indigenous from *indigenista* to *indígena,* from paternalistic to accompaniment, in the 1970s and 1980s.[18] In its most specific form, guidelines for this indigenism included (1) defending the land, (2) learning the indigenous languages, (3) motivating self-determination, (4) equipping the community for contact with outsiders, (5) recovering cultural memory, (6) providing hope, and (7) stimulating alliances.[19]

Liberation theology also emerged in Latin America in the 1960s as a way of proposing that the church, as a people and an institution, exert an active role in society. This way of thinking contrasted to the Latin American Catholic Church's previous role as an otherworldly, fiesta-bound institution. Liberation theology centered its concerns in a preferential option for the poor, weak, and vulnerable. Its theologians advocated social change, action to promote justice, and emphasized communities with lay and clerical leadership as the basis of action.

To describe Latin American religious thought, especially the theology of liberation, to those with little knowledge of Latin America is a daunting enterprise. Alessandra Stanley, based in Rome and writing in 2001 for the New York Times Service, reported that John Paul II had crushed liberation theology.[20] Such statements come as a shock to many Latin Americans, particularly those theologians who carry on with the task of refining liberation theology. They are aided by more than seven hundred dissertations and countless publications that have contributed to its elaboration.[21] Liberation theologians continue to write statements about a maturing theology, not knowing that it is dead.[22] Liberation theology can claim two important contributions to

present-day theologizing throughout the world: method and context. Both are
salient here. Liberation theologians emphasize an inductive method: begin with
a description of the world and the church within it, reflect on the situation
from a biblical perspective, and act to bring the world and the church more in
harmony with this biblical vision. Liberation theology also took the lead in
what is today called contextual theology, a theology of utmost importance to
many missiologists.[23] Contextual theology attempts to express Christian faith in
distinct languages, thought patterns, and other cultural expressions.

The creators of liberation theology were Latin American religious think-
ers, many of whom had been trained in Europe and the United States in the
1950s and 1960s. They included two commonly recognized progenitors, Gustavo Gutiérrez in Peru and Juan Luis Segundo in Uruguay. They joined a core
group of about one hundred theologians in a joint venture to formulate this
new theology, especially in the 1970s.[24] An Argentine Methodist trained at
Union Theological Seminary in New York, José Míguez Bonino, became the
most prominent among Protestant theologians in the group. Latin Americans
quickly bonded with theologians from other regions of the world to form the
Ecumenical Association of Third World Theologians in the 1970s. By and
large, the missionaries working in Latin America were not the creators of liberation theology.[25] However, Catholic, and some Protestant, missionaries were
among liberation theology's main consumers.[26]

Just as liberation theology was beginning to hit its stride in Latin America, missionaries of all denominations came under severe criticism from academics and activists in the region. The Barbados 1971 Conference of the
International Work Group for Indigenous Affairs served as a lightning rod,
bringing the subject of religion and the indigenous to the attention of the
world.[27] Delegates to the conference charged that governments, international
agencies, and missionaries were participating in programs of ethnocide in
Latin America.[28] While the charges were leveled specifically about non-
Andean Indians, the implications reached to include relations generally with
missionaries, churches, and indigenous peoples. The Barbados Conference repeated a position that some anthropologists had long held: missions were instruments of cultural imperialism.[29]

The Barbados conference not only served as a wake up call for the
churches, it also helped to launch the international indigenous rights movement.[30] Anthropologists and indigenous activists at that meeting established
themselves as catalysts for a transnational movement. Their activities opened
up an era of globalized actions in relation to the nation-state and Indian rights
movements. In part as a response to Barbados, religious institutions played a
critical role in this process. In the last third of the twentieth century some religious bodies responded extensively to the perceived need to aid tribal leaders in organizing to pressure governments for their rights and privileges as full

citizens. The World Council of Churches throughout the 1970s flew Indian leaders to regional meetings. Between 1970 and 1981 the Brazilian Catholic bishops sponsored fifteen meetings, bringing together hundreds of indigenous leaders from about two hundred groups. From these international conferences to local assets provided through religious organizations, the critical networks, resources, and ideological frameworks for Latin America's indigenous resurgence were formed.

The corps of Latin American liberation theologians has diminished in energy and creative formulations due both to aging, and to the strong and effective opposition of more conservative elements within the Catholic Church. However, the impact of liberation theology continues to be felt in Latin America. Liberation theology has been established both in church documents and in a generalizing trend of the Latin American church to promote justice. Alison Brysk, in the best account of Indian movements as a transnational enterprise, found that liberation theology "played a critical role in establishing indigenous movements and remains a key referent in areas."[31] According to Brysk, "concerned clergy were the most frequent (and periodically successful) interlocutors for Indian interests" in Latin America.[32] In other words, liberation theology radiated out from its academic setting to facilitate the empowerment of Latin American Indians. Spurred by many of the tenets of liberation theology, thousands of missionaries have served the indigenous poor in Latin America and maintained their loyalties to their churches through selfless service.[33]

From Liberation Theology to Indigenous Theology

A second link between liberation theology and indigenous mobilization relates to the theologians and missionaries themselves. In the 1980s and 1990s, some theologians within the liberationist tradition began working at indigenous think tanks and began to rediscover the value of culture that many missionaries and liberation theologians had ignored earlier. These theologians entered into the long process of listening to the indigenous and elaborating intellectually what they heard.

A number of missionaries in Bolivia and elsewhere in Latin America also began to develop a theological perspective with a greater focus on the value of local culture. In this view, culture has the central position for description and explanation. Some early forms of liberation theology were seen as ignoring culture, emphasizing the strictly socioeconomic aspects of Latin America. Further, culturalists believed that the liberationist perspective may have brought failure to many indigenous development projects because the projects were based on socioeconomic analysis that excluded cultural factors. Some members of this sector saw liberation theology as looking for a socialist world that never came.[34]

In the end, both liberationists and culturalists helped to foster the growth of indigenous theologians, who would eventually bring about a fuller elaboration of *teología india*. Indigenous theology became a major derivative of the liberationist movement.[35] Some indigenous theologians also began to appear in print, not so much as liberationists, but as part of a small wave of theologians of inculturation. The Zapotec theologian Eleazar López and others helped to make the Fourth Latin American Bishops Conference in Santo Domingo (1992) a new stage in the church's awareness of the indigenous. Since then, Domingo Llanque in Peru, Enrique Jordá in Bolivia, a small group of indigenous theologians from the Catholic University, Cochabamba, and others have joined in the effort to create indigenous theology based on Andean, Mayan, Zapotec, or other indigenous cosmologies.[36] Stephen Judd traces the evolution of this nascent theological movement in his chapter on indigenous theology.

The Evangelical Challenge

As religious changes were fundamentally altering the Catholic Church in Latin America in the 1960s and 1970s, evangelical Protestantism began experiencing its first period of rapid growth in the region. Although Protestantism has a long history in Latin America,[37] early missionaries met with little success in their attempts to promote Protestant growth, primarily due to cultural barriers. The loss of China as a mission field brought more missionaries into Latin America in the 1960s, and, in some cases, local religious leaders broke from their mother churches and abandoned some of the cultural practices that had previously limited their success in gaining converts.

While most observers had their eyes on the historical Protestant congregations with a longer history in the region, the real growth among evangelicals came from the Pentecostals.[38] Pentecostal churches stressed faith healing, charismatic acts, and a millennial message focused on the imminent coming of the "end times." These churches grew most rapidly among Latin America's indigenous groups, as local Pentecostal pastors worked with missionaries to translate the Bible into indigenous languages and to make their services more culturally relevant. Many other non-Catholic groups also had success evangelizing to the indigenous, including the Mormons, Jehovah's Witnesses, and Seventh-Day Adventists.

The distribution of evangelical groups among Latin America's Indians varies widely between and within countries. In the Andes, some entire indigenous communities have become Adventist, while others have joined historic Protestant missions. Still others remain staunchly Catholic. In Central America and Mexico, it is commonly asserted that Pentecostalism is most prevalent among the indigenous, though hard numbers are rarely cited. In the countries under consideration in this study, the percentage of indigenous evangelicals ranges from 10 to 25 percent.

As our case studies make clear, the impact of evangelical groups on indigenous societies has also been mixed. Protestant missionaries have been accused of fomenting local divisions, supporting repressive governments, and destroying indigenous culture. At the same time, Protestant mission organizations have played a critical role in promoting literacy, education, and other services that have translated into political resources among indigenous peoples. As is often the case, the interactions between religion and indigenous politics defy simple characterizations and linear explanations.

UNDERSTANDING LATIN AMERICA'S INDIGENOUS RESURGENCE

Indian political movements in Latin America burst into public consciousness with sudden force in the early 1990s. With little warning, Indians in Ecuador engaged in a week-long uprising that brought the nation to a standstill in 1990. Also in 1990, Bolivian Indians began a thirty-four-day march to La Paz, the capital, with ominous determination. In the first light of 1994 Indians in Chiapas rose up fearlessly against an authoritarian Mexican government.[39] Indigenous groups would no longer accept their customary subaltern status in these countries. In Guatemala, too, and in Peru, to a lesser extent, Indians were making demands for recognition of their rights in new ways. Mexican and Guatemalan Mayas, Ecuadoran Quechuas, Bolivian Aymaras, and other Indians in the Americas called for a new vision of autonomy in a world of globalization.[40]

At the broadest economic level of analysis, the precipitant factors for the indigenous resurgence included the growing integration of the world economy, shifts from industrial production to financial capital as the basis for accumulation, and diminishing resources devoted to subsistence production throughout the world. In Latin America, the expansion of agribusiness added to the pressures of population growth on indigenous subsistence farmers, bringing increased food dependency as well as rapid urbanization. For large numbers of Latin America's Indians, the growing informal sector of the economy became the most likely source of employment.

In the midst of this social and economic dislocation, economic and ideological support shifted away from the modernization paradigm of indigenous assimilation into national society.[41] As state-funded projects aimed at indigenous incorporation gave way to policies of structural adjustment, decentralization, and privatization, indigenous groups were increasingly cut off from traditional modes of interest mediation and access to state funding. Peasant organizations lost political clout, agricultural subsidies were cut, and markets for land transactions were liberalized. Latin America's indigenous peoples found themselves without their traditional forms of political representation precisely at the moment that their traditional means of economic survival were in jeopardy.[42]

The shift in the 1990s to what Deborah Yashar has called "neoliberal citizenship regimes" in Latin America both exacerbated the negative economic trends for indigenous people and provided an ideological opening for increased indigenous mobilization. Adopting elements of the neoliberal discourse, indigenous groups have recently focused attention on their long-denied individual and civil rights. At the same time, the neoliberal emphasis on the decentralization of the state has led to a devolution of power to more local units, allowing indigenous groups to argue for greater indigenous local autonomy as well. Indigenous organizations are thus armed with dual logic for mobilization, calling their governments to task for the failure to guarantee individual rights while demanding recognition and legal status for their group and ethnic identities.[43]

At this critical juncture of economic crisis and ideological opening, indigenous activists have found key support for their agenda in the international realm. The International Labor Organization's (ILO) Convention 169 commits those states who sign it to ensure the economic, cultural, labor, and land rights of indigenous people. Along with the United Nations (UN) and Organization of American States Draft Declarations on Indigenous Rights, the ILO Convention 169 has spurred a series of constitutional reforms recognizing the multicultural nature of Latin American societies.[44]

Faced with threats to their economic livelihood and cultural autonomy, Latin America's Indians have responded with a series of new ideological and international tools. When Subcomandante Marcos and his companions rose up in Chiapas, emails were streaming from their headquarters to friends, protectors, and collaborators in Mexico City, Minneapolis, and Boston. When Ecuadorian Indians took up defense of their cause, they did so in New York and Geneva conference rooms as well as in the streets of Quito. International organizations, secular and religious nongovernmental organizations, and transnational advocacy networks served as resources and conduits for the new voices of indigenous activism.

The 1994 uprising in Chiapas also confirmed a shift away from the kind of national-popular revolution that dominated much of twentieth-century Latin American political ideology (as in the examples of Cuba and of the Sandinistas in Nicaragua). In Chiapas and elsewhere, Indians are mobilizing around their distinctively indigenous identity. As Charles Hale notes, "Indigenous peoples now increasingly advance their struggles through a discourse that links Indian identity with rights to territory, autonomy, and peoplehood—rights that run parallel to those of the nation-state itself."[45]

As the effects of a globalized economy reached into Latin America's high plateaus and lowland jungles during the 1990s, indigenous groups responded with remarkable vigor. Across the Americas, shifting economic and political forces sparked indigenous mobilization. Once mobilized, Latin America's Indians have utilized a new set of resources to promote their cause, demanding cultural and individual rights framed through the politics of identity, while increasing their transnational ties to nongovernmental and international organizations. This potent confluence of processes, tools, and tactics continues to buttress Latin America's indigenous resurgence.

Academics Catch up with Events

Veteran anthropologists and other social scientists with thirty or more years experience in Latin America began to call attention to the new indigenous militancy, as the new level of activism in the 1990s seemed to surprise even them.[46] Carol Smith, writing in 1991, described a Maya national movement so young "that it is difficult to know exactly what it is and where it is going,"[47] Richard Adams wrote three years later of the changing political status of Mayas, who had a "great deal of organization" and "a potential for being effective politically."[48] In 1996 Edward Fisher and McKenna Brown wrote that this Indian movement marked the beginning of a new era of studies.[49] By 1998, the outlines of this movement were clearer. Kay B. Warren, a leading scholar, wrote a full-scale treatment of Guatemala in her *Indigenous Movements and Their Critics: Pan-Maya Activism in Guatemala*.[50] What was becoming evident was that Indians no longer depended largely on outsiders as their interlocutors with larger society. Pan-Mayanism, as other Indian movements, had its own public intellectuals.

As attention to the indigenous resurgence became more widespread, academics began to explore the growing field of indigenous rights. Alison Brysk led the way. She had framed in 1994 one of the most careful and acclaimed analyses of the Argentine human rights situation.[51] She then turned to the indigenous rights movements.[52] Through a series of publications ending in her masterful *From Tribal Village to Global Village: Indian Rights and International Relations in Latin America,* Brysk showed the impact of Indian rights movements on world politics.[53] Indian movements helped to reform the United Nations in its policies, to strengthen international law regarding minority rights, and to control the reach of transnational corporations into Indian domains. She argued that marginalized Indians have responded to globalization with new, internationalized forms of identity politics that are reconstructing power relations. In doing so, Brysk traced a wide dynamics of interstate relations, global markets, and transnational civil society.

While Brysk outlined the transnational implications of indigenous mobilization, Donna Van Cott and others explored the implications of Indian activism for the new democracies of Latin America formed after military rule.

Societies where Indians had large numbers could not simply go back to the same power relations that existed before military government. Indians would not and will not allow this to occur. Looking at Guatemala and the Central Andes in 1998, John Peeler concluded that "the last generation has seen an unprecedented emergence of indigenous people as mainstream actors."[54] Xavier Albó, Deborah Yashar, Christian Gros, Donna Van Cott, Rachel Sieder, David Maybury-Lewis, Kay Warren and Jean Jackson, Ronald Niezen, Frank Salomon, Stuart Schwartz, and their colleagues have demonstrated an evolution of contemporary state politics and new policy outcomes forged in conflict by Indian activists.[55]

This struggle led to new constitutional provisions for Indian rights in Colombia and Bolivia. As Donna Van Cott has argued, Indian activism has led to constitutional reforms that espouse a more local, participatory, and culturally diverse society in Latin America.[56] Colombia and Bolivia have created multicultural constitutional frameworks that recognize customary law, collective property rights, and bilingual education. Other countries with strong indigenous movements have also won important concessions that redefine the relationship between the state and Indian groups.[57] But the fight is far from over, as statutes mean little in practice without further political pressure. Further, substantial legislation with enforcement policies has yet to be created in Mexico and Guatemala, the two countries with almost half the Indians of Latin America. Only a noteworthy start in a long and painful conflict has begun in those countries.

The Understudied Role of Religion

The grand man of research in Indian cultures, Rodolfo Stavenhagen, stated in 1997 that Indian movements were "questioning and challenging the basic premises on which the Nation-State has been built in Latin America for almost two centuries."[58] As Stavenhagen and others have noted, Indians in Latin America have made these recent challenges with the aid of outside support. Religious networks and institutions have played a key role in fostering this process. The acknowledgment by anthropologists and other social scientists of this religious support is a turn-around from the sort of accusations made at the 1971 Barbados conference.

As the leading authorities on indigenous activism in Latin America highlighted the recent upsurge in mobilization, they also alluded to the role of religion as an antecedent to indigenous movements. However, the field remains open for investigation, as few observers have probed the links between religion and indigenous activism. In the pages that follow, the contributors to this volume argue that Indian insurgency cannot be understood without recourse to religious variables. Religion forms a major component of indigenous life and culture, provides resources and motivations for public action, and serves as a transnational link to state and non-state actors who can advocate for indigenous causes. Religious ideas, networks, and organizations form a critical part of ethnic identities.[59] Religious ideologies provide a groundwork for the framing of movement issues. Religious institutions enhance the acceptance of movement positions, provide social legitimacy, and help to ward off repression. Religion furnishes narratives for movements, providing a rationale for action and a foundation for collective identities and group solidarity.[60]

CASES AND THEMES

Because the topic of religion and indigenous mobilization has been understudied, it is particularly well suited to the case study approach. The strength of this approach lies in the excellent qualitative information that can be gleaned from seasoned investigators with significant experience in their respective areas of inquiry. Our contributors were free to choose the theoretical and methodological framework best suited to their case, allowing for a breadth of disciplinary perspectives and a greater richness of ethnographic detail. It is out of such detail that informed hypotheses and credible cross-case generalizations emerge.

The cases included in this volume were chosen both for their representative character and thematic breadth. For the most part, we included case studies from the countries representing the greatest number of indigenous people (Mexico, Guatemala, Bolivia, Peru, and Ecuador). The Paraguayan case is the exception to this rule, but merits inclusion because most Paraguayans speak Guarani and profess an Indian cosmology and spirituality.[61]

We begin with the case of Ecuador, where the 1990 indigenous uprising first focused attention on Latin America's indigenous awakening. This mobilization has continued and multiplied, as January 2000 witnessed the indigenous uprisings that deposed president Jamil Mahuad. Alison Brysk outlines the religious antecedents of these indigenous mobilizations, detailing the connections between religion and civil society in the Ecuadoran case.

Edward Cleary's comparative treatment of the Bolivian and Peruvian cases follows, providing important insights for understanding the role of contextual factors in conditioning the trajectory of indigenous movements in Latin America. While a context of political authoritarianism limited the emergence of a coherent indigenous mobilization in Peru, both Bolivia and Peru have well-established connections between religion and the indigenous, resulting in the emergence of a unique indigenous theology movement. Cleary pays special attention to the role that church-founded intellectual and cultural centers and indigenous catechists have played in developing the intellectual basis for indigenous political activism in the region. René Harder Horst's chapter completes our focus on the Andes, highlighting the fluidity of indigenous religion in the understudied case of Paraguay.

We include two chapters on the Guatemalan case to highlight both the historical detail of Catholic-indigenous interactions and the more recent interactions between Christian theology and Mayan cosmovision. Bruce Calder's chapter takes a historical approach, detailing the critical interactions between the Catholic Church and the Maya from the 1940s through the 1990s. Calder points to the key role that the Catholic Church played in setting the stage for the Mayan revindication movement. Virginia Garrard-Burnett's contribution to this volume expands upon her earlier work, exploring the interactions between Catholic and Protestant religion and Mayan cosmovision. She argues that indigenous theologians are now fashioning new theological forms in Guatemala that valorize and provide support for indigenous political movements.

In Mexico, we focus on the two states where indigenous activism has been most pronounced, Chiapas and Oaxaca. Kristin Norget argues that the efforts of the Oaxacan progressive church to be more open in its discourse and practice to the traditions of indigenous communities reflect an unprecedented democratization of Catholic culture. She warns us that in practice, however, indigenous theology may represent a partial continuation of paternalistic and authoritarian relations between the church and indigenous Oaxacans.

Christine Kovic takes a different approach, emphasizing the key role that Bishop Samuel Ruiz played in Chiapas as an interlocutor for indigenous peoples as well as the ideological and practical support that religion has provided for indigenous mobilization. She details the specific workshops, collective labor projects, health promotion programs, language programs, educational opportunities, and peasant cooperatives sponsored by the Catholic Church in Chiapas.

Stephen Judd's chapter provides us with the outlines of the emergent indigenous theology movement developing in Latin America. Though in its incipient stages, Judd argues that this theological movement has the potential to fundamentally alter the way indigenous Christians frame their religious practice and beliefs. As Judd explains, this process is already underway.

Timothy Steigenga concludes the volume, providing some comparative generalizations and outlining the theoretical implications of the individual cases. The primary thesis put forward in this volume is that religion has fundamentally influenced indigenous culture and politics and that Latin American religion has been altered in the process. Our inquiry focuses on the impact of religious and cultural mixing, the effects of religious institutions, beliefs, and practices on indigenous social movements, and the general fluidity of religious practice and complexity of religious politics in Latin America.

First, each of our authors notes that religious and cultural mixing has played a role in the recent indigenous resurgence. As this blending of practices and beliefs occurs, cultures, traditions, and strategic needs shape and refine religious practices. Mayas of Guatemala, Aymaras of Bolivia and Peru, and other indigenous groups have selectively appropriated aspects of outside religions to meet their spiritual, physical, and emotional needs. They have forged their own expressions not only of Catholicism, but also of Pentecostalism and historical Protestantism.

This creation of *una iglesia indígena* (an indigenous church) was both sought and unanticipated. The Catholic Church abandoned its policy of assimilation of Indians into a Eurocentric church in the wake of Vatican Council II. The church allocated considerable resources into a policy of inculturation, providing Christianity with an Aymara or Maya face. Released from centuries of (not always successful) control, Indian religion has acquired much greater identity under a enlarged Catholic canopy. To a large degree, the Catholic Church has succeeded in a spectacular fashion in its efforts of forming una iglesia indígena. Whether its bishops and authorities in Rome are ready for the new expression of assertiveness in religious culture is another matter.

The birth of an indigenous church among Latin America's growing evangelical population has been more complicated. While some historical Protestant churches have been positively engaged in their own version of inculturation theology (as Virginia Garrard-Burnett's chapter demonstrates), Pentecostalism continues to generate significant conflict within some indigenous communities (as evidenced in contributions from Alison Brysk and Kristin Norget).

Second, the chapters of this volume point to the resources and roles that religion has provided for indigenous mobilization. From education and language translation to advocacy and strategic protection, religious institutions have facilitated identity-based social movements for indigenous rights. The skills, networks, resources, and spaces of religious institutions combined with powerful religious messages of equality and dignity to form the foundation for political mobilization. As indigenous groups faced repression while making their new demands, religious workers and missionaries who stood with them became potent symbols of their cause. When religious actors became the target of government repression, local and international actors became involved in promoting the cause of indigenous rights.

Finally, the chapters contained in this volume demonstrate the remarkable fluidity of the religious marketplace in Latin America as well as the complexity of religious politics. Opening a wider window on this flexibility reveals a world seldom analyzed by previous descriptions of Latin American religion. A wider ecumenism is being forced on Catholic and Protestant pastoral workers. As René Harder Horst explains, some Paraguayan Catholic leaders now recognize Protestant theology as a valid expression of the divine. Interaction of indigenous peoples has broadened interdenominational practices because native peoples do not recognize what they consider arbitrary "white" divisions.

From the level of national politics to neighborhood to micro (family) based relationships, understanding relations of religion and politics requires the careful attention to context, beliefs, organizational structures, religious practices, on one hand, and power relations, advocacy, and political gains and losses, on the other. The authors in this volume have taken great care not to broadly generalize from religious to political variables. Rather, they trace the interactions of beliefs, actions, organizations, and outcomes in each case, demonstrating the roles and resources that religious groups have provided for indigenous movements seeking autonomy and a voice in their respective political systems.

In sum, the new voice that is being heard in Latin American politics and religion comes from indigenous movements. Participants in these movements have become important political actors, have forced demands for Indian rights on governments, and have changed constitutions to open national societies to ethnic demands of some 40 million Indians. Religion is a central part of this insurgency. Religion is a fuel that helped to ignite these demands, and in the process the nature of religious practice in Latin America has been fundamentally altered. The impact of these changes will be felt well into the present century.

NOTES

1. A more complete version of Jerónimo's story in his own words may be found in the introduction to Allan F. Burns, *The Maya in Exile: Guatemalans in South Florida* (Philadelphia: Temple University Press, 1993).
2. Such a definition is in line with United Nations policies on defining the indigenous. See Donna Van Cott, *The Friendly Liquidation of the Past: The Politics of Diversity in Latin America* (Pittsburgh, Pa.: University of Pittsburgh Press, 2000), 208.
3. Exceptions can be found frequently for groups or individuals who made their way to other regions. Thus, the Quechua established their culture in mountainous areas but many have migrated, especially through contemporary, government-sponsored colonization projects, to tropical regions.
4. For sources and range of estimates, see David Maybury-Lewis, "Lowland Peoples of the Twentieth Century," in *The Cambridge History of the Native Peoples of Latin America,* vol. 3, part 2, ed. Frank Salomon and Stuart B. Schwartz (New York: Cambridge University Press, 1999), 875.
5. María de los Angeles Romero Frizzi, "The Indigenous Population of Oaxaca from the Sixteenth Century to the Present," in *The Cambridge History of the Native Peoples of the Americas,* vol. 2, part 2, ed. Richard E. W. Adams and Murdo J. MacLeod (New York: Cambridge University Press, 2000), 302–345.
6. Estimates vary due to questionable census data and varying definitions across countries. See Rachel Sieder, ed., *Multiculturalism in Latin America: Indigenous Rights, Diversity, and Democracy* (New York: Palgrave Macmillan, 2002). Also see Van Cott, *The Friendly Liquidation.*
7. Sieder, *Multiculturalism in Latin America,* 1. Also see statistics from the World Bank (www.worldbank.org).

8. Justo González, "Voices of Compassion, Yesterday and Today" in *The New Face of the Church in Latin America,* ed. Guillermo Cook (Maryknoll, N.Y.: Orbis Books, 1994).

9. Written communication from Luis Joliceour, anthropologist and rector of the Facultad de Teología, Cochabamba, Bolivia.

10. See John Watanabe, *Maya Saints and Souls in a Changing World* (Austin: University of Texas Press, 1992), 9.

11. Richard Wilson, *Maya Resurgence in Guatemala* (Norman: University of Oklahoma Press, 1995), 22, citing various sources.

12. Popular religion has been extensively explored by many social scientists. See especially Anna L. Peterson, Manuel Vásquez, and Philip J. Williams, *Christianity, Social Change, and Globalization in the Americas* (New Brunswick, N.J.: Rutgers University Press, 2001) and Manuel Marzal, *Tierra encantada: Tratado de antropología religiosa en America Latina* (Madrid: Trotta, 2002).

13. The percentage of Catholic missionaries in some countries has been extraordinarily high. By 1970, missionaries formed 60 percent of clergy in Peru and in Bolivia, 75 percent.

14. In the 1950s Latin American delegates at a key meeting in Chimbote, Peru, recognized that most Latin Americans were only nominally Catholic, with only a minimum of religious instruction. See *Tercera Semana Interamericana de Acción Católica* (Lima and Chimbote, 1953).

15. This great struggle to wrest Indians away from heterodoxy through Catholic Action and native catechists was immortalized in Kay B. Warren, *The Symbolism of Subordination: Indian Identity in a Guatemalan Town* (Austin: University of Texas Press, 1978) and in Hans C. Buechler and Judith Maria Buechler, "Combating Feathered Serpents: The Rise of Protestantism and Reformed Catholicism in a Bolivian Highland Community," in *Amerikanistische studien: Festschrift für Hermann Trimborn,* vol. 1 (St. Augustin: Hans Völker u. Kultern, Anthropos-Inst., 1978).

16. The chief institutional leadership of the Catholic Church lies in the Consejo Episcopal Latinoamericano (CELAM). Established in 1955, CELAM only began to exercise great influence in Latin America after the Second General CELAM Conference at Medellín (1968).

17. Edward L. Cleary, *Crisis and Change: The Church in Latin America Today* (Maryknoll, N.Y.: Orbis, 1985), 23–33, 78. See "CELAM," *The Encyclopedia of Religion and Politics,* vol. 1 (Washington: Congressional Quarterly, 1998), 113–114.

18. See esp. Consejo Episcopal Latinoamericano, *De una pastoral indigenista a una pastoral indígena* (Bogotá: Consejo Episcopal Latinoamericano, 1987); and José Alsina Franch, compiler, *Indianismo e indigenismo en América* (Madrid: Alianza Editorial/Quinto Cententario, 1990). See also Bishop Julio Cabrera Ovalle, El Quiché, "Desafíos de la pastoral indígena en Guatemala"; and Bishop Gerard Flores Reyes, "Una experiencia concreta: La Verapaz," both in *Misiones Extranjeras* 116 (March–April 1990), 122–129 and 152–156, respectively, and Giulio Girardi, *El derecho indígena a la autodeterminación política y religiosa* (Quito: Ediciones Abya-Yala, 1997); and Giulio Girardi, *Los excluídos: Constituirán la nueva historia: El movimiento indígena, negro y popular* (Quito: Centro Cultural Afroecuatoriano, 1994).

19. Drawn from Brazil's Conselho Indigenista Misionario. See Juan Bottasso, ed., *Las misiones salesianas en un continente que se transforma* (Quito: Centro Regional Salesiano, 1982), 195.

20. *International Herald Tribune* (May 22, 2001).

21. Among the more than 700 doctoral dissertations written on liberation theology, see, for example, Guillermo César Hansen, "The Doctrine of the Trinity and Liberation Theology: A Study of the Trinitarian Doctrine and Its Place in Latin American Theology," Th.D diss., Lutheran School of Theology, Chicago, 1995.

22. See appraisals of contemporary liberation theology in Enrique Dussel, *Teologia da*

Libertação: Um panorama de seu desenvolvimento (Petrópolis: Editora Vozes, 1999 [Spanish edition: Mexico, 1995]); and Leonardo Boff, José Ramos Regidor, and Clodovis Boff, *A Teologia da Libertação: Balanço e perspectivas* (São Paulo: Editora Atica, 1996).

23. See Series on Faith and Cultures: *Contextualizing Gospel and Church,* forthcoming from Orbis and edited by Robert J. Schreiter.

24. For a full description of the core of liberation theologians see Christian Smith, *The Emergence of Liberation Theology: Radical Religion and Social Movement Theory* (Chicago: University of Chicago Press, 1991).

25. Among major creators of liberation theology, Jon Sobrino, a Jesuit, was born in Spain.

26. In Brazil and Chile, in Catholic Churches where reforms were taking place before Vatican II, many foreign clergy and religious women reinforced progressive tendencies. In countries where native clergy were notably conservative in the 1970s, as Nicaragua, foreign clergy tended to take the lead in implementing liberation theology.

27. See Miguel Alberto Bartolomé, *Declaration of Barbados* (Rooseveltville, N.Y.: International Work Group for Indigenous Affairs, 1971).

28. The role of the World Council of Churches in the Declaration of Barbados and the evolution of anthropologists' views, as those of Guillermo Bonfil, are detailed by Andrew Walls and Lannin Senneh in their Prospectus for the 11th Yale-Edinburgh Group on Non-Western Christianity, July 12–14, 2001 meeting at New Haven.

29. What gave the conference added rhetorical force was funding from the World Council of Churches. The council had been advised by anthropologist Georg Gruneberg from the University of Berne. This apparently solid front of criticism began to weaken, however, through the 1970s.

30. The second Barbados Conference of the International Work Group for Indigenous Affairs took place in 1977 and issued a revised declaration signed by Indian representatives as well as anthropologists.

31. Alison Brysk, *From Tribal Village to Global Village: Indian Rights and International Relations in Latin America* (Stanford: Stanford University Press, 2000), 194.

32. Brysk, *From Tribal Village,* 9.

33. Jeffrey Klaiber, "Catholic Church," in *Encyclopedia of Latin American History and Culture* (N.Y.: Scribners; Simon and Schuster; Prentice-Hall, 1996), vol. 2, 33.

34. Luis Jolicoeur, "Teología y culturas aymaras," *Teología y Vida* 36 (1995): 226.

35. Indigenous theology is taking its place alongside other theologies spawned by liberation theologians or inspired by liberation methodology, such as feminist-womenist theology of liberation.

36. Of the second generation of indigenous theologians, Nicanor Sarmiento (from Bolivia, but working in Labrador, Canada) was chosen to give the key presentation at the major Symposium on the Dialogue about Indian Theology at Riobamba, Ecuador, in October 2002.

37. Perhaps as many as 160,000 missionaries worked in the region at one time. P. G. Cabra, "Los religiosos y la evangelización de América Latina," *Iglesia, Pueblo y Culturas* 32 (January–March 1994): 125.

38. Historical or mainline Protestant denominations include Anglicans, Lutherans, Methodists, Baptists, and Presbyterians. In Latin America, most proselytizing non-Catholic groups are referred to as "evangelicals" in common usage.

39. Richard N. Adams, a major authority on Central American Indians, noted in 1991 that "ladino fears of potential indigenous rebellion continues to be strong." Richard N. Adams, "Strategies of Ethnic Survival in Central America," in *Nation-States and Indians in Latin America,* ed. Greg Urban and Joel Scherzer (Austin: University of Texas Press, 1991), 202.

40. June C. Nash, *Mayan Visions: The Quest for Autonomy in an Age of Globalization* (New York: Routledge, 2001).

41. Rodolfo Stavenhagen, "Indigenous Peoples and the State in Latin America: An Ongoing Debate," in *Multiculturalism in Latin America: Indigenous Rights, Diversity, and Democracy,* ed. Rachel Sieder (New York: Palgrave Macmillon, 2002), 24–44.

42. See Deborah J. Yashar "Democracy, Indigenous Movements, and the Postliberal Challenge in Latin America," *World Politics* 52 (1999): 76–104.

43. See Yashar, "Democracy."

44. Rachel Sieder, introduction to *Multiculturalism in Latin America: Indigenous Rights, Diversity, and Democracy,* ed. Rachel Sieder (New York: Palgrave Macmillon, 2002), 3–6. Also see Donna Lee Van Cott, ed., *Indigenous Peoples and Democracy in Latin America* (New York: St. Martin's Press, 1994), 17, 262.

45. Charles R. Hale, "Cultural Politics of Identity in Latin America," *Annual Review of Anthropology* 26 (1997): 567–590. See also Francesca Polletta and James M. Jasper, "Collective Identity and Social Movements," *Annual Review of Sociology* 27 (2001): 283–305; and Judith A. Howard, "Social Psychology of Identities," *Annual Review of Sociology* 26 (2000): 367–393.

46. Richard N. Adams and others tended to stress cultural survival. See, for example, Adams, "Strategies of Ethnic Survival in Central America," 181–206.

47. Carol A. Smith, "'Culture Is More Than Folklore': Maya Leaders Insist on Self Determination," mimeograph.

48. Richard N. Adams, "A Report on the Political Status of the Guatemalan Maya," in *Indigenous Peoples and Democracy in Latin America,* ed. Donna Lee Van Cott (New York: St. Martin's Press, 1994), 155 for quotation, 155–186 for chapter.

49. Edward F. Fisher and R. McKenna Brown, eds., *Maya Cultural Activism in Guatemala* (Austin: University of Texas Press, 1996), 1.

50. Kay B. Warren, *Indigenous Movements and Their Critics: Pan-Maya Activism in Guatemala* (Princeton, N.J.: Princeton University Press, 1998).

51. Alison Brysk, *The Politics of Human Rights in Argentina: Protest, Change, and Democratization* (Stanford: Stanford University Press, 1994).

52. She and her husband took a trip to Bolivia as a diversion from research in Argentina. See Brysk, *From Tribal Village,* ix.

53. Brysk, *From Tribal Village,* ix. Brysk's earlier chapter was considered a seminal work on Indian rights as a transnational movement: "Acting Globally: Indian Rights and Information Politics in the Americas," in Van Cott, ed., *Indigenous Peoples,* 29–51.

54. John Peeler, "Social Justice and the New Indigenous Politics: An Analysis of Guatemala and the Central Andes," paper for Latin American Studies Association International Congress, 1998, 14.

55. In addition to references in other endnotes, see Xavier Albó, *Pueblos indios en la política* (La Paz: Plural Editores, 2002); Deborah Yashar, "Indigenous Protest and Democracy," in *Constructing Democratic Governance, Latin America and Caribbean,* ed. Jorge Domínguez and Abraham Lowenthal (Baltimore: Johns Hopkins University Press, 1996), 87–105; "Contesting Citizenship: Indigenous Movements and Democracy," *Comparative Politics* 31, no. 1 (October 1998): 23–42; Christian Gros, *Políticas de la etnicidad: Identidad, estado y modernidad* (Bogotá: Instituto Colombiano de Antropología e Historia, 2000); Van Cott, ed., *Indigenous Peoples*; Rachel Sieder, ed., *Multiculturalism in Latin America: Indigenous Rights, Diversity, and Democracy* (New York: Palgrave Macmillan, 2002); David Maybury-Lewis, ed., *The Politics of Ethnicity: Indigenous Peoples in Latin American States* (Cambridge. Mass.: Harvard University Press, 2002); Kay Warren and Jean Jackson, eds., *Indigenous Movements, Self-Representation, and the State in Latin America* (Austin: University of Texas Press, 2002); Ronald Niezen, *The Origins of Indigenism: Human Rights and the Politics of Identity* (Berkley:

University of California Press, 2003); and Frank Salomon and Stuart B. Schwartz, eds., *The Cambridge History of the Native Peoples of the Americas*, vol. 3, *South America*, part 2 (New York: Cambridge University Press, 1999). Ediciones Abya-Yala in Quito has published a number of volumes on the indigenous and their movements.

56. Van Cott, *The Friendly Liquidation*.

57. See Van Cott, *The Friendly Liquidation*, table 4, 266–268.

58. Rodolfo Stavenhagen, *CEPAL Review* 62 (August 1997): 63.

59. Darren E. Sherkat and Christopher B. Ellison, "Recent Developments and Current Controversies in the Sociology of Religion," *Annual Review of Sociology* 25 (1999): 369.

60. This has been a consistent theme in Daniel Levine's influential work. See esp. his *Popular Voices in Latin American Catholicism* (Princeton, N.J.: Princeton University Press, 1992). Anna Peterson, *Martyrdom and the Politics of Religion: Progressive Catholicism in El Salvador's Civil War* (Albany, N.Y.: State University of New York Press, 1997).

61. Bartomeu Melia, "The Guarani Religious Experience," in *The Indian Face of God in Latin America,* ed. Manuel Marzal et al. (Maryknoll, N.Y.: Orbis, 1996), 170–216.

CHAPTER 2

From Civil Society
to Collective Action

THE POLITICS OF RELIGION IN ECUADOR

Alison Brysk

IN THEIR long and continuing struggle for rights, Ecuador's Indians have mobilized through, with, under, and against religious institutions. The debate on the role of religion in Ecuador's indigenous movement partakes of a wider conversation concerning the interaction between religious institutions and civil society in Latin America.[1] Are religious beliefs an opiate of the masses and religious institutions a partner of elite-dominated, ethnocentric regimes? Or can faith serve as a font of personal empowerment, while religious networks build civic alternatives to exclusionary or weak states? What is the political impact of the identity of Latin America's major religious actors? Does the history, structure, or beliefs of the Catholic Church or particular Protestant denominations produce patterned political consequences? More specifically, how do particular religious forces affect the political consciousness, mobilization, and rights of indigenous communities?

Religious actors and indigenous communities are both part of civil society, the terrain of social organization and political contention outside the formal government structure. Political scientists traditionally see civil society as a source of political attitudes and resources. In addition, it is increasingly recognized that civic institutions may also mediate between individuals and their governments, or even exercise direct power over citizens in lieu of or in tandem with state institutions. Civil society's political power will be seen in authoritative control of the assets, behavior, and identity of individuals; education and mobilization for collective action; and direct attempts to influence the policies of states and international organizations. Civil society thus can be both a source and a target of political action, as well as an interlocutor between state and citizen.[2]

Since Ecuador's religious institutions were politically organized before indigenous communities had mobilized for political action, the initial interaction is the influence of religious actors on indigenous society. The most important general roles of religious institutions in political life are to build political consciousness, establish social networks, expand notions of rights, and channel or represent a community's relationship with state authorities. In addition, weak states such as Ecuador have historically delegated some of their functions to religious institutions—such as education or social welfare. Such religious institutions then become an alternative source of local authority. And as indigenous communities began to mobilize a formal political movement, religious authority became a legitimate target for political mobilization by indigenous movements.

In order to evaluate the outcome of this interaction, it is helpful to consider broader patterns of the political impact of transnational civil society on indigenous communities. Comparative research suggests that authority organized around ideas will have the most beneficial impact on indigenous rights when the civic force is more structurally autonomous from states, has an ideology compatible with indigenous self-determination, and exhibits a pattern of learning through interaction with indigenous communities.[3] Careful analysis of these factors should overcome the "opiate versus liberator" dichotomy, as well as permit a more neutral analysis of particular religious institutions. As structural autonomy and religious ideology change over time, this type of analysis also suggests a dynamic relationship between religious institutions and indigenous communities and leads one to expect the political impact of religion to evolve with shifting social relationships and emerging indigenous agency. This approach stands in contrast to analyses that predict the political impact of religious groups based on their manifest theology and/or internal structure.

We can apply this rubric for the impact of civil society to the Catholic Church and Protestant missionaries in Ecuador. While the Catholic Church was historically less autonomous than Protestantism, by the 1980s liberationist Catholics faced fewer structural constraints than U.S.-sponsored Protestant missionaries, since the Catholic Church was no longer directly dependent on state patronage. Similarly, Catholic notions of human dignity were quite compatible with indigenous rights, once they were translated into a multicultural idiom. On the other hand, despite generic Protestant norms of individualism, Protestant missionaries in Ecuador were originally imbued with a Eurocentric ethos that gave short shrift to indigenous self-determination. However, the anthropological experiences and perspectives of certain groups such as World Vision fostered a learning process with indigenous communities.

BACKGROUND: THE UNHAPPY MARRIAGE
OF CHURCH AND STATE IN LATIN AMERICA

The conquest of America's indigenous peoples was carried out with cross and sword, yet the Catholic Church was also the first advocate for Indian rights in the Americas. It is also the oldest and largest transnational organization and the most consequential member of civil society throughout Latin America. During the period of colonization, patterns of principled resistance were set by sectors of the church. Dominicans such as Mexico's Bartolomé de las Casas challenged Spain's ideological legitimation of conquest and lobbied for changes in the legal status of Indian subjects; many consider de las Casas the first exponent of truly universal human rights. One study concludes, "There is a close correlation between the demands of the missionaries and theologians and the laws dictated by the [Spanish] kings."[4]

Nevertheless, the mainstream of the Catholic Church supported and benefited from the status quo domination of Indians until the mid-twentieth-century appearance of liberation theology. New tendencies like a preferential option for the poor coincided with a renewed transnational opening of the Latin American Church and the "contact conversion" of clergy who had been working in indigenous areas to a more multicultural orientation.

Reflecting the historical pattern, as late as the 1970s, indigenous movement representatives at a church-sponsored continental conference complained that the church had been used by the state to (forcibly)integrate indigenous peoples, had divided communities through missionary work, and even in its latter-day outreach had failed to consult thoroughly with Indian constituents. Sympathetic clerics from eight countries concluded with surprise that the Indian leaders seemed to value the church for its social work, not its theological role. In response, by the 1980s Ecuador's church had adopted a resolution to serve as a mediator between indigenous movements and the state and as a source of information and support on Indian rights.[5]

The interloper seeking to woo Latin Americans away from the Catholic Church is Protestantism. Protestantism and associated foreign missionary influence have been strongest in many of Latin America's most Indian countries and zones. For example, Ecuador's Chimborazo Province in the highlands Indian heartland is at least 20 percent Protestant, while the national Protestant population is less than 5 percent.[6] Criticisms of the political influence of Protestant fundamentalism on indigenous communities focus somewhat on active manipulation, but more frequently on the encouragement of political passivity and a "Protestant ethic" of capitalist individualism replacing traditional patterns of reciprocity and communal identity. There is widespread evidence that foreign missionaries and ideologies have promoted passivity and undermined village solidarity, although it is difficult to separate these influences from the general process of modernization and increasing international contact. Aside from several dramatic cases of direct political influence, the general impact of missionaries seems to operate through shifting social capital, rights, and roles. One disgruntled Ecuadorian evangelical Indian reported, "They [missionaries] prevented us from going out to protest, saying you just had to pray, now [anyway] we go out when there are problems, we have to see the brothers who are hungry or who are maltreated on busses." New social patterns introduced by missionaries unwittingly undermined traditional expressions of communal identity and sources of "social capital." "The *minga* [village communal work party] is done on Sundays. The Mormons don't participate because [their religion] prohibits work on that day." While individualism may well empower future leaders, there is clearly an inherent conflict between traditional and modernizing logics. Another Indian convert affirms, "I appreciate [my] culture, the tradition of the ancestors, but when and if it doesn't interfere with the economy."[7]

The most egregious case of political manipulation linked to foreign missionaries was found in Guatemala, where conservative evangelicals gained power through influence over a president (Ríos Montt) who pursued a genocidal civil war in Indian villages during the 1980s. In several other cases, politically conservative American fundamentalists have served as patriotic surrogates for U.S. interests in the region. But Latin American nationalist and leftist fears of a continent-wide campaign of theological imperialism proved exaggerated and were superceded by local Latin American takeovers of evangelical congregations and associations.[8] True indigenous Protestantism has played a surprising variety of roles, from quiescence to militancy.

INDIGENOUS POLITICS: COLLECTIVE ACTION IN ECUADOR

Ecuador's 1990 Indian uprising (*el levantamiento*) was historically and regionally unprecedented. For over one week, indigenous peoples rose up to shut down the country with occupations, demonstrations, and roadblocks. Versions of the 1990 uprising were repeated in 1992, 1994, 1997, 1999, and 2000. The demonstrations were organized by a national Indian rights confederation, CONAIE, which united indigenous groups from the Andes to the Amazon.[9]

In June 1990, instead of celebrating the solar equinox with the festival of Inti Raymi, Ecuador's Indians occupied Quito's main cathedral, shut down roads and markets throughout the nation, took over disputed lands, and even kidnapped some unpopular local officials. For movement leaders, the mark of their success was that for the first time in history, Ecuador's president negotiated directly with indigenous citizens. Some economic measures were taken, such as the establishment of a government fund for the purchase of contested lands and some increase of social services in certain communities.

In 1992, thousands of Amazonian Indians marched across the Andes to Quito, demanding territory, reduction of the border security zone, and indigenous management of the Yasuní National Park (which overlaps Indian territories). The month-long pilgrimage was sponsored by the Indian rights organization of Pastaza Province (OPIP—Organizacíon de los Pueblos Indígenas de Pastaza). While two thousand participants left the Pastaza capital of Púyó, their numbers had swelled to between five and ten thousand by the time they arrived in Quito, as highland peoples along the route joined in solidarity. Ecuadorian police monitored but did not suppress the 1992 march, and when the contingent arrived in Quito, the mayor offered them permission to camp in the capital's Central Park while they negotiated their demands with the president. The president accepted and extended the persuasive logic of the protestors, announcing, "These just demands are not against our government, but rather a reaction to five hundred years of oppression." The marchers had labeled their event "500 Kilometers of Resistance"—echoing the continental anti-quincentenary "500 Years of Resistance." In the course of the two-week negotiations, which included the Indian movements CONAIE, OPIP, and CONFENIAE (Confederacíon Indígena de la Amazonia Ecuatoriana), protesters also occupied the Ministry of Social Welfare and the Land Reform agency (in both cases, they were peacefully removed but not arrested). In the end, they received over a million hectares of territory—about 60 percent of their demand—split between three organizations. The march also secured a reduction of the border security zone, which contained about a third of the local Indian population.[10]

In 1994, massive civil disobedience protested the new Agrarian Law, which would roll back land reform—and the law was modified. The 1994 agrarian initiative passed by President Sixto Durán Ballén flouted the attempts of indigenous and peasant groups to introduce a comprehensive rural development package in the legislature. But Ecuador's Indians once again took to the streets in massive protest for nine days, blocking roads and cutting off food supplies to the cities. In the Amazon, they blockaded oil facilities. For the first time, all of the national-level indigenous organizations mounted a united front, including the traditionally accomodationist evangelical groups. The Durán Ballén government's initial response was to declare a state of emergency and mobilize the armed forces. There were some arrests and confrontations, and a mob backed by local elites sacked and burned the regional headquarters of the Indian movement in the province of Cañar. CONAIE had direct discussions with the World Bank and Inter-American Development Bank and brought in both the O.A.S. Human Rights Commission and Rigoberta Menchú's Iniciativa Indígena por la Paz—which indigenous leaders credit with making the government more amenable to negotiation.[11] In response to the uprising, Ecuador's president established a commission to amend the law; the commission included landowners' interest groups, legislators, church mediators, and both CONAIE president Luis Macas and CONAIE's secretary of lands Nina Pacari. As a result of the negotiation, forty articles of the Agrarian Law were amended and five new articles were introduced, including a new treatment of the public status of water rights, regional differentiation of the status of unused land, some remaining land redistribution, and government funds for rural retraining—including promotion of traditional indigenous agricultural techniques.

Recent waves of Indian mobilization in Ecuador have explicitly linked ethnic mobilization with resistance to adjustment. Indigenous groups mounted several strikes against government economic measures in 1993 and 1994. Rural Indian organizations were the major participants in a 1995 general strike called by a labor-peasant coalition to protest cuts in government social programs. In 1996, Indians protested for greater resources for the government bilingual education program.

In 1996, Ecuador's Movimiento Pachakutic elected a bloc of eight deputies to Ecuador's fractured eighty-eight-member legislature—in the same election that brought the ill-fated Abdalá Bucaram to the presidency. Bucaram's intense corruption, personal instability, and imposition of unpopular economic adjustment programs quickly alienated large sectors of Ecuador's citizenry. It was the Indian movement that spearheaded street protests and coordinated the widespread challenge to Bucaram that winter. By February 1997, the Ecuadorian Congress had voted to impeach Bucaram—by a margin of ten votes. Seven of those votes came from the Movimiento Pachakutic.

In August 1997, another full-fledged uprising occurred. This time the issues were renewed crisis in the Rural Social Security program and the government's delay in convening a promised Assembly for Constitutional Reform. Once again, tens of thousands of Ecuadorian Indians demonstrated, erected roadblocks, and took over public offices throughout the country. This time, they were part of a wider "Social Movement Coordination" and the protests were joined by peasants, oil workers, students, and leftist activists. The activists planned an autumn protest march along the 500-km length of Ecuador's oil pipeline, which carries crude from the Amazon over the Andes to coastal refineries. After forty-eight hours of protest, the president pledged new resources to the Rural Social Security Fund and the release of funds to the newly created Indigenous Development Council. The Assembly for Constitutional Reform, a longstanding demand of the indigenous movement, was brought forward to precede the presidential elections scheduled for 1998.

At the local level, almost a dozen indigenous mayors and scores of council members have assumed power in some regions, including Ecuador's third largest city (Cuenca). A procession of executive offices have served as channels and advocates for indigenous voice. In 1994, the Indigenous Office of the

Ministry of Social Welfare was upgraded to a Secretariat of Indigenous Affairs, reporting directly to the president (headed by an indigenous professional not associated with the movement). Following the 1996 elections, President Bucaram changed the new secretariat (SENAIN) to a cabinet-level ministry and appointed Amazonian indigenous co-directors from CONAIE and COICA (Coordinadora Indígena de la Cuenca Amazónica). After the demise of his government, the ministry was replaced by the Council for Indigenous Development under the direction of CONAIE officer Pacari. All of these agencies have been under funded and somewhat isolated from other bureaucracies, but important in establishing indigenous corporate presence. In 1998, Nina Pacari was elected to Congress as leader of the indigenous Pachakutic Party and became the second vice president of the Congress.

On January 21, 2000, the rising tide of indigenous protest spilled over into a direct attempt to take power, through indigenous movement participation in an abortive coup attempt by populist junior military officers. The indigenous movement had come to spearhead popular-sector anti-austerity protests and established relationships with a broad array of opponents of then-President Jamil Mahuad. After Indian movement protesters occupied the presidential palace, Congress, and Supreme Court, the military announced a three-man junta headed by Lt. Col. Lucio Gutiérrez—and including the head of CONAIE. When Ecuador's Congress, local business elites, and the international community balked, the junta collapsed in favor of replacing Mahuad with his vice president. Although coup leaders were sanctioned, episodes of Indian protest continued with widespread support.

After his release from jail, the pro-peasant military officer dismissed for his role in the coup, Lucio Gutiérrez, ran for president in 2002. With the endorsement of CONAIE and the Pachakutic Party, Gutiérrez was elected president on a populist program. As he assumed office, the new president designated CONAIE co-founder and Pachakutic Party congressional representative Nina Pacari as Ecuador's foreign minister. Gutiérrez also named former CONAIE president Luis Macas as Minister of Agriculture and Ranching, a key post for Indian's land rights concerns. This unprecedented influence of indigenous leaders in Ecuador's government is somewhat mitigated by Gutiérrez's simultaneous selection of a U.S.-educated banker as Minister of Economy and several military officers in other key administrative positions. At the same time, a December 2002 indigenous kidnapping of oil workers from contested territories demonstrates the persistence of the structural conflict between the Ecuadorian state's international dependence on oil revenues and its capacity to provide indigenous rights. Nevertheless, the new president's pledges of poverty reduction, popular participation, and multiculturalism offer the potential for Ecuador's indigenous movement to translate its program into action—a mere dozen years since it emerged as a national political force.

CIVIL SOCIETY: RELIGION AS BUILDER
OF INDIGENOUS COMMUNITY

Religious institutions helped build the indigenous movements which later led the protests and campaigns as well as the establishment of programs for local self-determination. The Italian-based Salesians were strong supporters of self-determination in the Shuar region and founders of the Shuar Federation. During the nineteenth century, Latin American governments often requested the presence of Italian Salesians, since the order was new, emphasized technical training and other modernizing activities, and was dedicated to working with the emerging urban working classes—there are more than four thousand Salesians in Latin America.[12]

The Salesians were drawn into this special relationship with the Shuar by two factors. The Salesians' original mandate from the state, to serve urban migrants to the Amazon, stimulated colonization and attendant cultural pressure on the Indians. This inadvertent displacement of vulnerable Indians by the Salesians' laboring flock dismayed the progressive clerics. So, the Salesians established Indian boarding schools to integrate the Shuar—but these were later criticized for their culturally destructive effects. The Salesians also started around fifty conventional and over two hundred radio schools. Father Juan Botasso, an Italian Salesian who had served among the Shuar, went on to found the Abya Yala Press, a bookstore, archives, and the Dom Bosco media center in Quito. Another Italian Salesian, Adriano Barale, founded an Amazonian aviation service for the order; it provides the Shuar Federation with air ambulance service, meat marketing from Shuar ranches, and over forty-seven thousand flights in the isolated region. The inspiration for the service came from competing oil company and Protestant transport systems which often excluded both Catholic missionaries and Shuar; the planes were paid for by congregations in Italy, Germany, and the United States.[13] Yet another Salesian initiative was the establishment of a hostel for migrant Indian workers in Quito, echoing the founder of the order's work in nineteenth-century Italy. Juan Botasso helped found the program in 1974; it is currently run by another Italian Salesian. The project, which has housed over 13,500 Indians, is heavily funded by the Inter-American Foundation and emphasizes the provision of legal services to migrants.[14]

Some elements within the national structure of the Catholic Church also raised consciousness and nurtured the burgeoning Indian rights movement. In the Ecuadorian highlands, Monseñor Leonidas Proaño became known as "the Bishop of the Indians." In an unprecedented opening to this ignored constituency, Proaño held regular grassroots assemblies, organized radio literacy campaigns, returned church lands to Indians, and constructed an Indian community meetinghouse (with French funds). The bishop founded an agricultural cooperative and development association which adumbrated the government's land reform program (CEAS); Proaño discussed the problem with then-President Camilo Ponce Enríquez. Proaño became famous for his substitute priestly garb: the denigrated poncho of the highlands Indian. He started an indigenous seminary and trained large numbers of Indian pastoral agents—many also active in community organizations. The bishop also assumed the liberation theology pedagogy of "see, judge, and act" and was influenced by the Brazilian Paulo Freire.[15] As his longtime assistant recounted, "Bishop Proaño said that the first thing we must give back to the Indians is their voice [su palabra]."[16]

At a 1976 international conference sponsored by Proaño on indigenous issues, the Ecuadorian police arrested seventeen visiting Latin American archbishops, four North American bishops, and Proaño himself. While this incident marked the level of domestic opposition to Indian rights and the probable involvement of Brazilian and Chilean intelligence services, the resultant public and world repudiation limited the state's repressive capacity.[17] One of the imprisoned priests reported: "Later we were visited by the Cardinal, by the Nuncio. . . . Then the Embassies began to come. The German Ambassador established himself there to see what was happening because there were also Germans, a Lutheran and others. So then [the government] was seen badly, they had 'blown it' [metido la pata], and they began to worry about treating us well."[18] In 1986, "the Bishop of the Indians" was nominated for the Nobel Peace prize. In 1988, he was awarded a posthumous Human Rights prize by the United Nations General Assembly, commemorating the fortieth anniversary of the Universal Declaration of Human Rights.

The church has continued to "accompany" Ecuador's Indians in their long march toward recognition and participation—sometimes literally. Church congregations, personnel, and community organizations supply blankets for marchers, presses for newsletters, and new messages of dignity and self-assertion. At the latest demonstrations in 2002, in which thousands of Indians from throughout the region occupied Quito to protest plans for hemispheric free trade, priests said mass in a local park before the marchers turned and entered the Ministerial Summit.[19]

The emerging Protestant challenge initially undercut indigenous mobilization, but later indigenous Protestants lent their organizational strength to Indian rights. In some areas of Ecuador, during the 1980s, Protestant missionaries promoted the establishment of "apolitical" rival evangelical indigenous associations which shadowed the emerging Indian rights movement groups and competed for state recognition at the local and regional levels. However, some of the indigenous evangelical groups broke from their foreign sponsors by the 1990s and assumed either a more neutral or supportive stance toward the Indian rights movement. Simplistic views of fundamentalism as opiate are challenged by developments such as the leading role played by Indians from Ecuador's Chimborazo Province—the most Protestant area of the highlands— in the 1990 indigenous uprising.[20] In 1995 FEINE, Ecuador's national con- federation of fourteen provincial evangelical associations began to actively collaborate with CONAIE under a new leadership. From the late 1990s, FEINE aligned with a separate national-level confederation (FENOCLE), but the Protestant organizations continued to join national Indian rights and anti- adjustment protests and to question government policies. Although evangeli- cal Indian individuals and congregations are somewhat less likely to mobilize politically than their Catholic peers, the web site of their national organization (FEINE) lists political reform as one of its principal goals.

Between Civil Society and State: The Church as Interlocutor

The Catholic Church quickly moved beyond the role of movement mid- wife to actively broker and mediate between restive indigenous populations and their political targets. Leonidas Proaño died in 1988, but his followers es- tablished a foundation (Fundación Pueblo Indio), a study center (CEDIS), a development agency (FEPP), and a human rights movement (CEDHU). Each of these organizations has served as an important resource for indigenous Ecuadorians: CEDHU's reports have pressured the Ecuadorian government in human rights cases, while FEPP has presided over an important land reform program linked to debt relief. Just as important, this network of church-based advocates has served as intermediary between the Ecuadorian indigenous movement and the government during periods of conflict. CEDHU's leader is a U.S.-educated Ecuadorian Maryknoll sister, Elsie Monge, whom Proaño brought back to Ecuador following work in Guatemala and Panama. During CONAIE's 1990 Indian uprising, the mediating commission was composed of Elsie Monge; Proaño's successor, Monsignor Víctor Corral; and a representa- tive of SERPAJ—a pan–Latin American grassroots human rights movement based in liberation theology and Ghandian "active non-violence."[21]

When Ecuador's indigenous movement launched the 1990 uprising, the public space they took over was one of Quito's main churches, Santo Domingo. In the national protests that followed in 1992 and 1994, church oc- cupations became part of the protest repertoire—as did clerical mediation. When the 1994 protests against agrarian counter-reform broke out, a hard- line president declared a state of siege. Former CONAIE president Luis Macas relates that when indigenous leaders meeting in Quito learned that arrest war- rants had been issued, they sought—and received—sanctuary in the National Bishops' Headquarters [Obispado].[22] The church then brokered the Agrarian Reform accord which settled the 1994 protests.

This mediating role has continued in subsequent waves of protest, and even in resolving the 2000 coup attempt. In a typical example, early 2001 rural protests and blockades resulted in food shortages, looting, several deaths, and a government declaration of a state of siege. The mediating commission which sought to restore order and acknowledge indigenous grievances was composed of the Catholic Church, human rights organizations, the United Nations mission in Quito, and the Association of Municipalities.[23] While the Latin American branch of the mainline Protestant World Council of Churches has occasionally worked with the Catholic Church on local inter-religious conflicts, Protestantism's weak historic role in Ecuador and the decentralization of the newer evangelical churches active in indigenous communities have diminished the possibilities for meaningful Protestant mediation of national-level indigenous protest.

Church as State? Religious Institutions as Delegated Authorities

We must also consider the direct political impact on indigenous communities when religious authorities substitute for weak states, usually by providing services at the local level. It is important to recognize that the provision of scarce vital services in isolated underserved areas may grant a civic group significant power—unmonitored and unelected. While Catholic missions and orders exercised great influence through the mid-twentieth century, especially in the Amazon, Catholic temporal power was diminished by the gradual implementation of constitutionally mandated separation of church and state, waves of land reform, philosophical changes in the church, and Catholic inability to staff remote rural outposts. Thus, in Ecuador the religious force which has assumed local authority or filled power vacuums has been Protestantism—usually foreign-sponsored evangelical missionaries.

For example, the (Protestant) missionary aviators of Alas de Socorro are still the main form of transport in the Ecuadorian Amazon—Ecuador's Ministry of Health pays 80 percent of their costs for air ambulance service, and the missionaries run 650 flights each month. Wings of Mercy has also placed a network of sixty radio sets in jungle villages, facilitating but also monopolizing communications in the region. While Indian rights organizations complain that the missionary aviators discriminate against them in the provision of services, the director claims to follow a strict set of guidelines and rate structure which favor only missionary work and medical emergencies. Stating that as foreigners the aviators must avoid politics, he explained that they will not transport political candidates, but will fly in polling personnel at government request. Similarly, Wings of Mercy will fly foreign oil company personnel in for "community development" or out for medical reasons, but they do not provide transport for routine oil company business operations. The director did recount that on "a handful" of occasions, communities had requested that the missionaries not bring in a particular visitor—some of these requests may have included activists and thus reflected local conflicts.[24]

The most notorious historic cases of this relationship of delegated authority involve a Protestant group, closely linked to the United States, with a
high level of theological ethnocentrism, targeting vulnerable rainforest Indians. The Summer Institute of Linguistics (SIL) is a fundamentalist Protestant
educational organization affiliated with the Wycliffe Bible Translators, with
more than six thousand members in forty-four countries in 1992. A core element of their belief system is the evangelical imperative to translate the Bible
into every known language and to convert maximum numbers of "unreached
peoples." From their U.S. supporters, the SIL derived ample material resources
for jungle aviation, communication, and well-equipped bases, backing from
Republican politicians and California businessmen, and a professional training
institute at the University of Oklahoma. Initial support was also provided by
expatriate coffee processors in Guatemala's Indian highlands, and later by the
Rockefellers, Standard Oil, the timber company Weyerhauser, and U.S. AID. In
return, the organization helped quell incipient Indian protest at the 1959
Inter-American Indian Conference with the expertise of missionary linguists,
surveyed Indian areas ripe for "development" in Brazil, and played a support
role for U.S.-backed counter-insurgency efforts in Ecuador, Peru, and Colombia. The entrepreneurial and visionary founder, Cameron Townsend, tirelessly
cultivated Latin American leaders for the cause. Through these connections,
the SIL was given jungle training facilities in Mexico's Chiapas region, widespread military cooperation, and authorization to administer bilingual education programs by Latin American governments throughout the Amazon
basin.[25]

Townsend gained such widespread acceptance in large part because he
could offer Latin American states something more important even than jungle
aviation: a program for the acculturation of "unreached" citizens. For the
Summer Institute to do its work, it had to gather dispersed tribal groups into
villages where they could attend school. Missionaries translated national an-
thems into native languages and helped states to count and register citizens.[26]
Contact with transplanted North Americans and their trade goods facilitated
Indians' integration into a cash economy. The missionaries' campaigns against
traditional dress, festivals, and marriage customs brought natives closer to their
Hispanic neighbors. And of course, training in Spanish and Christianity made
Indians better workers, soldiers, and citizens.

Nevertheless, by the 1980s, the Summer Institute was expelled from
Brazil, Ecuador, Mexico, and Panama, and restricted in Colombia and Peru, as
a result of a new nationalist coalition and vision. In Ecuador, a 1980 campaign
linked the Catholic Church, nationalist intellectuals, anthropologists, and an
emerging indigenous movement in opposition to the missionaries' control of
bilingual education. In a typical 1983 statement, Ecuador's Bishop of the Indians concluded, "Our evangelical brethren are contributing with all their ef-

forts, except [a few] honorable exceptions, to the maintenance of North American imperialism."[27] Accusations of SIL ties to the CIA were so persistent that the U.S. Embassy issued a denial in 1981.[28]

A crucial case became the SIL's "pacification" of the jungle Huaorani from the late 1950s, when oil was discovered in their area. In the initial attempts to contact the fierce and threatened hunter-gatherers, five American missionaries were speared. Their martyrdom captured the world's imagination through articles in *Life* magazine and a 1957 twenty-seven-city U.S. speaking tour by the sister of one of the victims—Rachel Saint—who appeared on "This Is Your Life" and the Billy Graham crusade with successful Huaorani converts. Through classic techniques of dropping gifts and broadcasting messages from helicopters, sending converted Huaorani back into unacculturated areas, and offering selective access to medical care and trade goods, the SIL's Rachel Saint established a local suzerainty. In 1969, she persuaded the Ecuadorian government to establish a Huaorani protectorate, moving many of the Huaorani "out of the way" of oil development. There, even missionary anthropologists reported that the Huaorani suffered a typical syndrome of cultural collapse, including epidemics, economic dependency, and social breakdown. The SIL itself removed Saint from her area in 1973, but she later returned to a neighboring zone, controlling access to radio communications, air traffic, and medical care in her enclave until her death in 1994.[29]

The resistance claimed that the SIL's mission of acculturation actually represented a form of "ethnocide"—the deliberate destruction of a culture. The new concept had been developed in a series of UNESCO and NGO (Nongovernmental Organizations) conferences, with influence from anthropologists at the Barbados meetings (who had directly demanded the exit of the SIL from Latin America). The main weapon of the Ecuadorian indigenists was an information campaign, revealing the extent and impact of the SIL's activities. This was combined with a legitimacy challenge to the state to assume its responsibilities in education and promote a *national* identity. The Summer Institute of Linguistics was formally expelled from Ecuador in 1980 (although a token presence remained). Remnants of SIL presence were protested in every subsequent Indian uprising. The missionaries' Quito headquarters, which had been leased from the municipality, were turned over to the national evangelical Indian rights group FEINE.

The SIL's ultimate legacy in the tribal village is ambiguous and contested. While SIL "villagization" of Ecuador's Huaorani contributed greatly to their physical and political deterioration, the SIL's anthropologist James Yost helped train the Huaorani in political skills to confront oil development pressures. The linguists' presence, airstrips, and "pacification" clearly facilitated subsequent activities of multinational resource extraction,[30] with all of its attendant consequences for indigenous health, welfare, and autonomy. But the missionaries themselves educated Indians about their legal rights and sometimes helped them to secure independent territories.

The Protestant evangelical development organization World Vision had a similar experience of delegated local authority in Ecuador, with a very different long-term outcome. Between 1979 and 1985, World Vision provided more than $4.7 million in aid to Ecuador.[31] But the experience of World Vision in Ecuador also illustrates the reconstruction of an acculturating agenda by mobilized indigenous communities. World Vision, globally active since the 1950s, appeared in Ecuador shortly after the expulsion of the Summer Institute—producing persistent rumors that the development organization was a secret surrogate for the missionary linguists. The organization's campaigns were supported by influential Americans such as board member Senator Mark Hatfield (Republican from Oregon). Although World Vision was based in a sector of the North American evangelical community similar to that of the SIL, it was populated by distinct personalities, did not engage in direct proselytization, and operated initially through child sponsorship programs and associated U.S. television campaigns. World Vision also concentrated on Indian areas, but while the Summer Institute sought out the "unreached peoples" of the Amazon, World Vision concentrated on the highlands poverty of syncretistic Chimborazo.

Like the Summer Institute, World Vision insisted that its humanitarian mission was a form of witness separable from its theological agenda. World Vision also was granted Ecuadorian government contracts during the 1980s for reforestation, water, rural electrification, and small production projects in Ecuador's Indian highlands. These contracts followed a period of competition between state development agencies and the better-funded North Americans, usually to the detriment of the bureaucratic and struggling state programs. State officials complained that World Vision outbid their programs, conditioned community aid on a monopoly of presence, and even induced villagers to destroy competing projects. One villager explained, "By necessity, we would ask the Devil himself for help, because the State hasn't given [us] anything. We don't look at the religion but at the community's needs."[32]

The biggest difference between World Vision and the Summer Institute as transnational agents, and that which ironically produced the most community conflict, was World Vision's channeling of resources through local members of Indian villages. World Vision's work was influenced by newer anthropologically influenced norms among missionaries, norms which stressed respect for local cultural values and the proselytizing efficacy of reliance on local authorities.

By 1982, World Vision had moved beyond the particularistic allocation of funds to sponsored families and begun to fund community-wide development programs. Funds were generally given to Indian evangelical congregations or emerging Protestant political associations to distribute. In several cases, World

Vision employees held simultaneous posts in municipal administration. This led to conflicts between traditional (Catholic) and evangelical sectors of Indian communities, including destruction of project property and even violence, along with widespread maladministration of funds. This generated bad publicity, notably an extensive study commissioned by the Ecuadorian government Ministry of Social Welfare and conducted by a respected Ecuadorian think tank. Local Indian organizations such as Imbabura's FICI [home of the weaver-merchant Otavalos] mobilized in protest. In response, World Vision appointed a new director in 1987—for the first time, an Ecuadorian national. New guidelines for management and distribution were drafted, anthropologists were hired, and the organization withdrew from several particularly conflictual communities.

The ultimate effects on indigenous movements and community activism were mixed, but displayed a surprisingly positive range of outcomes. In the highlands community of La Compañía, the conflict over World Vision unexpectedly promoted a reconciliation of religious divisions: the village elected a new council with a Catholic president, evangelical vice president, and Mormon treasurer. In Tocagón, a court case brought by World Vision for wrecking projects strengthened the role of the indigenous movement FICI as a defender of the community's rights, although others turned to Compassion International—a more overtly and preferentially evangelical patron. In Palugsha, the construction of a drinking water system brought together both religious and territorial factions. The canton of Otavalo sued World Vision for withdrawing committed resources—and won back a development fund of 13 million sucres to be administered by local councils. On the other hand, conflicts continued in some zones and some communities which rejected the entrance of World Vision on principled grounds were incorporated when the NGO hired former Indian movement leaders.[33]

Renewed criticism from the strengthening indigenous movement led World Vision to again reorganize in 1990, even bringing in some former academic critics as administrators. About fifty people left the Ecuador office, as the international headquarters in Monrovia, California, was also decentralized. World Vision signed agreements with local Catholic Churches and coordinated local provision of services with overlapping NGOs. Perhaps the most important change is that project plans were submitted for approval by the target community, and the communities were invited to designate the project administrator. Some of the evangelical Indians who had gained experience in World Vision projects went on to become active in Indian rights movements. One analyst links the small-project model introduced by the NGO to subsequent development strategies of those indigenous community organizations.[34]

While improvements in communication and transportation have diminished the physical isolation of indigenous zones, a decade of financial and political crisis has exacerbated the Ecuadorian state's withdrawal from a range of localities and social service functions. Thus, delegation of local authority to nongovernmental forces will continue, and some of those civic powers may well be religious forces.

A final trend is the physical withdrawal of large numbers of indigenous Ecuadorans via migration. Continuing intense internal and international migration has attenuated many indigenous Ecuadorians' ties to *all* community-based institutions, including churches. At the same time, as some immigrants' resources and networks recirculate through local communities, diasporas have become in some cases—like Otavalo—a third alternative to church and state organizations and identities. As indigenous communities become transnational, relationships with religious institutions of all kinds are more selective and self-determined, yet religious affiliation may persist or even grow as a source of bonding across borders.[35]

CONCLUSIONS

The Ecuadorian indigenous experience with religion shows that civil society matters—politics are forged by civic identities, challenges are supported by civic networks, policies are mediated by civic interlocutors, and authority is exercised by civic administrators. But it also suggests that religious structure matters as much as religious content. It has been the *role* as much as the beliefs of religious forces that made the difference between oppression and liberation. This suggests that indigenous peoples, advocates, and scholars may want to focus less on theology and more on religious actors' relationship to state power.

But the political impact of religious forces on Ecuador's indigenous community has also changed over time, with a general evolution in social context mirrored by the internal trajectory of both major religious forces. At the broad historical level, religion has moved from opiate to liberator to increasing political independence. Both Catholicism and Protestantism have followed this pathway, despite very different theologies and structures, over distinctive time periods corresponding to their historical scale of active presence in indigenous communities. In the current period, as the Indian rights movement has emerged as an independent and influential national political force, religious preferences, programs, and networks have a much less predictable relationship to political behavior.

The current scenario in Ecuador suggests an intensification of both of these trends: evolving religious independence, but ongoing relationships between states and their churches—with potentially contradictory consequences. On the one hand, the indigenous movement that has come of age and entered national power does not reference or reflect religious institutions or affiliations. In this sense, we should expect a trend of growing religious independence parallel to the general experience of other ethnic constituencies around the world, as they modernize and gain broader opportunities for political participation. Overall, this means that religious institutions may become active around particular issues or in particular regions, but become less relevant to mobilization and mediation at the national level.

On the other hand, the trend of globalization may increase the influence of certain religious groups and identities. The decentralization and privatization catalyzed by economic crisis and mandated by international lenders recreate the traditional power vacuum of underdevelopment—which is now urban as well as rural. Among other things, this means *more* power for religious groups as delegated service providers. Globalization also seems to increase the attractiveness of Protestantism (especially Pentecostalism) as an identity, which is widely perceived as "more international" despite Catholicism's historic and structural transnationalism. In a country that has adopted the U.S. dollar as its national currency, it makes sense to worship the brand of deity that is referenced on the greenback. However, increased identification with and knowledge of the United States may also encourage more secular attitudes and less engaged varieties and interpretations of Protestantism.

The interaction of these trends is difficult to predict, and the picture is further complicated by newer minority religions that have become important in particular locations or issues—including Mormonism, Baha'i, and resurgent interest in pre-Christian indigenous religious practices. Religion's influence on indigenous politics in Ecuador is likely to be increasingly situational and less systematic. What is certain is that civil society will continue to matter— through, with, under, and against politics.

Notes

1. Please see the introduction to this volume; Timothy Steigenga, *The Politics of the Spirit: The Political Implications of Pentecostalized Religion in Costa Rica and Guatemala* (Lanham, MD: Lexington Books, 2001); Edward Cleary and Hannah Stewart-Gambino, eds., *Conflict and Competition: The Latin American Church in a Changing Environment* (Boulder: Lynne Rienner, 1992); and Edward Cleary and Hannah Stewart-Gambino, eds., *Power, Politics, and Pentecostals* (Boulder: Westview Press, 1997).

2. On civil society, see Jean Cohen and Andrew Arato, *Civil Society and Political Theory* (Cambridge: MIT Press, 1992); Thomas Carothers, "Civil Society," *Foreign Policy* (winter 1999–2000): 19–29; Alison Brysk, "Democratizing Civil Society in Latin America," *Journal of Democracy* 11, no. 3 (July 2000).

3. Alison Brysk, *From Tribal Village to Global Village: Indian Rights and International Relations in Latin America* (Stanford: Stanford University Press, 2000).

4. A. Calderón, "El papel de los misioneros y los antropólogos," in *Antropólogos y misioneros. ¿Posiciones incompatibles?* ed. Juan Botasso (Quito: Editorial Abya-Yala, 1986), 113.

5. Juan Botasso, *Las misiónes Salesianas en un continente que se transforma* (Quito: Centro Regional Salesiano, 1982), 201–203; Arquidiócesis de Quito, *Plan Pastoral de la*

Arquidiócesis de Quito, 1995, 101, 115; Conferencia Episcopal Ecuatoriana, *Lineas pastorales,* Quito, 1994, 115.

6. Susana Andrade, *Visión mundial: Entre el cielo y la tierra* (Quito: Editorial Abya-Yala, 1990), 24; Alvin Goffin, *The Rise of Protestant Evangelism in Ecuador, 1895–1990* (Gainesville: University Press of Florida, 1994).

7. Andrade, *Visión mundial,* 56, 83, 67.

8. David Stoll, *Is Latin America Turning Protestant?* (Berkeley: University of California Press, 1990).

9. The following section is based on Brysk, *From Tribal Village.*

10. Norman Whitten, Dorothea Scott Whitten, and Alfonso Chango, "Return of the Yumbos: The Indigenous Caminata from the Amazon to Andean Quito," *American Ethnologist* 24, no. 2 (1997): 355–391.

11. Interviews, October 26, 1995.

12. Botasso, *Las misiónes Salesianas,* 15, 17.

13. T.E.A. Arroyo, *Diez años servicio Aéreo Misional Misión Salesiana de Oriente 1975– 1985* (Quito: Servicio Aéreo Misional, Procura Misión Salesiana, 1985).

14. Botasso, *Las misiónes Salesianas,* 71; Patrick Breslin, *Development and Dignity* (Rosslyn, Va.: Inter-American Foundation, 1987), 56.

15. L. Proaño, *Luchador de la paz y de la vida* (Quito: FEPP-CEDIS, 1989).

16. Interview, July 1995.

17. Goffin, *The Rise of Protestant Evangelism,* 117.

18. Proaño, *Luchador de la paz,* 24.

19. EFE News Service, October 30, 2002.

20. Goffin, *The Rise of Protestant Evangelism,* 131.

21. Ibid., 121, 131.

22. Interview, May 18, 1997.

23. Spanish CRE Satellite Radio web site, Guayaquil, February 5, 2001.

24. Interview, August 31, 1995.

25. F. Barriga López, *Las culturas indígenas ecuatorianas y el Instituto Lingüístico de Verano* (Quito: Ediciones Amauta, 1992); Stoll, *Is Latin America Turning Protestant?*; B. Colby and Charlotte Dennett, *Thy Will Be Done: The Conquest of the Amazon, Nelson Rockefeller, and Evangelism in the Age of Oil* (New York: HarperCollins, 1995); P. Aaby and S. Hvalkof, *Is God an American? An Anthropological Perspective on the Missionary Work of the Summer Institute of Linguistics* (Copenhagen: International Working Group on Indigenous Affairs, 1981).

26. Barriga López, *Las culturas indígenas ecuatorianas,* 117.

27. Proaño, *Luchador de la paz,* 78.

28. Barriga López, *Las culturas indígenas ecuatorianas,*: 287.

29. David Stoll, *Fishers of Men or Founders of Empire? The Wycliffe Bible Translators in Latin America* (London: Zed Press with Cultural Survival, 1982).

30. Colby and Dennett, *Thy Will Be Done.*

31. Goffin, *The Rise of Protestant Evangelism,* 84.

32. Andrade, *Visión mundial,* 67–68.

33. Ibid., 57, 59, 68, 90.

34. Ibid., 85–88; interview, June 27, 1995.

35. See David Kyle, *Transnational Peasants: Migrations, Networks, and Ethnicity in Andean Ecuador* (Baltimore: Johns Hopkins University Press, 2000).

CHAPTER 3

New Voice in Religion and Politics in Bolivia and Peru

Edward L. Cleary

BOLIVIA'S INDIGENOUS have made themselves into the newest political force in the country. They are able to command attention in ways that rival most groups in the country. They have brought about constitutional changes and threaten more. Peru's indigenous have yet to form a strong national movement, but they present a new face to Peru's political classes. Increasingly, they no longer accept the subordinate status imposed on them for centuries.

In June 2002 indigenous groups again drew national attention with a march across the main arteries of Bolivia. More than a thousand marchers made their way across hundreds of kilometers in an effort to wrest concessions both from the government and from political parties. This was a repetition of the watershed 1990 March for Land and Dignity. The indigenous chose in 2002 to mount a challenge to government and political parties at a most vulnerable time of scheduled national elections. They were making it clear that the Bolivian nation had to hear them out about unfulfilled promises.

Behind these processes that virtually no politician or social scientist predicted are Catholic and Protestant churches. Whereas charges were raised at the 1971 Barbados Conference that missionaries were contributing to ethnocide, missionaries in Peru and Bolivia have provided the needed external boost to indigenous political activism and to the creation of a native intellectual force.[1]

The resurgence of Indian populations in Latin America is strongly evident in Bolivia and Peru.[2] Investigation of both countries shows the reasons for the resurgence: the struggles to revitalize what were considered dying traditional cultures and the crucial role that religion has played. Churches provided key resources needed for fostering ethnic identity and for stimulating indigenous political activism.

In the process, a distinctive Indian theology is being born. Indian theology grows from grassroots efforts. Seven intellectual and cultural centers, with libraries and world-renowned experts, anchor these efforts. Indians have found the intellectual resources that have been unavailable to them for centuries.

The comparison of Peru and Bolivia, two key indigenous countries, points to important differences. Despite relative equality in Peru and Bolivia in terms of resources for cultural and political activism, the achievements in Bolivia exceed those in Peru. In a word, the relative strength of indigenous movements depends in strong measure on structural and institutional constraints, as well as opportunities encountered, in the religious field and in respective societies.

This chapter is divided into four thematic sections. The first section deals with conflicts in religious ideology. The second section addresses the emergence of an indigenous church and the individuals who facilitated it in this part of the Andean region. The next section deals with the emergence of indigenous political activism. The chapter ends with a discussion of major achievements and with a comparison of Bolivia and Peru.[3]

CLASHES OF RELIGIOUS IDEOLOGY

An ideological war—a religious ideological war—has been waged on the Altiplano and Amazonian region for more than thirty years. The thousands of square kilometers of upland Peru and Bolivia, the focal point of this study, contained areas so remote that few signs of modernity (graded roads or clinics) and few tax collectors were present. Yet even before 1970 a great influx of ideas coming from outside was taking place. Nor were the peoples of the Altiplano, where the majority of Indian peoples live, passive peasants. By the 1960s many rural Indian men and women lived part of their lives in towns and cities. Many served in the military, traveled to other parts of their countries, and listened frequently to radio with news of the outside world.

Two types of religious ideology flooded into the Altiplano and clashed, especially from the early 1970s. First, Mormons, Pentecostals, and a wide range of churches, sects, and cults brought clashing religious messages to a nominally Catholic population. They also brought demands of "true faith" and promises of healing and salvation. One impact on many indigenous persons was confusion and division.[4]

The second religious conflict took place within Catholicism. The presence of Catholic clergy in the remote areas of Peru and Bolivia has waxed and waned over the five hundred years of Catholicism in these countries. When modern missionaries reached remote Andean areas in the early 1940s, they found the church in decline, with few priests ministering there. Missionaries from mostly North Atlantic countries began taking over many parishes and missions in the region. The church gained organizational strength, multiplying jurisdictions and responsibilities. To traditional indigenous religion, missionaries counterposed orthodox Catholicism. Where missionaries had a steady and thick presence, their impact was often strong. Hans and Judith Buechler have described the changes they affected in the Altiplano as "reform Catholicism,"[5] alterations in religiosity brought on by changes in the Catholic Church in the 1960s.

EMERGENCE OF INDIGENOUS CHURCH AND NEW ETHNIC IDENTITY

Vatican Council II (1962–1965) and the Latin American Bishops' Medellín Conference (1968) led to changes, this time toward modernity and away from traces of traditional practices. Bishops, priests, and catechists began taking harder stands against traditional practices that seemed to them to have little to do with essential Christianity. At least one diocese in the heart of Aymara country, bordering on Lake Titicaca, forbade the celebration of Catholic masses within certain traditional celebrations, as carnival. For a period of some years meetings to plan church strategies were often marked by strong disagreements.[6]

During this period liberation theology became *un paradigma hegemónico,* a hegemonic paradigm, for many missionaries. Theology of liberation, as a modernizing and rational element in religious thought, was seen not just as condemning traditional practices as out of touch with a modern understanding of Scripture, but also as portraying traditional practices as the continuation of the dominance of mestizo political and economic control and the subordination of Indian peasants.

But liberation theology guided only a sector of missionaries and the native religious. Others were aware of liberation theology but did not follow closely its principles. Instead, they were driven by another impulse, forming an indigenous church. This was the overarching policy, shared also by most liberationists, in most, or a large part, of indigenous territory. The church changed its policy, as noted in the introduction to this volume, from an *indigenista* to *indígena,* from paternalist to accompaniment.[7] Thus, the main thrust of missionaries and other religious workers among the very large Indian populations of Peru and Bolivia was creating an indigenous church. This represented a major change: instead of working to incorporate Indians within a unified culture, the church turned to providing the basis for other than Eurocentric cultural expressions of Christianity. In attempting this, missionaries and others found the basis for an Indian theology.

Further, those involved in the monumental task of creating an indigenous church were deeply concerned about the lack of what was called by them "religious knowledge." Left without benefit of clergy for decades, many indigenous peoples did not have an orthodox understanding of Christianity. Questions were increasingly raised about whether Indian communities (and many other Latin Americans) had ever been properly instructed in fundamental aspects of Catholicism.[8] Out of this discussion came the conviction of need of a New Evangelization. This became the policy emphasis of John Paul II and the Latin American bishops at their Santo Domingo General Conference (1992).[9]

Long before the Santo Domingo meeting, those interested in establishing an indigenous church had focused on training native teachers, catechists, to begin this epic task. Thousands of catechists were educated in myriad centers. To extend geographically the efforts of the catechists, to reinforce their teaching, and to increase survival skills (as improved farming methods and health precautions), Catholic and Protestants alike employed citizens' media, especially low-range radio stations and radio schools, described below.[10]

At root, the policy shift to an indigenous church meant, first of all, regard for promoting native languages for worship and instruction. It also meant supporting political self-determination, equipping communities for contact with outsiders, recovering cultural memory, and stimulating alliances. All these objectives had implications for political involvement.

Intellectual Resources for Indigenous Peoples

Indian religion was truly in crisis, in danger of being overwhelmed by the avalanche of foreign religions and torn by internal divisions among Catholics. Despite the remoteness of the Altiplano, the Indian peoples had been through other invasions and internal divisions brought on by outsiders. The invasion of Inca rulers and then the Spanish were only two of these incursions. What distinguishes the present period from others in which Indians were assaulted by outside influences and what anchors the Catholic Church's presence in indigenous areas are catechists and intellectual centers placed throughout or near the Altiplano in the larger Andean region.

These centers grew from a larger impulse in the Latin American church: a conviction that each culture has its own integrity that must be known and respected by missionaries. The centers appeared in the Andean region of South America and in Guatemala and Mexico. Through these centers, bishops and missionaries hoped to form native religious leaders for an indigenous church. Further, some centers helped raised political consciousness in indigenous communities and encouraged the indigenous to organize to struggle for their own rights.[11] They conceived this as the self-emancipation of the poor.[12]

Crucial Role of Catechists

More was at stake than finding indigenous persons to act as translators of liberation theology. Indeed, some missionaries and even more bishops had neither personal inclination nor time to absorb liberation theology. Rather, virtually all agreed to the formation of an indigenous church. Lacking a native clergy, the indigenous church could have catechists. Catechetical centers trained persons especially in understanding the Bible. These centers became something similar to indigenous seminaries. For at least fifty years the practice of having a native catechist in each rural settlement area has grown. Under the impact of missionary presence religious life has changed in many areas of the Andean region. The hegemonic hold of fiesta sponsorship has diminished to a considerable degree. In some areas it is gone entirely.

The contemporary history of Bolivia and Peru is being played out in an entanglement of local and global forces. Indigenous ethnic groups are interacting with national political forces as well as international market penetration. Fundamentally, the situation touches upon personhood and identity, an interaction of religion, persons, community, nation, and the parts of the larger world that affect Bolivian and Peruvian agriculture, commerce, and economic lives. Viewed from the underside, catechists act as a major factor in affecting changes in personhood among the indigenous in Peru and Bolivia.

Catechists are lay specialists, mostly volunteer actors in Aymara, Quichua, and other indigenous communities. Missionaries have been important in indigenous revitalization, but catechists are equally or more important. They recruit and lead. They act as intermediaries between missionaries and communities. They act as a new layer inserted between original layers of a religious organization, that is, between priest and congregation. They have become increasingly important actors in the wide, intense, and influential discourse of ethnic identity that has been taking placing in the Peruvian and Bolivian Altiplano.

Catechists began to see themselves as protagonists of their interpretation of Christianity, not objects of evangelization. In doing so, they discarded their role as buffers between larger society and communities to become translocal intermediaries. Religious actors joined and fostered in the turning outward of indigenous communities from isolation to the occupation of contentious public space.

Basic conceptions of personhood and agency are important in this transformation toward political activism. Catechists are helping Aymaras to define their personhood proactively as persons capable of interacting with the state instead of fatalistically hanging back from full political participation or, more accurately, operating in their own world, more or less apart from a citizen's participation in the nation. Equally, the reinterpretation led by catechists of "community" is important for indigenous who, to a greater or lesser extent, define themselves through participating in a community. Thus, Aymaras and other ethnic groups began conceiving themselves as a people on the march toward greater independence or autonomy within the nation.

In sum, catechists help reshape indigenous ethnic groups by leading small groups to reinterpret their place in society through the Bible and their ethnic cosmologies. Further, in some areas of the Altiplano, catechists form networks within their own circle. These networks help to overcome the antagonism between indigenous communities built up over centuries of feuds over land and other issues. They have become meta-Aymaras or meta-Quichuas

Both Catholic progressives and conservatives have promoted access to the Bible. Reflection on the Bible takes place at Sunday liturgies or more commonly in weeknight meetings of small communities. Catechists, *presidentes de la comunidad,* or leaders of the Word of God, facilitate the meetings, but those in attendance are expected to offer their interpretation of the Bible passages.

These communities are by no means all base Christian communities promoted by enthusiastic followers of liberation theology.[13] But, for the sake of example, presume the case of a small community where the catechist and members have picked up ideas from liberation theology. Exposure to the Bible and the exposure of liberation-theology-oriented pastoral agents in interpreting the Bible contributed to indigenous Catholics' political consciousness, especially in the late 1980s and early 1990s.[14]

However, whether small community leaders are liberationists or not, indigenous readers interpret the Bible in extremely complex ways. Their biblical reflections are more than folk liberation. The indigenous churches have cosmologies that guide them to interpretations that look and sound different from liberation theology. Thus is being born a theology of inculturation that may lead to *teología india,*[15] as noted by Stephen Judd in his chapter within this volume.

Pivotal Centers

Seven remarkable centers grew from missionary efforts in the region and revitalized Catholic universities in Peru and Bolivia, where missionary anthropologists and religious studies experts focused their activities. These well-placed centers anchored a theological and pastoral indigenous revitalization. Five began as free-standing centers near Puno, Cuzco, and Sicuani, in Peru, and La Paz and Oruro, in Bolivia.[16] Two other places were not so much centers as well-defined emphases at the Catholic University in Lima, headed by Manuel Marzal, and at the Bolivian Catholic University's theological campus in Cochabamba, with Hans van den Berg, Luis Jolicoeur, Francisco McGourn, and Juan Gorski.

The major figures staffing these centers were principally missionaries. Many had advanced graduate training in anthropology or religious studies. A large part of their own and the centers' financial support came from their overseas congregations or foreign-mission collections. All made strenuous efforts to include indigenous members as part of their teams, looking for the day when the centers would be fully conducted by native talent.[17] In their founding, one center was from U.S. Maryknoll Missioners (Puno), one French Dominican (Cuzco), two Spanish Jesuit (Lima and La Paz), one French Canadian Oblate (Oruro), and two alliances of mostly religious orders (Cuzco and Cochabamba).

Several centers have significant collections of research materials on indigenous religions. The Catholic University of Bolivia's campus at Cochabamba may have the best collection of ethnographic materials in the Andean region. Members of these centers have been extraordinarily productive.[18] The academic nature of their work and their influence on a wider world can be seen in the long lists of their works that are routinely collected at Harvard and University of California, Berkeley, libraries and the Library of Congress.

The members of these centers conducted anthropological and historical research and engaged in theological reflection. To a greater or lesser extent members of centers other than Cochabamba absorbed the method of liberation theology. They took seriously the first step of liberation theology: to describe the universe in which Indians lived. To do this, center members had to listen to indigenous people describe religion as they experienced it. The second step of liberation theology is biblical reflection. Thousands of hours were spent by researchers and indigenous peoples discussing the Andean or biblical understanding of native religious practices. Ten to twenty-five years have been spent by individual researchers in this process. The director of the Andean Pastoral Center, María José Caram, O.P., described the effort of the noted Southern Andean Church as cultivating "a spirit of contemplation and listening and trying to put aside paternalistic and materialistic attitudes."[19]

The major figures differ considerably in how they came into this enterprise. Diego Irarrázaval experienced firsthand and early in his life (he was a deacon and not yet ordained a priest when he left Chile) how leftist Catholics had committed serious failures. He recognized, for example, that the movement of Christians for Socialism did not give sufficient attention to the divisions it caused within the church. In Peru, where he was working as a missionary, Irarrázaval emphasized listening rather than organizing. He built up an impressive body of work on indigenous religion based on what he observed.[20]

Irarrázaval never lost his enthusiasm for liberation theology; indeed, it was the driving force that led him to the poorest of Latin America. "Here [among the indigenous] liberation theology has borne its fruit: believing communities and men and women missionaries who are fully committed to the cause of the continent's poor."[21] By the 1980s he began seeing Indian religion as inculturated liberation: communities finding salvation from evil and sin and confronting local customs that cause self-destruction.

On the Bolivian side of the Andes, Xavier Albó has become what one longtime observer has called a "twentieth-century reincarnation of Bartolomé de Las Casas, a one-man publishing industry, and the country's most intellectual activist in the area of indigenous issues."[22] Albó came to occupy this position from a somewhat different path than Irarrázaval. To prepare himself for establishing or working with an Indian center, Albó, a Catalan Jesuit priest, obtained a Ph.D. in anthropology and social linguistics at Cornell University. Albó, for the most part, eschewed working with other professionals, choosing instead to mentor talented Indian activists and intelligentsia.

An Emerging Theology of Inculturation

Missionaries were strategically placed to have a major hand in shaping a theology of inculturation.[23] They sought out remote areas where the majority of Indians live. Missionary groups remained there with enduring commitment to hear and to understand native languages and conceptions of God and Jesus, death and resurrection. Missionaries had resources, intellectual and economic, for drawing in teams of experts and organizing activities. Further, as foreigners they were acutely aware of the need of cultural adaptation, whereas national clergy frequently did not conceive of the indigenous as the "other," a central concept in dealing with culture.

Under the hand of missionaries, liberation theology began to take a decided turn. In a sense, missionaries and indigenous spokespersons forced theologians of liberation to reconsider traditional forms of thought as expressing, in an imperfect but important way, the face of God.[24] Or, stated from the other side, Indians forced changes in prevailing Christian theology. Popular religion and traditional religion were seen as having strongly positive as well as negative qualities.[25] On the part of the indigenous, liberation theology had to be extended to include cultural liberation.[26] This was a major missing element in liberation theology,[27] as noted in the introduction.

Three larger aspects of liberation thus emerged in missionary-indigenous discussions of liberation. First, development of all forms of life to their full potential is liberating. Second, liberation would strengthen community solidarity, not weaken it as Christian churches have done by bringing division to communities. Third, in the case of Aymara people, liberation would mean liberation of the Aymara nation.

A second stream of indigenous religious thought, a culturalist view, developed vigorously alongside the much better known liberation theology. Both streams lead to the elaboration of indigenous theology. Instead of beginning analysis from the world of miners and other workers, many persons carried on their reflections from what Luis Jolicoeur calls "a cosmovision totally distinct from the world of work." For him, people working within the cultural framework found this social struggle not the most fundamental or inclusive. It was not as if these academics and indigenous leaders rejected the workers' struggle or did not recognize its value. They thought something else more important. However, while Jolicoeur believed the culturalist view could exist peacefully with a liberationist perspective, Albó made it clear that he strongly disagreed with the culturalist perspective, as taking the support away from political activism.[28]

Juan Gorski has provided a succinct statement about Indian theology from a culturalist perspective, one that has been published in several languages due to widespread interest in the topic.[29] Together, Luis Jolicoeur, as rector, and Hans van den Berg, Frank McGourn, and Gorski, as professors, form the basis for perhaps the strongest indigenous theology center in Latin America. The Instituto Superior de Estudios Theológicos (Higher Institute for Theological Studies) forms part of the Catholic University of Bolivia campuses at Cochabamba. To these are affiliated the Institute of Applied Anthropology, Institute of Missiological Studies, and Library of Ethnography. Graduates from Cochabamba have published careful studies extensively on indigenous cultures, far beyond Bolivia.[30] In contrast to Guatemala, the Bolivian church includes large numbers of indigenous seminarians. In the racist context of Bolivia the shame of being indigenous has given way to cultural pride. The intellectual basis for an indigenous church is taking place for the first time in five hundred years.

The Bolivian and Latin American bishops have been key players in this effort. For some years the bishops were not attuned to indigenous cultural questions. But, following pressures from priests and catechists of the indigenous church and responding to the indigenous complaints about the celebration of Columbus's "discovery," the bishops have strongly backed Indian initiatives since the early 1990s.[31]

Protestants number about 10 percent of Bolivian and Peruvian populations, with concentrated groupings in the highlands and Amazonian regions. While Protestants have not created indigenous intellectual centers similar to the Catholic ones described, some provided a generalized thrust toward political empowerment. Notably, Adventists encircled Lake Titicaca, providing schools that have had a positive impact on an almost exclusively indigenous student body. Fernando Stahl, a pioneer Adventist educator, has emerged as a major figure in designing education for indigenous empowerment.

In a word, Catholic and some Protestant churches provided an intellectual basis toward empowerment of Indians, furnishing centers, schools, and informal educational opportunities aimed at creating an indigenous church. This, in turn, served as a fundamental basis for political activism.

Emergence of Indigenous Political Activism

Whereas only a small number of formal indigenous organizations existed in the 1960s, since then, hundreds of indigenous associations of all types not only sprung up but also made their impact felt locally, nationally, and internationally. Indeed, a few prescient political scientists pointed to a transnational indigenous movement that was making its voice heard at the Organization of American States and the United Nations.[32] The movement improved political negotiating capacity of Indian groups in their own countries.

During the first two-thirds of the twentieth century the Peruvian and Bolivian states and political parties made strong efforts to eradicate the "ethnic question." Both countries attempted to turn their indigenous population into peasants. *Campesino* (peasant) replaced *indio* (Indian). *Indígena* (indigenous) was reserved for the people from eastern forest region. Use of "community" was dropped in favor of union, cooperatives, or agricultural producers. Political parties, from the right and the left, wanted to put an end to the idea of ethnic identities acting in opposition to the state. As Albó mentions, the Peruvian and Bolivian states wanted to be universal and monopolistic in their control.[33] It has not worked. Indians held onto their identity through communitarian space, rituals, and local politics. As Víctor Hugo Cárdenas has pointed out, a close reading of indigenous history shows that indigenous communities have a quality of being mini-states.[34]

Peruvian and Bolivian intellectuals largely ignored Indian culture as part of the national patrimony. Two prominent Andean intellectuals broke with this tradition. Fausto Reinaga published *La revolución india* in 1969 to the great discomfort of his Bolivian colleagues. The Peruvian intellectual of world renown, Anibal Quijano, raised the question of ethnic identity in 1980 in terms of *cholo*.[35] But in the 1990s, the almost exclusively non-Indian intellectuals no longer had the floor to themselves. To the great surprise of Peru and Bolivia's educated classes, Indian intellectuals not only existed but they stepped forward confidently into the public sphere. The assimilationist model, in the indigenous view, was dead.

Beginnings of Political Activism in the Andean Region

None of the indigenous rights movements would have appeared as readily or in the form in which they have appeared without outside help. The impulse to organize and to act in the public sphere in new ways came from anthropologists and from the churches, especially from missionaries.[36] The first notable indigenous political movements appeared in Ecuador. The political assertiveness of the Shuar peoples, supported by Salesian missionaries, began in the early 1960s. Their activism refracted into peoples of the neighboring Peruvian Amazon region. The first notable Peruvian congress of indigenous, Congreso Amuesha, took place in 1968. This was followed by the formation of the Council of Aguarana and Huambisa and then the Front for the Defense of the Native Shipibo Communities. By the beginning of the 1980s the three groups had pulled together into the Interethnic Association for the Development of the Peruvian Jungle (AIDESEP). The united group went on to become the principal voice of eastern Peruvian Indians.

The Bolivian National Revolution (1952) depended upon indigenous participation and their armed groups to enter and to continue in the presidential palace. Indians were rewarded by being declared campesinos (peasants), instead of the (then) deprecatory indio (Indian). They were given their own ministry within the government, the Ministry of Peasant Affairs. The leaders of the Movimiento Nacional Revolucionario (MNR), the party of the revolution, and Bolivia's other political leaders of the 1950s through the next decades pushed a policy of integration, not cultural pluralism. But the revolution unleashed far greater active lower-class participation in national life than had been the case in Bolivia. With the opportunities afforded by the revolution and with foreign aid monies, indigenous built and staffed thousands of new primary schools. Thereafter Bolivians achieved a pace of improved literacy and student enrollment unmatched even by Brazil.[37] The stage was set in Bolivia for the momentous change back from campesino to indio.

In the 1960s in the Bolivian highlands, after his contacts among Indian communities where he had done doctoral field research, Xavier Albó began gathering around him native speakers and investigators to form CIPCA (Centro de Investigación y Promoción del Campesinado, or Center for Investigation and Promotion of Peasants). This activist think tank nurtured the Katarists. In turn, the Katarists spawned a family of parties and movements. When possible, Albó submerged his talents, hoping that others would take leadership positions.

The CIPCA group included Víctor Hugo Cárdenas, who became a major figure in Bolivian politics. Cárdenas translated and familiarized himself with North American and European anthropologists and historians who wrote about the Andean region. This gave him the capacity of making a more profound critique of Eurocentric development paradigms, one that foresaw the disappearance of Indian culture.[38]

Oblate priests from French Canada established the Institute for Development, Investigation, and Popular Peasant Education (INDICEP) in the mining center of Oruro. INDICEP, along with Albo's CIPCA, strongly nurtured and supported a core group of Aymara intellectuals, the Katarists. With the Oblate priest Gregorio Iriarte as adviser, the Katarists appeared dramatically on the public stage at Tihuanaco, the premier indigenous site in Bolivia, with a carefully crafted statement called the Tihuanaco Manifesto in 1973. Cultural assimilation and exclusive education in the Spanish language were all condemned. Due to the military dictatorship in power when the manifesto was solemnly read in the Latin American fashion, the controlled national media paid little attention. However, with the help of the progressive church and some clandestine groups, the manifesto received serious attention at the grassroots.

A few years later, with state authoritarian controls diminishing, Albó helped young Aymara leaders found the Tupac Katari Center, which fostered an enlarged Katarista movement. Within a relatively brief time the movement took over most of the official government peasant unions and organized its own union. Aymaras asserted themselves with a degree of political sophistication and independence not seen since Inca times. They also broadened the labor movement to bring together urban and mine workers with rural workers. They had a much larger target, though, than labor rights. They took aim at the state,[39] presenting their demands about unequal treatment from the state for agricultural prices, credit, education, and health. They proposed a series of revindications about the nature of ethnicity and the basic racial definitions of national society. The Katarists helped move what had been in Bolivia a cultural-awareness movement to one with political goals.

By contrast, organizing in the Bolivian lowlands received much less attention of outsiders because of the earlier, stronger, and much better reported indigenous political activity in the highlands. Both the Katarist organizing and the experience of Peruvian lowland organizations influenced the Indigenous Center of Eastern Bolivia (CIDOB). CIDOB started in 1982 and acquired a misleading name as the Confederation of the Indigenous Peoples of Bolivia, pretentious in that the group represented relatively small groups in the tropics, while the Unified Confederation of Peasant Workers of Bolivia (CSUTCB) in the Andean region was, in fact, the principal indigenous organization in the country. Nonetheless, CIDOB pulled together a coalition of disparate Indian groups from Bolivia's tropical regions, including the Assembly of the Guaraní People.[40] Padre Albó and colleagues supplied the assembly with training in weapons of research and action for Guaraní leaders.

National March and the Media

CIDOB moved the national spotlight toward them in the most dramatic way possible in Bolivia. In 1990 they marched hundreds of kilometers across the main highways of Bolivia, moving toward La Paz and demanding "territory and dignity." By that time many short-range but often interconnected radio stations established themselves as primary agents in communication for Indian peoples. Through decades of gaining an indigenous audience, stations ingrained in indigenous peoples the habit of following local and national news through transistor radios. Thus, news of the national march quickly spread.

Many dozens of these *radioemisoras culturales,* mostly short-range stations that spread through the Bolivian and Peruvian Altiplano, were created by Catholic and Protestant churches. They were fundamental instruments in cultivating indigenous languages and promoting indigenous culture. In a largely oral culture they were ideally suited to their task. While the seven Indian intellectual centers and many catechetical centers contributed to the formation of an indigenous intelligentsia, the radio stations carried on a humble, largely unnoticed task of diffusing indigenous culture and of reinforcing a sense of indigenous worth.

Use of citizens' media, especially the networks of community radio stations, has been a vital endeavor of the churches. Many of the Catholic stations were created under the impulse of the progressive church. Clemencia Rodríguez has traced the connection between liberation theology and hundreds of citizens' media in Chile but believes these typical of what hundreds of Latin American Catholic bishops, priests, nuns, and believers made possible elsewhere.[41] In Rodríguez's view, hundreds of Catholic collectives created their own citizens' media projects from Patagonia to Rio Grande. She summarizes: "They explored participatory and horizontal communication, concientization (consciousness raising) and action-research methodologies, all aimed at one goal: the transformation of passive, voiceless, dominated communities into active shapers of their own destiny."[42] These efforts came to play in making the putatively inert mass of Indians ready to support an indigenous surge to power.

The 1990 march meant walking long distances at extreme altitudes for peoples from the lowland tropics. Marchers continued on to a crown point 4,700 meters above sea level (above 14,000 feet) outside of La Paz. There they received a symbolic embrace from the directorate of Bolivia's major indigenous organization, CSUTCB, and together the enlarged column marched to La Paz. It was a triumphal entrance for a people who thought themselves overlooked and forgotten in a nation intent on entering a globalized economy. More than symbolic gains were made. This march brought about passage of government decrees that for the first time in history recognized indigenous rights to hold their territorial rights.

Explaining the Emergence of Indigenous Activism

Beyond the intentions of missionaries or indigenous peoples, structural changes were taking place within Latin American nations in the 1980s. Two changes can be noted and they appear contradictory. First, more political space was allowed for political activity by citizens at the grassroots once military and authoritarian controls lessened. Second, the states that emerged from authoritarian governance attempted reforms that fell heavily on the poor and especially the indigenous peoples. The reforms were stabilization and structural adjustment programs. New democratic governments advanced neoliberal reforms by reducing budgets for agriculture, education, health and other social services, and programs of protecting peasant lands, access to credit, and agricultural subsidies. In sum the indigenous faced diminishing resources from the state while real wage income in the agricultural sector from the 1980s decreased by 30 percent by 1992.[43]

In contrast to diminished help from the state and greater poverty, indigenous people hoped that in democratization indigenous peoples would take

their place as full citizens, with educational and other benefits. A reflective indigenous awareness was growing. For the first time in modern history increasing numbers of young indigenous people passed through the formal
educational system and obtained positions as teachers, doctors, and agrono-
mists. The Adventist schools in the Lake Titicaca area were especially adept at
providing education that empowered Indians.[44] Their graduates began taking
on local political leadership positions decades ago and have advanced to become national legislators.

The emergent leadership focused on underlying causes of poverty. Primarily, they reacted to two generalized failures. First, they witnessed on their
own terrain the failure of traditional development plans. Second, they became increasingly aware that the modern nation-state was flawed in its foundations.[45] As a result of these failures, indigenous persons and groups felt that
they had been treated as second-class persons. They were deprived of their
rights, treated as minors. In some areas they were treated as wards of the state.
Indigenous persons tended to react to this treatment by self-negation, in
essence, agreeing with treatment afforded them by mestizo classes above
them. Some saw themselves as unschooled and largely ignorant of the ways to
prosper economically in their own societies. Many indigenous built walls
around themselves and their communities, fostering or maintaining a culture
of resistance.[46]

To remedy this situation indigenous leaders proposed the goal of a multicultural and polyethnic state. They also honed arguments about specific issues.
They sought more clearly defined legal status, a new status of indigenous peoples within a democratic society. Many indigenous peoples consider the right
to land essential to their survival. They looked for ways to foster cultural identity beyond resistance. Hence, in a number of places efforts have been made to
facilitate a cultural rebirth, especially in terms of indigenous languages and literature. They look for ways to safeguard their community organizational life
and customary laws. Lastly, Indian leaders aim to achieve greater self-determination and greater voice in national politics.

ACHIEVEMENTS AND CONTRASTS BETWEEN
BOLIVIA AND PERU

The most prominent achievement is the new voice that indigenous
groups have gained in national and local politics. Contrary to some expecta-
tions, revolutionaries and leftists were typically not useful in fostering indigenous cultural interests. In Bolivia the Movimiento Nacional Revolucionario
(MNR), the architect of the 1952 social revolution and frequently the gov-
erning party, fostered assimilation of indigenous groups and undermined their
cultural identity. Another strong party, the Movimiento Izquierdista Revolucionario (MIR), kept cultural themes out of its policy statements until the in-

digenous broke into public consciousness through dramatic long marches, as the 1990 March for Territory and Dignity.

Within a relatively short time following the election, the first government of Gonzalo Sánchez de Lozada (1993–1997) with his Indian vice president Víctor Hugo Cárdenas (one of Albó's protégés) promoted in 1994 the amendment of the first article of the National Constitution to define Bolivia as a multiethnic, multicultural state.[47] The government also led the successful drive to recognize as legal native forms of government, such as the *allyu* or *mburuvicha*. The Law of Popular Participation (1994) created smaller units of government that brought government resources to native units of government. In an optimistic view, Kevin Healy believes that "Bolivia has begun to re-define itself."[48]

The 1995 Law of Decentralization provided for administrative independence at the local and provincial levels. Through these two moves President Gonzalo Sánchez made bold steps toward taking power away from central government and placing decisions and financial resources in the hands of local authorities.[49] While the government directed these initiatives toward the nation as a whole, indigenous were among the most active in seizing on the opportunities for self-determination offered them. They had to enter into competition with entrenched local politicians, a difficult political initiation into rough-and-tumble politics. In places like Concepción, in the heart of CIDOB country, they battled manipulations, like trucking in voters from other towns.

Marcela López Levy judges that the two laws (1994 and 1995) constitute "the most ambitious attempt on the continent to bring power to the people." The laws creating stronger municipalities generated a synergy of grassroots indigenous organizations and municipal power. In the important elections that followed decentralization, 464 indigenous leaders were elected to the municipal council. This represented 29 percent of those elected in the country and 62 percent in the Oruro department, a center of Aymara and Quechua culture. More than a quarter served as mayor for at least part of their term as counselors. In the same year 9 of 130 national deputies were elected to Congress. One of their number, Evo Morales, went on to receive the second largest numbers of votes in the 2002 national presidential election.

Whatever progress Indians made at the local level, their major achievement has been the constitutional conception of the nation as a multiethnic state. They also contributed mightily to a widespread multicultural and bilingual educational system, establishment of new government agencies to serve the indigenous sector, acceptance of indigenous culture as part of the national patrimony, and the coming from shadows to prominence in national politics.

However successful indigenous have been in Bolivia, Andean indigenous movements are at the beginning of their challenges to exclusion from full citizenship. In neighboring Peru the ten-year reign of Alberto Fujimori (1990–2000) continued the suppression of cultural pluralism and indigenous cultural patrimony. But now even Peru may be headed toward policies that favor its Indian history and populations. In 2001 Peru elected Alejandro Toledo, the first indigenous person as president in its history. In general, indigenous groups have made what Alison Brysk considers "tremendous gains" in the struggle for specific goals, such as land rights, recognition of communal life, and language rights in five Indian nations.[50]

Peruvian and Bolivian Contrasts

Peru and Bolivia offer contrasts in organizing interests of indigenous populations. Whereas Bolivia has one of the most vigorous Indian rights movements in the hemisphere, Peru does not have a national movement and has little cohesive international presence.[51] Nonetheless, Peruvians made three major advances in law, with hopes that practical implementation might follow. Peru recognized the multicultural nature of the nation in the Constitution of 1993. In the same year Peru ratified International Labor Convention 169 on Indigenous and Tribal Peoples. Both instruments granted indigenous peoples and peasant communities the right to participate in decisions that affect them and in national decision-making processes. Both instruments recognize a third legal advance for campesino, *rondero,* and indigenous communities: the right to administer customary law. However, to date, lack of a national movement meant laws were not well implemented.[52]

Why the difference? The Peruvian Catholic Church, similar to Bolivia's, made widespread advances in fashioning persons and communities turned toward obtaining their rights as individuals and as communities. Missionaries, catechists, and intellectual-cultural centers operated in Peru. Further, despite the conservative character of the national church leadership, the Peruvian Bishops Conference through CEAS, the Episcopal Commission for Social Action, played an influential role in helping to obtain recognition of customary law. Local churches organized workshops to try to assure implementation. Despite these influences, no national indigenous mobilization arose.

The political authoritarianism of President Alberto Fujimori (1990–2000) and the widespread, prolonged internal war waged by Sendero Luminoso and other Marxist guerrillas stifled formation of a national movement. Despite the efforts of Catholic, Adventist, and other religious groups, campesino and indigenous organizations lacked the political opportunity that would ignite a national social movement.[53] Authoritarian legacies continued through subordination of rural groups to military control, and lack of independence of the judiciary blocked the implementation of the favorable legal instruments.

Despite lack of national mobilization, indigenous groups played substantial political roles in Peru. The groups differ markedly depending on whether they are based in the highlands or the Amazon. In the highlands indigenous groups began gaining their rights under the Augusto Leguía government. In the 1920s the Leguía government extended legal recognition to indigenous communities. These communities expanded and consolidated these rights through court decisions.

Marxist and populist parties in Peru, intent on class-based politics, put heavy emphasis on calling Peru's indigenous "peasants." Indigenous elites and masses in centers such as Cuzco strove for de-Indianization through the 1920s to 1990s.[54] The leftist military government of Juan Velasco Alvarado intensified this campaign after 1968 when it took power. Indians accepted the term "peasant" as a slightly more exulted status than indio, as they did in Bolivia after the revolution of 1952. The difference between the two countries hinged on a reversal in Bolivia where campesinos became indios again.[55] Orin Starn, viewing the politics of protest in the Andes, observes that "most Peruvian villagers would be confused or insulted to be called by the old name [indio]."[56]

Velasco's military government sought to achieve stability in the country by reducing the great disparities in land holdings. Family dynasties held ownership of vast territories. To prevent a bottom-up revolt the military broke up large estates and created peasant cooperatives. While the inefficient economies of these cooperatives largely failed, the indigenous peasants found the rural class structure turning more in their favor. As John Peeler has noted, "the result . . . has been "a rather highly organized but fragmented peasantry."[57]

The plagues that descended on all classes in Peru, but especially on its peasantry, were two brutal guerrilla movements, the Sendero Luminoso (Shining Path) and the Movimiento Revolucionario Tupac Amaru (MRTA). Peruvian peasant activism took shape as a very large movement for self-protection. Indian communities began in 1976 to form groups for night patrol against bandits that marauded the countryside. This grassroots initiative responded to the perceived incapacity of the government to provide essential protection. In northern Peru the *rondas* attempted to make up for the absence, inefficiency, or corruption of authorities who neglected the poor and responded to the wealthy.

In the northern Andean region some three hundred thousand men joined the rondas campesinas, peasant patrols, covering an extensive area of the northern Peruvian Andes. They also created a system of public discipline and punishment of crime. After the Indians took a measure of power through the rondas, they were no longer intimidated by local or national authorities. They stood up to authorities, wresting from them a measure of accountability. They forced government officials to respond to situations they would have previously ignored unless bribes or tributes were paid. In the process Indians and some officials with whom they had to deal saw Indians as persons with full rights of citizens. Liberation theology had a hand in this. Small Christian communities provided the organizational structure, the religious symbols, and what Lester McGrath–Andino calls the "messiah mechanism" for empowering the masses.[58]

Throughout his study of the rondas, Starn was struck by the "impress of Christianity," especially through the participation of Catholic catechists and Protestant pastors.[59] In the southern Andean region Catholic leaders, through the Institute for Andean Pastoral Activity, and Adventists, through their schools, implemented a policy of empowerment. Their message became this: Do not remain on the sidelines; we want to hear your voice in building Peruvian democracy.

In sum, Peruvian highland indigenous peasant organizations managed to retake lands that had been taken from them and supplanted local authorities with their own members. They became, as María Isabel Remy says, "valued interlocutors with the state."[60]

Peru's Amazonian region was affected by guerrilla warfare, globalization of drug and other trade, and reforms initiated by the military governments after 1968. In contrast to Andean communities' emphasis on economic goals, Amazonian leaders centered their attention on cultural integrity and autonomy. Through aid and mentorship from the churches, anthropologists, and transnational groups, as Cultural Survival, indigenous peoples have organized well enough to begin to engage the Peruvian state.

Social movement analysts dealing with Peru may have missed something by concentrating on national and transnational movements and by tending to abstract from lower-level political actors and activities. By contrast Donna Lee Van Cott emphasizes grassroots movement, defining the Indian rights movement as "groups working for change in the status and conditions of Indians as a distinct cultural group." As John Peeler argues, "It is still largely the case in Peruvian consciousness that to be peasant is to be indigenous and to be indigenous is to be a peasant."[61] In sum, both Andean peasant and Amazonian indigenous groups and actors have taken on considerable political roles in Peru.

CONCLUSION

Indigenous discourse in Peru and Bolivia stands at a crossroads between human rights, democracy, and nation-states.[62] Indigenous groups, at the top and bottom of their organizations, now challenge the assumptions that national elites and national societies have made since nation-states were created in Latin America almost two hundred years ago. They publicly question state policies that have maintained Indians in their inferior status in society. Religious beliefs, commitments, and resources foster ethnic identities, and they help provide ideological and other resources for pushing indigenous demands in conflicts toward economic justice and political rights. Latin America's indigenous and their theologians are constructing indigenous theology that acts as an ideological asset for defending their rights. They wish to be treated as men and women with full rights to education, employment, and public voice.

NOTES

1. See Miguel Alberto Bartolome, *Por la liberación del indigena: Declaración de Barbados* (Cuernavaca: Centro Intercultural de Documentación, 1971).

2. Among surveys of Bolivia and Peru see especially: Xavier Albó, *Pueblos indios en la política* (La Paz: Plural Editores, 2002), "Andean People in the Twentieth Century," in *The Cambridge History of the Native Peoples of the Americas*, vol. 2, part 2, ed. Frank Salomon and Stuart B. Schwartz (New York: Cambridge University Press, 1999), 765–871, with extensive bibliography, and "Bolivia: From Indian and Campesino Leaders to Councillors and Parliamentary Deputies," in *Multiculturalism in Latin America: Indigenous Rights, Diversity, and Democracy,* ed. Rachel Sieder (New York: Palgrave Macmillan, 2002), 74–102; David Maybury-Lewis, "Lowland Peoples of the Twentieth Century," in *The Cambridge History* vol.2, part 2, ed. Salomon and Schwartz, 872–947; Donna Lee Van Cott, various works, esp. "Constitutional Reforms in the Andes: Redefining Indigenous-State Relations," in *Multiculturalism*, ed. Sieder, 45–73; Diego Garcí-Sayán, various works, esp., *Tomas de la tierra en el Perú* (Lima: Centro de Estudios y Promoción del Desarrollo, 1982); and Raquel Irigoyan Farjardo, "Peru: Pluralist Constitution, Monist Judiciary—A Post-Reform Assessment" in *Multiculturalism*, ed. Sieder, 157–183.

3. This chapter is based, in part, on interviews in Bolivia and Peru from 1958 to 2002, and from a network of scholars established while editor of *Estudios Andinos* (1970–1976).

4. Xavier Albó, "The Aymara Religious Experience," in *The Indian Face of God in Latin America,* ed. Manuel Marzal et al. (Maryknoll, N.Y.: Orbis, 1996), 153–155.

5. Hans C. Buechler and Judith Maria Buechler, "Combatting Feathered Serpents: The Rise of Protestantism and Reformed Catholicism in a Bolivian Highland Community," in *Amerikanistische studien: Festschrift für Hermann Trimborn,* vol. 1 (St. Augustin: Hans Völker u. Kultern, Anthropos-Inst., 1978).

6. Susan Rosales Nelson, "Bolivia: Continuity and Conflict in Religious Discourse," in *Religion and Political Conflict in Latin America,* ed. Daniel H. Levine (Chapel Hill: University of North Carolina Press, 1986), 222.

7. See esp. Consejo Episcopal Latinoamericano, *De una pastoral indigenista a una pastoral indígena* (Bogotá: Consejo Episcopal Latinoamericano, 1987); and José Alsina Franch, compiler, *Indianismo e indigenismo en América* (Madrid: Alianza Editorial/ Quinto Cententario, 1990).

8. See, for example, Edward L. Cleary, *Crisis and Change: The Church in Latin America Today* (Maryknoll, N.Y.: Orbis, 1985), 5.

9. John Paul II, "Opening Address," 41–60, and "Message to Indigenous People," 156–160, and Latin American Bishops' Conference, "Conclusions," nos. 136–140 in document, in Alfred T. Hennelly, *Santo Domingo and Beyond* (Maryknoll, N.Y.: Orbis, 1993).

10. Other expressions of citizens' media include low-cost mimeographed publications and instructional videos.

11. For a vividly presented case study see June C. Nash, *Mayan Visions: The Quest for Autonomy in an Age of Globalization* (New York: Routledge, 2001), passim.

12. See, for example, Michael Lowy, "Sources and Resources of Zapatism," *Monthly Review* 49, no. 10 (March 1998): 1–5.

13. Younger missionaries tended to promote a culturalist rather than a liberationist view. Interview with Andrew Orta, February 29, 2003.

14. See, for example, Barry J. Lyons, "Religion, Authority, and Identity: Intergenera-

tional Politics, Ethnic Resurgence, and Respect in Chimborazo, Ecuador," *Latin American Research Review* 36, no. 1 (2001): 7–48.

15. Edward L. Cleary, "Birth of Latin American Indigenous Theology," in *Crosscurrents in Indigenous Spirituality: Interface of Maya, Catholic, and Protestant Worldviews,* ed. Guillermo Cook (New York: E. J. Brill, 1997), 171–188.

16. Instituto de Estudios Aymaras, Chucuito, near Puno, Peru, was founded by Frank McGourn, M.M., as part of the Prelature of Juli, under the care of Maryknoll Missioners; Centro de Estudios Regionales Andinos Bartolomé de Las Casas, Cuzco, was founded by Dominicans, the Province of Toulouse, and has been extended to include Escuela Andina de Postgrado; Instituto Pastoral Andino, Sicuani, originally was situated in Cuzco and was created largely by missionary bishops of the Southern Andes; Centro de Investigación y Promoción del Campesinado, La Paz, was founded by Jesuit Xavier Albó and maintained ties to Centro de Teología Popular; and Instituto de Desarrollo, Investigación, y Educación Popular Campesino, Oruro, was founded by Canadian Oblates.

17. For indigenous views see Nicanor Sarmiento Tupayupanque's *Los caminos de la teología india* (Cochabmba: Editorial Verbo Divino, 1999); Enrique Jorda, "La cosmovisión amara en el diálogo de la fe: Teología desde el Titicaca," doctoral diss., Faculty of Theology, Pontifical Catholic University, Lima; Domingo Llanque Chana, *La cultura aymara: Desestructuración o afirmación de identidad?* (Lima: Idea/Tarea, 1990); and Calixto Quispe et al., "Religión aymara liberadora," *Fe y Pueblo* 4, no. 18 (1987). For a summary view of indigenous theology from Mexico, see interview with Mario Pérez in *Latinamerica Press* 33, no. 25 (July 9, 2001): 3–4.

18. See, for example, the works of Manuel Marzal, Xavier Albó, Diego Irarrázaval, Esteban Judd, Miguel Briggs, Hans van den Berg, Luis Jolicoeur, and others. See equally *Pastoral Andina, Allpanchis, Aymar Yatiyawi, Abya Yala News, Revista Andina, Fe y Pueblo, Búsqueda Pastoral,* and publications of CIPCA (Centro de Investigación y Promoción del Campesinado). Some publications extend beyond the Peruvian-Bolivian subregion.

19. María José Caram, "The Shape of Catholic Identity among the Aymara of Pilcuyo," in *Popular Catholicism in a World Church: Seven Case Studies in Inculturation,* ed. Thomas Bamat and Jean-Paul Wiest (Maryknoll, N.Y.: Orbis, 1999), 79.

20. See, for example, Diego Irarrázaval, *Inculturation: New Dawn of the Church in Latin America* (Maryknoll, N.Y.: Orbis, 2000); and other books by him: *Teología en la fe del pueblo* (1999); *Cultura y fe latinoamericanas* (1994); *Rito y pensar cristiano* (1993); and *Tradición y provenir andino* (1992).

21. Irarrázaval, *Inculturation,* 61.

22. Kevin Healy, *Llamas, Weavings, and Organic Chocolate: Multicultural Grassroots Development in the Andes and Amazon of Bolivia* (Notre Dame, Ind.: University of Notre Dame Press, 2001), 70.

23. Inculturation as an ideal implies the embodiment of the Christian message within a specific culture. Inculturation is a neologism, resisted in its early use and now commonly accepted in theological circles. The closest equivalent in anthropological usage may be acculturation.

24. Albó repeats St. Augustine's description of religion outside of Christianity as "seeds of revelation," in Albó, "The Aymara," 122.

25. See Irarrázaval, *Inculturation,* on programmatic advances, 50–52.

26. Jorda, "La cosmovisión aymara."

27. Andrew Orta treats this aspect at length in several publications. See, for example, his "From Theologies of Liberation to Theologies of Inculturation," in *Organized Religion in the Transformation of Latin America,* ed. Satya R. Pattnayak (Lanham, Md., University Press of America, 1995), 97–124.

28. Interview, Washington, D.C., September 8, 2001.

29. Juan Gorski, "La teología india y la inculturación," the Spanish version is in *Yachay* (Cochabamba, Bolivia) 23 (1998): 72–98.

30. Publications available through Editorial Verbo Divino, Cochabamba.

31. See sections 243–251, *Conclusions, Fourth General Conference of Latin American Bishops* (1992), and Stephen Judd, "From Lamentation to Project: The Emergence of an Indigenous Theological Movement in Latin America," both in *Santo Domingo and Beyond,* ed. Alfred T. Hennelly (Maryknoll, N.Y.: Orbis, 1993).

32. Alison Brysk believes that Protestant churches did not systematically but only episodically play a mediating role in the Indian transnational movement. She argues that the Catholic Church is not on equal footing with other social forces and stands between state and society in Latin America. She also observes that Protestant churches also lack tight transnational structures needed for systematic mediation. See Alison Brysk, *From Tribal Village to Global Village: Indian Rights and International Relations in Latin America* (Stanford: Stanford University Press, 2000), 209, nt. 14.

33. Albó, *Pueblos indios,* 181.

34. Ibid., 182.

35. Anibal Quijano, *Dominación y cultura: Lo cholo y el conflicto cultural en el Perú.* (Lima: Mosca Azul, 1980).

36. Among the most important external agencies, missionaries are commonly cited. See, for example, Brysk *From Tribal Village,* passim; Rodolfo Stavenhagen, "Indigenous Organizations: Rising Actors in Latin America," *CEPAL Review* 62 (1997): 63–75; and Rachel Sieder, introduction to *Multiculturalism in Latin America: Indigenous Rights, Diversity, and Democracy,* ed. Sieder (New York: Palgrave Macmillan, 2002).

37. See the assessment of the gains of the Bolivian Revolution, especially see Herbert S. Klein "Social Change in Bolivia since 1952," in *Proclaiming Revolution: Bolivia in Comparative Perspective,* ed. Merilee Grindle and Pilar Domingo (Cambridge, Mass.: Harvard University Press, 2003), 232–258.

38. Healy, *Llamas,* 69.

39. For a view of one the principal indigenous leaders, see Víctor Hugo Cárdenas, "Cambios en la relación entre los pueblos indígenas y los estados en América Latina," in *Pueblos indígenas y estado en América Latina,* ed. Virginia Alta et al. (Quito: Editorial Abya-Yala, 1998), 27–38.

40. An account of the history of CIDOB is provided by political leader Vicente Pessoa in "Procesos indígenas de participación política y ciudana en los espacios de gobierno y desarrollo municipal," in *Pueblos indígenas,* ed. Alta et al., 169–203.

41. Clemencia Rodríguez, "The Bishops and His Star: Citizens' Communication in Southern Chile," unpublished manuscript.

42. Ibid.

43. James W. Wilkie, Carlos Alberto Contreras, and Katherine Komisaruk, eds., *Statistical Abstract for Latin America,* vol. 31 (Los Angeles: UCLA Latin American Center Publications, 1995), 990, table 3107.

44. For further description see Charles Teel, "Las raíces radicales del Adventismo en el Altiplano Peruano," *Allpanchis* 33 (1989): 209–248.

45. The wider relations of state and culture are too lengthy to pursue here. For a recent discussion see George Steinmetz, ed., *State / Culture: State Formation after the Cultural Turn* (Ithaca, N.Y.: Cornell University Press, 1999).

46. For forms of resistance see James C. Scott, *Weapons of the Weak: The Everyday Forms of Resistance* (New Haven, Conn.: Yale University Press, 1985).

47. For an assessment of this process see Donna Lee Van Cott, *The Friendly Liquidation of the Past: The Politics of Diversity in Latin America* (Pittsburgh: University Pittsburgh Press, 2000).

48. Healy, *Llamas,* 121.

49. See Marilee S. Grindle, *Audacious Reforms: Institutional Invention and Democracy in Latin America* (Baltimore, Md.: Johns Hopkins University Press, 2000), 94–146, for the mechanisms and politics of reform.
50. Brysk, *From Tribal Village,* 282 and 246–282, passim.
51. Ibid., 269.
52. Yrigoyen Fajardo, "Pluralist Constitution," in *Multiculturalism,* ed. Sieder, 157–183.
53. Xavier Albó explores alternative explanations for lack of a national movement in *Pueblos indios,* 216–225.
54. María de la Cadena, "Race, Ethnicity, and the Struggle for Indigenous Self-Representation: De-indianization in Cuzco, Peru, 1919–1992," Ph.D. diss., University of Wisconsin-Madison, 1996.
55. See, for example, Xavier Albó, "El retorno del indio," *Revista Andina* 9, no. 2 (1991): 299–345.
56. Orin Starn, *Nightwatch: The Politics of Protest in the Andes* (Durham, N.C.: Duke University Press, 1999), 32.
57. John Peeler, "Social Justice and the New Indigenous Politics: An Analysis of Guatemala and the Central Andes," paper for the 1998 Latin American Studies International Congress, 10.
58. Lester McGrath-Andino, "The Social Spirituality of Latin American Base Christian Communities," Th.D. diss., Boston University, 1995.
59. Starn, *Nightwatch,* esp. 90–91; see also Irigoyan, "Peru," 164 and 176.
60. María Isabel Remy, "The Indigenous Population and the Construction of Democracy in Peru," in *Indigenous Peoples and Democracy in Latin America,* ed. Donna Lee Van Cott (New York: St. Martin's Press, 1994), 117.
61. Peeler, "Social Justice," 12.
62. See remarks of Stavenhagen, "Indigenous Organizations," 75.

CHAPTER 4

Breaking Down Religious Barriers

INDIGENOUS PEOPLE AND CHRISTIAN
CHURCHES IN PARAGUAY

René Harder Horst

INTERACTION WITH indigenous people has altered both
Catholic and Protestant religious organizations in Paraguay. Although missionaries have worked in this area since the seventeenth century, only recently
have the Christian denominations begun to learn from and change as a result
of their contacts with indigenous people. This chapter will show five ways in
which indigenous peoples in Paraguay have interacted with and altered Christian denominations during the last thirty years. By opposing the complicity of
Christian churches with state attempts to control indigenous means of production and ways of life, as well as by refusing to relinquish their land, traditions, and worldviews, indigenous peoples have changed the practice of
Christianity in Paraguay.

First, the most significant lesson indigenous people have contributed to
churches is that they consider themselves to be different from other subaltern
peoples and refuse to be viewed as *campesinos,* or peasants. Indigenous protestors have stressed time and again that their people do not "melt down" as part
of the national lower class.

Second, regardless of well-intentioned work by liberation theologians on
behalf of lower classes in Latin America, the Catholic Church has often mis-
takenly neglected to differentiate between the various "oppressed" peoples
among which they minister. Indigenous peoples have not only distinguished
themselves, they have also forced the church to recognize the validity of minority theologies and different cultural practices as honest expressions of
Christian faith.

Third, if religious leaders take seriously the implications of indigenous
examples, they will no longer be able to maintain traditional separations
between religious denominations. Some Catholic workers in Paraguay now

recognize Protestant theology as a valid understanding of the divine. Interaction with indigenous people has broadened interdenominational parameters because many native people consider these traditional boundaries to be arbitrary and "white" divisions.

Fourth, rising participation of indigenous people and languages in the Catholic mass has encouraged the inclusion of the vernacular in popular worship and in translated scriptures. The resulting rise in religious acceptance and the broader religious outreach have contributed to ethnic pride movements among several indigenous peoples in Paraguay.

Finally, large denominations that militantly stood up for indigenous land rights and opposed regime abuses and development schemes have broadened traditional spheres of religious influence from proselytism to political defense and from economic dependency to independent self-determination. This chapter will follow these five themes as they developed chronologically throughout the Alfredo Stroessner regime (1954–1989) and will argue that indigenous peoples have altered religious organizations.

PARAGUAY AND ITS INDIGENOUS PEOPLES

By 1960, there were only between sixty and seventy thousand indigenous people in Paraguay who considered themselves distinct from the majority population. Seventeen different indigenous ethnicities, from five language families, were divided geographically by the Paraguay River. East of the river, indigenous people belonged to the Tupí-Guaraní language family and spoke some form of Guaraní. In the northern Amambay region the Paï Tavyterã still practiced subsistence horticulture, though they no longer lived in large traditional communities. The Avá Guaraní, culturally closest to Paraguayan peasants, lived in the eastern region. Both had contact with peasants and even worked as peons on ranches or sold *yerba mate* to outsiders. In the central east lived the Mbyá, who still fled from the national society and resided in small isolated agricultural communities. The Ache, who used a form of Guaraní language but hunted and gathered in small nomadic bands, lived in a few forested outposts in the central eastern regions. Some Tupí-Guaraní had also migrated west of the river in pre-Columbian times, and the Western Guaraní and the Guaraní Ñandeva, both Guaraní speakers, still lived along the border with Bolivia.

In the dry western Chaco region lived a variety of non-Guaraní ethnicities from four different linguistic families. The Ayoreode and Ïshïro were members of the Zamuco language group and traditionally inhabited the northern Chaco, the first closer to Bolivia and the Ïshïro nearer the Paraguay River. The larger Enlhit, Angaité, Sanapaná, Guan'a, and Enenlhit ethnicities belonged to the Lengua-Maskoy linguistic group and lived in central and eastern areas of the Chaco between the Mennonite Colonies and the Paraguay

River. The Yofuaxa, Nivaklé, and Mak'a shared Mataco-Mataguayo linguistic ties and traditionally lived in central and southern areas of the Chaco. Finally, the Toba-Qom, of Guaicurú linguistic ancestry, had resided in the southeastern Chaco.[1] The western tribes shared ties with natives elsewhere in the Gran Chaco, an area covering parts of western Paraguay, northern Argentina, southeastern Bolivia, and southwestern Brazil.

The indigenous ethnicities had distinct histories of interaction with national society and with other native peoples, but all shared the legacy of discrimination and inadequate access to legal protection. Some tribes actively avoided interaction with Paraguayos, but in the eastern region, especially, a few ethnicities shared close linguistic and cultural traits with nationals. By mid-century, every indigenous tribe had increased contacts with the national population and had also lost most of their territory as settlers and ranchers extended crops, cattle, and cut lumber near indigenous settlements. Accelerated economic development caused significant changes within indigenous communities as they maneuvered transitions of cultural, political, and religious adaptation and changes.

When Alfredo Stroessner took power in a coup in 1954, he had no interest in these indigenous peoples. The agreement he forged between the Colorado Party and the Paraguayan military became the basis for his political longevity.[2] Over the years the dictator remained in control through adept administration, periodic waves of repression, and by tolerating corrupt business opportunities for the upper class.[3] The principal goal of the dictatorship became the development of the nation's economic potential, primarily through the sale of hydroelectric energy to neighboring Brazil and Argentina, as well as an active black market in cheap industrial goods and cars. Stroessner paid attention to indigenous peoples and the Catholic Church in Paraguay only when they came in the way of his economic goals or challenged his authority.

CATHOLICS, PROTESTANTS, AND INDIGENOUS PEOPLE IN THE 1960S

Until the 1960s, Christian denominations in Paraguay held a fairly traditional view of indigenous people and cultures. When Jesuit proselytism began in the early seventeenth century, Catholic missionaries depicted the indigenous people as savages and children in need of conversion.[4] Protestants shared these demeaning attitudes; when the Anglican South American Mission Society began to proselytize in the eastern Chaco in 1888, workers designated the first indigenous people they contacted as barbarous, weird, and savage.[5] The state also held this view. When Stroessner's regime created an *indigenista* agency (the Department of Indigenous Affairs or DAI) to integrate indigenous people in 1958, it was patterned after the Mexican model and depicted the Indians as defenseless, helpless, miserable, and unorganized.[6] It would be years before international contact gradually improved pejorative attitudes toward indigenous peoples in Paraguay.

The dictator had not been in power very long, however, when changes became obvious in the Catholic Church, both internationally and in Paraguay. At the Second Vatican Council (1962–1965), Pope John XXIII called his congregation to defend human rights as a new way to evangelize the modern world.[7] When Latin American bishops met at Medellín in 1968, they agreed to emphasize social justice to defend subaltern rights. The shifts in the wider church soon changed the Catholic approach to proselytism in Paraguay. Before Medellín bishops had encouraged missions to evangelize indigenous peoples quickly and teach them how to farm, ignoring that Guaraní subsistence already traditionally depended on raising crops.[8] Following the Episcopal conference, bishops canceled plans for proselytism and instead began to stress economic assistance to indigenous people.[9]

The new approaches to mission strategy also reflected a sense of past failure. Career Catholic missionary José Seelwische recognized that previous church efforts to proselytize had not succeeded among indigenous people: "The Catholic attempt to convert the pagan *indígenas,* civilizing and educating them towards a Christian way of life [had] not succeed[ed] in any way, and many missionaries felt their work was impossible." In his view, Catholics had failed to "convince the *indígenas* to abandon their superstitions, pagan rituals, and primitive customs." To correct these mistakes, Father Seelwische argued, after Vatican II missionaries learned to respect indigenous cultures, tolerate religious freedom, and instead preached universal salvation for all people.[10]

Indigenous Responses to Protestant Proselytism in Western Paraguay

While the Catholic Church took stock of its success and failures in the region, a growing Protestant influence was making itself visible in Paraguay. By 1960, Mennonites directed the largest evangelistic effort among indigenous people. German Mennonite settlers had first arrived in Paraguay from Canada in 1926, followed by others from the USSR in 1930 and 1947. Thirty years later the hardworking settlers enjoyed prosperous enclaves.

The Mennonites employed Enlhit from the eastern Chaco, many of whom converted and settled among them by 1935.[11] On the other hand, the Mennonites refused to settle the Nivaclé, a group of semi-nomadic gatherers from southwestern Chaco. The Nivaclé, who also arrived in search of work, were turned away because the Mennonites saw them as culturally unprepared for agriculture.[12]

When the worst drought in thirty-three years hit Western Paraguay in 1962 and completely damaged crops, Mennonite farmers laid off their laborers and conditions deteriorated until indigenous people grew desperate. The drought brought to a climax the Nivaclé discontent at being consistently denied land. In September 1962, nearly seven hundred desperate Nivaclé rose up in arms against the Mennonite settlers, marched to colony headquarters, and demanded equipment and land. Native women, who made economic choices in matriarchal Nivaclé society, led the uprising because the rebel chief had promised women that once they left the colonies they would regain their authority. Mennonite administrators calmed the Nivaclé but gave them no land, so the indigenous people "stomped out of the colonies in anger."[13]

The Nivaclé who left the Mennonite Colonies then approached Catholic missionaries for relief. The Catholic Church resettled five hundred Nivaclé at the Santa Teresita mission near Mariscal Estigarribia, west of the Mennonites. Unlike the Mennonites, Catholic priests encouraged the Nivaclé to farm and made land and tools available to them. The Nivaclé were willing to turn to whichever mission could provide them with drought relief, regardless of the particular denominational teaching they received in the process. For people in difficult conditions, it appears as though doctrinal differences are less important than food.

Once they were through the worst of the drought, Mennonites created new native settlements that included some of the Nivaclé people. By 1963, the immigrants built four agricultural communities composed of thirty-six indigenous villages. Mennonites offered work programs, built health centers and schools, and granted credit to encourage indigenous people to farm. Concurrently, Mennonite evangelism resulted in the creation of one dozen indigenous churches by the early 1960s. Religious proselytism and proximity to the colonists significantly altered indigenous ways of life, especially as it shifted power from the women to men.[14] In effect, as the regime had hoped when it first encouraged religious proselytism, life near the Mennonites helped integrate the indigenous people into wider markets and labor pools as it introduced non-indigenous worldviews and ways of life.

The Anglican Church also saw widespread indigenous adherence in Paraguay. Between 1964 and 1970 most of the Enlhit tribe joined the Anglican Church.[15] Earlier waves of conversion had occurred between 1899 to 1910 and 1926 to 1936, when western Enlhit moved from the central mission compound of Makthlawaiya to a new mission station. The indigenous Anglican component continued to grow, and by 1985 several thousand indígenas came to form 90 percent of the Paraguayan Anglican Church.[16]

Still, within their Chaco cultural context as traditional immediate-return hunter-gatherers, the indigenous people largely viewed missionaries as sources of provisions and did not clearly differentiate between Christian denominations. This perception grew as indigenous conditions deteriorated and missionaries provided for all indigenous needs during religious training at

mission compounds. Anglicans built cattle ranches and created small indus-
tries, such as carpentry and leather shops at the central mission at Makthlawaiya, where they employed and also fed as many as one thousand Enlhit
people.[17]

Events between 1953 and 1959, when a conservative interdenominational
Protestant group from Florida called New Tribes Mission briefly managed
Makthlawaiya, confirm that denominational differences actually mattered little to the Enlhit. In this period, nearly the entire indigenous population of the
mission was re-baptized as followers of the New Tribes Mission, regardless of
earlier Anglican membership. The conversions were primarily a pragmatic response, as the Enlhit explained that they had joined New Tribes because
American missionaries traveled in two airplanes while their British predeces-
sors had gotten around only by horse and oxcart. The day after Anglicans took
ownership of the mission again, in 1963, the Enlhit asked for the reintroduc-
tion of the Anglican communion service and aligned themselves again with
the new source of provisions.[18]

The enthusiastic Enlhit response to Protestantism was, in part, economically motivated. Such wholesale conversion, however, can only be fully understood by recognizing the extent to which the native people continued to
distinguish traditional religious beliefs from their adoption of Christianity. To
secure economic benefits, the Enlhit deliberately hid traditional spirituality
from the missionaries while displaying a façade of orthodox Anglicanism. The
yohoxma, or religious healers, learned to sing quietly and continued healing
ceremonies without missionary knowledge, even at the mission stations.
Whenever the Enlhit wished to drink or dance they left the mission for a
time, following what anthropologist Stephen Kidd has called an "excellent
understanding and parallel rejection of many aspects of the missionary message. Their success has been predicated on following a dual strategy of hiding
their traditional culture and mastering an acceptable Anglican discourse."[19]
This compartmentalization and juxtaposition of values seems to fly in the face
of dominant theories of practice such as Bourdieu's concept of the subcon-
scious habitus, but cultural strategies native to the Chaco help explain the
practice. Given their hunter-gathering tradition, the Enlhit viewed the missions as new sources of economic abundance and their teachings as new rituals necessary to procure the provisions. Still, observers clearly regarded the
concealment of tribal customs and even the portrayal of doctrinal orthodoxy
to have been purposeful and conscious deception of the missionaries and as
necessary to continue access to mission resources. As Kidd and missionaries
discovered, the Enlhit expounded theology to give excellent impressions of
doctrinal orthodoxy and even acted as converts to convince missionaries of
their legitimate beliefs.[20] Even if this was a strategy rooted in the cultures na-

tive to the Chaco, the example highlights the creativity commonly seen in indigenous resistance to outside impositions.

The Enlhit adoption of the Anglican message allowed them to secure financial assistance from the mission but continue traditional beliefs and rituals in secret. Not only did indigenous people overlook differences between various denominations, they found creative ways to accept the beliefs of the new dominant powers into their own faith and worldviews. At the level of consciousness, then, the example of the Enlhit adoption of Christianity seems to differ from other examples of indigenous religious change, most notably the age-old layered and syncretic Mayan adaptation of new beliefs into their own tradition of multiple cults and supernatural beings with a resulting mixture of codes.[21] The dissimilarity between these cases is cultural: sedentary Mayan strategies of survival versus the hunting and gathering practices of the Chaco peoples. Without casting a judgment on the legitimacy of their religious experience, then, at one level the Enlhit therefore "appropriated" Christianity for their own purposes and still subverted the missionaries' original intent by limiting their power to control.

Mennonite missionaries farther west reported similar surges in conversions and cultural change. Starting in the late 1960s, almost all indigenous settlements within the Mennonite Colonies experienced messianic movements as they joined new Mennonite Church structures. While in part an effort to improve economic conditions, growing participation of Nivaclé and Enlhit in native Mennonite churches was also an indigenous attempt to restore harmony and well-being to a rapidly changing way of life.[22] Anthropologist Elmer Miller has shown that Toba and Pilagá tribes in the Argentine Chaco used Pentecostal revivals to reduce communal tensions that resulted from contact with non-Indians.[23] In much the same way, indigenous people in the Mennonite Colonies used massive religious revivals to invoke the spiritual forces they believed had made the Europeans successful farmers. Indigenous people understood their relationship with Mennonites within the context of rituals they had previously employed to control their world, such as spiritualizing hunting and gathering. After moving to a sedentary life among the Mennonites, indigenous people transferred their traditional worldview to the relationship with their new overseers and providers and came to believe that correct fulfillment of the new religious rites would bring them economic success.[24] Baptism into the Mennonite churches, then, had not altered their traditional religious cosmology. The Enlhit and Nivaclé continued tribal spirituality even as they fulfilled Protestant rituals.

Indigenous people in the Chaco thus greatly increased participation in Anglican and Mennonite churches by 1965. The regime was delighted with this turn of events, for, as a result, indigenous people often settled in permanent locations and started to farm.

Indigenous Spirituality Alters Catholic Proselytism

Even as Protestant missionaries reported a rise in indigenous conversions, the Catholic Church radically changed its mission approach as a result of increasing contact with indigenous people. In the 1960s, growing anthropological awareness began to make the Paraguayan Catholic Church more tolerant of indigenous cultures. Central in this transition was a Jesuit named Bartomeu Melià, who had earned a Ph.D. in anthropology in Strasbourg. Melià's fieldwork among the Avá and Mbyá Guaraní of Eastern Paraguay in 1969 completely changed his view of proselytism, for his encounter with Guaraní spirituality showed that indigenous people already led profoundly spiritual lives without professing Christianity. Prayer, justice, contemplation, and mysticism were foundations of the Guaraní historical consciousness, Melià argued, and had permeated indigenous society with so-called "Christian" principles such as mutual respect and relative economic and political equality to such a degree that it was unnecessary to catechize them because they already led profoundly religious ways of life. Instead, he urged priests to learn from the Guaraní experience with respect and humility.[25]

As general secretary of the Catholic Missions Team between 1972 and 1976, Melià tried to bring Catholic proselytism in line with Vatican II and Medellín.[26] The Jesuit instructed missionaries to foment traditional indigenous religious expressions rather than conversion to Christianity. Religious workers began to encourage the Guaraní to once again practice their tribal rituals. After missionaries of the Divine Word Order applied Melià's advice at the eastern mission of Akaraymí, for instance, the Avá Guaraní recommended the visible practice of their long-supressed *jeroky ñembo'é,* or prayer dances. Greater tolerance at Akaraymí encouraged a wave of tribal ethnic identification that eventually spread to other Avá Guaraní communities.[27] By the mid-1980s, Guaraní communities again expressed their commitment to traditional religious values and customs. Similar church-sponsored encouragement of expression of ethnic identity was also evident elsewhere, as in Chiapas, Mexico, where Bishop Samuel Ruíz and the workers of Catholic Action created women's groups and encouraged tribal fiestas and music.[28] In Paraguay, Melià's anthropological awareness encouraged missionaries to support indigenous cultural distinctiveness, and greater toleration slowly led to a rise in ethnic identification and pride within Guaraní indigenous communities of eastern Paraguay.

INDIGENOUS RIGHTS, POLITICAL ACTIVISM, AND RELIGIOUS DENOMINATIONS IN THE 1970S

While the church slowly began to foment indigenous religious expressions, the international community focused on human rights in Paraguay. German anthropologist Mark Münzel began to study the Ache people in the winter of 1971 at the new reservation where the regime was trying to settle the three Ache groups. The scholar and his wife lived for the better part of a year at the reservation. There they witnessed the malnutrition, abuse, and death of the Northern Ache that the overseer Pereira and his armed indigenous assistants had brought to the camp by truck and kept as prisoners.[29] When Münzel spoke out on behalf of the Ache the dictatorship expelled him from the country. Convinced by his rude treatment that Stroessner was trying to cover a sinister plot to exterminate Paraguay's indigenous peoples, the anthropologist denounced the regime in Europe.[30] Critics of Stroessner took advantage of Münzel's momentum to embarrass the regime. The Catholic Church especially used the case to position itself firmly behind indigenous rights and against the dictatorship.

The international community, meanwhile, had begun to focus on indigenous situations and rights. In January 1971, anthropologists gathered in Barbados to discuss indigenous conditions in Latin America. In their Declaration of Barbados, the scholars accused states of genocide and called on churches to stop missionary activities. The religious response to this admonition took place in Paraguay in March of 1972, when the World Council of Churches and the Evangelical Union in Latin America (UNELAM) assembled missionaries and anthropologists. The resulting Document of Asunción apologized for past religious ties to oppressive structures and called on churches to help end all forms of discrimination. Religious agencies pledged to support indigenous organizations, study native religious values, and defend indigenous human rights through the media.[31]

Indigenous conditions and the growing campaign to defend them focused the Catholic Church in Paraguay on indigenous rights in a new way. In May 1972, even before Münzel left the country, the Catholic University hosted a conference on the situation of native peoples, where the anthropologist himself called on Paraguayans to help improve deteriorating Ache conditions.[32] In response, Paraguayan scholars and Catholic activists began to use the Ache ordeal to criticize the integration policy and the dictatorship. The director of anthropology at the Catholic University, Miguel Chase Sardi, also a recipient of a prestigious Guggenheim fellowship in 1971–1972, depicted the integration policy for the Ache as genocidal.[33] Bartomeu Melià denounced settlement efforts as "ethnocidal" and positioned the Catholic University and the church itself firmly behind the growing criticism of the dictatorship.[34] At Melià's encouragement, the bishop's conference notified the Holy See in Rome about recent Ache deaths.[35]

In this atmosphere of repression and resistance the church organized a National Missions Team (ENM) to channel its work on behalf of indigenous peoples. The controversies that this new approach generated led the new office to annually gather bishops, priests, and lay workers to plan the Catholic mission action among indigenous populations. Beginning in 1972, the new agency emphasized support for land claims and improved living conditions, as well as respect for indigenous identities and cultures.[36] The work of the ENM reflected a clear departure from the previous pattern of church support for the regime in Paraguay.

The Stroessner regime now faced a predicament: while it had intended to use missions to help integrate the indigenous people, its traditional ally, the Catholic Church, had begun to defend indigenous rights and use them to criticize state policies. The dictatorship instead turned to the Protestant denominations, which still cooperated with plans to make indigenous people join the peasantry as small farmers and wage earners. Both Anglicans and Mennonites had long tried to make indigenous people in western Paraguay into good workers and participants in the market economy. Thus the regime's integration program at this early stage coincided closely with their mission goals. Late in 1973, when Ayoreode peoples began leaving the New Tribes mission complex at El Faro Moro to beg for work and food in the nearby Mennonite colonies, the regime used Mennonite and military guards to return and confine the indigenous people once more to the mission site.[37]

Meanwhile, Miguel Chase Sardi and Bartomeu Melià designed a program to assist indigenous leaders in defending their rights, taking charge of their own future, and constructing new economic infrastructures.[38] Chase Sardi presented the project, named Marandú, the Guaraní term for information, at the 1972 United Nations Conference on Human Environments. His promises to inform indigenous people and national society about each other won endorsement from the International Work Group for Indian Affairs.[39] The Catholic University launched Marandú in April 1974, and workers presented programs in ten indigenous communities throughout the country.[40]

As the foreign investigation into Ache conditions escalated and the church began its advocacy work, the regime turned to its most common method of handling dissent, the use of what in Guaraní is known as *mbareté,* or direct force. In April and May 1974, Minister of Defense General Marcial Samaniego summoned state cabinets, religious agencies, educational institutions, and even the U.S. embassy to a series of meetings and forced them to sign a statement denying that genocide had taken place.[41] "There was great manipulation," recalled Melià, in relation to how the minister used threats to coerce their compliance.[42] Immediately, Catholic workers declared to the press that they had signed this disavowal against their free will and bishops called for an "exhaustive investigation of this matter with particular regard to the situation of several Indian groups in Paraguay, whose survival is seriously imperiled." In a statement signed by Melià, the ENM announced, "based on concrete evidence, properly investigated, the existence of cases of genocide against the Ache Indians" has been documented.[43]

Pan-Indigenous Organization and the Catholic Church

Sponsored by the church, Marandú responded to and assisted with indigenous attempts to organize. In October 1974, the project hosted thirty indigenous leaders from different countries at the Parlamento Indioamericano del Cono Sur. For three days leaders met at the Catholic University in Asunción to discuss socioeconomic conditions and finally issued a strong call for improved attention to the indigenous question by national governments. Leaders in Paraguay formed a pan-Indian council, by far the most enduring effect of the conference.[44] Participants accused missionaries and states of perpetrating five centuries of abuse and demanded health care and legal protection as a minimal reparation. The collective proclamation was a pointed demand that non-Indians respect indigenous languages and cultures, grant indigenous people equality in education and labor, and allow them to own property communally.[45]

Following the conference, chiefs began to refer to themselves as victims of national colonization and abuse when approaching the regime and missionaries. Toba Indians at the Cerrito Catholic mission for the first time accused missionaries of being "criminals who had and continue to destroy indigenous people."[46] Over the next years the Toba at Cerrito began to organize themselves and pressured authorities in Asunción to return their ancestral lands.

In February 1975, Marandú sent the leaders of the indigenous council to the Twenty-fifth Annual Latin American Congress at the University of Florida.[47] Later that year, three council delegates attended another encounter for indigenous leaders in Canada.[48] Professor of social ethics Lois Ann Lorentzen has shown that such transnational alliances enable subaltern communities to fight for their own social and human rights.[49] As a result of contact with indigenous people within other nations, back in Paraguay leaders called on the church to be more inclusive, supportive, ecumenical, and tolerant of different cultural expressions.

Indigenous People Influence Protestant Denominations

By 1976, meanwhile, Mennonites in the Western Chaco still managed the largest evangelism effort to indigenous people in Paraguay. The indigenous population in the colonies had grown rapidly to 9,500 people and actually outnumbered the Mennonites themselves. Nearly one-half of these indigenous people, however, continued to live at work camps with poor conditions and no access to land. While missionaries continued proselytism and ranchers hired them for fieldwork, indigenous people pressured colony administrators for farm land. In 1976, the Mennonites created the Indigenous-Mennonite Association for Cooperation Services (ASCIM), an agency to create stable agricultural settlements for indigenous laborers and "prepare the natives how to survive in a modernizing world, and become citizens of Paraguay."[50] The

new NGO (non-governmental organization) gave landless indigenous house-
holds a few head of livestock, a plow and cultivator, a wheelbarrow, seeds, and
wire to fence their field. By August 1976, indigenous people were settled in
forty-one villages within five "agricultural districts," farmed a total of 695
five-hectare fields, and marketed crops in cooperatives. Every village built a
school, and fifty-eight indigenous teachers instructed nearly 1,700 students.[51]
Genuine interest in the welfare of the indigenous laborers motivated the settlement project, but the prospect of cheap labor and the desire to proselytize
must have also influenced Mennonite efforts.

Mennonite administrators may have hoped that farming and Western
tools would change indigenous cultures and religious practices. Rather than
becoming capitalists overnight, indigenous people took advantage of settler
assistance to secure land, jobs, and thus reclaim some economic independence.
Rising mechanization did not increase crop yields because the total area that
indigenous people farmed actually decreased in direct proportion to the use
of new farming implements.[52] When indigenous people had land they raised
crops for immediate consumption rather than outside markets and were slow
to embrace values of accumulation.[53]

While the indigenous people initially rejected certain forms of capitalist
production, they enthusiastically responded to further Mennonite proselytism.
During the 1970s, religious fervor within indigenous settlements grew so intense that it produced veritable messianic movements. Often entire settlements joined the Mennonite Church at once. Anthropologists have made clear
that religious faith grows dramatically especially when it provides means of
satisfaction for those with needs amidst a rapidly changing world.[54] Through
their religious revivals, indigenous groups in the Mennonite Colonies may
also have sought access to the spiritual forces they believed had given economic success to the Mennonites, in an attempt to additionally improve their
own socioeconomic situation.[55]

The literature on Protestantism in late twentieth-century Latin America
sheds some light on the mass indigenous conversion to Protestantism in western Paraguay. Jean Pierre Bastian has shown that rural Mexican peasants employed new Protestant sects to express both political and social dissent.
Peasants used the new religious expression to create the vision of a world that
contrasted sharply with the surrounding dominant society. The search for religious autonomy also contributed to conflicts over land occupation.[56]

Joanne Rappaport has argued similarly that the Páez and Guambiano
communities of southern Colombia successfully discarded unhelpful elements
in outside religious expressions. Additionally, studies in religion change among
Mayas in Central America show that contrary to common criticism along We-
berian lines, Protestantism served not as a "broker between [them and] en-
croaching modernization," but in some cases as a means for new communities

of indigenous believers to "intentionally reconstruct and reinforce ethnic identity."[57] Rather than stifle their militancy, these indigenous people found that participation in Evangelical sects strengthened movements to reclaim tribal territories.[58]

In Ecuador, Quichua peasants used the Protestant Gospel Missionary Union to improve their social status while revalidating a distinct indigenous ethnic identity. According to anthropologist Blanca Muratorio, "Protestantism has been of fundamental importance in reviving the Quichuas' interest in their own language . . . and they talk about it with a renewed sense of pride."[59] Receiving biblical literature in their own language revived the peoples' interest in identifying themselves as Quichua. For the Quichua, Protestant affiliation became an "alternate ideology," a form of resistance to integration that legitimated continued national oppression.[60]

Evangelical Denominations and Indigenous Ethnic Identity

As had peasants in Mexico, Colombia, and Ecuador, indigenous people in Paraguay also found that participation in Evangelical denominations offered advantages. Widespread adoption of Evangelical practices helped them resist regime pressures for integration. Because surrounding Paraguayos were Catholic, Protestantism provided indigenous people in the Chaco clear religious and cultural barriers with which to distinguish themselves from other peasants. Indigenous communities used Protestant rituals to reorganize their rapidly changing societies. Participation in Mennonite churches offered converts new communal ties and encouraged wider tribal organization. An Enlhit leader named Selhejic argued that Christianity had brought positive changes to his community: "Then many of my countrymen were converted, so that soon the dances and drunkenness in our town were silenced. Instead of that we sang Christian hymns and we entertained ourselves with games taught by the missionary. We accepted these games with great satisfaction, because they served to promote unity and better understanding of community members."[61]

Testimonies suggest that indigenous people felt participation in what they called *cultos evangélicos* strengthened their unity as a people. Baptisms, harvest rituals, and weddings replaced former tribal rituals and provided social interaction, bonding between relatives, and younger leadership in their new setting. Indigenous people therefore employed the cultos, over time, to strengthen their indigenous political and communal fabric.

From the Mennonite Colonies, indigenous evangelists spread their new faith to communities on ranches throughout the Chaco. Soon, 80 percent of adults near the Mennonite Colonies had joined the native Mennonite Church.[62] Indigenous leaders used evangelism to unite tribal members in an unprecedented manner. By 1980, there were seventeen native Mennonite congregations with a baptized adult membership of 3,500. Both Nivaclé and

Enlhit created formal church conferences that by the early 1980s had over 1,000 adherents each. The Enhlit called their religious organization the United Evangelical Churches and had 2,000 registered members by 1982.[63]

Not surprisingly, it was Enlhit laborers and extended families from the Mennonite Colonies, including church members, who in the late 1970s began a concerted demand for ancestral lands. In December 1981, when two Guaraní Ñandeva groups recovered 7,500 hectares of tribal land at Laguna Negra through ASCIM, they organized five agrarian villages and named them Bethlehem, Canaan, Timothy, Damascus, and Emaus.[64] Their use of biblical names for their settlements shows a connection between their desire to recover land in order to raise crops and their adoption of the Evangelical Protestant faith.[65]

Indigenous people also employed Protestant missions to further their resistance to state integration pressures by reasserting the use of tribal languages. In *Translating the Message,* historian Lamin Sanneh has shown how scriptural translation into vernacular languages provides a strong sense of importance to minority ethnicities and was closely linked to cultural revitalization and struggles for ethnic and national independence in Africa and Asia.[66] So called "native-victims," Sanneh continued in a later article, could thus "turn to their own account the things to which Europeans introduced them, including mother tongue literacy."[67] In Paraguay it was precisely during the mid-1970s, when indigenous people were converting en masse to Protestant churches, that larger missions translated scriptures into indigenous tongues and emphasized their use. Mennonites had translated significant portions of New Testament scriptures into Nivaclé and Enlhit by the late 1960s, and this literature provided indigenous people with the pride of having the "word of God" in their own language. Later, as indigenous evangelists learned to read and speak publicly to spread their Christian faith to other communities, translated texts served as an incentive for education.[68] Use of indigenous languages grew throughout the 1970s, immediately prior to the large western indigenous claims to land.

As Brigit Meyer has argued about Protestantism in nineteenth-century Kingdom of Krepi (today Ghana) though, at the grassroots Christianity cannot be reduced to the intentions and actions of missionaries. Rather, in Paraguay as in Krepi, the indigenous appropriation of Christianity "transcended the opposition they seemed to be trapped in," and in "the process of making Christianity their own . . . [they] subverted the missionary ideas."[69] Translated scriptures empowered the Enlhit and encouraged their tribal organization. The power of church officials to control indigenous Christians was extremely limited.

In 1976 the Anglican mission reversed its earlier decision to use only Guaraní language with the Enlhit, a choice they had made to encourage indigenous integration into national society.[70] Anglicans began to urge use of the New Testament in the indigenous vernacular, and soon the Enlhit once again expressed themselves publicly in their own language. Younger Enlhit promptly began to "show a confidence and dynamism which help[ed] them compete" in local job markets, that could "be attributed in part to their . . . literacy in their own language."[71] As linguist Gabriela Coronado Suzán has shown, language can serve as a very important support for indigenous communal organization and additionally as a means to exclude outsiders from the tribe.[72] The Enlhit benefited from bilingual education, translated scriptures, and the resulting ethnic pride that both produced in their society. During the 1980s they became one of the most militant indigenous peoples to demand ancestral lands from the government.

Indigenous Land Rights and Christian Advocacy

Meanwhile, land tenure disparities in Paraguay had reached severe proportions. Landless peasants and indigenous peoples alike were desperate. The rising market for cash crops led to large regime projects to extend cotton, soybean, mint, and rice production in the Eastern Border Region, often onto indigenous lands. At the same time, a spontaneous surge in peasant land takeovers overwhelmed the area. By 1976, the regime had issued ninety thousand land titles to peasants from the Central Zone for four million hectares in eastern Paraguay.[73] Many new arrivals saw indigenous territories as theirs for the taking. Additionally, in the late 1970s, three hundred thousand colonists from Brazil with agricultural experience and credit moved into the area. Colonization soon overwhelmed the regime program and spilled onto indigenous lands.[74]

The regime continued development efforts, such as the Caaguazú and Caazapá Projects, that completely altered the eastern countryside and further pushed indigenous peoples off their territories. To complicate matters, peasants organized themselves into leagues to reclaim their properties. As the church extended legal defense to both peasants and indigenous people, it often found itself hard pressed to divide loyalty between groups struggling to farm on the same land.[75]

Growing tensions between peasants and indigenous people provided the church with another important lesson: indigenous people do not melt down into the national peasant underclass. This had not always been the case. By the late eighteenth and early nineteenth century, historian Thomas Whigham has shown, indigenous people from the former Jesuit missions lived in twenty-one *pueblos de indios* under Franciscan or secular rule and gradually entered mainstream society and became peasants. This was especially the case after 1848, when in the name of a new liberal order President Carlos Antonio López divided their communal lands and disestablished the indigenous villages.[76] Some isolated communities remained outside official control, however, and in these settlements indigenous people resisted integration and instead continued tribal religious practices and communal farming. Since the peasantry used the Guaraní language, it was these religious beliefs and shared agriculture, in fact, that provided the clearest cultural differences between indigenous people and Paraguayan campesinos.

In the late 1970s, as their living conditions and access to land grew even more difficult, indigenous peoples began to pressure religious organizations to help them recover land. Indigenous people initiated these contacts, and the weight of their lobbies was critical in encouraging religious groups to represent their demands to the state. This was especially the case of the Catholic Church, which had adopted a somewhat less confrontational approach to the Paraguayan regime following the 1979 Puebla Episcopal Conference.[77] In the case of Paraguay, the church focus on peasants and indigenous rights attracted less regime censorship than outright calls for regime change. In this sense, the Catholic Church could portray itself as socially active without risking direct reprisals from the Stroessner regime.

Beginning in 1977, three indigenous communities, from the Chaco, that had lost their lands in the previous decade began to press the regime to return the territory they claimed as ancestral. Two groups of Toba Maskoy, one squatting at the Mennonite Colonies and another from the upper Paraguay River town of Puerto Casado, sought to recover territory at Casanillo and Riacho Mosquito. Their conditions were so difficult that women from the first group had even aborted their fetuses to show their despair.[78] At nearly the same time a Toba Qom community, nearer to the capital at Cerrito, began to lobby for the return of the land from which the DAI itself had forcefully evicted them in September 1969.[79] The three groups found ready allies in their struggle in the Catholic Church, which pressured the regime to solve the land problems or face responsibility for genocide.[80] However, none of these communities won their battles for land. After the regime had expropriated Casanillo for the Maskoy, the powerful Casado Company used its influence to ask the army to remove the Enenlhit at gunpoint to a barren plot further west.[81] In another upset, the Toba Qom also lost their struggle for homelands despite support from the Catholic Church and the regime's National Indigenous Institute (INDI).

DEFENSE OF INDIGENOUS PEOPLES INFLUENCES DENOMINATIONS IN THE 1980s

The loss of Casanillo in January 1981 proved a wake-up call for the Catholic Church. It was at this point that bishops reaffirmed the important contributions of indigenous cultures to national society and promised again to support indigenous religious expressions as "adequate sacraments of salvation."[82] Finally, church leaders firmly pledged to uphold indigenous claims for land and issued a plan for social action that positioned the Catholic Church firmly behind indigenous, peasant, and labor groups.[83] At the same time, the pledge may also be interpreted as a church attempt to reestablish influence within indigenous communities, for in conclusion the bishops cited examples of indigenous groups that had found fulfillment in Catholicism.[84]

Possible secondary motives aside, the church upheld its commitments to defend native land claims: during the 1980s, Catholic lawyers were involved in dozens of legal battles over land between indigenous communities and individual ranchers or the regime. One state effort that uprooted dozens of Mbyá settlements was the Caazapá Development Project, a $54.3 million program to increase agricultural production, started in 1982.[85] Despite church attempts to defend these communities, the dictatorship and the World Bank developed forested areas and displaced as many as four hundred sedentary families of Mbyá horticulturists.[86] Catholic lawyers also lobbied on behalf of Avá Guaraní communities evicted in 1982 by the Itaipú hydroelectric plant, and again raised the charge of genocide.[87] To solve this conflict, the Catholic Church and other non-governmental organizations (NGOs) purchased land and resettled two Avá Guaraní communities, Vacaretangué and Kiritó, out of harm's way.[88]

The long legal battle between three Mbyá communities located within the eastern Mennonite Colony of Sommerfeld also occupied much of the Catholic Church's energy. To clear Mbyá off of land the Mennonites from Manitoba had purchased in 1946, the prosperous settlers burned indigenous homes and destroyed their crops with bulldozers throughout the 1980s. The ENM (National Missions Team) and other NGOs legally defended five Mbyá communities. After a prolonged judicial battle, the Andres Rodriguez government finally expropriated 1,457 hectares from Sommerfeld for the Mbyá in 1989.[89]

Legal defense of indigenous communities visibly altered the Catholic Church. In August 1983, the ENM published a new pastoral program to direct Catholic interaction with indigenous people. Written by Jesuit Antonio Dorado González and Oblate José Seelwiche, the plans decreed indigenous people capable of "elaborating their own future, history and salvation."[90] The priests proclaimed a significant internal change within the church, literally, "a conversion by the indigenous world." The church's urgent mission, insisted the ENM, was to eliminate dominant national prejudices rather than alter the indigenous peoples. To accomplish this task, the Catholic Church promised to promote interdenominational ecumenism, publicize indigenous conditions, and continue to defend indigenous lands.[91] The document shows concrete evidence that indigenous peoples had profoundly changed the goals of Paraguay's Catholic Church.

Meanwhile, increasing indigenous demands for self-determination and land also changed other denominations. By the mid-1970s, the Enlhit of the

Eastern Chaco, completely frustrated with the regime's refusal to return the land the state had sold out from under them, turned to churches for help. Because they were Anglican, the Enlhit pressured their denomination to enable them to settle again on tribal lands.[92] Anglican overseers, who had still hoped to integrate Enlhit further into national society as small ranchers, decided after a significant policy reversal to help settle them instead on large communally owned tracts of land and give them cattle and land titles to help encourage self-determination. The mission designed a project called La Herencia, meaning inheritance or legacy, which over the next ten years purchased three hundred thousand hectares, in three properties, for three hundred Enlhit families to settle and farm.[93] As administrator Ed Brice recalled, the abrupt change was a response "to what Indians were requesting at the time" and led the Anglican church into a "whole process that proved to be quite fruitful for the Enlhit" since they used communal land ownership as a unifying tool for their people.[94]

Unlike the indigenous people, peasants did not farm communally. Still, the lack of land also forced campesinos to organize, and by 1985 they had formed over ten groups to represent their struggles, including the Paraguayan Peasant Movement and the National Union of Peasants. Supported by the Catholic Church, these organizations encouraged peasants to use communal marketing to further agricultural self-sufficiency.[95] In the first ten months of 1985, peasants invaded thirty-one private properties and forced nearly 300,000 Brazilian settlers from the country by taking their land.[96] The notable absence of indigenous people from these peasant groups, as well as the practical impossibility of serving both sides when they competed for the same land, proved a lesson to the church about rifts between peasants and indigenous people.[97]

By this time, the Catholic Church had become the outspoken advocate for a group of Toba Maskoy from Puerto Casado, along the Upper Paraguay River. The Casado Company had extracted tannin from the Chaco for nearly a century with a largely indigenous labor force. By the 1980s, though, as the hardwood *quebracho* trees dwindled and company work ground to a halt, workers lived in desperately poor conditions. In 1983, the Maskoy sent their leaders to the capital on six occasions, where with Catholic legal support they negotiated for the return of lands from the Casado Company and addressed high regime authorities through the newspapers.[98] The Catholic Church became the strongest defender of the Maskoy land claims, possibly because they had accepted Catholic proselytism at the Salesian María Auxiliadora mission along the Upper Paraguay River.

The bishop at Puerto Casado, Alejo Obelar, was a trusted ally of the Maskoy in their struggle for Riacho Mosquito and placed church legal services at their disposal.[99] Major newspapers, even those usually pro-regime, daily supported the Maskoy claim.[100] In 1984, two hundred citizens, the

Paraguayan Lawyers College, and the Catholic University all lobbied on behalf of the Maskoy.[101] The Maskoy had by 1985 created important alliances with other NGO's, but the church was their most active advocate. As support for the dictatorship crumbled in 1985 with the economic downturn, the church used the Maskoy claim to criticize the ruling party.[102] By January 1987, as Paraguayos staged anti-regime demonstrations, the Catholic Church brought the Maskoy struggle to the forefront of public attention. When a large labor union began to champion the Maskoy claim, the Catholic Church presented three thousand additional signatures in support of the Maskoy to Congress and launched a "national campaign" on their behalf.[103] Labor unions, base ecclesial communities, and peasant organizations added their support to the church and ten thousand people signed another petition for the prompt return of the Maskoy lands. Finally, on July 30, the Senate unanimously expropriated 30,103 hectares at Riacho Mosquito for three hundred Maskoy families, citing as sufficient cause the "long and painful process of the *indígenas.*"[104] The return to ancestral homelands restored economic self-sufficiency and encouraged the Maskoy to identify again with their indigenous heritage. Chief René Ramírez considered the campaign a great victory, for the people began to use their own languages and once again practice dances and tribal religious traditions that had declined while among non-Indians.[105] Catholic support was critical in this indigenous success.

Such national support on behalf of an indigenous community was impressive. Still, there is no escaping the fact that NGO allies and the Catholic Church itself also employed indigenous rights to further their own causes. Catholic leaders used the Maskoy case to publicize their own opposition to the regime and to position the church as a champion of subaltern requests for political and economic change.

Indigenous Spirituality amidst Cultural Change

Meanwhile, indigenous people continued to identify with their indigenous worldviews and religious practices in the midst of the growing threats to their resources and lands. At the end of August 1987, religious and political leaders from eighteen Avá Guaraní communities met at Fortuna after having expelled a regime attack on their timber. Together the chiefs formulated a response to outside threats:

> We have prayed . . . four days and nights. We have dialogued much about . . . [the] culture . . . our God and our ancestors have left for our own way of life. We have also seen that we cannot give it up, we the guaraní [*sic*], as it is a gift from our God. We also see attempts to introduce another culture among us, which destroys members of our community, our descendants, because it weakens them. Therefore, after much exchange, we have

decided these points: In all Guaraní-Chiripá communities we must strengthen our Guaraní culture; we need to revitalize our dances. We the Guaraní need to live like Guaraní if we wish to be authentic.[106]

The indigenous declaration was a strong and united resolve to resist outside pressures for change. Such expressions of indigenous identity and tribal religion stand as testaments to the results of the Catholic Church resolve to encourage indigenous spirituality rather than force an outside set of beliefs upon the indigenous peoples.[107] Attempts to identify with tribal religious beliefs and communal landholding were also therefore unified indigenous rejections of state development, outside religion influence, and coerced integration.

Rising Indigenous Support for the Catholic Church

As Catholic Church leaders may have hoped, the prolonged Catholic legal advocacy increased indigenous support for the Catholic Church in Paraguay. In December 1987, eight different native ethnicities participated for the first time in the annual pilgrimage to the Virgin of Caacupé, where they read scriptures in their own languages to the entire assembly. An Enenlhit man from Puerto Casado declared his devotion to Catholicism to reporters: "I believe in God, the Virgin, we are Catholics. We pray much and have faith. We always pray the rosary and ask to receive our lands, we tried for so many years and for so long that finally we received them."[108] Lucio Alfert, vicar of the Chaco, decried the theft of indigenous lands and promised that despite former exclusion, indigenous people were now finally to be considered full members of both the church and state.[109]

In August 1987, the Catholic Church announced that Pope John Paul II would visit the following year and would meet indigenous groups at the Santa Teresita Mission in the Chaco.[110] With the promise of a papal visit, demonstrations against the dictator reached an unprecedented level. Throughout the year, frustration in both popular and Colorado Party spheres escalated as people responded to the worsening economy and politicians tried to decide who would succeed the dictator. Protestors demanded an end to state repression, corruption, and the growing economic crisis. Amidst growing conflict within his official Colorado Party, the dictator tried to diminish negative publicity and cancel the papal encounter with native peoples, but the pope insisted on meeting with Paraguay's indigenous people.

In the afternoon of May 17, 1988, seven hundred indigenous people from Brazil, Paraguay, and Argentina welcomed Pope John Paul II to the Chaco at the Santa Teresita Mission. Enenlhit leader René Ramírez, experienced from his people's long struggle for land, presented their message to the pontiff. The chief proudly concluded what the indigenous people had asked him to convey to the pope: "Whites say we should become civilized. We invite the whites to be civilized and respect us as people, respect our communities and our leaders, respect our lands and our woods, and that they return even a small part of what they have taken from us. Indigenous people wish to be friends with all Paraguayans. We wish for them to let us live in peace and without inconveniences."[111]

Ramírez's address serves as another example of indigenous attempts to help shape the church. The chief listed the difficulties indigenous people faced in daily struggles for food and work and showed that that indigenous people still did not consider themselves to be members of the national society. The oration focused on the loss of indigenous land, and Ramírez accused the regime of working against indigenous land rights. "The white authorities who should defend us instead defend those who purchased our land with us still living there. The whites have created a law in our favor. The law is good; they do not apply it in our favor," Ramírez concluded.[112] The speech was a powerful repudiation of the regime's attempt to clear indigenous peoples off their lands and integrate them into the national society. Even more importantly, the address to the pope made public the long indigenous struggle to reclaim land and the significant support churches had given to the indigenous communities.

In his accustomed sympathetic tone, Pope John Paul II responded to the indigenous people with a strong message of comfort and support: "Your desires for improved social conditions are just. Above all you wish to be respected as persons and that your civil and human rights be recognized and honored. I know the great problems you face; in particular your need for land and property titles. For these I appeal to a sense of justice and humanity by all those responsible to favor the most deprived."[113] The indigenous encounter with the pope not only buttressed the indigenous cause because of the recognition they received in the media; the event also showed evidence that indigenous requests for legal support had altered the Catholic Church, which had become the strongest advocate for justice to indigenous communities and land claims. Clearly, indigenous people had influenced Christian denominations in Paraguay.

CONCLUSION

In the years that followed the collapse of the Stroessner regime in January 1989, indigenous people in Paraguay continued to struggle to protect their lands and resources. They achieved a notable legal success in 1992 with the inclusion of an entire chapter on indigenous rights in the new Constitution. A strong indigenous lobby supported by the Catholic Church was responsible for this improvement in Paraguayan legislation. Still, the new law has remained largely un-enforced and indigenous conditions have continued to deteriorate. The loss of land has figured most prominently in their worsening situation. Mennonites, Anglicans, and the Catholic Church have supported the indigenous efforts to improve their conditions. Due to the deteriorating economic situation in Latin America as a whole, however, it will take much more than religious inclusion to better the situation of Paraguay's indigenous peoples.

This chapter has shown five ways in which indigenous peoples have changed Christian denominations in Paraguay over the past thirty years. The most significant point indigenous people have emphasized is that they are different from the peasants, that their beliefs, cultures, and worldviews set them apart from the national lower classes. While state and churches alike in Paraguay have traditionally glorified the race mixture process that created a unique national population, indigenous peoples that managed to continue a semi-independent existence throughout the twentieth century obviously have no intention of following the earlier example of accommodation and identity change.

Second, indigenous people have forced churches to recognize the validity of minority theologies and different cultural practices as honest expressions of Christian faith. In a manner similar to the African Independent Churches and syncretic expressions elsewhere in Brazil and Central America, indigenous people in Paraguay have shown that they already knew God's message in their own cultural expressions and tribal religious rituals prior to the arrival of the missionaries. The more that denominations can learn to recognize spiritual truth already incarnated within indigenous religious expressions, the more they will be able to connect with and learn from indigenous spirituality in an experience potentially meaningful to all of the peoples involved.

Third, indigenous examples have encouraged churches to lay aside the traditional separations among the denominations and the minority peoples themselves and in the process discard what indigenous people have seen as arbitrary and often even "white" divisions. For indigenous people caught within rapid social change and divorced from a means of independent subsistence, doctrinal differences between denominations mattered far less than the economic benefits they might secure from these new sources of provisions and labor. Additionally, as indigenous people discovered ways in which the new church structures served to unite and restore cohesion to their people, they appropriated outside religious identities to organize their own people into new and meaningful associations. While these indigenous church structures fit initially into traditional denominational boundaries, there is a good possibility that in the future, as with the African Independent Churches, they will form the foundation for more authentic indigenous denominations that reflect their own cultural needs and desires.

Fourth, increased indigenous participation in the mass and church events has encouraged the inclusion of the vernacular in popular worship and translated scriptures. Religious acceptance and growing ecumenical outreach has contributed to ethnic pride movements in several large tribes in Paraguay.

Similar to what occurred in Africa and in Central America, it has by and large not been missionaries and denominations that have encouraged these movements to restore vitality to ethnic differences and identities. Rather, indigenous people themselves took advantage of the religious organizations they had at their disposal and used them to build new tribal structures that could create unity and cohesion for their own people, as well as a greater sense of religious satisfaction in a new cultural context.

It is in this way that indigenous people themselves must be the acknowledged as the initiators and the strength behind attempts to recover and defend tribal lands from state development. Those denominations that militantly defended indigenous land rights against state development schemes widened the scope of religious influence to include legal protection and support for independent indigenous self-determination. Religious organizations may have had their own interests as well as those of the indigenous peoples in mind when they lobbied for indigenous land rights. Nevertheless, the desire to increase religious influence within indigenous communities will never completely explain the risks that the Catholic Church took in the face of considerable regime opposition in its defense of the Mbyá, the Toba Maskoy, and dozens of other land claims in recent Paraguayan history. Clearly, the voices of indigenous people in Paraguay have encouraged religious denominations to adopt a new position and to include indigenous people as equals within their midst. Echoes of these resurgent voices and experiences may ultimately encourage people everywhere toward greater inclusiveness, toleration, and a broader understanding of divine grace.

NOTES

1. One of the most recent studies of indigenous peoples in the Chaco is by John Renshaw, *Los indígenas del Chaco paraguayo, Economía y Sociedad* (Asunción, Paraguay: Intercontinental Editora, 1996), 46–56. I am indebted to outside readers Ed Cleary and Tim Steigenga for helpful suggestions, as well as to my father, Willis Horst, and mother, Byrdalene Horst, for their insight and experience with missions and indigenous peoples in Paraguay.

2. R. Andrew Nickson, "Tyranny and Longevity: Stroessner's Paraguay," *Third World Quarterly* 10, no. 1 (January 1988): 239.

3. On Stroessner's rise to power see Paul Lewis, *Paraguay under Stroessner* (Chapel Hill: University of North Carolina Press, 1980), 63–72. See also Hugh M. Hamill, introduction to *Caudillos, Dictators in Spanish America,* ed. Hugh M. Hamill (Norman and London: University of Oklahoma Press, 1992), 18.

4. José Sanchez Labrador, *Paraguay Católico: Harmonioso entable de las Misiones de los Indios Guaranis,* 1772, vol. 1, 331, La. Mss., Lilly Library, Indiana University, Bloomington, Indiana.

5. W. Barbrooke Grubb, *An Unknown People in an Unknown Land* (London: Seeley, Service and Co. Limited, 1913), 20–21 and ff.

6. Decreto #1,343, *Por el cual se crea el Departamento de Asuntos Indígenas,* Asunción, 1958, 1; DAI documents, 20, National Indigenous Institute (hereafter cited as INDI), Asunción, Paraguay. See also appendix to Decreto #1,343, DAI documents,

n.p., INDI. On indigenism, see Hector Díaz Polanco, *Indigenous Peoples in Latin America: The Quest for Self-Determination* (Boulder: Westview Press, 1997); and Alcida Ramos, *Indigenism: Ethnic Politics in Brazil* (Madison: University of Wisconsin Press, 1998).

7. Scott Mainwaring and Alexander Wilde, eds., *The Progressive Church in Latin America* (Notre Dame: University of Notre Dame Press, 1989), 10.

8. Paraguayan Episcopal Conference (CEP) to archbishop, March 25, 1965; Dr. Gómez Fleitas to Dr. Fracchia, October 14, 1967, ENM (Equipo Nacional de Misiones) (currently CONAPI) Archive, Paraguayan Episcopal Conference, Asunción, Paraguay (hereafter cited as ENM Archive).

9. Meeting between Catholic administrators and Alfonso Borgognon, December 14, 1967, ENM Archive.

10. José Seelwische, O.M.I., "Los Misioneros y la Autogestión de los Pueblos Indígenas," manuscript, 1991, ENM Archive.

11. Wilmar Stahl, *Escenario Indígena Chaqueño, Pasado y Presente* (Filadelfia, Paraguay: A.S.C.I.M., 1982), 91.

12. Jacob Loewen, "From Nomadism to Sedentary Agriculture," *América Indígena* 26, no. 1 (January 1966): 27.

13. Ibid., 28.

14. Ibid., 36.

15. Stephen Kidd, "Religious Change: a Case-Study Amongst the Enxet of the Paraguayan Chaco," MA thesis, University of Durham, 1992, 111.

16. Ibid., 111.

17. Ibid., 112.

18. Ibid., 116–117.

19. Ibid., 118.

20. Ibid., 119, 121.

21. On the Maya, see, for instance, Gary Gossen, *Telling Maya Tales: Tzotzil Identities in Modern Mexico* (New York: Routledge, 1999), 184.

22. Cristóbal Wallis, "Cuatros Proyectos Indígenas del Chaco," manuscript, Salta, Comisión Intereclesiástica de Coordinación para Projectos de Desarrollo (ICCO), 1985, 41, Anglican Church Archive, Asunción, Paraguay.

23. Elmer Miller, *Los Tobas Argentinos, Armonía y Disonancia en una Sociedad* (Buenos Aires: Siglo Veintiuno Argentina Editores, 1979), 131.

24. Walter Regehr, "Mennonite Economic Life and the Paraguayan Experience," 37, Archive of Walter Regeher, Neuland, Paraguay.

25. Alejandro E. Kowalski, "Aceptar al otro como Constituyente de uno mismo," in *Despues de la Piel, 500 Años de Confusión Entre Desigualdad y Diferencia,* ed. Alejandro E. Kowalski (Posadas: Departamento de Antropología Social, Universidad de Misiones, 1993), 37–39.

26. Bartomeu Melià, *El Guaraní: Experiencia Religiosa* (Asunción, Paraguay: Universidad Católica, 1991), 9.

27. Miguel Chase Sardi, *Situación Sociocultural, Económica, Juridico-Política Actual de las Comunidades Indígenas en el Paraguay* (Asunción: Universidad Católica, 1990), 278.

28. Lois Ann Lorentzen, "Who Is an Indian? Religion, Globalization, and Chiapas," in *Religions/Globalizations, Theories, and Cases,* ed. Hopkins, Lorentzen, Mendieta, and Batstone (Durham: Duke University Press, 2001), 94.

29. Mark Münzel, *The Aché Indians: Genocide in Paraguay* (Copenhagen: International World Group on Indigenous Affairs, 1973), 52. See also Mark Münzel, "Manhunt," in *Genocide in Paraguay,* ed. Richard Arens (Philadelphia: Temple University Press, 1976), 29.

30. Mark Münzel, *The Ache: Genocide Continues in Paraguay* (Copenhagen: IWGIA, 1974).

31. Adolfo Colómbres, ed., *Por la Liberación del Indígena* (Buenos Aires: Ediciones del Sol, 1975), 31–36.

32. "Persigue Hoy Conferencias sobre Indigenismo en la Universidad Católica," *ABC*, May 31, 1972, n.p.

33. Miguel Chase Sardi, "Apéndice, 1972, para la situación reciente de los Guajakí," *Suplemento Antropológico* 6 (1971): 37. Chase Sardi visited the United States between September 1, 1971 and August 31, 1972. Gordon Ray, Guggenheim Memorial Foundation, to Garret Sweany, Consul, U.S. Embassy in Asunción, New York, August 25, 1971, INDI, File 122.2, CEE, 1959–1973.

34. Chase Sardi published his report on recent Aché conditions in the *Suplemento Antropológico* 6 (1971): 37; Miraglia in the *ABC* (July 23, 1972) 1; Melià did so in an interview with *La Tribuna* entitled "Melià: Los Indios Están en Estado de Cautiverio," February 7, 1972, 13. See Münzel, *The Aché Indians*, 61.

35. "La CEP Estudia Informe Sobre Masacre de Indios," *La Tribuna*, June 30, 1972, 6.

36. Serafina de Álvarez, Director of CONAPI, formerly ENM, correspondence, Asunción, July 26, 2002.

37. Ejercicio del Año 1973, Asunción, January 8, 1974, DAI note #3, INDI, Carpeta Memorias, 4.

38. John Renshaw, "Paraguay, the Marandú Project," *Survival International Review* 1, no. 15 (spring 1976): 15.

39. Miguel Chase Sardi and Branislava Susnik, *Indios del Paraguay*, manuscript, Asunción, 1992, 312, later published in Madrid by MAPFRE América, 1995.

40. "Proyecto 'Marandú: Se Busca Informar a Líderes Indígenas de Todo el País," *ABC*, April 23, 1974, 9.

41. Infanzón to Bartomeu Melià, Asunción, April 17, 1974, INDI, File 110, CEE, 1974; "No hay genocidio en el Paraguay porque no hay intención de destruir grupos indígenas," *ABC*, March 9, 1974, 7.

42. Bartomeu Melià, interview, Asunción, April 19, 1995; "Declaración sobre Genocidio en la República del Paraguay," INDI, File 110. CEE, 1974. See also Infanzon to Professor Jaime María de Mahieu, Buenos Aires, Asunción, May 11, INDI, ibid.

43. CEP statement, May 8, 1974, cited by Arens, *Genocide in Paraguay*, 142.

44. "Se inició ayer en San Bernadino reunión de líderes indígenas de la selva tropical," *ABC*, October 9, 1974, 14. The World Council of Churches Program to Combat Racism and the Inter-American Foundation funded this event. Adolfo Colombres, *Por la Liberación del Indígena* (Buenos Aires: Ediciones del Sol), 248.

45. "Parlamento Indio pidió se devuelva tierras a tribus con títulos de propiedad de las mismas," *ABC*, October 15, 1974, 9.

46. Angel Llorente and Antonio Carmona, "Parte Crónica de el Proyecto Marandú, Proyecto de la Interamericana Fundation [*sic*]," monograph, Asunción, Chase Sardi Personal Archive, 24.

47. "Dos aborígenes paraguayos participarán por primera vez en un congreso en EE.UU.," *ABC*, February 11, 1975, 6.

48. "Retornaron Indígenas que participaron en congreso mundial," *ABC*, November 8, 1975, 11.

49. Lorentzen, "Who Is an Indian?" 88.

50. Wilmar Stahl, "Chaco Native Economies and Mennonite Development Cooperation," manuscript, Filadelfia, ASCIM, 1994, 13; Wallis, "Cuatro Proyectos Indígenas," 39.

51. "Los Indígenas del Chaco Central trabajarán sus propias chacras," *ABC*, August 2, 1976, n.p.; "Las Comunidades Indígenas cuentan con 41 escuelas," *ABC*, August 4, 1976, 15.

52. Wallis, "Cuatro Proyectos Indígenas," 45.

53. Walter Regehr, "Mennonite Economic Life and the Paraguayan Experience," monograph, Archive of Walter Regehr, Neuland, Paraguay, 1990, 38–39.

54. Sidney Greenfield, "Population Growth, Industrialization, and the Proliferation of Syncretized Religions in Brazil," in *Reinventing Religions, Syncretism and Transformation in Africa and the Americas*, ed. Greenfield and Droogers (Lanham: Rowman and Littlefield Publishers, 2001), 66.

55. Wallis, "Cuatro Proyectos Indígenas," 41.

56. Jean Pierre Bastian, *Protestantismo y Sociedad en México* (Mexico City: Casa Unida de Publicaciones, 1983).

57. Virginia Garrard-Burnett, "Identity, Community, and Religious Change among the Mayas in Chiapas and Guatemala," *Journal of Hispanic/Latino Theology* 6, no. 1 (1998): 73.

58. Joanne Rappaport, "Las Misiones Protestantes y la Resistencia Indígena en el Sur de Colombia," *América Indígena* 44, no. 1 (January–March 1984): 124.

59. Blanca Muratorio, "Protestantism, Ethnicity, and Class in Chimborazo," in *Sacha Runa: Ethnicity and Adaptation of Ecuadorian Jungle Quichua*, ed. Norman Whitten (Urbana: University of Illinois Press, 1976), 520.

60. Muratorio, "Protestantism, Ethnicity, and Class in Chimborazo," 522.

61. Wilmar Stahl, *Escenario Indígena Chaqueño* (Filadelfia: A.S.C.I.M., 1982), 78.

62. Wilmar Stahl, interview, Filadelfia, May 11, 1995.

63. Stahl, *Escenario Indígena Chaqueño*, 102.

64. "Proyecto Guaraní-Ñandeva, Informe de Actividades para el período Septiembre 1981–Febrero 1982," Filadelfia, February 1982, AIP and Servicio Profecional Anthropológicos EPSAJ Archives, Asunción.

65. Miguel Chase Sardi et al., *Situación Sociocultural, Económica, Jurídico-Política Actual de las Comunidades Indígenas en el Paraguay* (Asunción, Paraguay: CIDSEP, Universidad Católica, 1990), 188–193. See also, Wallis, "Cuatro Proyectos Indígenas."

66. Lamin Sanneh, Professor of World Christianity at Yale Divinity School, *Translating the Message: The Missionary Impact on Culture* (Maryknoll: Orbis Books, 1989), 124.

67. Lamin Sanneh, "The African Transformation of Christianity: Comparative Reflections on Ethnicity and Religious Mobilization in Africa," in *Religions/Globalizations, Theories, and Cases*, ed. Hopkins et al., 108.

68. Stahl, *Escenario Indígena Chaqueño*, 99.

69. Brigit Meyer, "Beyond Syncretism, Translation, and Diabolization in the Appropriation of Protestantism in Africa," in *Syncretism/Anti-Syncretism: The Politics of Religious Synthesis*, ed. Charles Stewart and Rosalind Shaw (London and New York: Routledge, 1994), 48, 63.

70. While most nationals in Paraguay used Guaraní for their intimate language of choice, the indigenous tongue was native to Eastern Paraguay and not to the Chaco west of the Paraguay River. Fostering the Enxet use of Guaraní had therefore been an Anglican tool for further integration rather than the support of an indigenous language.

71. Ed Brice, former director of Anglican Project La Herencia, personal correspondence, December 31, 1996.

72. Gabriela Coronado Suzán, "Políticas y Prácticas Lingüísticas como mecanismo de dominación y liberación en America Latina," in *Democracia y Estado multiétnico en América Latina*, ed. Casanova and Rosenmann (Mexico City: Jornada Ediciones Centro de Investigaciones Interdisciplinarias en Ciencias y Humanidades/UNAM, 1996), 63–91.

73. Werner Baer and Melissa Birch, "Expansion of the Economic Frontier: Paraguayan Growth in the 1970s," *World Development* 12, no. 8 (August 1984): 786.

74. Baer and Birch, "Expansion of the Economic Frontier," 787. See also R. Andrew

Nickson, "Brazilian Colonization of the Eastern Border Region of Paraguay," *Journal of Latin American Studies* 13, no. 1 (May 1981): 111.

75. Serafina de Álvarez, director of CONAPI, Asunción, interview in Asunción, May 24, 2001.

76. Thomas Whigham, "Paraguay's Pueblos de Indios, Echoes of a Missionary Past," in *The New Latin American Mission History*, ed. Erick Langer and Robert Jackson (Lincoln and London: University of Nebraska Press, 1995), 179.

77. Miguel Carter, *El Papel de la Iglesia en la Caída de Stroessner* (Asunción, Paraguay: Imprenta Salesiana, 1991), 110.

78. Father José Seelwische, interview, Asunción, June 29, 1995. Historian Barbara Bush has documented this extreme tactic of resistance in colonial Caribbean society, where slaves employed herbal abortifacient techniques from Africa to end pregnancies when living conditions became too adverse. Barbara Bush, *Slave Women in Caribbean Society, 1650–1838* (Bloomington: Indiana University Press, 1990), 141–149.

79. Francisco Cáceres, Toba Qom chief, interview, Cerrito, July 6, 1995.

80. P. W. Stunnenberg, *Entitled to Land* (Saarbrücken and Fort Lauderdale: Verlag Breitenback Publishers, 1993), 105.

81. "INDI impidió ocupación de las tierras de Casanillo, En el Kilómetro 220, la tierra es inhóspita," *ABC,* January 6, 1981, 13; "Traslado es forma de genocidio," *ABC,* January 9, 1981, 13.

82. José Seelwische, O.M.I., "Una interpretación del indígena desde las categorías de la Iglesia," *Acción* 13, no. 51 (August 1981): 23–25. See also, "El indígena como persona," *Última Hora,* August 8, 1981, 7; "El indígena es una persona adulta, madura y educada," *Hoy,* August 7, 1981, 15.

83. R. Andrew Nickson, "Tyranny and Longevity: Stroessner's Paraguay, *Third World Quarterly,* 10, no. 1 (January 1988): 246.

84. "Carta de los Misioneros Católicos a todos los Pueblos Indígenas del Paraguay," Asunción, December 1, 1981, Archives of the Catholic National Missions Team, AENM, 2–3, 7.

85. "Se prepara un proyecto de desarrollo rural de Caazapá," *ABC,* August 7, 1980, 16.

86. Ramón Fogel, *El Proceso de Modernización y el deterioro de las Comunidades Indígenas* (Asunción: Centro Paraguayo de Estudios Sociológicos, 1989, 62–64.

87. "Reasentamiento debe ser una prioridad," *Hoy,* March 11, 1982, 15.

88. "Indígenas pedirán indemnización en tierras a Itaipú Binacional," *ABC,* February 26, 1982.

89. See, on the Mbyá-Sommerfeld conflict, René Harder Horst, "Las comunidades indígenas y la democracia en el Paraguay, 1988–1992," *Suplemento Antropológico* 36, no. 2 (December 2001): 126.

90. Fathers Antonio Dorado González and José Seelwische, "Plan de Pastoral de la Iglesia Católica para los Indígenas del Paraguay," manuscript, August 1983, 12, Paraguayan Episcopal Conference, Asunción, Paraguay.

91. Ibid., 36–37.

92. Wallis, "Cuatro Proyectos Indígenas," 28.

93. *Ibid.*

94. Ed Brice, interview, Asunción, Paraguay, March 23, 1995.

95. *Paraguay: Repression in the Countryside,* Americas Watch Report (Washington: Americas Watch Committee, 1988), 38–39.

96. Ibid., 27.

97. Serafina de Álvarez, Director of CONAPI, interview, Asunción, May 24, 2001.

98. Enenlhit chief René Ramírez, interview, Asunción, Paraguay, May 21, 2001. See also "Nuestro pueblo no puede seguir así," *Última Hora,* January 5, 1984, 10.

99. Enenlhit chief René Ramírez, interview, Asunción, Paraguay, May 21, 2001. See also *Diálogo Indígena Misionero*, 35, no. 11 (April 1990): 3.

100. "Maskoy: No ejecutaron hasta ahora la mensura," *Noticias*, April 27, 1985, 13.

101. Two-hundred Public Citizens to General Martínez, INDI, Asunción, October 4, 1984, Archive of the Catholic Church National Missions Team, CONAPI.

102. John Hoyt Williams, "Paraguay's Stroessner: Losing Control?" *Current History* 86, no. 516 (January 1987): 26. See also René Harder Horst, "The Catholic Church, Human Rights Advocacy, and Indigenous Resístance in Paraguay, 1969–1989," *Catholic Historical Review* 88, no. 4 (October 2002): 738.

103. "Nuevas muestras de solidaridad para con Maskoy," *Hoy*, July 22, 1987, 21; "Otras 3,000 firmas dan su apoyo a los maskoy [*sic*]," *Última Hora*, August 21, 1987, 16.

104. "Senado aprobó expropiación," *El Diario*, July 31, 1987, 11.

105. Enenlhit chief René Ramírez, interview, Asunción, Paraguay, May 21, 2001.

106. "Debemos vivir como Guaraní," *Diálogo Indígena Misionera* 8, no. 27 (December 1987): 12.

107. On indigenous spirituality see Pablo Richard, "La Palabra de Diós en las Pequeñas Comunidades de Base, Vida y Pensamiento," *Revista Teológica de la Uinversidad Biblica Latinamericana* 21, no. 1 (first semester 2001): 182.

108. "Emotiva Presencia de Indígenas hubo en Caacupé," *El Diario*, December 7, 1987, 8–9.

109. "Harán misa en idioma de indígenas," *El Diario*, November 26, 1987, 20. See Horst, "Las comunidades indígenas y la democracia," 90–91.

110. "El Papa estará con los indios," *El Diario,* August 31, 1987, 18.

111. René Ramírez, "Discurso de bienvenida dirigida a su santidad Juán Pablo Segundo," mimeograph, Mariscal Estigarribia, May 17, 1988, AENM, Asunción.

112. Ibid.

113. "Juan Pablo II se pronuncio a los indígenas," *Diálogo Indígena Misionero* 9, no. 29 (July 1988): 15.

CHAPTER 5

Interwoven Histories

THE CATHOLIC CHURCH AND THE MAYA, 1940 TO THE PRESENT

Bruce J. Calder

SCHOLARS FAMILIAR with the contemporary life of the Guatemalan Maya have noted a marked shift in Mayan identity in recent decades. The results of this shift became particularly visible by the mid-1970s, as the Maya involved themselves in a movement for socioeconomic and political change which swept Guatemala; they engaged the outside world in a variety of new ways, including participation in a guerrilla war. Despite severe government repression of both the movement for change and the Maya generally in the late 1970s and early 1980s, the Maya seemed to reemerge stronger than ever. By the early 1990s there was clearly a dynamic "movimiento Maya" (Mayan movement, also called the Pan-Mayan movement), an effort to preserve and strengthen the Mayan people and their culture and to reshape the Mayan relationship to the surrounding world on a basis of equality. Explanations of how these changes came about cover a full range of social, economic, and political factors. But they inevitably include the role which the Catholic Church played in Indian communities in recent decades.[1]

This chapter examines the Catholic-Mayan relationship from the 1940s to the 1990s. It begins with a sketch of the church among the Maya in about 1940 and then details the forces which gradually modified the situation in the 1950s and 1960s, particularly Catholic Action and the arrival of large numbers of foreign missionaries. The developments of this period were of great importance to what followed in the 1970s and later. Social and political change, much of it encouraged by Catholic activity (in such forms as education, community organizing, and leadership training), provided a solid base for the innovations of the 1970s. While the ideas of liberation theology and its associated pastoral activities influenced and partly transformed that base, it remained an essential influence during the radicalization and mobilization which

93

marked Mayan society (and Guatemalan society generally) in the 1970s and during the severe repression which followed. Since then it has continued as a foundation for the creation of new structures and movements, of which the movimiento Maya is one.

The contemporary relationship between the Catholic Church and the Indian communities of Guatemala has roots deep in the colonial and post-independence periods, particularly in the anticlerical policies of the Liberal regimes of the later nineteenth and early twentieth centuries. The sixteenth-century church, a central institution in the process of conquest, set the tone of the future relationship by working to replace Mayan religion with Spanish Christianity and to Hispanicize Mayan culture in general, an effort which was as much about political sovereignty as it was religion. Under both Spanish and Guatemalan rule the basic characteristic of the relationship was domination, sometimes exploitative, sometimes paternal and protective. In the society which emerged, religion was an integral part of a race-based socioeconomic and political system, one in which European whites and later Guatemalan ladinos (the non-Maya) were nearly always in charge.

What allowed Mayan cultural survival was their will to resist and the long-term ineffectiveness of the Spanish and Guatemalan states—the Spanish-speaking authorities, both civil and clerical, gradually withdrew from many isolated rural and Indian areas and tried to exploit them from a distance, leaving the Indians to lead many aspects of their lives as they wished. While economic pressures on Mayan communities increased in the nineteenth and twentieth centuries, Liberal anticlerical reforms greatly debilitated the Catholic Church and created an enlarged space for Mayan religious practices.

CATHOLIC-MAYAN RELATIONS, 1940 TO THE 1960s

The weakness of Catholic institutions under the Liberals deeply affected the religious status quo in the rural, indigenous areas of Guatemala between the 1870s and the 1940s. Following the reforms of the 1870s, which disestablished the church, seized nearly all of its assets, and sent a large portion of its personnel into exile or retirement, there were just a handful of priests and no nuns in rural areas.[2] With priests in just a few of the largest towns, the influence of formal Catholicism in Indian communities was limited. These priests, moreover, labored against nearly impossible odds. Parishes were huge, with many thousands of parishioners spread out over wide expanses of territory, often in tiny villages which were extremely difficult to reach. Most communities saw priests very infrequently, perhaps once or twice a year.[3] This remained the typical situation in most of Indian Guatemala well into the 1950s and 1960s.

Anticlerical critics of Catholicism would have said that the church, though weak, was an institution which continued to exploit the Indians. In a certain sense, even from the Catholic point of view, this was true, since rural Catholicism was on a fee-for-services basis; the priests' survival depended on their charging for masses, baptisms, marriages, processions, and virtually all other ritual functions. This enabled rural priests, though poor by the standards of the wealthy, to maintain a standard of living which was far above most of their parishioners.

In 1943 a priest newly arrived in Huehuetenango from the United States portrayed the old system with little sympathy: "A greedy clergy of none too reputable origin, taking advantage of the dire scarcity of priests, imposed a price for every priestly function and even went to the limit of inventing ministrations for profit."[4] Anthropologist Ruth Bunzel noted of a much beloved priest in Chichicastenango that, except for one local landowner, the priest "lives better and more lavishly and has greater economic security than any other person in town."[5] A priest's income also enabled him to maintain his status within the ladino minorities which had formed a dominant sector in many Indian communities since the nineteenth century. The priests, along with ladino officials, landowners, and merchants, played a central role in the ladino power structure; they were outsiders, ladinos themselves, or foreigners (usually Spanish though occasionally from other countries).[6]

The Redevelopment of Rural Catholicism, 1940s–1960s

In the 1940s there were two principal developments affecting the relationship of the Catholic Church and Mayan communities. The first was the gradual arrival of foreign missionaries in the clerically underserved rural areas of the country, a process which began with a trickle of new personnel in the late 1930s, increased somewhat after 1944, and became a veritable flood after 1954. The second was the formation in the 1940s of Acción Católica Rural, a movement within the church to revitalize Catholicism in rural areas. Both these developments are partly associated with the slight softening of the long hostile relationship between the Catholic Church and the state under the dictator Jorge Ubico in the 1930s. This trend continued in the period 1944–1954 after the collapse of Liberalism led to change-oriented, "revolutionary" governments under Presidents Juan José Arévalo and Jacobo Arbenz, who seemed less concerned with anticlericalism and generally favored increased openness and democracy. The Guatemalan church benefited from this changing situation under the leadership of an energetic new archbishop, Mariano Rossell Arellano, appointed in 1939.[7]

Acción Católica Rural

Acción Católica Rural developed in the early 1940s under the patronage of the new archbishop and under the direct leadership of an auxiliary bishop of the Archdiocese of Guatemala, Rafael González Estrada. Its central feature was its stress on the formation of lay catechists, who worked as priests' helpers and, in Mayan areas, served a critical role as translators. They taught elementary aspects of Christian doctrine and practice to widely scattered rural communities.

The obvious purpose of this project was to revitalize and modernize Catholicism in rural areas. In Indian communities, where the related phenomena of ecclesiastical neglect and syncretism had created a Catholicism which in many cases was little influenced by priests, it would work to reassert the church's control and to replace what church leaders saw as a paganized Catholicism with an orthodox European version.[8] For this reason the lay catechists were supposed to be under the strict control of priests and bishops, although there is evidence that some of the early catechists were very zealous and operated nearly on their own, taking the initiative in proselytizing in towns and villages where Acción Católica was unknown, much like the Protestants of later years.[9] This owed to the great scarcity of clergy; later, as there were more priests, the catechists' independence seems to have diminished, only to increase once again in the 1970s under the influence of the Second Vatican Council.

Soon after its founding, in the mid to late 1940s, a second goal of Acción Católica Rural emerged; it was to provide a counter-influence to the growing involvement of the secular state in rural areas. More particularly, it was meant to create some organizational and philosophical basis for resistance on the local level to what Archbishop Rossell and many in the Guatemalan elite saw as a drift toward communism within the Guatemalan government and its economic and social projects.[10]

One should note that Rossell's anticommunism, whatever its political result, was not intended by him as a cover to preserve the privileges of the rich. It was Rossell's sincere though paternal belief that a responsible society had to make efforts on behalf of the poor and exploited. In this he reflected twentieth-century Catholic social doctrine, going back to the 1891 encyclical, *Rerum Novarum,* which was critical of both socialism and unbridled capitalism. The archbishop identified (and publicly condemned) exploitation and poverty as reasons for the alleged receptivity to radical ideas in Indian communities.[11] But most of his elite allies had little interest in heeding his calls for social and economic change, which generally depended on the implementation of paternalistic schemes by landowners and employers themselves.

One area of social change in which Archbishop Rossell himself took some initiative was in the area of education. In an environment which generally depreciated the need for schooling the country's indigenous population (and, indeed, questioned the aptitude of Indians for formal learning), Rossell set out to provide one of the first opportunities for Indian education. In the 1940s he created the Instituto Indígena Santiago, soliciting the support of wealthy Catholic laymen to support his effort.[12] The purpose was to train young Indian men as teachers who would then return to their home villages. Some years later, in 1965, the archdiocese opened a companion school for young Indian women, the Instituto de Nuestra Senora del Socorro.[13]

The New Foreign Presence

A second impetus to change the relationship between the Catholic Church and the indigenous population of Guatemala resulted from the activities of new groups of foreign priests (and later nuns) who began working in Mayan communities in the 1940s. By 1966 foreign religious workers had come to constitute 85 percent of the clerical population of Guatemala, with the percentage even greater in many rural Mayan areas than elsewhere.[14] Because of the innovative religious and social orientation of many of these new arrivals, plus their outside financial support, they had a major impact on the Catholic Church and on the communities in which they served. The increasing clerical population was paralleled by institutional growth, with the number of dioceses (or dioceses in formation) expanding from three in 1950 to twelve in 1969. Since nearly half of these new jurisdictions were in the western highlands (and a number of others had significant indigenous populations), the Maya and their localities received ever greater amounts of attention.

Among the first of the newly arriving missionaries were the U.S.-based Maryknolls, who in 1943 began to work in the Department of Huehuetenango, a heavily Mayan area on the northwestern Guatemalan border next to the Mexican state of Chiapas.[15] The Maryknolls initiated their work with ordinary pastoral activities, including Acción Católica, but soon branched out into social endeavors. The rural primary schools and clinics which they created in Mayan communities became a model for other missionary groups operating in places outside of Huehuetenango. In the late 1950s the Maryknolls invited the Christian Brothers to open a high school, thus opening the way for a limited number of indigenous students to go on to university education.[16]

The system of education created by the Maryknolls was part of a larger project. They came to believe that modernization and development were essential to their work, both practical and religious, in Indian communities. They believed that the creation of schools, clinics, cooperatives, credit unions, improved transportation, and agricultural innovation would enable the Maya to better their lives economically and in the long run to integrate more advantageously into national structures which had previously served to exploit them.[17] In religious terms, schools and literacy offered a way to facilitate Catholic religious life in Mayan communities; education offered the prospect of better-prepared catechists and, in the future, groups of Indian priests and nuns who could replace the missionary structure.

Developmentalism, the name which was later attached to the Maryknoll's habit of promoting social and economic goals along with religious ones, became the dominant paradigm in the rapidly growing missionary sector of the Catholic Church in the later 1950s. Interest in developmentalism was greatly increased in the 1960s with the advent of the Cuban Revolution. This event caused a redoubling of the missionary efforts in Latin America by the Vatican, which poured in personnel and money from the wealthy Catholic communities of Europe and North America. It also frightened U.S. policy makers into creating the Alliance for Progress, which provided considerable additional resources, many of which were channeled through Catholic institutions.[18]

One important aspect of the Catholic development projects financed by the U.S. government was leadership training. A large number of individuals from rural areas, many selected by Catholic priests from among their catechists, participated in leadership development programs in Guatemala (such as the Center for Rural Leadership Training (CAPS) at the Jesuit's Universidad Rafael Landívar) and in the United States (such as at Loyola University in New Orleans). These programs were designed to create grassroots leaders trained to promote health care, education, cooperatives, modern agriculture, and other development projects on the local level.[19]

Dovetailing with Catholic development efforts was the work of the Catholic-related Christian Democratic Party.[20] The party, like the revolutionary governments of the 1944–1954 period, sought to involve the indigenous population in national politics, thus to build a political base for itself in the heavily Mayan western highlands. Though the party was institutionally separate from the Catholic Church by the early 1960s, its historical and philosophical connections created a continuing spirit of alliance. Catechists and other active Catholics were frequently involved as party activists; although priests, especially foreigners, generally avoided open involvement in politics, they gave tacit and occasionally direct support to these activities.[21]

Since one of the Christian Democrats' primary goals was the training of rural leaders, there was a natural connection between Christian Democratic organizers and catechists, who were often articulate men who were willing to question the status quo. The party provided its training both in Guatemala and in Germany, supported by funds from the West German government.[22] One important result of this political organizing (as well as Catholic development projects) was that many Maya communities rapidly developed a group of educated and trained local leaders who came from outside the traditional leadership structure of Indian society.[23]

Conflicting Visions, Community Factions

The fact that foreign personnel brought their own ideas about religious work and about the proper functioning of society caused friction and conflict both within clerical circles and with various elements of the laity. In Mayan communities, depending on the situation, problems could develop with either the ladino minority or the Mayan majority (and not infrequently with elements of both). In many cases foreign priests developed considerable prejudice against the ladinos and in favor of the Mayan population. This prejudice was partly based on an innate sympathy for the underdog and partly on perceptions (and misperceptions!) about the cultures of the two groups. Comparing the ladinos to the Maya, foreign religious workers often stereotyped the ladinos as only superficially religious, without the strong spiritual orientation of the Indians; they especially objected to the attitudes of male ladinos, whom they saw as generally indifferent to religion (or worse, anticlerical) and often immoral and unethical in their personal lives. One missionary reported in 1952 from a village in Huehuetenango, "Fortunately a very small percentage of the people are ladinos. If this were not the case, the work here would be very discouraging."[24]

Foreigners, though they carried ideas of racial and cultural superiority from their own societies, sometimes reacted against the racist distinctions which governed ladino-Mayan social relations and upon which the ladino minority depended to help maintain their political and economic dominance of village life. In church activities, for example, many priests wanted Indians to participate in religious activities with ladinos on an integrated and equal basis, but the ladinos usually preferred to maintain their separate groups. Worse, the ladino minority rejected the concepts of democracy and majority rule, causing intense Indian-ladino struggles over matters of local prestige, money, and power, such as control of the committees for the maintenance of the church.[25]

Another cause of conflict with the ladinos was the missionaries' work in community and human development projects. These efforts had obvious racial and political implications in Indian communities because Guatemala's deep inequalities of wealth and power often translated into a stark division between the ladino minority and the Indian majority. It seemed obvious to most foreign religious workers that the group which most desperately needed assistance with development was the Indian population. Moreover, some missionaries began to conclude that the general poverty of the Maya was no accident, that it had come about during centuries of systematic exploitation. It was also clear that a variety of institutions and structures remained in place, perpetuating this exploitation in the twentieth century, and that ladinos, either locals or outsiders, were usually the ones who benefited.[26]

In this socioeconomic context, a parish school which tried to educate Mayan and ladino children equally or a credit union which sought to offer an alternative to the local money lender was a menace to ladino interests. Thus missionary development projects often led to local tensions, to confrontations, and sometimes to the intervention of civil governors or the military on behalf of ladino landowners or merchants who saw their profits or power threatened. On several occasions beginning in the 1960s local elites managed to have priests expelled from their parishes or even from the country.[27]

Priest-parishioner conflict was not, however, limited to ladinos. It often arose between foreign missionaries and their Indian parishioners as well, most frequently over the key elements of Mayan religiosity, the lay brotherhoods (*cofradías*), and the traditional religious beliefs and practices (*costumbre*). The cofradías, originally organized by Catholic priests in the colonial period, had moved far from Catholic orthodoxy and control. During the long absence of priests, they had become the guardians of the syncretistic Mayan-Catholic tradition; they also came to control the church, the church's property, and community ceremonial life. Frictions which arose from this state of affairs had long been an element in Catholic-indigenous relations but they were minimized by the fact that before the 1940s priests were few, overworked, and largely dependent upon community cooperation and financial support. Probably most important, they seldom spent time in most communities.[28]

The arrival, beginning in the 1950s, of large numbers of foreign missionaries, many of whom came from North America and northern Europe, appreciably changed the relationship between the church and Mayan religious traditionalists. Many of the new priests had an activist agenda, were independent of local financial support, and were determined to control religious life in the areas where they lived and worked. This, plus their ignorance, misunderstanding, and lack of sympathy for the religious aspects of Mayan culture, eventually led to attacks on the traditional religious practices known as costumbre, which they saw as paganism or, at best, unorthodox beliefs and practices. They also worked actively to undermine Mayan priest practitioners. In the process they frequently alienated the cofradías and other followers of the Mayan religious tradition.[29]

Among the Maya, foreign clerics found both allies and opponents. The priest's usual base of support and the organizational basis of his struggle for orthodoxy and control was Acción Católica. He used this new group to separate his followers from the traditional religious life of the community, while he attempted to provide them with a new understanding of Catholic doctrine and ceremonial life. At the core of the organization were the catechists, who served as his chief agents of proselytization. In opposition were the members of the cofradías and other followers of traditional ways.[30] In some instances a deep hostility grew up between the two factions and on more than a few occasions the cofradías and their supporters ran priests out of town with threats or violence. In these situations, the priest could count on the backing of his bishop and, on some occasions after 1954, of the state in the form of the governor or even the military.[31]

In many or perhaps most Mayan towns and villages, the contest between these two forces was very gradually won by the priest as he gained converts to Catholic Action. His victory debilitated and sometimes destroyed the traditional religious system, driving costumbre underground and contributing (often with other forces) to the gradual weakening of cofradías. Nonetheless these struggles left lasting divisions in many communities, divisions which would have important implications in later years.

Aside from the divisive results of the church's program in Mayan areas, there were other problems. One of the most obvious was that there were virtually no Catholic priests of Mayan descent, neither among the Guatemalans, nor (obviously) among the foreigners. In the 1940s and 1950s there was only one identifiable Indian priest in Guatemala.[32] A second problem was that both Guatemalan and foreign priests were often extremely insensitive to indigenous ways. Because there was little or no seminary preparation relative to Mayan language and culture, new priests, whether Guatemalan ladinos or foreigners, arrived ignorant of both.[33] Except in a few individual cases of ethnologically or linguistically oriented priests, there was little conscious effort to learn more. This is hardly surprising. Aside from the racism which influenced many clerics, their training emphasized the Eurocentric, hierarchical, clerical, paternal notions which dominated the Catholic Church before the Second Vatican Council. There was scarcely a thought of learning from the laity, Maya or otherwise.

By the 1970s a modern, European-style Catholicism appeared to be ascendant institutionally, although there was wide variation from community to community. The word *institutionally* is important here. While the Catholic Church and its priests had recaptured control of the churches and probably had the formal allegiance of the majority of the Indian population, it has become very clear over the years that traditional Mayan beliefs and practices continued to exist beneath the surface of Catholic orthodoxy, remaining an integral part of the lives of many if not most Mayan Catholics. Apart from this dual structure, a variety of Protestant denominations and churches began to develop, slowly at first and with great rapidity after 1970. Thus there came to exist a variety of religious practices in Mayan areas.

Major developments in the religious life of Guatemala occurred in the decades beginning with the 1940s. It is likely that among the most important of these in the long run were the changing Catholic-Mayan relationship and the creation of new religious structures in rural areas; they are not only important elements in the history of mid-twentieth-century Guatemala but are also critical to understanding the better known and more dramatic developments of later decades.

MOBILIZATION AND RADICALIZATION IN CHURCH AND SOCIETY: 1960S TO THE LATE-1970S

During the mid-1960s to the late-1970s a second phase of the post-1940 relationship between the Catholic Church and the Maya unfolded. The forces of change which Acción Católica, developmentalism, and Christian Democracy had put into motion in Mayan communities were augmented by new phenomena, particularly liberation theology and the church's "preferential option for the poor." In this period a significant minority of those in the church and many in Mayan communities developed a new outlook and a new approach to both religious and secular affairs. Parts of the Catholic Church and many of its existing programs in Mayan areas were transformed and, to some degree, radicalized. Many Catholic Maya were motivated to become participants in a widespread mobilization of the poor and disenfranchised which swept Guatemala after 1975. Even though this led the ruling coalition of the elite and military to unleash a brutal campaign of violence which devastated both Mayan communities and many programs of the Catholic Church, both survived. By the mid-1980s both were again participating in an equally vital, if more cautious, movement for change. Central to this is the movement for Mayan revindication.

In regard to the Catholic-Mayan relationship itself, the experience of the violence of the late 1970s and early 1980s led a variety of groups and individuals to reexamine the earlier practices of the Catholic Church. Critics from both the church and the Mayan community found value but also grave shortcomings in the past policies of the Catholic Church in both its developmentalist and subsequent liberationist phases. In particular they condemned the church's long campaign to devalue and undermine traditional Mayan culture, particularly its many religious aspects. Numerous modifications to church policy based on an effort to show greater respect for indigenous culture, including a tentative exploration of the possible "Mayanization" of Catholicism, have resulted. At the same time there have been Mayan initiatives, such as an effort to revitalize the traditional Mayan priesthood, which are independent of the Catholic Church.[34]

The primary cause of these developments within the Catholic Church was the program of change initiated by the Second Vatican Council (1962–1965) and by the 1968 Latin American bishops' conference in Medellín, Colombia. New elements began to take their place alongside of (and frequently mixed with) the old. The innovations involved both theological and practical aspects, having to do with liberation theology, the "preferential option for the poor," and a reorientation of pastoral work. A second major cause of the events which unfolded in this period had nothing to do with religion. Rather, it was the failure of Guatemalan governments after 1954 to solve any of the basic social and economic problems which affected Guatemala's impoverished majority, combined with the use of fraud and repression to block the political path to change.

The New Paradigm: Liberation Theology

In rural Guatemala the growing influence of liberation theology brought change to the two dominant movements of earlier decades, Acción Católica and the developmentalist model of missionary work. When this transformation occurred, it brought organizational changes, an increased emphasis on the role of the laity, and a shift in the content of the church's message. In some cases Christian base communities (*comunidades de base*) emerged; these small local Catholic lay groups were responsible for conducting the religious life of the community during the frequent periods when no priest was available. The new groups expanded the role of the catechists, who moved from being mere assistants to being intermediaries between the priest and the base communities and sometimes acting in his stead (directing religious services in distant communities and distributing communion, for example). For the first time some women began to serve as catechists and, more commonly, as leaders of base communities. In terms of the message there was also a shift. The former focus on orthodox Catholic practice and individual moral and spiritual matters increasingly transformed into a concern with broader issues, particularly those of social, economic, and political justice. What remained unchanged was the traditional three-step methodology (see–judge–act) of Acción Católica.[35]

The reader should note that, except in some clerical circles, the actual term "liberation theology" was used infrequently in Guatemala and least of all in public. This probably resulted from the extremely polarized and dangerous political environment, as well as from the fact that Accíon Católica was very well established, especially in Maya areas. Yet the liberationist concepts and practices were very definitely present and led to widespread changes in Guatemalan religious life. Similarly, other terminology associated with liberation theology was not widely used. There were Christian base communities in Guatemala, but they were not usually referred to as base communities, especially in rural areas where Catholic Action had been strong. Luis Samandú and Oscar Sierra note that often in Guatemala the "new pastoral model" of liberationist clergy "was supported on the base of Acción Católica," that, in other words, the structures of Catholic Action were modified to accommodate new ways of thinking and acting. Similarly, the leaders of what were in essence base communities were most often referred to as *catequistas* and less often as *delegados de la palabra* (delegates of the word). Liberationist institutions were collectively identified as associated with *la Iglesia de los pobres* (the church of the poor).[36]

While the rise of liberation theology is associated with the decline of the dominance of the developmentalist model of missionary work, development projects continued (and some continue even today). But other factors were at work. The decline occurred, at least in part, because some of the main advocates of developmentalism themselves began to question whether their efforts would ever make a substantial difference to the lives of most poor Guatemalans as long as the politics and economy of the nation continued to be controlled by an elite which seemed indifferent to the general welfare. This realization opened them to new approaches. The liberationist idea was both to promote new religious perceptions and to bring broad social change by applying religious values to the everyday struggles of life. The new focus was on *concientización* (roughly, consciousness raising) and local empowerment, on liberation of self and community from the un-Christian political and economic structures which led to oppression and poverty.

The message of liberation theology, adopted by some of the church's most active and articulate members, both Guatemalan and foreign, became a major force and certainly affected the church's work. But it remained a minority position. While there was great enthusiasm for liberation theology by some bishops, priests, and nuns, there was resistance or disinterest by others.[37] There was a similar reaction among the Maya. Though some embraced the new theology or its practices enthusiastically, its sociological and intellectual approach apparently left others feeling that it lacked a meaningful spiritual dimension. Thus some ignored it, continuing with old forms of Catholicism as best they could, and others became alienated, sometimes turning to the Catholic charismatics or to the new Protestant Pentecostal churches which began to appear in increasing numbers in the 1970s.[38]

Liberation theology could nevertheless have dramatic implications in Mayan areas. Concientización and empowerment, plus the socio-political nature of the message, served to encourage a process of change which had begun in previous decades under the revolutionary governments of 1944–1954 and then under Catholic foreign missionaries. This process was also encouraged in Mayan communities by the continuing activities of the Christian Democratic Party, which had strong ties to the Catholic Church. The Christian Democratic emphasis on political education and mobilization among the Indian masses since 1960 had not only produced local branches of the party but new Mayan leaders and affiliated groups such as cooperatives and the Christian Democratic peasant leagues, the Ligas Campesinas.[39]

Gradually, as other parties imitated the Christian Democratic effort, Mayan towns and villages saw the formation of modern, competing political parties and the election of Indian officials at the local (and later the national) levels. With competing political parties, patterns of allegiance began to emerge which were sometimes related to religious criteria. The Christian Democrats were often associated with the Acción Católica faction and, by association, the local Catholic priest. In addition, some evidence shows that other parties, such as the Partido Revolucionario or the ultra-conservative Movimiento de Liberación Nacional, were more likely to be close to religious traditionalists. But since local factionalism, rather than national ideological or political issues, was frequently the basis of these religious-political connections, the general patterns were likely of great complexity.[40]

Thanks to the extension of formal politics into rural areas, the Maya were becoming politically mobilized, broadening and deepening a process which had begun under the revolutionary governments of 1944–1954. While this was important in itself, Indian political involvement was one of several factors, including the activities of modernized Catholicism, which fostered communication between Mayan villages and linguistic groups, as well as with ladinos and other non-Maya. Political workers, catechists, cooperative leaders, rural union organizers, and health workers began to participate together in meetings, workshops, and training at the diocesan, regional, national, and even international level.

Mayan Cultural and Political Mobilization

The breaking down of old barriers helped to produce several new phenomena in the later 1970s. One of these was the many-faceted *movimiento Maya* (Maya movement), which had a primarily cultural focus (though there were clear political implications as well). Another, more obviously political, was Mayan involvement in the general mobilization of Guatemala's "popular sectors," particularly their key role in the new peasants' organization, the Comité de Unidad Campesino (CUC, the Committee for Campesino Unity). Also critical was increasing Mayan support for and participation in the guerrilla organizations which began to operate in the western highlands in the 1970s.[41]

A nascent Mayan movement began to emerge in the mid-1970s, the result of the gradual process of the redefinition of Mayan identity in the 1960s and 1970s. It had various roots, some within Mayan culture itself and some, like the changes wrought by foreign missionaries, external. This shift was not only important for how Maya viewed themselves and their possibilities, but for the way they dealt with the ladino and outside world.

Several early manifestations of the Mayan movement emerged in the 1970s in connection with the efforts of various individuals in some of the dioceses to create a *pastoral indígena,* a sensitive and coherent pastoral policy for working in Mayan communities. One of the leaders of this work was Jim Curtin, a Maryknoll priest who organized what he called the Comisión de Pastoral Indígena. Curtin viewed education as essential; he organized seminars in order to educate church personnel about indigenous culture and the various forms of oppression—economic, social and political—which affected the Maya.[42] Among the participants in one of the seminars was one of the few indigenous Catholic nuns, a young K'iche' (Quiché) Mayan woman who worked as a primary schoolteacher.[43] What she learned in the seminar, she says, caused a conversion, completely changing her perception of herself and her people. Wanting to spread this message, she began to speak at meetings and workshops and on local Catholic radio stations with Mayan audiences. In addition she became a teacher in Father Curtin's seminars, becoming a visible leader in the Indian consciousness field. Then she worked, not without opposition, to create a center within her religious congregation to train Mayan girls as Catholic nuns in a way which would not alienate them from their home culture (which had been her own painful experience). Finally, working in the later 1970s, she organized a traveling team to promote Mayan consciousness throughout the western highlands. The team was based in the K'iche' village of Zunil, Quezaltenango, where the Catholic priest, a German missionary, provided moral and financial support to the project.[44]

Father Curtin and the Comisión de Pastoral Indígena also created a cultural center to serve the needs of Maya working and living in Guatemala City. The center became a vital institution, promoting Mayan culture and serving as a focus for a variety of educational and service activities to a clientele which ranged from market women to university students. But all of this activity was brought to an end, literally destroyed, by the violence of the late 1970s and early 1980s, with its promoters all forced to flee the country.[45]

Another major shift in the 1970s, intimately related to the Mayan movement, was the increasing participation of the Maya in popular organizations which operated on both the local and national levels. The Maya most often became involved because they were active Catholics, members of Acción Católica and of base communities, or because of church and/or Christian Democratic ties to cooperatives and peasant unions.

Certainly the most important of these, both in terms of Mayan participation and of its impact on national events, was a new peasant organization, the Comité de Unidad Campesino (CUC, the Committee for Campesino Unity), which originated among the K'iche', both in their home Department of El Quiché and in Escuintla (a coastal department to which many Quicheans migrated seasonally to work on the sugar plantations). Heavily represented among the leaders and followers of the CUC were Mayan catechists and activists from other Catholic organizations. In addition there is evidence that members of several Catholic religious orders were also involved behind the scenes in the formation of the CUC. Phillip Berryman, one of the best informed observers of these events, has observed that CUC "emerged mainly from the work of church groups and continued to maintain strong church ties."[46]

In one sense the importance of the CUC lay in the fact that it was an organization which could mobilize a large number of individuals in support of social and economic change, as it proved in a massive and successful 1980 strike against south coast sugar plantations. Its importance in another sense was that Maya participation and leadership signified direct engagement in national events and the transcendence of a variety of economic, social, and ethnic differences, including the usually vast divide which separated Indian and ladino. This was also true of Mayan involvement in the expanding guerrilla movement around 1980.[47]

The mobilization and partial radicalization which occurred in the Catholic Church and in Mayan communities in the 1970s did not occur in isolation. Despite periodic waves of repression, a significant number of para-political popular organizations emerged which represented the views of labor, urban slum dwellers, reformist intellectuals, Catholic and Protestant religious activists, and others. This activity multiplied greatly after the great earthquake of 1976, which brought immense devastation and socioeconomic dislocation, particularly to poorer communities and to the Mayan towns of the western highlands, laying bare the deep social and economic inequities of the country. Meanwhile, on the political front there was also increased vitality, both among reformist parties such as the Christian Democrats and the United Front of the Revolution (FUR) and parties of the left, whose activities remained clandestine.[48]

In the mid-1970s Guatemala's ruling coalition of elite and military interests decided that the gathering forces of change were becoming a serious threat to the status quo. Not only was the organization and mobilization of Guatemala's rural and urban masses proceeding apace, but there were various indications of the revitalization of Guatemala's long moribund guerrilla movement, this time in the heavily Indian western highlands. The ruling military responded to these perceived threats in the traditional way, with violence. Two of the principal targets were the Catholic Church and the Maya.

The Violence, 1978–1984

The savage repression of the late 1970s and early 1980s has become known generally by a matter-of-fact but brutally correct name, *la violencia*. In Mayan towns and villages this involved the murder and disappearance of many individuals; some of them were activists of one sort or another but many were uninvolved in the processes of change. In some areas entire towns suffered near extermination as they became the targets of a scorched-earth policy carried out by the military, a policy which involved the killing of many thousands and the eradication of some four hundred Mayan villages. Hundreds of thousands fled, seeking refuge in mountain hideaways, in the cities, and in foreign countries.[49]

The violence was not narrowly targeted, yet there was a certain logic to it. For the Catholic Church the weight of the repression tended to fall on activist clergy and laity, particularly those who were associated with liberationist views and outreach to the poor. Fifteen priests were murdered between 1978 and 1985, as well as thousands of catechists and other lay workers; at the same time threats and the general climate of terror forced thousands more into flight or inactivity. But as in society generally, the repression was not narrowly targeted. Virtually all programs and institutions, religious and secular, which the ultra-conservative right associated with change or with assistance to Guatemala's impoverished majority, particularly the flourishing cooperatives, were seen as subversive and their leaders and participants targeted.

The reason that the protagonists of the violence focused on the Maya and the Catholic Church are relatively clear. Parts of both groups participated, directly and indirectly, in the process of social and political mobilization which culminated in the mid to late 1970s. The church was the main outside actor in many Indian communities and had been responsible for the organization of schools, clinics, and cooperatives, as well as for the training of non-traditional leaders, the organization of liberationist lay religious groups, and the promotion of egalitarian social and economic ideas. Mayan Catholic activists were also frequently associated with the Christian Democratic Party, another targeted institution.[50]

Similarly, church members and organizations, as well as the members of Mayan communities, were centrally involved in the growing political and economic protests of the 1970s. A series of strikes and demonstrations shook the confidence of Guatemala's rulers and reinforced their inclination to see all opposition as subversion. Among the offending activities were the widespread demonstrations of solidarity surrounding the strike of Indian and ladino miners at Ixtahuacán; a series of street protests which condemned economic and living conditions (both before and after the earthquake of 1976); the marches which protested mass murders, individual killings, and other abuses of human rights; and the massive strike organized by CUC on the sugar plantations of the south coast in 1980. In addition there were local protests, such as the demonstration over land seizures which led to the army massacre in Panzós, Alta Verapaz, in 1978.[51]

Even more provocative in the eyes of Guatemala's rulers, there were sometimes direct connections between organizations which had ties to Mayan communities and the Catholic Church (such as the CUC) and the expanding guerrilla war of the later 1970s. Both Indian activists and even a few Catholic priests were directly or indirectly implicated and it soon became clear that many communities supported or at least tolerated the guerrillas' activities.[52] Each of these associations gave the repressive forces of the Guatemalan government additional excuses for their broad attack on Catholic institutions and Mayan communities in the late 1970s and early 1980s. Both suffered tremendous losses.

The violence quickly and deeply affected the relationship between the Catholic Church and the Maya. There were three principal results. One was that the church withdrew from large areas of the Indian western highlands. In one case this withdrawal involved an entire diocese and department, that of El Quiché; more typically the withdrawal was partial. Nearly everywhere the more progressive, more activist clergy felt compelled to flee the rural areas, either to Guatemala City or to other countries. Those who remained maintained a tense existence in provincial capitals or in other larger towns, greatly restricting their activities and abandoning work in isolated villages altogether.

The countryside became the realm of the army, the death squads, and the guerrillas. The church's projects, whether developmental or liberationist, crumbled because it was precisely these projects and their leaders which the forces of repression targeted for elimination. Cooperatives, seen as some form of socialism by ultra conservatives, and lay religious groups identified with the theology of liberation suffered especially. But all independent institutions, even schools and clinics, were under suspicion; and those associated with them, teachers, community health workers, and various others, were regularly kidnapped and murdered. Beyond this targeted violence, there was a generalized violence, an atmosphere of terror which prevented the normal operation of even the most innocent institutions.[53]

A second major result of the violence was that religious institutions in all but the larger towns reverted to the de facto control of the local populations. This meant that the local representatives of Catholic Action or of the base communities became responsible for the maintenance of local Catholic life with little or no guidance from priests or nuns. But because the repressive forces had often marked these more progressive lay religious leaders, many had to flee or were forced into virtual inaction. The result was that there was an increased space for a resurgence of the cofradías and the traditional practices of costumbre.

A third result was a marked expansion of Protestantism, especially of the Pentecostal churches, which begun a rapid growth in the aftermath of the 1976 earthquake. There has been considerable controversy over the factors which facilitated the expansion. While this is a very important question, it will not be explored in detail here, both for reasons of space and because there is now a sizeable literature exploring the issue. Suffice to say that some analysts, including many within the Catholic Church, have posited a simple and direct relationship between the growth of Pentecostalism and the repression of the Catholic Church and progressive Catholics (as well as the arrival of large numbers of well-financed foreign Pentecostal missionaries) during the violence. But many subsequent studies, with which this author generally agrees, have argued that in most cases the reasons for these conversions are much more complex and that, at best, the violence is one factor among many (most of which are religious and social rather than political).[54]

IN THE AFTERMATH OF THE VIOLENCE, 1985–1990s

The violence had a great impact on both the Catholic Church and the Maya. Both parties were changed, the situation had changed and, as a result, their relationship changed. The last section of this chapter will examine this from two perspectives. The first will treat the church's introspective analysis of past pastoral policies and how, in light of the disasters brought on by the violence, these policies and the projects which with they were connected collapsed so entirely and with such great loss of life. The second will examine how the church responded to the new situation with a new agenda designed to help end the violence and to encourage the construction of a new society in which violence would be much less likely.

In the late 1980s and 1990s there were still strong links between the Catholic Church and the Maya. But an important change was taking place. New Mayan leaders, many of them produced by the church's earlier activities, were emerging, often in response to the situation caused by the violence. They were increasingly independent actors, creating new structures and organizations, focused on issues both cultural and political (e.g., human rights), which were national in scope. As a result, the Catholic Church and the Maya were becoming more equal entities, with the Maya increasingly standing on their own on the national stage rather than being represented by others.

Reevaluating Catholic Policies

In the mid-1980s a partial decline in the level of repression allowed religious workers to begin to work more freely in Guatemalan villages. Their return to scenes of suffering and devastation caused Catholic pastoral workers and the hierarchy to begin a gradual reexamination of the relationship of the church and the Maya in light of the violence. Bishops, priests, nuns, and the laity, among them ladinos, Mayas, and foreigners, participated in this informal but serious process of reflection. The resulting analysis posited that fundamental errors underlay some of the pastoral policies of the Catholic Church in the period of the 1940s to the 1970s.

The ladinos and foreigners who had been working in indigenous communities (many of them progressives) were motivated both by guilt at what had happened to those with whom they had been working and by their desire to understand how disaster had overtaken the church's seemingly successful work in rural areas. On the indigenous side a major motivating factor was a growing Mayan self-consciousness and self-confidence. This in turn was part of an expanding movement for Mayan revindication in Guatemala, particularly a desire to preserve their culture and to have some control over the institutions which affected their lives.

Out of the process of reevaluation came not only a critique of past church policies but also an effort to formulate new ones. The past did seem to hold some possible models for the future—Maryknoll Father Curtin's pre-violence work with Mayan culture is one pertinent example. Many dioceses created new offices for designing and implementing a pastoral indígena, a policy focused specifically on Mayan issues. In 1990 the Episcopal Conference created an official Comisión Nacional de Pastoral Indígena.

The post-violence reconsideration of pastoral policy convinced many that a major error had occurred when Catholic pastoral workers had created Acción Católica (and later, liberationist lay communities) in opposition to traditional Mayan religious life. This had caused ongoing conflict and resulted in deep divisions in many communities. In some places these divisions led to deadly confrontations during the violence and opened the community to the penetration of destructive outside forces, especially the army and its civilian allies.[55]

A second major problem was that a variety of Catholic policies had weakened or even destroyed important aspects of indigenous culture and of the Maya's belief in themselves. Obviously, this problem had its roots in the conquest, but it had continued in less dramatic ways in the second half of the twentieth century. Catholic contributions to the erosion of Mayan culture (which were just some of a number of modernizing, sometimes global, erosive forces) resulted especially from the active opposition of many priests and Catholic Action to the cofradías and costumbre. But similar results came from other common elements of Catholic pastoral policies and attitudes. For example, Catholic religious workers, particularly priests, were often paternal or elitist. They seldom acquired the language of the people among whom they worked, expecting the Maya to learn Spanish (and Mayan children in Catholic schools to study in Spanish). When in later years there began to be Indian candidates for the priesthood or for the male and female religious orders, their training either ignored or even depreciated Mayan culture. This frequently had one of two negative effects: It either discouraged Indian candidates from religious vocations or, even worse, alienated successful Indian candidates from their own culture and community. Many are the personal stories of Mayan students who felt disoriented, marginalized, and depressed during their training. Still worse, upon graduation and their entrance into pastoral life as a priest or a nun, some felt superior to and out of place among their own people, even their families. This type of preparation also had the effect of producing ladino priests largely unacquainted with and insensitive to indigenous culture.[56]

Increasing sensitivity to the Maya also involved changing pastoral activities so that they would serve the Maya and their communities in terms of their own cultures. The new approach committed the Catholic Church to respecting and even accommodating popular religiosity, including costumbre and the cofradías, as a means of more effective evangelization and a way of recuperating social cohesion within the community and Mayan culture. In the 1990s this spirit of accommodation sometimes included even the Catholic charismatics, who had been treated intolerantly by many progressive priests. But, not surprisingly, it did not normally extend to the growing number of Pentecostal Protestants, who continued to be seen by Catholic clerics as interlopers and a major threat.

Another change was to insist that all pastoral workers learn the language of the people with whom they worked and that they use it in church-related institutions such as schools and clinics. Beyond this, religious personnel were urged to adopt the practice of *inserción* (insertion). The idea of insertion, which the Conferencia de Religiosos de Guatemala (the Conference of Religions in Guatemala, usually called CONFREGUA) began to push in 1985, was that the religious would live within rather than outside of the communities which they served and they would work to become part of community life. The idea was to make them more sensitive to Mayan culture and to help transform them from outsiders to insiders in indigenous communities; this was to make them more committed to the people and more effective in their work.[57]

A further shift in Catholic practice, which represented an attempt to address the perennial shortage of priests as well as the Protestant advantage of having locally born ministers, was the redoubling of efforts to encourage religious vocations in Mayan communities. To ensure that these vocations led to the eventual return of effective pastoral workers to the community, the training of priests and nuns began a dramatic shift in the 1980s (though not always smoothly). For the first time, there were classes on indigenous cultures and languages for both Indian and ladino students. Seminary leaders also took measures to help Indian students adjust successfully to their new environment, which had often been alienating because many students were unaccustomed to living in a dominantly ladino (or if the student went abroad, foreign) environment, because they encountered the insensitive or even racist attitudes of faculty and students, and because many were inadequately prepared for a rigorous academic program by their previous schooling. To discourage an over-adaptation to ladino culture, seminaries attempted to keep Mayan students in close contact with their home communities, both socially and in terms of sending them back on work assignments. Similar experiences for ladino students sensitized them to Indian culture and values. In addition to the modification of existing training programs, religious leaders also created several new programs which focused entirely on Indian students.[58]

The process of accommodating Catholic practice to Mayan culture has varied greatly, ranging from the superficial to the radical. The use of indigenous textiles for liturgical vestments and decoration of the church, an easy first step, has long been common. Another project promoted the composition of liturgical music in Mayan languages and for Mayan musical instruments (primarily the marimba), a step which at first provoked a surprising amount of clerical resistance because of the marimba's connection to Mayan ceremonial life before Acción Católica.[59] Later measures, especially significant because they reversed long-standing policy, promoted the increasing involvement of traditional religious organizations, especially the cofradías, in official Catholic ceremonial life. Similarly, some priests have tried to incorporate Mayan ceremonies, such as those having to do with planting, harvesting, and the changing of the seasons, into church services. While much of this was long underway in some of the dioceses, it became official church policy in 1992 when the bishops issued their pastoral letter, "Quinientos años sembrando el evangelio" (five hundred years of spreading the gospel) in 1992. This long document, which ranged from cataloging the many injustices suffered by the Maya over the centuries (some at the hands of the church, for which the bishops apologized) to making progressive proposals for the future, included the creation of "una Iglesia auténtica Madre-Maya, . . . una Iglesia autóctona" (an authentic Mother-Maya church, an indigenous church) within Mayan culture and under greater Mayan control.[60]

The language of the pastoral letter was meant to include, to some degree, the most radical form of accommodation, the movement to create a Mayan theology within Catholicism or a Mayan Catholicism. These projects fall under the rubric of *inculturación* (inculturation). This small movement is made up of a few Catholic intellectuals (one of them, for example, a European Jesuit who teaches at the Universidad Rafael Landívar, another a Dominican priest with long experience among the Q'eqchi' [Kekchí] of Verapaz) and a small number of other Catholic priests, many of them young Maya who work in Mayan communities. While there is a range of thinking within the movement, the fundamental thrust involves rethinking and restructuring Catholicism for the purpose of changing its European elements (intellectual concepts, cultural referents) to Mayan ones, to move from a *Roman* Catholicism to a *Mayan* Catholicism. The only inviolate principle, say some of its advocates, would be the divinity of Christ.[61]

Such thinking has led some of its partisans into difficulties with Catholic orthodoxy; those few priests who first tried to create some kind of preliminary amalgam of Catholic and Mayan ideas and practices in their pastoral work were in and out of trouble with their bishops. For the bishops (and for some Mayan cultural nationalists) it is a short step from thinking about a Mayan-Catholic fusion to an attempt to recreate a Mayan religion apart from Catholicism. This is obviously unacceptable to Catholic authorities.

Into the 1990s: Resolving Problems of War and Peace

The second major development in Catholic-Mayan relations in the post-violence period was a dramatic shift in the agenda of the Catholic Church as it attempted to deal with the results of the violence of the preceding years, violence which had destroyed the lives of many thousands of its members and much of what its pastoral workers had created in previous decades. I have written elsewhere that the agenda of the Catholic Church in Guatemala changed significantly in the 1980s, that the issues which had been the focus of a progressive minority in the 1970s became the agenda of the hierarchy and thus the church's official policy in the late 1980s. I have also argued that an essential reason for this shift was the experience of the extreme violence of the late 1970s and early 1980s, which continued at a reduced level throughout the 1990s. Facilitating this changing agenda was the continuing influence of Vatican II, the bishops' conferences at Medellín (1968) and Puebla (1979), and, among the religious, the activities of the Conference of Latin American Religious (CLAR).[62]

The focus of the new agenda (which did not abandon old goals, but shifted them to a back burner) was ending the violence, aiding refugees, and establishing the concepts of human rights and the rule of law. Equally important was an emphasis on reforming aspects of politics and society which promoted the use of violence. Thus the Catholic hierarchy began to show considerable concern for democracy, the cultural rights of the Maya, and more equitable forms of social and economic development. All of these matters were eventually included in the peace accords, in no small part because both the church and the Maya were involved in the peace process.

The shift in the 1980s also had roots in the past, both in the international Catholic Church (for example, the "social encyclicals," beginning with Leo XIII's *Rerum Novarum* in 1891) and the Guatemalan church itself, as with Archbishop Rossell Arellano's mixture of anti-communism with calls for social justice, especially for the Maya, in the 1950s. Also, there was considerable development almost a decade earlier of what became the social and economic dimensions of the new agenda, evidenced particularly in the hierarchy's dramatic critique of Guatemala's underlying problems following the deadly earthquake of 1976.[63]

But the new agenda didn't emerge in its entirety until after the death of the conservative Archbishop Mario Casariego and his replacement with the relatively progressive Próspero Penados del Barrio in 1984. At that point, with the worst of the violence subsiding, the bishops began to speak and write regularly about the need for a lasting peace based on serious reforms. One of the first of these letters, "Para construir la paz" (June 1984), is representative of many which followed. Written in anticipation of the constituent assembly which would write the new constitution of 1985, the letter spoke quite directly about the problems of Guatemala. The bishops used a religious frame of reference as they condemned the country's "institutionalized violence" and its manifestation "in the unjust reality of economic and social differences . . . , in the prostration of our people, in their systematic marginalization from participation and making decisions and in the lack of effective civil liberties." They also denounced lack of basic freedoms, such as the rights to free expression, to association, to education, to work, to organize, and to life itself. They spoke of the urgent need for an end to violence and for democracy, human rights, and social and economic reforms. Playing no political favorites, they criticized "marxist materialism" and the "National Security Doctrine," both of which put the needs of the state above those of man.[64]

It was some time, however, before the hierarchy translated their verbal endorsement of serious reform into action on the national level. But their support of change did provide cover for other brave souls, some of them religious personnel and others unconnected to the church, to work for change. This was certainly the case with some of the first human rights organizations, particularly the Grupo de Apoyo Mutuo (GAM), an organization of relatives (ladino and Maya) of the disappeared, which Archbishop Penados and the national office of religious men and women, CONFREGUA, both openly supported.

The peace process, of which the Catholic Church was an early supporter, was essential to the church's relationship to the Maya in the late 1980s and 1990s. Beginning with the Esquipulas talks of 1986–1987, which mandated procedures for moving toward peace, the Catholic Church, some Protestant denominations, and a few ecumenical groups were among the most active of the civil society groups exerting pressure for a peace process in Guatemala.[65] In fact, the Catholic Church, writes Suzanne Jonas, was at first the only "articulated" institution which favored peace. Thus it was not surprising that the Catholic bishop of Zacapa, Rodolfo Quezada Toruño, became head of the National Commission of Reconciliation, the facilitating group mandated by the Esquipulas agreement in late 1987, and then of the National Dialogue; later he acted as coordinator for the actual peace negotiations, a position which he held until 1993. Quezada Toruño and the other organizers of the peace effort (which was generally opposed by the military and the political right) believed it was essential to include the Maya and their issues in the peace process and encouraged it. This was also facilitated by the Maya themselves, who created a number of organizations in the 1980s and early 1990s to advocate for human rights, refugees and other victims of the violence, as well as to advance Mayan culture, education, and other projects.

Among the most important of these were Mayan groups which today are well known, such as CONAVIGUA (representing widows), CERJ (human rights), CUC (rural workers), and CONDEG (the displaced). These and other Mayan organizations, frequently led by figures with past ties to Acción Católica or liberationist lay groups, joined with a wide variety of civil society groups (including Catholic and Protestant religious activists, unions, marginalized urban communities, human rights activists, and many others) to form a pro-peace movement. Using such tactics as grassroots education, demonstrations, and strikes, they had a considerable impact on the peace accords (though getting the military and the political right to honor them subsequently has proved an even greater challenge). In any case, the peace process brought the Catholic Church and the Maya together in a new kind of working relationship at the national level.[66]

Surviving and recovering from the violence in the early to mid-1980s also involved considerable practical (as opposed to policy) work in the urban barrios and rural communities, many of them largely Maya. Much of this work, such as providing "accompaniment,"[67] supplying food and shelter to victims, protecting survivors from further violence, publicizing and protesting atrocities, working with fleeing refugees, providing legal help, aiding widows and orphans, and creating money-making projects for survivors' self support, was carried out by Catholic pastoral workers, when the level of violence permitted it (which it often did not during the early 1980s).[68] The earliest institutional efforts to deal with these problems took place in CONFREGUA, whose members had long associations with Mayan communities, and in the individual dioceses, especially those in the predominately Mayan western highlands, where bishops, priests, nuns, and other pastoral workers also had deep connections. Members of these institutions, keeping low profiles, gradually created local responses to the disastrous human situation. Particularly noteworthy were the efforts of such bishops as Gerardo Flores in the Verapaces and Julio Cabrera in Quiché, who focused much of their pastoral effort on refugees and the displaced. Beginning in the mid-1980s, they and their pastoral workers provided accompaniment, material support, protection, legal help, and assistance with the many difficult problems of return and resettlement to local Maya, to those who had fled to other parts of Guatemala (called the "displaced"), and to those who had fled to Mexico (where individual Mexican bishops—most notably Samuel Ruiz in Chiapas—plus a host of NGOs and the United Nations picked up much of the burden). Especially notable were the efforts of Bishops Flores and Cabrera to legitimize, aid, and resettle those beleaguered refugees groups in the Guatemalan mountains called Comunidades de Población en Resistencia (the CPRs or Communities of Population in Resistance), which the army had decided were guerrilla supporters, best exterminated along with anyone who aided them.[69]

As the violence subsided, these kinds of activities increased and became the basis for national structures. CONFREGUA began this effort when its leaders established the Oficina de Servicios Multiples (Office of Multiple Services) in 1988–1989, which coordinated work by the religious on human rights, legal aid, refugees, and the problems of the displaced. Also, because many of CONFREGUA's members were foreign, it had access to economic support from abroad; in this regard it was able to channel funds both to its own projects and to the assistance projects of other organizations. In 1990 the bishops established what soon amounted to a national human rights office, the Oficina de Derechos Humanos del Arzobispado de Guatemala (Human Rights Office of the Archdiocese of Guatemala), and eventually the office of the Pastoral de Mobilidad Humana in 1992 to work on aid to refugees, repatriation, and resettlement.[70] The human rights office, divided between legal work and human rights education, has played an increasingly vital role in Guatemala since its founding, carrying on heroic work on behalf of the human rights of individuals and communities and a hard-fought campaign against impunity and for the rule of law. In 1994 it also created the Proyecto Interdiocesano de Recuperación de la Memoria Histórica, usually called REMHI (the Interdiocesan Project for the Recovery of Historical Memory), a very successful effort to document the tens of thousands of human rights crimes committed during the thirty-six-year civil war which ended in 1996, and helped sponsor the original exhumations of mass graves, nearly all of them of Mayan villagers. The murder of Bishop Juan Gerardi in April 1998, who directed these programs, stands as a backward testimony to their importance, both to those who want justice and change and to those who oppose them.[71]

CONCLUSION

Since the 1940s there have been dramatic transformations in the Catholic Church, in Mayan life, and in Guatemalan society generally. The changes to Catholicism, the dominant religion in Guatemala, and to the Maya, the majority of the population, are both notable. The church, which at the beginning of this period was small, weak, and very conservative, is now much larger, much more influential, and, while diverse, much more progressive in its outlook. The Maya, generally impoverished, frequently exploited, culturally oppressed, and having no direct voice in the major institutions which governed their lives, are in the midst of a renaissance; while still suffering the effects of centuries of marginalization and oppression, they are today mobilized and directly engaged with the larger society in order to obtain a place of equality for their culture, greater economic justice, and political influence at all levels.

Both the Catholic Church and the Maya have been major actors in their own transformations, but they have also interacted with each other. The church and the Maya have also been shaped by a variety of factors in the larger society, some of them deep in Guatemalan history and some of more recent vintage, such as the revolution of 1944–1954 and its aftermath of growing socioeconomic inequality, guerrilla insurgency, expanding U.S. involvement, the build-up of the army, dictatorship and repression, and other phenomena.

The original impetus for changes in the Catholic-Mayan relationship in this period, from the perspective of the church, was its effort to revitalize its relationship with Guatemala's indigenous population, to make more orthodox the Indian version of Catholicism, and to offer an alternative to what many church leaders saw as the Marxist materialist agenda of the revolutionary governments of 1944 to 1954. This activity was possible, ironically, because the revolutionaries of 1944 had allowed the Catholic Church to begin to recover, especially in terms of permitting the entry of a growing number of missionaries, from the massive blow it had suffered from the nineteenth-century Liberals. While the church was successful in these activities, greatly impacting many Indian communities, the long-term results of these changes were even more impressive (and sometimes, as in all human enterprises, quite unpredictable).

Perhaps the most impressive of these developments has been the Mayan movement for revitalization. While this movement has multiple causes, there can be no doubt that the church was one of the principal facilitating factors. Catholic education, leadership training, and political organizing in the period from 1950 to 1980, provided by the church itself and the church-related Christian Democrats, helped to create a class of Indian professionals, thousands of teachers, doctors, lawyers, priests and nuns, activists and organizers, as well as businessmen and women and a better-educated, more conscious, and more mobilized Indian peasantry. It also resulted in the capture of local and some-times regional political power by Indian-based political groups.[72]

Although this enterprise was very badly shaken by the brutal violence of the period 1978–1984, both the Maya and the Catholic Church gradually re-covered their vitality and their determination to work for change. In fact, as this essay has shown, the violence gradually drew the Maya and the church closer together. Preoccupied with many of the same major issues, basically the creation of a just society and lasting peace, they increasingly worked together in the 1980s and 1990s and continue to do so. In the process the Catholic Church has been as changed, in myriad ways, by its relationship to the Maya as the Maya have been changed by the church.

It must be emphasized that the Catholic-Mayan relationship is a work in progress. For all the recent Catholic support of reform, much remains at the level of good intentions. Where this relationship will lead in the future is hard to predict, not only because of the serendipity of human history, but because the Maya are now capable of creating their own agenda and of operating on their own. Empowered by the strength of their culture and by the experiences of the past fifty years, they increasingly have a voice in a society in which they have been marginalized for almost five hundred years.

NOTES

The author would like to thank Virginia Garrard-Burnett, William Malone, and Dennis Smith for their perceptive comments on the manuscript and the editors, Father Edward Cleary and Tim Steigenga, for their helpful advice and patience.

   1. Ricardo Falla, *Quiché rebelde* (Guatemala: Editorial Universitaria de Guatemala, 1980); Kay B. Warren, *The Symbolism of Subordination: Indian Identity in a Guatemalan Town* (Austin: University of Texas Press, 1989); Carol A. Smith, ed., *Guatemalan Indians and the State: 1540 to 1988* (Austin: University of Texas Press, 1990); Luis Samandú, Hans Siebers, and Oscar Sierra, *Guatemala: Retos de la Iglesia Católica en una sociedad en crisis* (San José, Costa Rica: DEI, 1990). See also Phillip Berryman's two books, *The Religious Roots of Rebellion: Christians in Central American Revolutions* (Maryknoll, N.Y.: Orbis Books, 1984) and *Stubborn Hope: Religion, Politics and Revolution in Central America* (New York: The New Press/Orbis, 1994).
   2. Mary P. Holleran, *Church and State in Guatemala* (New York: Columbia University Press, 1949), describes the Liberal anticlerical reforms and their twentieth-century

aftermath; see also Ricardo Bendaña Perdomo, *La iglesia en Guatemala: Síntesis histórica del Catolicismo* (Guatemala: Librerías Artemis-Edinter, 1996). Other books on the twentieth-century Guatemalan church include José Luis Chea, *Guatemala: La cruz fragmentada* (San José, Costa Rica: DEI, 1988); and Bruce J. Calder, *Crecimiento y cambio de la Iglesia Católica Guatemalteca, 1944–1966* (Guatemala: Seminario de Integración Social Guatemalteco, 1970).

3. A firsthand account of the difficult task facing Salesian priests in rural Alta Verapaz in the 1930s and 1940s appears in Luis Z. de León V., *Carchá, una misión en Guatemala* (San Salvador, El Salvador: Instituto Técnico Ricaldone, 1985), 67–93. Various anthropologists have noted the situation of the church in the rural areas before 1950. Among them, see Maud Oakes, *The Two Crosses of Todos Santos,* Bollingen Series XXVII (New York: Pantheon, 1951), 53; Oliver LaFarge, *Santa Eulalia: The Religion of a Cuchumatán Indian Town* (Chicago: University of Chicago Press, 1947), 79–82; Charles Wagley, "The Social and Religious Life of a Guatemalan Village," *American Anthropologist* 51, no. 4, part 2 (October 1949): 50, for various towns in Huehuetenango in the 1930s; Charles Wisdom, *The Chorti Indians of Guatemala* (Chicago: University of Chicago Press, 1940), 373; and John Gillin, *The Culture of Security in San Carlos,* Middle American Research Institute, No. 16 (New Orleans: Tulane University, 1951) 78, on San Luis Jilotepeque in the 1940s. See also Holleran, *Church and State,* 235–236.

4. Clarence J. Witte, "Thoughts and Jottings for October in Soloma," October 17–31, 1943, Maryknoll Archive, Maryknoll, N.Y.

5. Ruth Bunzel, *Chichicastenango: A Guatemalan Village,* Publications of the American Ethnological Association XXII (Locust Valley, N.Y.: J. J. Augustin, 1952), 88. Wagley, "The Social and Religious Life," 50 and 121, notes the fee-for-services system in Santiago Chimaltenango. In an appendix to Wagley's book, Juan de Dios Rosado, "Excerpts from a Diary of a Visit to Santiago Chimaltenango," 132–133, indicates that a priest visiting San Juan Atitán for a three-day fiesta took in $150 for two masses and numerous baptisms. Benjamin N. Colby and Pierre L. van den Berghe, *Ixil* Country (Berkeley: University of California Press, 1969), 121 and 134–135, report that during fiestas the priest performed "baptism in an assembly line system" at one dollar per head, twice or more the average local daily wage in 1967.

6. On the relationship of rural priests to their parishioners, see LaFarge, *Santa Eulalia,* 80–81 and Holleran, *Church and State,* 237. At least a few priests identified with their Indian parishioners, cooperating with cofradías and other elements of popular Catholicism. Bunzel, *Chichicastenango,* x, notes the famous case of Father Ildefonso Rossbach, a German-American priest who worked in Momostenango and Chichicastenango.

7. The irony of this situation is obvious since Rossell became one of the leading actors in the destruction of the revolutionary government in 1954. For more on Rossell Arellano and the development of the church during his twenty-five-year period as archbishop, see Chea, *Guatemala,* 67–98; and Bendaña Perdomo, *La iglesia,* 115–138.

8. Acción Católica Rural was originally known as the Apostolado Seglar de Educación. Agustín Estrada Monroy, *Datos para la historia de la iglesia en Guatemala,* vol. 3 (Guatemala: Tipografía Nacional, 1979), 545–546 and 556. Mariano Rossell Arellano, "Carta Pastoral sobre la Acción Católica," March 12, 1946. The various *cartas pastorales* (pastoral letters) were and are published by the individual dioceses at more or less the same time the letters are read in all Catholic Churches. The collective *cartas pastorales,* signed by some or all of the bishops, have been issued by the Conferencia Episcopal (CEG, the Episcopal Conference) since the early 1960s. These printed letters were widely circulated and most diocesan archives and research libraries hold some or all of them. The bishops' collective letters and *comunicados* (press

releases) through mid-1997 are also published in book form: Conferencia Episcopal de Guatemala (CEG), *Al servicio de la vida, la justicia y la paz* (Guatemala: Ediciones San Pablo, 1997).

9. Falla, *Quiché Rebelde*, 433–434; Warren, *Symbolism*, 95–97. Colby and van den Berghe, *Ixil Country*, 138–139, note the conflicts caused by Acción Católica militants.

10. Rossell, "Conferencia del . . . Monseñor Mariano Rossell Arellano . . . en el Tercer Congreso Católico de la Vida Rural, el 21 de Abril de 1955, en la Ciudad de Panama"; Warren, *Symbolism*, 88–89.

11. One example of Rossell's views is found in his pastoral letter of November 15, 1948, "La justicia social, fundamento del bienestar social." See also Estrada Monroy, *Datos*, vol. 3, 634–635, and Warren, *Symbolism*, 90–92.

12. Estrada Monroy, *Datos*, vol. 3, 634–635. Rossell Arellano, "Superación del indígena: Discurso del Arzobispo de Guatemala con motivo de la bendición del nuevo local del Instituto Indígena," January 22, 1949 (pastoral letter, see note 8).

13. Personal communication, Venancio Olcot, September 17, 1994.

14. Calder, *Crecimiento y cambio*, 59.

15. Spanish Jesuits had arrived earlier, in the late 1930s, but confined their work to Guatemala City. The Salesians, also present in the capital, began a tiny rural mission among the Q'eqchi's (Kekchí is the traditional spelling of Q'eqchi') of Alta Verapaz when they took over the parish of San Pedro Carchá in 1935; see de León V., *Carchá*, 67–78. Holleran, *Church and State*, 236, notes that by 1946 there were five male religious orders in Guatemala; most of their members worked in the capital city.

16. David C. Kelly, "Maryknoll in Central America, 1943–1978," 2–16 (mimeograph, personal copy). A few communities had government primary schools before the Maryknolls' arrival. H. Gerberman, "Guatemala-Ixtahuacán Diary for January 1952," (Maryknoll Archive), reported from Huehuetenango that it was necessary to create a new school because in the old one "the teachers were all ladinos and have no desire whatever of teaching Indians anything." An interview with Padre Joe Nerino, M. M., March 14, 1989, yielded a similar view of ladino-controlled schools in Aguacatán.

17. A Maryknoll brother, Felix Fournier, organized some of the first producer cooperatives and credit unions in Huehuetenango; see "Diary from Huehuetenango," December 1954, Maryknoll Archive. See also Kelly, "Maryknoll in Central America," 8.

18. State Department policy strictly forbade the use of the Catholic Church or other religious institutions as conduits for U.S. aid before the Kennedy administration; the policy changed dramatically in the early 1960s. Interview with Ed Marasciulo, May 28, 1993.

19. The Loyola program was directed at young leaders, both urban and rural, in such fields as politics, education, and labor. Interviews with Dennis Barnes, May 27, 1993, and Ed Marasciulo, May 28, 1993.

20. The Christian Democratic Party was itself the product of Catholic organizing in the 1950s; its chief promoter was Archbishop Rossell Arellano.

21. Interviews with Father Carroll Quinn, M.M., April 27, 1989, and Father Jim Scanlon, M.M., May 1, 1989. See also David Stoll, *Between Two Armies in the Ixil Towns of Guatemala* (New York: Columbia University Press, 1993), 57.

22. Calder, *Crecimiento y cambio*, 59. Interviews with Father Joe Nerino, M.M., March 14, 1989; Marco de Paz, September 6, 1989; Carlos Gelhert Mata, January 30, 1992.

23. The established leaders of Mayan villages were part of a political-religious hierarchy which was generally conservative in its orientation, avoiding ties to the world outside the village and acting to preserve traditional practices. It was this group which was under attack by modernizing priests and their Acción Católica followers. Its partisans often fought valiantly, and sometimes violently, to preserve the traditional system. See Calder, *Crecimiento y cambio*, 90–104.

24. H. Gerberman, "Guatemala-Ixtahuacán Diary for January 1952," Maryknoll Archive. Many missionaries recalled the existence of this bias in interviews. Colby and van den Berghe, *Ixil Country*, 138, report a similar attitude among Spanish priests working in the Ixil area in the 1960s. Some anthropologists have judged ladino religious culture to be weak in comparison to that of the Maya; for example, see Bunzel, *Chichicastenango*, 13, LaFarge, *Santa Eulalia*, 5, and Wisdom, *The Chorti Indians*, 372.
25. Interview with Father Joe Nerino, M. M., March 14–15, 1989.
26. Thomas Melville and Marjorie Melville describe the process of coming to this realization in *Whose Heaven, Whose Earth?* (New York: Knopf, 1971). Interview with Father Joe Nerino, M.M., March 14–15, 1989, regarding Aguacatán.
27. Calder, *Crecimiento y cambio*, 69–70; Stoll, *Between Two Armies*, 172.
28. LaFarge, *Santa Eulalia*, 80–81, describes this situation in Huehuetenango. Flavio Rojas Lima, *La cofradía: Reducto cultural indígena* (Guatemala: Seminario de Integración Social, 1988), provides material on the history of cofradías in San Pedro Jocopilas, El Quiché, and Guatemala generally. Women were also active in cofradías.
29. For example, Falla, *Quiché Rebelde*, 443–445, and Colby and van den Berghe, *Ixil Country*, 138. A Maryknoll priest describes his intolerant and even belligerent encounter with Mayan customs in Melville and Melville, *Whose Heaven*, chapters 6 and 7. One should note that the few Guatemalan priests were no more sensitive to Mayan culture, but they were less apt than foreigners to confront it directly.
30. Interview with Father Joe Nerino, M. M., March 14, 1989, regarding Aguacatán. Stoll, *Between Two Armies*, 47–53, describes the same in the Ixil area. There are various reports of over-zealous catechists causing friction; see Warren, *Symbolism*, 97–103; Colby and van den Berghe, *Ixil Country*, 138–139; Jim Handy, *Revolution in the Countryside* (Chapel Hill: University of North Carolina Press, 1994), 143; and John M. Watanabe, *Maya Saints and Souls in a Changing World* (Austin: University of Texas Press, 1992), 198–199 and 204.
31. Calder, *Crecimiento y cambio*, 99–100; Colby and van den Berghe, *Ixil Country*, 138; Roland H. Ebel, "Political Modernization in Three Guatemalan Indian Communiites" in *Community Culture and National Change*, ed. Richard N. Adams et al., Middle American Research Institute No. 24 (New Orleans: Tulane University, 1972); Falla, *Quiché Rebelde*, 444–445; E. Michael Mendelsohn, *Los escándolos de Maximón* (Guatemala: Seminario de Integración Social, 1965). Interviews with Evelio López, March 14, 1989, concerning Chiantla, and Father James Flaherty, M. M., May 1989, regarding Olintepeque. John Watanabe, "Enduring yet Ineffable Community in the Western Periphery," in *Guatemalan Indians*, ed. Smith, 195–299; and Watanabe, *Maya Saints*, 194–199. Watanabe found that in Santiago Chimaltenango there had been relatively little opposition to Acción Católica and that the catechists wielded considerable power as mediators between the priest and laity.
32. This priest, Celso Narciso Teletor, openly identified with his Indian origins, publishing various studies on Mayan language and culture. In the mid-1950s a second Indian priest, from a prosperous and educated Quiché family in Quezaltenango, was ordained. Interview with Marco de Paz, September 6, 1989.
33. Salesian missionaries in Alta Verapaz were part of a general pattern; they worked among the Q'eqchi' (Kekchí) Maya for more than thirty years before one of the priests learned their language. See de León V., *Carchá*, 129.
34. Both the Mayan and the Catholic innovations can be traced back to trial initiatives begun in the 1970s.
35. An analysis of three instances of changing pastoral policies is the main focus of Samandú, Seibers, and Sierra, *Guatemala*. Berryman, *Stubborn Hope*, 11–13, gives an example from Izabal; and Watanabe, *Maya Saints*, 198, an example from Huehuetenango.
36. Samandú, Seibers, and Sierra, *Guatemala*, 77–81 and 107–108.

37. Ibid., 171, notes that the continued presence of the conservative Archbishop of Guatemala, Mario Casariego, prevented concerted support for liberation theology and its associated practices at the national level, though some bishops were more supportive in their own dioceses. One of the main sources of support for liberation theology was among the leadership and members of CONFREGUA.

38. The Catholic charismatics, a movement dating from the late 1960s, maintained traditional Catholic doctrine but adopted certain practices from the early Christian church, such as healing by the laying on of hands and speaking in tongues. This movement has been popular in some Mayan communities, though it has often been rejected and even harassed by liberationist Catholics for its separatism and other-worldly emphasis; for these views see Samandú, Seibers, and Sierra, *Guatemala*, 122–125. In some circumstances, Mayan charismatics have switched their allegiance to Protestant Pentecostalism; Stoll, *Between Two Armies*, examines this process in the Ixil area.

39. Samandú, Seibers, and Sierra, *Guatemala*, 32–33; Arturo Arias, "Changing Indian Identity: Guatemala's Violent Transition to Modernity," in *Guatemalan Indians and the State*, ed. Smith, 234. The number and importance of the Ligas Campesinas is unclear, though Arias and other writers suggest that their existence was brief.

40. For some evidence suggesting these patterns, see Samandú, Seibers, and Sierra, *Guatemala*, 30; Falla, *Quiché rebelde*, 448–449 and 462ff.; Stoll, *Between Two Armies*, 57; and Ebel, "Political Modernization," 170–173 and 182–183.

41. Kay B. Warren, *Indigenous Movements and Their Critics: Pan-Mayan Activism in Guatemala* (Princeton: Princeton University Press, 1998), 1–32 and chapter 1; Edward F. Fischer, "Induced Cultural Change as a Strategy for Socioeconomic Development: The Pan-Maya Movement in Guatemala," in *Maya Cultural Activism in Guatemala*, ed. Edward F. Fischer and R. McKenna Brown (Austin: University of Texas Press, 1996), 56–68; Arias, "Changing Indian Identity," 231–235. For the general political and economic context, see Suzanne Jonas, *The Battle for Guatemala* (Boulder, Colo.: Westview Press, 1991), chapters 7–9.

42. Interview with Father James Curtin, M. M. (Los Altos, California), September 10, 1991. Arias, "Changing Indian Identity," 236–242, places great emphasis on the influence of Acción Católica and literacy projects in these developments.

43. The first spelling, K'iche', follows the modern orthography; the second is the traditional.

44. Interviews with name withheld, Mexico City, December 12, 1989, and Curtin, September 10, 1991. Father Curtin is a good example of a fairly typical pattern among missionaries; his attitude toward Mayan culture and religion, having been rather closed and paternal at first, shifted dramatically over the years.

45. Interviews with Father Tomás García (Retalhuleu), January 10, 1991, and Curtin, September 10, 1991. Arias, "Changing Indian Identity," 239. Some members of the Comisión Pastoral reconstituted the group in the late 1980s.

46. Interview with Curtin, September 10, 1991. Samandú, Seibers, and Sierra, *Guatemala*, 84; Berryman, *Religious Roots,* 337; Arias, "Changing Indian Identity," 248–255; Rigoberta Menchú, et al., "Weaving Our Future: Campesino Struggles for Land," 50–61, and Minor Sinclair, "Faith, Community and Resistance in the Guatemalan Highlands," 86–87, both in *The New Politics of Survival,* ed. Minor Sinclair (New York: Monthly Review Press/EPICA, 1995).

47. Susanne Jonas, *Of Centaurs and Doves: Guatemala's Peace Process* (Boulder, Colo.: Westview Press, 2000), 21–24; Stoll, *Between Two Armies*, 87–88; Rachel A. May, *Terror in the Countryside: Campesino Responses to Political Violence in Guatemala, 1954–1985* (Athens: Ohio University Press, 2001), chapter 6.

48. Jonas, *Battle for Guatemala*, 123–125; Miguel Angel Albizures, "Struggles and Experiences of the Guatemalan Trade-Union Movement, 1976–June 1978," *Latin American Perspectives* 7, no. 2–3 (spring–summer 1980): 146–149.

49. Two excellent sources (of the many available) on the violence are Ricardo Falla, *Massacres in the Jungle: Ixcán, Guatemala, 1975–1982* (Boulder, Colo.: Westview Press, 1994); and Human Rights Office of the Archdiocese of Guatemala, *Guatemala: Never Again!* (Maryknoll, N.Y.: Orbis Books, 1999), which is an abridged version of the four-volume REMHI report, *Guatemala: Nunca Mas!*

50. Samandú, Seibers, and Sierra, *Guatemala*, 56–62; Jonas, *Battle for Guatemala*, 148–149 and 163. The Catholic Church and organizations to which it had ties were also often involved in the organizations which formed the popular movement in urban areas.

51. Jonas, *Battle for Guatemala*, 123–129; Arias, "Changing Indian Identity," 243 and 248–250; Berryman, *Religious Roots*, 185–200.

52. Arias, "Changing Indian Identity," 254–255, states that a "vast majority of CUC militants" joined guerrilla groups, so many that CUC basically vanished for several years. Rigoberta Menchú et al., "Weaving Our Future," 63–64, also says that CUC was almost inoperative during 1982–1986, though she blames it on extreme repression. Both versions make sense.

53. Berryman, *Religious Roots*, 200–215. The atmosphere of paralyzing terror is a common theme in many interviews I conducted during 1989 and 1991–1992. Several recent works focus on the violence and its effects among the Maya: Linda Green, *Fear as a Way of Life: Mayan Widows in Rural Guatemala* (New York: Columbia University Press, 1993); Victoria Sanford, *Buried Secrets: Truth and Human Rights in Guatemala* (New York: Palgrave Macmillan, 2003), chapters 5 and 6; Clark Taylor, *Return of Guatemala's Refugees: Reweaving the Torn* (Philadelphia: Temple University Press, 1998), chapter 1 and *passim*. Warren, *Indigenous Movements*, chapter 4.

54. Edward L. Cleary, "Evangelicals and Competition in Guatemala," in *Conflict and Competition: The Latin American Church in a Changing Environment*, ed. Cleary and Hannah Stewart-Gambino (Boulder, Colo.: Lynne Rienner, 1992), 167–195; Berryman, *Stubborn Hope*, chapter 5; Virginia Garrard-Burnett, *Protestantism in Guatemala* (Austin: University of Texas Press, 1998), 117–124, 131–132, 154–161, 164–166; Green, *Fear as a Way of Life*, chapter 7; Samandú, Seibers, and Sierra, *Guatemala*, 62–65.

55. Interview with Padre Max Alvarado (Huehuetenango), March 14, 1989.

56. Interviews with Father Patrick Greene (Sololá), December 26, 1988; Father Jacobo Lucas (Quezaltenango), April 18, 1989; Bishop Gerardo Flores (Cobán), September 27, 1989; Father Tomás García (Retalhuleu), January 10, 1991.

57. Raquel Saravia and Santiago Otero, *Memoria y profecía: Historia de CONFREGUA, 1961–1996* (Guatemala: Ediciones San Pablo, 1997), 152–155. The authors note, however, that only 10 percent of the religious had opted for *inserción* as of 1995, ten years after the policy's inception.

58. Interviews with Brother Ramón Schuster (Cobán), March 2, 1989; Father Patrick Greene (Sololá), December 26, 1988. A Dominican priest with long experience among the Q'eqchi' (Kekchí) near Cobán, Carlos Berganza, seems to offer a bleak assessment of efforts to keep young Mayan priests connected to their culture; see Edward L. Cleary, "Birth of Latin American Indigenous Theology," in *Crosscurrents in Indigenous Spirituality: Interface of Maya, Catholic and Protestant Worldviews*, ed. Guillermo Cook (New York: E. J. Brill, 1997), 180–181.

59. Interview with Father Tomás García (Retalhuleu), January 10, 1991.

60. CEG, "Quinientos años sembrando el evangelio," August 15, 1992, in Conferencia Episcopal de Guatemala *Al servicio de la vida, la justicia y la paz* (Guatemala: Ediciones San Pablo, 1997), 572–630, especially 621. However, one researcher among the Q'eqchi' (Kekchí) in Verapaz about 1990 writes that "the attitude of most clergy suggests that the indigenizing of the liturgy is undertaken with the intention of making Q'eqchi's more Catholic rather than making Catholicism more Q'eqchi'."

See Richard Wilson, *Maya Resurgence in Guatemala: Q'eqchi' Experiences* (Norman: University of Oklahoma Press, 1995), 266.

61. Interview with Antonio Gallo, S.J. (Guatemala City), June 1, 1989. For a much fuller discussion of inculturation, see Virginia Garrard-Burnett, "'God Was Already Here When Columbus Arrived,'" in this volume. Also see the chapters by Cleary and others in *Crosscurrents in Indigenous Spirituality*, ed. Cook.

62. I have discussed this new agenda and its roots in several essays: See Bruce J. Calder, "The Role of the Catholic Church and Other Religious Institutions in the Guatemalan Peace Process, 1980–1996," *Journal of Church and State* 43 (fall 2001): 773–797. The others were presented at conferences of the Latin American Studies Association; these include "The Origins of the Human Rights Programs in the Guatemalan Catholic Church," (Miami, Florida, March 2000); "The Catholic Church and Democratization in Guatemala, 1960s–1990s," (Washington, D.C., September 2001); "The Catholic Church and Guatemala's Refugees, 1975–1996," (Dallas, Texas, March 2003).

63. "Unidos en la esperanza," July 25, 1976, in Conferencia Episcopal *Al servicio*, 126–159. Archbishop Mario Casariego did not sign this letter.

64. "Para construir la paz," June 10, 1984, in CEG, *Al servicio*, 349–378. The reader must remember that this was not the agenda of all Catholics, of clerics or the laity, in the mid-1980s, nor would it be in the future.

65. The Protestant individuals and denominations were generally from the "historical" Protestant churches, as opposed to the Pentecostals, who participated only slightly.

66. Calder, "The Role of the Catholic Church . . . in the Guatemalan Peace Process," 783–797; Warren, *Indigenous Movements,* chapter 2.

67. "Accompaniment" (*acompañamiento*) refers to the pastoral practice of being with those who are suffering from adversity, thus demonstrating concern and solidarity and providing human support.

68. These activities became quite difficult during the height of the violence, when Catholic pastoral workers (clerical and lay) and their projects, as well as others working for social and economic change, came under the same murderous attack as the Maya themselves. Some Protestant denominations were also involved in relief efforts. In the 1990s; the United Nations carried on large-scale projects with refugees and human rights monitoring.

69. Interviews with Alfonso Huet (Cobán), March 1, 1989; Bishop Gerardo Flores (Cobán), September 27, 1989; Bishop Julio Cabrera (El Quiché), May 20, 1999.

70. "Mobilidad Humana" (human mobility) refers to the movements of refugees.

71. Calder, "The Origins of the Human Rights Programs," 20–21; Arzobispado de Guatemala, *Oficina de Derechos Humanos del Arzobispado de Guatemala,* pamphlet (Guatemala: ODHAG, 1998).

72. It is important to note that Protestant churches, working on a smaller scale, also contributed greatly to the process of change in Mayan communities all during this period.

CHAPTER 6

"God Was Already Here
When Columbus Arrived"

INCULTURATION THEOLOGY AND THE
MAYAN MOVEMENT IN GUATEMALA

Virginia Garrard-Burnett

THIS CHAPTER will explore theological innovation and issues of identity and resurgence among the indigenous Mayan population of Guatemala. Specifically, this work will examine the efforts of Catholic and Protestant clergy to "inculturate" Christian theology; that is, to decontextualize Christian narratives from their Western cultural references and reposition them within a Mayan *telos,* or cosmovision. Inculturation theology, which has its roots in Vatican II, has a powerful presence in Africa and other postcolonial regions.[1] Yet in the case of Guatemala, inculturated, or, as in this case, Mayanized, theology represents a unique and self-conscious response to the historic repression of Guatemala's native indigenous population. As such, inculturated, Mayanized theology may be understood within the context of the efforts of Mayan intellectuals to create a coherent political movement through which to represent pan-Mayan political, social, and economic interests. But it also represents an effort to fully universalize Christianity by consciously framing Christian beliefs within the conceptual structures—embodied in humans' relations with one another, with the earth and cosmos, and with the Divine— of Mayan cosmovision.

Within Guatemala, teología Maya—sometimes also known as "incarnation" theology—is a direct project of a history of political subordination, genocide, and cultural resurgence. By some measures, Mayanized theology is as much a political gesture as it is a meaningful theology, for the authors of the theology are fully aware of the ways in which Mayan people have, over time, been able to appropriate a powerful means of domination and subordination (Christianity) and invert both the means and the message for their own strategies.

In this sense the decolonialized theology is much like other types of "liberating" religious discourses such as liberation theology or other theologies tied directly to the political and cultural agendas of subordinate groups. Examples include the black theology promoted by James H. Cone in the United States during the 1960s or feminist theologians within the Catholic Church today. This convergence brings to mind David Batstone's suggestion that "political discourse [naturally] has its theological counterpart. The coincidence of the political and the theological should come as no surprise; after all, theological discourse is responding to the same material culture that finds expression in political discourse."[2]

Of central significance to this project is an examination of the ways that local innovators adapt and reorganize imported religious systems for their own ends.[3] It begs the obvious to state that Christian missionary enterprises in Latin America have been, from the first colonial contacts, grounded in asymmetrical power relations and in the desire to reconstruct not only people's identities, but also their very consciousness. In their work on colonial Christianity in South Africa, John and Jean Comaroff describe religious cultural encounters as "a complex dialectic of invasion and riposte, of challenge and resistance . . . a politics of consciousness in which the very nature of consciousness [is] itself the object of struggle."[4] Given these high stakes and deep asymmetries, religion has remained a contested venue in Guatemala. But the struggle has never been completely one-sided. The object of Mayan theology is to invert and reinterpret the power relations and identity issues implicit in the Christian project for their own purposes.

Yet it would be a mistake to think of Mayan theology as nothing more than political rhetoric. Because Christianity has such a long and contested history in Guatemala, religion has often been used as a measure and metaphor for the deeply rooted contradictions and tensions that underlie so much of Guatemala's past and present; and, in fact, religion—and militant Christianity in particular—sometimes lies at the very heart of these contradictions. Obviously, the colonial, imperialist origins of Christianity, both Catholic (Spanish) and Protestant (North American), in a place like Guatemala carry enormous historical weight that cannot be overlooked. Yet Christianity in Guatemala long ago lost its foreign accent and acquired what R. S. Sugirtharajah calls a "vernacular hermeneutics," a local system of value, understanding, and interpretation.[5]

HISTORICAL CONTEXT

Because of the theology's overtly political genesis, some historical and ethnographic background is necessary to understand the context for its development. Guatemala is, along with Bolivia, one of the only nations in Latin America with an Indian majority (upwards of 60 percent of Guatemalans are indigenous); but its indigenous population has historically been the object of a virulent racism that has left them with some of the lowest social indicators in the hemisphere. In terms of religious identity, the majority (more than 60 percent) of Guatemalans are Catholic (both orthodox and practitioners of a Mayanized "folk Catholicism"), although the influence of U.S. missionaries and the rapid growth of independent, local Protestant churches has also resulted in a sizeable and expanding Protestant population that accounts for approximately 35 percent of the population, a figure that is higher in Mayan, as opposed to ladino (non-Mayan), parts of the country.[6]

Power in the country is vested in a small elite of primarily European origin and in the *ladinos,* a term which applies both to persons of mixed Indian-European descent and to acculturated indigenous people. Guatemala has historically been the richest nation in Central America in terms of economic and natural resources, but decades of political struggle severely retarded its economic advancement during the second half of the twentieth century. The nation suffered through an unevenly matched and bloody civil war between Marxist guerrillas (the Guatemalan National Revolutionary Unity, URNG) and the military-controlled government from 1961 to 1996. Although the struggle lasted for thirty-six years, the most concentrated period of violence occurred after a devastating earthquake in 1976 that exacerbated the nation's many social and political inequities. State repression and violence accelerated sharply between 1981 and 1982, corresponding to the scorched-earth campaign inaugurated by General Efraín Ríos Montt. This period is commonly referred to simply as *la violencia* (the violence).

Ríos Montt, a retired general noted for his membership in a neo-Pentecostal church with ties to the United States,[7] took power in a coup in March 1982 and was himself overthrown in August 1983. Since the late 1970s, the guerrillas had a substantial presence in certain parts of the country and were thought to have significant links to Cuba, Nicaragua's Sandinistas, and El Salvador's FMLN. The army also believed that the popular resistance enjoyed support among the indigenous population. The exigencies of this situation elicited the different governments' wholesale assault, patterned after the Maoist axiom to "drain the sea, in which the fish swim," which devastated the largely indigenous highlands. By 1983, the army had routed the armed resistance and, by its own count, had eliminated 440 indigenous villages entirely. Over the course of the thirty-six year war, some two hundred thousand Guatemalans died violently.

Of this total, some twenty thousand Guatemalans were killed between 1981 and 1983; upward of 80 percent of those were Mayan.[8] Many of those who died in what some have called the "Mayan holocaust" were Catholics who had been called to political and social activism through their involvement in liberation theology.[9] So invasive was the assault on Mayan lives and culture

128   VIRGINIA GARRARD-BURNETT

during this period that one elderly Mayan woman referred to it as *desencarnación,* the loss flesh, or loss of being.[10]

This grim period of genocide of the early 1980s still leaves a strong imprint of terror in the country, but it also elicited a wide variety of political and social responses. In 1986, believing the URNG to be all but defeated, the military permitted the return of civilian government to Guatemala, a period that Susanne Jonas has described as less a meaningful transition to democracy as a "necessary adjustment for trying to deal with Guatemala's multiple crises and to reestablish minimal international credibility."[11] Although crime increased dramatically under civilian rule, the economy gradually improved and the nation moved slowly toward peace. Following the directives of the Esquipulas Agreements, which resolved the Salvadoran and Nicaraguan conflicts in the late 1980s, the Guatemalan government and the military began peace talks with the URNG in 1990 in Oslo, Norway. This process eventually resulted in the signing of the final Peace Accords, which brought an end to the nation's thirty-six-year armed conflict in December 1996.

The Emergence of the Movimiento Maya and the Forging of the Peace Accords

Despite these significant advances, Guatemalans have found that the establishment of peace and the creation of civil society force reconciliation with the nation's history, including the horrific violence of the recent past and a long tradition of racism, in particular, the period of la violencia, with its disproportionate impact on indigenous lives. From the ashes of the Mayan holocaust, indigenous leaders began to reinterpret the recent violence in terms of racism and genocide, rather than through the lens of the Cold War and anticommunism. This reinterpretation demanded a wholesale reconsideration of the Mayan experience vis-à-vis the Guatemalan state and called for a fundamental reassessment of the role Mayan people might play in postwar Guatemalan society and culture. In the mid-1980s, Mayan intellectuals began to lay down a series of demands for the reconstruction of Mayan society based upon three principles: (1) the conservation of Mayan culture production, (2) self-representation and self-determination, and (3) the promotion of governmental reform within the framework of Guatemalan and international law.[12] The issue of cultural rights lay at the core of these demands, as a legal (rather than inchoate, or intuitive) premise, in the call for the legal recognition of indigenous culture as distinct from and fully equal to a hypothetical "national Guatemalan culture." The expectation was that the full recognition of these cultural rights would precipitate a mandatory improvement—both legal and de facto—in the human and political rights of the Mayan people.[13]

By the early 1990s, this activity known as the *movimiento Maya* (Mayan or Pan-Mayan movement) gained additional momentum through the events surrounding the Columbian quincentenary in 1992 and the award of the Nobel

Peace Prize to an indigenous woman, Rigoberta Menchú Tum, that same year. By 1993, the Mayan movement had become a full-blown political and social crusade by and for Mayan people to assert their own cultural and political rights.[14] Within this context, the crucial matter of "Maya culture"—given the diversity and pluralism found even within the *mundo Maya*—refers to enduring commonalities and "essences," defined as "a transcendent spirituality, ties to place, common descent, physical differences, cultural practices, shared languages(s) and common histories of suffering."[15]

The operative premise of the movement was that the fundamental construction of the nation was built upon ladino domination over indigenous people, a system that had too long perpetuated oppression and violence against Guatemala's native peoples.[16] The Mayan movement's goal was to completely reconfigure this power asymmetry, and thereby recover the Mayas' rightful place in the body politic.[17] It also sought to redefine Guatemala's national culture in pluralistic, rather than monolithic, that is to say, ladino terms. "A pluralistic Guatemalan culture," wrote Raxché, a noted Kakchikel intellectual, "would be a space for encounter and dialogue with conditions of equality between the different peoples that exist in the country."[18]

Central to these demands was the concept of cultural rights, which asserts that "culture" is a measurable asset, the sum of the material and spiritual production of a determined group, which distinguishes it from any other group. As such, a given group has its own "cultural capital." In the Guatemalan context, then, the political project of Mayan revitalization demanded that Mayan cultural capital no longer be subordinated to a general or universal "Guatemalan" (that is to say, ladino) culture, but that the system of values and symbols of Mayan culture be given at least equal status.[19] This, of course, included the rich symbolism and values embodied in traditional Mayan spirituality and cosmovision.

In the short term, the Mayan movement sought recognition as an influential sector in the forging of the Peace Accords. In the long term, its objective was recognition of the "multiethnic, pluricultural, and multilingual" nature of Guatemalan society and full political and cultural rights for Mayan peoples within civil society.[20] Without question, the Mayan movement was successful in this first demand, as evidenced by the 1996 the Peace Accords, which not only ended the military confrontation, but also conceded and protected, for the first time in Guatemala's history, specific cultural and political rights of the Mayan peoples.

Church people formed a critical sector in the forging of the peace accords.[21] As members of the National Reconciliation Commission (CRN) required by the Esquipulas II agreements, important actors, such as Bishop Rodolfo Quezada Toruño, served as the Catholic Church's representatives and as "conciliators" in the early years of the talks that lead to the agreements.[22]

Both Catholic and mainline Protestant (although no Pentecostal) institutions served as intermediaries between the government, and guerrillas, and the military, representing involvement from a wide range of church agencies, from the archbishop's Office on Human Rights, to the Guatemalan bishops' conference, to the Lutheran World Federation (which sponsored and facilitated the Oslo peace talks), to pastors of ecumenically oriented grassroots mainline Protestant churches who acted as liaisons between indigenous interests and the negotiating parties.[23]

It is in part because of the high degree of involvement of the religious sector in the crafting of the accords that religion came to be folded into the larger context of Mayan cultural integrity.[24] The issue of religion is addressed specifically in the 1996 Peace Accords in the *Acuerdo sobre identidad y derechos de los pueblos,* which offers protection of indigenous religious practices as a specific cultural right.[25] As a political strategy, the primary purpose of the new theology was to encourage a religious system or systems that support indigenous cultural rights within the larger context of Mayan resurgence.

For some Mayan activists, the conflation of cultural rights and religion demanded an outright repudiation of Christianity altogether. While Mayan spirituality has long coexisted fairly comfortably alongside Catholicism, most practitioners of *costumbre*[26]—highly localized festivals honoring the saints, healing practices, divination, and such overtly Mayan practices as rituals associated with the Mayan calendar—had either considered themselves to be Catholics or *brujos,* practitioners of old religion, or witchcraft. The Peace Accords, however, opened a social space for Mayan spiritual leaders to break off their tie to Christianity and return to an autochthonous spirituality they believe has retained its pre-Christian essence. In an interview published in December 1991, Demetrio Cojtí, a prominent Mayan intellectual, called upon activists to abandon Christianity as a gesture of Mayan cultural revindication. "The process of decolonization," explained Cojtí, "[is part of] the search for authenticity, the search for one's own ethnic identity in the purest form possible, [which] demands a return to one's own religion."[27]

Rising to this challenge, at least two organizations—the Grand Confederation of Native Councils of Daykeeper Principals of the Guatemalan Mayan People and Oxlajuj Ajpop: The National Conference of Mayan Spiritual Guides of Guatemala (established in 1993)—formed in the early 1990s with the shared objective to "recover, develop, promote, and diffuse the practice of [Mayan] spirituality in all its manifestations."[28] The formalized revival of Mayan spirituality thus falls clearly within the context of larger Mayan cultural and political mobilization and, as such, plays an important symbolic role.[29] As Mayan activist and binational scholar Victor Montejo has remarked, "The role of spiritual leaders has become a symbol for the revival and unification of Mayan culture nationally."[30]

For some activists, the formal affirmation of Mayan religion serves as a metaphor for Mayan cultural resilience. "You don't revive something that has never been dead," explained one adherent: "We have practiced our religion and observed our calendar without interruption since the time of the Conquest. But we have kept it to ourselves, hidden from outsiders. Now, after the destruction of many of our communities and the scattering of thousands of our people across the face of the earth, the time for secrecy has passed."[31]

Nevertheless, the position of a politically based Maya-Mayan religion remains somewhat ambivalent. Some have criticized it as the embodiment of the type of "invented tradition" described by Eric Hobsbawm, in which "ancient materials [are used] to construct invented traditions of a novel type for quite novel purposes."[32] On the other hand, there is little debate that Mayan spirituality is central to what Hobsbawn also describes as the "fund of knowledge," that which is carefully preserved in popular memory and has never been completely co-opted by any dominating discourse, namely Christianity or nationalism.

Given these complexities, it is difficult to assess the number of people who have abandoned Christianity for de-Christianized Mayan religion. The latter carries powerful political implications in its associations with the Mayan movement, but is also deeply resonant with familiar Mayan worldviews and with the often-covert everyday spiritual practices that many Maya had long quietly practiced at home.

Kay Warren, in her study of Pan-Mayanism, has suggested that "many" Maya are choosing to abandon Christianity for Maya-Mayan religion, where they can experience a spiritual life that is fully consistent with their heritage and worldview and which carries with it no colonialist baggage.[33] On the other hand, other observers assert that Maya-Mayan religion is primarily an elite phenomenon. As such, revitalized Mayan religion, at least in its "official" venues, at this point seems to be more popular with Mayan intellectuals associated with the Pan-Mayan movement than with everyday Mayan people. It is likely that for the latter, after such long association, they either no longer necessarily regard Christianity as a colonial imposition or are so accustomed to conflating, layering, and intermingling beliefs that they can no longer feel the need to separate one from the other. It is also possible that many people, long accustomed to making accommodations between Christianity and Mayan spirituality, may participate fully in the old-new rituals of Maya-Mayan religion without relinquishing their identities as Christians.[34]

Although the situation could change in the future, most Maya, then, still subscribe to a discursive identity as Christians (Catholic or *evangélico*).[35] This is true even if they adhere to a predominantly Mayan worldview, and, significantly, even if they regularly tap into what Montejo calls "the fund of knowledge preserved in the Mayan memory"—the rituals that have no Christian context, such as divination, fertility rituals, calendar-related day-keeping, reverence of sacred geographic sites, and the like.[36] As one observer notes, "[There are] today indigenous intellectuals who adhere to the religion of their ancestors not only as a force of [cultural] affirmation, but also as a protest against the Catholic religion of the invaders and of the more recent evangelists. Over all, the force of Catholicism and evangelicalism among the Maya people is still very rooted (*arraigadas*)."[37]

The Catholic Roots of Inculturation Theology

It is nearly impossible to separate the development of inculturation theology in Guatemala from the Mayan movement, although the roots of inculturation reach back long to the 1960s, before the Mayan holocaust. Its origins are found in the Second Vatican Council (1962–1965), specifically in the document *Ad Gentes,* which calls on those who work among people of non-Christian cultures to "recognize, enjoy, and respect the seed of the Word" that those cultures contain. *Lumen Gentium* reiterates this sentiment, in inviting the faithful to "recognize and value all the good that is planted in the heart and mind of human beings and in the rights and cultures of all people."[38] At the pivotal Latin American bishops' conference held in Medellín, Colombia, in 1968, the prelates, led by Bishop Samuel Ruiz of Chiapas, affirmed the presence of "seeds of the Word of God" in non-Western cultures and called for the recognition of God's presence in civilizations before the arrival of Christianity. Yet despite the staggering implications of such a radical departure from traditional notions of orthodoxy, the message of inculturation was largely lost within the broader mandate for the preferential option for the poor—a class, not race-based, reinterpretation of the Gospel—and the political momentum of liberation theology.

However, it was precisely this momentum in the late 1960s and 1970s that eventually thrust inculturation theology to center stage, as clergy and Catholic activists, galvanized by their participation in liberationist Christian base communities, began to suffer heavy recriminations for their political involvement. The serious oppression of Catholic (and non-Catholic) activists in the political struggles in Central and South America—the core of what many considered to be the "Catholic heart" of Latin America—compelled the church to place new moral emphasis on human rights in general and indigenous rights in particular.

This new focus of concern was evident at the highest level. Upon assuming the papacy in 1979 John Paul II reasserted the church's concern for non-European cultures within the church in his encyclical *Redemptoris Missio,* in which he offered the first specific definition of inculturation theology. "Inculturation signifies the intimate transformation of the authentic cultural values through the means of their integration into Christianity," the pope wrote, "and to Christianity's taking root (*radicación*) into diverse cultures.[39] In a somewhat belated response, the Latin American Episcopal Council (CELAM) in 1987 formed the Indigenous Pastoral Commission in 1987.[40] The culmination of these efforts came at the Fourth General Conference CELAM, Santo Domingo, 1995, which, thanks to strong leadership on the part of Guatemalan and Bolivian bishops, generated a series of final documents that, in the words of Edward Cleary, "creat[ed] a sense of anticipation for a fully developed indigenous theology."[41]

Although the appeal of inculturation theology was obvious for a place such as Guatemala, where ancient Mayan beliefs continue to coexist tenaciously alongside Christianity, it did not take root there immediately, despite these larger church initiatives. This was due in part to the ascension of a political and theological ultra-conservative, Mario Casariego, to archbishop of Guatemala in 1964; he served until his death in 1983. Despite the archbishop's long, conservative shadow, a group of bishops established the Episcopal Conference of Guatemala (CEG) in 1969, a liberal body which was created in part to temper Archbishop Casariego's repudiation of Catholic social justice concerns and liberation theology.[42] In September 1968, the bishops returned from Medellín and convened a national-level *pastoral de conjunto* to broach the idea of a *pastoral indígena*. In 1970, several key Guatemalan-based priests began to meet with Mexican clergy in a series of workshops and discussions on how best to reveal an "Indian face" in the church.[43]

In the early 1970s, a group of (primarily foreign) Dominican clergy in Alta Vera Paz began to apply the study of anthropology to increase their sensitivity to Western cultural biases in their pastoral work,[44] but this work "did not have defined criteria [for a new type] of Christian formation" such as would eventually be found for inculturation theology.[45] In 1973, clergy sponsored a pastoral week (*semana de pastoral*) to examine the possibilities inherent in a "pastoral indígena"—at that time, conceptualized primarily as conducting the liturgy, preaching, and translating of hymns into indigenous languages. Within a few years, however, these concerns would be seared away by the hot winds of destruction—first, the 1976 earthquake, followed by the horror of la violencia—and clerical attention diverted from inculturation to the very survival of their people.[46]

Toward a Theology for Survivors

Unlike the political violence that occurred during earlier periods of the thirty-six-year-long civil war, the war of counterinsurgency that took place in the early 1980s struck disproportionately hard in the predominantly indigenous areas of the country, particularly affecting the departments of El Quiché, Alta Vera Paz, and Huehuetenango, as well as San Marcos and Chimaltenango, to the west and south. Here, the military believed the URNG enjoyed substantial support, particularly among the Mayan population.

Although no area of the country was immune from the violence, the department of El Quiché suffered perhaps most grievously at the hands of the security forces during this period. In 1980, after the assassination of a third Catholic priest and the deaths of hundreds of Catholic lay activists, the bishop of the Diocese of El Quiché, Juan Gerardi, suspended all pastoral work in the diocese.[47] Ecclesiastical services were not fully restored until 1987, when Julio Cabrera was ordained bishop of El Quiché.[48]

Horrified by the level of trauma he found among the survivors of what many called the "church of the catacombs" and troubled by substantial inroads made by Protestant churches during the 1980s in the region, Cabrera sought out a different theological paradigm to both bring spiritual consolation to the suffering and bring them back into the fold of the Catholic Church. In October 1990, Cabrera and other bishops and clergy met in El Quiché to reaffirm the diocese's commitment to a pastoral indígena and to demand a pastoral letter from the CEG to address both the issues of the recent violence and the issues raised by the upcoming Columbian anniversary.[49] In May 1992, Cabrera formally introduced inculturation theology to the Diocese of El Quiché in a sermon preached in Santa Cruz del Quiché, in which he proclaimed, "The unique Gospel of Jesus has to live in accordance with the manner of being of every people (*pueblo*), or every culture. And because of this, the catholicity of the Church does not mean that everyone think and live in the same manner, but rather that all express the same faith according to their own manner of being. . . . The Quiché[50] people have . . . enriched the Catholic Church not only because it has given numerous martyrs . . . but it also gives an example of how to live the faith, within a Maya culture."[51] This affirmation placed Bishop Cabrera in the vanguard of inculturation theology within the Catholic Church in Guatemala. In 1988, a group of priests who had been active in the 1970s established the ad hoc Comisión de Pastoral Indígena de Guatemala (COPIGUA),[52] which the officially sanctioned Comisión Nacional de Pastoral Indígena de la Conference Episcopal de Guatemala replaced in 1990.

But by far, the most ringing endorsement came in 1992, when the Guatemalan Episcopal Conference issued a collective pastoral letter entitled "El nuevo compromiso de la Iglesia: La carta pastoral colectiva: '500 años sembrando el Evangélio.'" This remarkable document, released to coincide with the five-hundred-year anniversary of Columbus's arrival in the Americas, first asked pardon for the errors committed by the church over the course of its long history with Guatemala's indigenous people, the "five centuries of planting watered with the tears, lamentations and the blood of the indigenous martyrs." Secondly, it stated that the Guatemalan church "assumed the *mundo indígena*" and would support the ways in which Mayan people could express their faith within an autochthonous church.[53]

Following the publication of "500 años sembrando el Evangélio" and fed by the energy of quincentenary, inculturation theology gained ground quickly in Guatemala, particularly since its challenges so closely complemented the emerging Mayan movement. On the actual anniversary of the Columbian "discovery," October 12, 1992, Pope John Paul II offered an address in which he lamented the human rights violations committed in the name of Christianity five hundred years earlier and offered his concern for the "pitiable" conditions of indigenous people today.[54] That same year, a group of Swiss Dominicans, working closely with Spanish and Mexican *hermanos* and some secular anthropologists, established the Fray Bartolomé de las Casas Center Ak'Kután (new dawn, in Q'eqchi' Maya) to work with Q'eqchi' cofradias (traditional religious brotherhoods), catechists, and other Q'eqchi' lay people in Alta Verapaz. In 2000, Guatemalan Jesuits began an additional inculturation project among the K'iche'.[55]

In general terms, such projects were less linked to the Mayan movement than they were tied to the church's desire to mend the large rents in its "spiritual canopy" made by the serious disruptions to church, community, and family caused by the war, the incursions made by Protestant conversion, and the rifts within the church between traditionalists, catechists, and charismatic Catholics. In effect, inculturation theology was thought to be able to provide a multi-radiant bridge to link not only Mayan worldview(s) and Christian orthodoxy, but also divergent cultures. Thus, the theology was believed to have the potential not only to bridge the ladino-indigenous social chasm, but also to cross the fissures that divided conservative Mayan *costumbristas* from progressive catechists within the church.[56] In 1995, CEG codified the challenges into the formal Plan Nacional de Pastoral Indígena.[57]

Yet the Roman Catholic Church was not the only entity energized by the new pastoral plan. Among the bridges built were ecumenical ones, an impulse fed by a series of diocesan, regional, and international conferences and workshops that permitted Protestant participation, but also fed by the fact the ecumenical Protestants, particularly from Presbyterian churches, had worked alongside Catholics in the CNR (National Reconciliation Commission) and had served as vocal spokespersons for Mayan cultural rights during the peace talks. Perhaps characteristically, Protestant involvement has been more on an individual than a denominational basis, although the mainline denominations have participated, particularly the Iglesia Evangélica Nacional Presbiteriana de Guatemala (IENPG), which has long had a powerful minority current of ecumenical involvement, concern with social justice issues, and, in recent years, direct ties to the Mayan movement.[58] In 1992—the year of the quincentenary—Mayan Presbyterians began to question historic racism in the church,[59] and Mayan Presbyterian leaders, most notably indigenous pastors, began to publish in journals and organize seminars, and workshops (following the Catholic model and often involving ecumenical participation) to bring a Mayan theology to their own churches.[60]

The leadership by Mayan pastors—almost unheard of in the Catholic Church, where very few priests are actually Mayan themselves—lent an immediate sense of authenticity. From a perspective of self-representation (a central goal of the Mayan movement), this gives Mayan Protestants, particularly some prominent Kakchikel Presbyterian pastors, a high visibility and influence in the inculturation theology movement. In some respects, the influence of these pastors exceeds that of their own denomination, or even the influence of mainline Protestantism, as opposed to Pentecostalism, altogether.

For Presbyterian inculturationists, theological innovation is being produced largely by the Conferencia de Iglesias Evangélicas de Guatemala (CIEDEG), a liberal Protestant organization that is dominated by Mayan Presbyterians. Vitalino Similox, a Kakchikel Mayan Presbyterian pastor who served as an intermediary for ecumenical church people associated with the URNG and was a negotiator during the Oslo peace talks, helped to found CIEDEG in the mid-1980s. CIEDEG was conceived to provide both ecclesial and political space for church people involved in the political struggle; but under Similox's leadership, CIEDEG shifted its focus primarily toward political concerns. Similox has been involved as an activist in the Mayan movement, and he ran for vice president of the republic for the Alianza Nueva Nación (ANN), a leftist party, during the 1999 presidential elections.[61]

As a Mayan activist, a leftist, and a Presbyterian pastor, Similox can be seen as the embodiment of the convergence between the Mayan movement and Mayanized theology. On the other hand, Similox and the other Presbyterian activists are by no means representative of all Mayan Protestants, especially Pentecostals, who, more engaged with politics than they were a decade ago, nonetheless tend to consider themselves to be "apolitical." Although CIEDEG does include a small Pentecostal membership, in general Mayan Pentecostals also tend to be dubious of inculturation theology, which they consider to be a dangerous revival of atavistic cultural practices that were abandoned when they were "born again."[62]

While CIEDEG is dominated by the Presbyterians, its membership also includes congregations from many other denominations, including a handful of Pentecostals (who make up the vast majority of Guatemala's Protestants, both Mayan and non-Mayan), non-Pentecostal fundamentalists, and independent Protestant denominations. As with the Catholic dioceses where inculturation theology has taken root, the common denominators of membership in CIEDEG are ethnicity and a shared geography of terror, in that nearly all the participating congregations are located near or in areas where military reprisals and massacres of civilians during the civil violence of the early 1980s took place and therefore loom large on the landscape of local memory.[63] While the founding mandate of CIEDEG was to help in the implementation of peace and reconciliation in the region (*camino de Shalom,* or Shalom road), its leaders, following the lead of Catholic churchmen, recognized a need to confront the implications of Guatemala's real history in theological terms.

THE MAYA THEOLOGY OF INCULTURATION

In the beginning, the movement toward indigenous theology in Guatemala grew from the top down, nurtured by clergy, both Catholic and, to a lesser extent, Protestant, who generated workshops, study groups, literature for use by church groups, political documents, and other means to engender a Mayan-based Christology in which to contextualize basic Christian beliefs within a larger system of Mayan cosmology, cultural values, and worldview.[64] The object of such directed thinking—guided by questioning, listening to, and recording local religious specialists and everyday believers who described their grassroots beliefs and worldview—is to help recognize the distinctness of the indigenous worldview, which differs in fundamental ways from the structure and cosmology of Western religious ideas.

As such, inculturation theology is not interested in promoting "syncretism" (essentially, the co-mixing of two religious forms, often at the cost of orthodoxy and authenticity for both religions), but, rather, it tries to grasp what Curt Cadorette has called the "gestalt"—the totality of material, patterns of thought and systems of organization, symbolic configurations, and religious feeling that make the Mayan worldview unique.[65] As such, the Mayan worldview is clearly influenced by half a millennium of contact with European culture and religion, but it is not fully subsumed by either. Frank Saloman (writing from an Andean context) has described this as "cultural doubleness," wherein two parallel systems confronted one another and could not be integrated as long as both modes of discourse retained their essential integrity."[66] What inculturation theology seeks to do, then, is to identify points of potential conjuncture between the two systems.

Mayan Cosmovision

At the most basic level, Mayanized theology attempts to reconcile Christianity with the three central elements of Mayan spirituality: peace with the natural world that sustains life, peace with other people (including the dead), and peace with the deity/deities.[67] Beyond these relatively broad elements are four key theological concepts that are integral to Mayan spirituality. The first of these is the belief in one God, but prayer to many saints/gods (in the words of one theologian, "monotheistic but polypraxis").[68] These sacred beings are often considered to be present in spatial geography, particularly in mountains, which provide a sacred landscape visible in nearly every corner of Guatemala. As Edward Cleary has insightfully noted, it only makes sense that such ancient sacred entities would retain their pre-Hispanic significance because so many of the same symbols and realities—mountains, animals, sky—are still there.[69]

An example of this is the case of the Tzuultaq'a, the force of the mountains revered by the Q'eqchis'.[70] More than animistic spirits and something less than a deity or set of deities, the Tzuultaq'a is representative of divine energy and power. For traditional Q'eqchis', the Tzuultaq'a is an ever-present and often capricious force, capable of great and fearsome actions. But for inculturationists, the Tzuultaq'a is "the witness of God, reflecting the power and glory of God. It is created by God, and is precious to him. The Tzuultaq'a is alive, and is the intermediary between God and men. . . . We can say that the Tzuultaq'a is the visible presence of the invisible God, the nearer presence of a distant God."[71]

The second principle central to Mayan spirituality is the concept of "soul shifting." This can refer to rebirth, either through the transference of a soul from an ancestor to a gestating or newborn child, or the return of an element of the soul from Xibalba (the Otherworld) or even heaven or hell. While there is no real uniformity in the form soul shifting may take, there is, in all Mayan cosmovision, a strong underlying concept of continuity and obligation from one generation to another.[72] This sense of integral continuity is also tied to the individual, who assumes his or her place within the cycle of the ancient Mayan calendar (*tzolkin,* in K'iche'), now simplified from Classic times to a 260-day long count and a 20-day short count of day names. Although the specific combination of days is reflected in rituals and festivals associated with each day (and which often correspond to the Catholic liturgical calendar), the larger significance in terms of the soul's continuity is the day on which a person is born. This helps determine one's fate and is useful for divination purposes throughout life. Even more important, the date of birth links a person directly to the ancestors who have been born or died within 260 days (a complete calendar cycle, but also the length of a human pregnancy) of that day.[73]

Closely related is a third central concept of "centeredness." This refers to a person's metaphysical place in the community, within the extended family (including the dead), and even in the Mundo (literally, world), defined as both the physical earth and the cosmos. Mayan notions of center are found in symbolic representations that reach back to the Classic Period: the ceiba tree, the umbilical cord (or naval), or the Milky Way. It is also visually illustrated in the ritual performance of the *voladores* (in the Dance of the Flyers), who slowly spiral down and out from a tall pole by their feet.[74] Q'eqchi' Maya conceptualize this notion of centeredness as "heart" (*'ool,* or the core of a tree), a person's center, which matures and changes as a person moves through the course of life. The heart forms the "central pivot" of both the body and a person's social relations, which extend in the four cardinal directions, and is responsible for coordinating reciprocity with the temporal world and the cosmos.[75]

Finally, the fourth theological concept is of "complementary opposites," what anthropologist Victoria Reifler Bricker has called "metaphorical cou-

plets."[76] This is the pairing of either related or contradictory objects to constitute balance and harmony: hot and cold, wet and dry, upper and lower, male
and female, red and brown, temporal earth and cosmos. The importance of
metaphorical couplets is found spatially—the human body, for example, is divided into the upper and lower half, as well as left and right halves, while
Mayan spatial relations in the home or as related to local geography are
thought of in terms of pairs or multiples of two.[77] The correct balance of complementary pairs is thought to bring about harmony and wellness, but the
pairings do not equate in Mayan thinking with morally weighted dualistic
concepts such as "good" and "evil."[78]

From Cosmovision to Inculturation

Inculturated theology attempts to incorporate these spiritual values as
much as possible into a Christian scheme, but it also demands a reexamination
of fundamental Christian images, symbols, and archetypes through the lens of
traditional Mayan cosmovision(s). This means, at the most basic level, that theology should be expressed in a language that can be easily understood—literally, in the most widely spoken Mayan languages (Kakchikel, Mam, and
K'iche', Q'eqchi'), but also figuratively, through the utilization of symbols,
myths, and iconography that are locally understood, valued, and interpreted.

The reasons for embedding Christian theology within Mayan culture are
partially strategic: "How can a Maya accept the Good News of the Gospel," a
Mayan theologian asks rhetorically, "if the person who is evangelizing practi-
cally requires him to give up what is essential to the profundity of his life, and
annul the spiritual and cultural heritage of his ancestors?" But this question
also suggests a postmodern reinterpretation of Christianity's claims to unique
revelation through the triune God and the person of Jesus Christ. Instead of a
salvation narrative based on traditional Christian notions of sin and redemp-
tion, Mayanized theology insists upon recognition of the "persistent historic
presence of God in our cultures: in the myths, the rituals, the customs, in the
community, the services, organizations, in the families, in the humanistic conception of the human being, and in the Earth, as a point of reference in the
Universe."[79]

Yet Mayanized theology is by no means universalistic. It embraces a traditional Christology which affirms Jesus Christ as "the Savior; without Him
there is not hope . . . without him there is no eternal salvation, there is no
human face of God outside of Christ." However, within this understanding is
that caveat that "the event of Jesus, the Christ," is not the exclusive possession
or the private property of any culture . . . the Gospel transcends whatever
[human] forces attempt to contain it in . . . whether they be cultural or religious."[80] Nevertheless, inculturationists are equally quick to add that indigenous theology is not merely Western Christianity that has been retrofitted

with politically correct Mesoamerican elements.[81] Instead, it is an effort to recognize the presence of God inherent in Mayan culture throughout history and to valorize the ways in which Mayan cosmovision has honored and continues to honor God's presence. In specific terms, one Mayan theologian, Ernestina López Bac, has explained the following four points as the "heart" (a theological reference, not simply a semantic choice) of indigenous theology: These include, according to López, the notions that (1) God is here with us, (2) *God values us and does not seek to destroy our culture* (emphasis mine), (3) God is our comrade, friend, and brother, (3) we can feel God's pulse of love (*latidos de amor*) in all places, and (4) God is that for which we live: the heart of the people (*corazón del pueblo*), heart of the sky (*corazón del cielo*), heart of the earth (*corazón de tierra*), and our Mother and Father.[82]

In a pamphlet published in *Prensa Libre,* Guatemala's most widely read daily newspaper, shortly before his entry into the presidential race, CIEDEG's Similox argued that Christianity not only transcends, but actually valorizes indigenous cultures: "God loves all cultures and his salvation does not signify the denigration or renunciation of cultural and historic identity." Evangelization does not signify the announcement of the "absence of God" in a culture, but [rather] it is an announcement of the good news of 'his presence.' "[83] An evangelical pastor framed the equation more succinctly "God was already here," he observed simply, "when Columbus arrived."[84]

"Decoding" Christianity from Mayan Sources

In his 1998 treatise entitled *Religion Maya: Fuente de resisténcia milenaria,*[85] Vitalino Similox outlined areas for cultural recovery within Mayan Christianity, so that, in his words, "the Maya may drink from his *own* well."[86] Specifically, the theology demands a fundamental reassessment of theology within the framework of five Mayan cultural paradigms. These include the following:

1. The recovery of Mayan cultural values, particularly the emphasis on the community over the individual.
2. The reintegration of religion into everyday life, not just relegated to the Sabbath. Traditional Mayan spirituality is not so much a system of dogma, but more a systemic spirituality that touches every aspect of life; more a "way of being" than a religion per se; therefore, indigenous theology calls for a fuller integration of faith into the quotidian details of life.[87]
3. The abandonment of the most obviously foreign cultural elements in worship. "Evangelization has been [tantamount to] acculturation," writes Similox. "We received hymns, not only in a different language, but also in another mentality."[88]
4. The creation of a "Mayan hermeneutics," which includes the utiliza-

tion of symbols, rites, and myths of ancient Mayan culture, whenever possible, to convey Christian allegory.

This last challenge, in particular, exposes a double hermeneutic puzzle because ancient Mayan religious symbols and imagery are buried so deeply beneath the symbols and myths of the dominant culture. The task, then, is to "decode from Mayan sources, such as the ancient chronicles to decipher the true meanings of the ancient messages."[89]

The heuristic tool for this task is the *Popol Vuh: The Book of Council,*[90] the holy text of Mayan sacred narratives, handed down orally and codified into holy writ in the K'iche' language after the arrival of the Spaniards, between 1554 and 1558.[91] The *Popol Vuh,* which, like many sacred texts, freely mixes allegory, myths, heroic epics, history, and revelation, begins with the Mayan creation story and ends with the arrival of the Spaniards. Although it is not the only Mayan text to survive the conquest—the *Annals of the Kakchikels* and the *Books of the Chilam Balam* form two other important references[92]—the *Popol Vuh* is, arguably, the most enduring, comprehensive, and influential Mayan narrative. As a sacred text, it continues to be used not only by the K'iche', but also by non-literate and non-K'iche'-speaking people, who have used dance and ritual to preserve and transmit its messages to the present day.[93]

One of the central concerns for inculturationists, whether Catholic or Protestant, is the position that the *Popol Vuh* holds as a sacred text for Mayan Christians. This is not a matter to be taken lightly, as the answer has to do with the very nature of Mayan spirituality within a Christian context. Within the Catholic context, the *Popol Vuh* is considered by many to be *ojer tzij,* literally, the "prior word" (as compared to the Bible, the "Word of God"), and is sometimes read during the mass—a practice that in Chiapas earned an investigation from the Vatican's Congregation of the Faith.[94] Despite Rome's concerns, the practice effectively reconciles some of the basic tensions implicit within inculturation theology, namely, if the seeds of faith were present before the arrival of Christianity, then where is Christianity's uniqueness? And secondly, if Christianity does indeed offer the "way, the truth, and the light," how does one reconcile the salvation of the elders and the ancestors—so vital to the Mayan worldview—those who nurtured the seeds of the faith before the arrival of the Word?

For inculturated Mayan Protestants—whose theological gaze tends to be sharply focused on the Bible as the literal and immutable Word of God—the issue of the reconciliation with the *Popol Vuh* becomes even more acute. From a theological binary perspective, the *Popol Vuh* is either sacred (of God) or idolatrous (demonic); it cannot be both. Thus, the *Popol Vuh* must be reconciled with Christianity as part of the canon of sacred texts, a unique revelation of the divine to the Mayan people.

Of particular concern to Mayan inculturated Christians (and the topic of several workshops and journal articles) has been the nature of God as portrayed within the *Popol Vuh*. In an effort to place the traditional Mayan sacredness within an acceptable Christian narrative framework, Mayan exegetes argue that the *Popol Vuh* clearly portrays one monotheistic Being, though described by many names to convey God's many diverse attributes.[95] Early explanations of multiple deities, in the inculturationists' view, stem from colonialist, Eurocentric, "Christocentric, and ecclesiocentric" misunderstandings of the nature of the divine.

The centrality of the *Popol Vuh* as a source of not just revelation but specifically Christian revelation is illustrated in the discourse of a rural Mayan evangelical pastor; his discourse underscores not only his concern with the reconciliation of holy texts, but also the reconciliation of worldviews—a deep concern for the ancestors (Mayan) and their eternal salvation (Christian).

> I found that in the Bible, it says you have to have respect, right? In the Bible, it also says to honor the father and the mother, no? And there is one God, God the father, etc. In Mam [the pastor's Mayan language group], that is "elder," right? But the concept is the same. . . . So I think that it is possible to see that the people before [pre-Christian Mayans] had the concept; it's much clearer that there was religion and there was faith in God [in the New World] maybe in the time of Abraham—we don't know, right? Because unfortunately, we don't have the dates. Our ancestors had a great book (the Popol Vuh), but our enemies [the Spanish friars] burned [it], right? . . . [W]hat I want to say is that in reading the Bible, I arrived at the conclusion that they [the ancient Mayan ancestors] had it, when they were here on the earth, carrying a faith in the kingdom of God.[96]

Beyond the exegesis of the *Popol Vuh*, the theology also prescribes the incorporation other integral material elements of Mayan culture as utensils of worship; these might include the pine-resin incense, colored votive candles, the use of three as a symbolic number, pine branches as liturgical decorations, the cross as representative of an ideogram of the cardinal points of the earth rather than as Jesus' execution instrument, and the libation of holy spaces with grain alcohol as occurs during syncretic rituals or in the ancient healing practices. Because such Mayan sacred elements serve such a similar function as the symbology used in traditional Catholic ritual (candles, incense, images), it has been relatively easy for the church to reintegrate them into the mass, albeit with some concern for movement down the slippery slope of inculturation back to old-time syncretism, in which Mayan and Christian elements were fused without common doctrinal reference. Even so, Mayan Catholic inculturationists have identified this as one area in which "the Church's respect toward these symbols has been one of the successes of recent years."[97]

"Double Paganization": Pentecostal Perspective

The issue of material elements in worship is one that is much more easily accommodated by Catholics than by Protestants. Indeed, it is the specifically the reappropriation of the material aspects of Mayan religious culture that proves a serious sticking point for many Mayan Protestants regarding inculturated theology. Typically, Mayan Protestants, particularly Pentecostals, assiduously avoid the use of somatic features such as incense, candles, and alcohol. They shun these elements as "idolatrous" practices associated with syncretism, demons, and, worse still—in their way of thinking—Catholicism, which many Mayan converts, justifiably or not, negatively associate with spiritual domination and a repudiated pagan past. As Mayan theologian Antonio Otzoy explained, "It was not long ago when Protestantism came; we were all Catholics then, and they would tell us, 'you are all pagans because you are Catholics.' "[98]

Otzoy has suggested that the longstanding sublimation of Mayan religious forms within Catholicism has produced a fierce Protestant bias against what he calls the "double paganization" (*doble paganización*) of Mayan spiritual imagery.[99] Thus, the central challenge for Protestant Mayanized theology is to reclaim the patrimony of Mayan religious language, rituals, and symbolism not so much from the pre-Christian past, but from its strong association with Catholicism. The explicit inclusion of Mayan material elements is a point which definitely separates "inculturated" Mayan Protestants from their "non-inculturated" counterparts, but it is also a starting point for ecumenical dialogue between Mayan Protestants and Mayan Catholics, who may determine that cultural concerns transcend denominational differences.[100] In the meantime, the issue of double paganization looms large for Mayan evangélicos, especially Pentecostals, who find it difficult to extricate precisely which elements of "Mayaness" are not inconsistent with their paradigmatic "new life."

This issue illustrates as well as any the disconnect that exists between the discourse of Mayanized theology, articulated as it is by well-educated Catholic clergy, Mayan pastors, and intellectuals, and everyday Mayan Protestants, who as yet remain somewhat reticent in their acceptance of inculturated Christian theology. This is most apparent among the Pentecostals, who recoil at any formal reconciliation between a type of spirituality that they now consider idolatrous and the "Christian way" (*camino cristiano*). By in large, at the moment, inculturation theology remains primarily a Catholic and mainline (that is, non-Pentecostal) Protestant phenomenon, which means that the majority of Mayan Protestants who are Pentecostals still lie, for the most part, outside the theology's parameters. There is some evidence, however—such as the handful of Pentecostal churches in El Quiché that have joined CIEDEG and the increasing number of Pentecostal contributors to the religious journal *Voces del*

Tiempo, where many of the debates around inculturationist issues take place—that this is changing.

Nevertheless, at present, inculturation theology requires a serious stretch to conventional notions of salvation and orthodoxy, a stretch that many Pentecostals are not yet prepared to make. For Mayan Pentecostals, the hermeneutic problems of inculturation theology are not necessarily linked to the issue of reconciling cultural and ethnic identity with Christianity—to the contrary, much of the discourse of Pentecostalism is built around the idea of God's unique revelation and distinct blessing to Guatemala. The large-scale Pentecostal revivals that took place during the 1980s and 1990s, notably the "La hora de Dios para Guatemala" and "Jesus es Señor de Guatemala" campaigns, certainly did not purposefully valorize Mayan culture. However, both of these movements were predicated on the notion that God had a plan to redeem the nation's deep, historical suffering by pouring out his specific and unique blessings on Guatemala and its people per se. This message was understood by many Mayans to have specific reference to their own tragic history as a people and may have contributed to Pentecostalism's rapid spread through Mayan regions during this period.[101]

Instead, inculturation theology's greatest obstacle for Mayan Pentecostals is that it challenges their conceptual framework of salvation, which is built around the watershed Pentecostal experience of "baptism in the Holy Spirit," an irreversible binary opposition of life before and after salvation by Jesus Christ. To see the "seeds of the Word" implicit in life prior to this life-altering event, therefore, is impossible for most Pentecostal converts. As one Mayan Pentecostal pastor put it, "We don't even have the language to talk about these things."[102]

Yet the pull of Mayan cultural and spiritual identity remains strong, even for Pentecostals. This seems particularly true for Mayan evangélicos who are long established in their conversions or who have been brought up in a Protestant church. With more distance from the conversion experience, some Mayan evangélicos are beginning to seek out ways to bridge whatever cognitive dissonance they may feel between their religion and their culture. For them, the accommodation of the full spectrum of Mayan beliefs—cosmovision, Catholicism, and Pentecostalism—becomes more a matter of spiritual discernment than of theological or political debate.

An example of this process is found in the K'iche' town of Nahualá, a town of strong religious sentiments, where American Protestant missionaries were threatened with dismemberment as recently as the 1920s.[103] In recent years, as David Parkyn has observed, evangélicos have become the most skilled craftsmen of wooden *santos,* the images central to local religious practice. They excel in this culturally resonant craft, despite the fact that Protestants believe the santos to be idolatrous—that is, totems of both Catholicism and Mayan religion. Historically, Protestants have shunned the images and have, for decades, burned them in public displays of conversion. Although *santeros evangélicos* claim that the carving of saints is simply a way of making a living, their careful craftsmanship and the fact that they have added images (particularly from the life of Jesus) to the standard repertoire of carvings suggests a larger reconciliation of beliefs. As one Nahualense carver explained, "We are a people of faith." He said, "When I practice the evangélico faith I also remain true to the Catholic faith and the *costumbre*. . . . Because we still worship the Mayan God, the harvest is abundant. And because we worship the *católico* saints, the basic needs of life—for health, peace, and sustenance—are provided. But now the evangélicos have brought us joy. This once was a village with an abundant harvest but no joy. Now the evangélicos have taught us to worship with joy."[104]

Thus, there is growing evidence that at the grassroots level even Pentecostals are beginning to accommodate their indigenous worldview with religious beliefs. This is apparent in the daily practice of religion—from Pentecostal *acciones de gracias,* prayer services held at the planting and harvest of corn, to the faith healing (*sanación*) that provides an analog to ancient shamanic practices associated with fertility, illness, and mental problems. Even the common phrase used by Maya Pentecostals, *camino cristiano,* while resonant with Christian imagery, is also rich with Mayan religious symbolism of journey, crossroads, and the divine "white path" of the cosmos, the Milky Way.

CONCLUSION

In conclusion, inculturation theology is clearly tied to the larger project of Mayan revitalization and the politics of the Pan-Mayan political movement, but its implications reach much farther than the political moment. In the immediate sense, both revitalized Mayan religion and inculturated theology work, serve, and share the strategic goals of the *movimiento Maya,* including that of self-determination, although in practical terms the utility of religion in this context seems to be more symbolic than concrete. More importantly, both Mayan-Maya religion and inculturation theology validate the ultimate of Mayan cultural capital—cosmovision—by affirming its powerful spiritual integrity both within and outside the paradigm of Christianity.

While Mayan-Maya adherents cast off Christianity as a colonial artifact, by contrast, proponents of inculturation theology tend to be enthusiastic Christians who see themselves in the vanguard of religious change. As a relatively new movement, inculturation theology has not yet fully permeated the stratum of everyday believers; at present, its main proponents are Catholics (both clergy and some laypeople), prominent mainline Protestants, and a limited number of Pentecostals. Nevertheless, the larger object of "decolonializing" and reconciling long-held beliefs with their new religion holds great promise for Mayan Christians, both Catholic and Protestant alike. For them, inculturation theology holds a potential that reaches far beyond political expediency. It is perhaps in this fashion that Mayanized theology is making the transition from its genesis, as the theological counterpart to a political discourse, to a vernacular hermeneutics in which is embedded a culturally meaningful narrative of salvation.

NOTES

1. See Sidney M. Greenfield and André Droogers, eds., *Reinventing Religions: Syncretism and Transformation in Africa and the Americas* (London: Rowman and Littlefield Publishers, 2001).
2. David Batstone, "Charting (dis)Courses of Liberation," in *Liberation Theologies, Postmodernity, and the Americas,* ed. David Batstone et al. (London: Routledge, 1997), 159.
3. I use the phrase "religious systems" here with some caution, and with a caveat offered by David Lehmann, who writes that "there are not grounds for taking the fixed integrity of a religious system for granted or even for believing that religious ensembles, sub-cultures or institutions can be thought of as systems at all. However, the self-image of a religious institution or subculture as possessing its own integrity, or the images it produces of the other as a distinct system, are interesting and important because religion in the modern world is evidently a marker of identity and a mechanism for the production of group/identarian boundaries. David Lehmann, "Charisma and Possession in Africa and Brazil," paper, Cambridge University, 2000, 2.
4. John Comaroff and Jean Comaroff, *Of Revelation and Revolution: Christianity, Colonialism, and Consciousness in South Africa,* vol. 1 (Chicago: University of Chicago Press, 1991), 250.
5. Rasiah S. Surgirtharajah, *The Bible and the Third World: Precolonial, Colonial, and Postcolonial Encounters.* (Cambridge: Cambridge University Press, 2001), 175.
6. This is a rough estimate, extrapolated from David Stoll, *Is Latin America Turning Protestant? The Politics of Evangelical Growth* (Berkeley: University of California Press, 1990), 337. Although there are more recent estimates, this figure seems to hold true.
7. "Neo-Pentecostalism" refers to the charismatic movement that swept through the mainline Protestant and the Roman Catholic churches in the early 1970s, as distinct from the Pentecostal movement that grew out of the "holiness movement" of the late nineteenth and early twentieth centuries. By the late 1970s, the neo-Pentecostal movement had generated the formation of large, charismatic, interdenominational or nondenominational churches that no longer affiliated with the mainline denominations. Neo-Pentecostal churches typically subscribe to charismatic practices as encouraging members to experience the "baptism of the Holy Spirit," manifested by such behaviors as speaking in tongues, faith healing, or ecstatic behavior (such as dancing, "holy laughter," falling to the floor when "slain in the Spirit," and the like) during church services. With the expansion of media-based ministries (including not only radio and televangelism, but also media-based worship centered on highly produced music and Powerpoint presentations), neo-Pentecostal churches have also embraced what is often called "health and wealth theology," a theology centered on the belief that God rewards the faithful with material bounty. (See Samuel Berberian, *Dos décadas de Renovación: Un análisis histórico de la renovación carismática en America Latina (1960–1980),* (Guatemala: Ediciones Sa-Ber, 2002).
8. There are two official summations of the violence that occurred over the course of the civil war and its effect on the human population. The first (REHMI) was provided by the Roman Catholic Church. See Oficina de Derechos Humanos del Arzobispado de Guatemala, *Informe Proyecto Interdiocesano de Recuperación de la Memoria*

Historica (REMHI), vol. 1–4 (Guatemala: Oficina de Derechos Humanos del Arzobispado de Guatemala [ODHAG], 1998). The second summation (CEH) was provided by the United Nation–mandated Comisión de Esclaramiento historico. A useful English summary of this report is found in Paul Kobrak and Herbert F. Spirer, *Guatemala: Memory of Silence*. (Washington, D.C.: AAAS Science and Human Rights Program, 1999).

9. The REHMI report, in particular, gives a strong sense to the extent to which members of Catholic Action were targeted as "subversives."

10. The word, *desencarnación,* comes from the grandmother of Antonio Otzoy (see body of text), as she reflected upon the implications of the violence on the Mayan people. I have borrowed this term from Matt Samson, who notes that Kline Taylor has reflected at some length on the notion of "defleshment" in a collaboration she did based with Antonio Otzoy: "Toward a Revolution of the Sun: Protestant Mayan Resistance in Guatemala," in *Revolution of Spirit: Ecumenical Theology in Global Context,* ed. Nantawan Boon Prasat (Grand Rapids: William B. Eerdmans Publishing Company, 1998), as cited in C. Matthew Samson, "The Martyrdom of Manuel Saquic: Construction Mayan Protestantism in the Face of War in Contemporary Guatemala" (*Le Jait Missionaire,* forthcoming, 2003), 17, note 21.

11. Susanne Jonas, *Of Centaurs and Doves: Guatemala's Peace Process* (Boulder: Westview Press, 2000), 7, cited in C. Matthew Samson, "From War to Reconciliation: Guatemalan Evangelicals and the Transition to Democracy, 1982–2001," manuscript, 7.

12. Edward Fisher and R. McKenna Brown, eds., *Maya Cultural Activism in Guatemala,* Critical Reflection on Latin America Series (Austin: University of Texas Press, Institute of Latin American Studies, 1996), 13.

13. Rudolfo Stavenhager, *Derecho indígena y derechos humanos en América Latina* (Mexico: Instituto Interamericano de Derechos Humanos, El Colegio de Mexico, 1988), 295.

14. See Victor Gálvez Borrell and Alberto Esquit Choy, *The Mayan Movement Today: Issues of Indigenous Culture and Development in Guatemala* (Guatemala City: FLACSO, 1997); Kay B. Warren and Jean E. Jackson, "Introduction: Studying Indigenous Activism in Latin America," in *Indigenous Movements, Self-Representation, and the State in Latin America,* ed. Warren and Jackson (Austin: University of Texas, 2002).

15. Warren and Jackson, *Indigenous Movements,* 8. Warren offers these words of caution about essentialism: "Discourses of racial difference and inferiority are another form of essentialism, and their virulence in Latin America reminds us that essentialism can be coercively imposed by the state as well as deployed by indigenous groups as a form of resistance to demanding political imaginaries and policies."

16. For a concrete statement of Mayan demands, see *Rajpop'ri Mayab' Amaq, Consejo de Organizaciones Mayas de Guatemala, Rutz'aqik rutikik qamaya' xeel: Rujunamil ri Mayab' Amaq pa rub'inib'al runuk'ik re Saqk'aslemal: Construyendo un futuro para nuestro pasado: Derechos del pueblo maya y el Proceso de Paz* (Guatemala: Editorial Cholsamaj, 1995).

17. Waqi' Q'anil (Demetrio Cojtí), *Ub'anik ri una'ooj uchomab'aal ri may' tinamit: Configuración del pensamiento político del pueblo maya,* part 2 (Guatemala: Editorial Cholsamaj, 1995), 125.

18. Raxché (Demetrio Rodríguez Guaján), "Maya Culture and the Politics of Development," in *Maya Cultural Activism,* ed. Fischer and Brown, 83.

19. Rudolfo Stavenhagen, "Derechos humanos y derechos culturales de los pueblos indígenas," in *Los derechos humanos en tierras maya: política, representaciones y moralidad,* ed. Pedro Pitach and Julian López García (Madrid: Sociedad Española de Estudios Mayas, 2001), 374.

20. Consejo de Organizaciones Mayas de Guatemala (COMG), "Qasaqalaj Tziij, Qakemoon Tziij, Qapach'uum Tziij, Identidad y derechos de los Pueblos Indígenas

(propuesto de consenso, 13 junio 1994)," in *Construyendo un Futuro para Nuestro Pasado: Derechos del Pueblo Maya y el Proceso de Paz* (Guatemala: Editorial Cholsamaj, 1995).

21. For a comprehensive account of the role of the church in the accords, see Bruce J. Calder, "The Role of the Catholic Church and Other Religious Institutions in the Guatemalan Peace Process, 1980–1996," *Journal of Church and State* 43 (autumn 2001): 773–797.

22. Paul Jeffery notes that according to the Guatemalan daily *Prensa Libre*, "It was the Catholic church . . . that led the call for a national dialogue and created an environment in which citizens could state their interests and put forward proposals for peace. In effect, the participation of the Catholic church contributed to the socialization of the topic of peace," *Prensa Libre*, January 7, 1988. See Paul Jeffery, *Recovering Memory: Guatemalan Churches and the Challenge of Peacemaking* (Uppsala, Sweden: Life and Peace Institute, 1998), 13–14.

23. Jeffery's study, *Recovering Memory*, provides an excellent account of the role of the religious sector in the Oslo accords.

24. See Consejo de Organizaciones Mayas de Guatemala (COMG), "Qasaqalaj Tziij, Qakemoon Tziij, Qapach'uum Tziij, Identidad y derechos de los Pueblos Indígenas (propuesto de consenso, 13 junio 1994)," in *Construyendo un Futuro para Nuestro Pasado: Derechos del Pueblo Maya y el Proceso de Paz* (Guatemala: Editorial Cholsamaj, 1995). This document states that one of the fundamental elements of Mayan identity is "a cosmovision that is based on one's relation with the universe, mother nature, the earth as a source of life and maize as a marker (*eje*) of one's culture that has been transmitted from generation to generation through its material production; and thorough the means of oral tradition, in which the woman has played a determining role" (60).

25. Mayan journalist Estuardo Zapeta notes that "some Mayan elders have protested the recognition of Mayan spirituality in the reforms by arguing that Mayan religion is not negotiable." Zapeta, as quoted in Kay B. Warren, "Voting against Indigenous Rights," in *Indigenous Movements,* ed. Warren and Jackson, 172.

26. Liberally, "custom." The word *costumbre* was first used widely by foreign anthropologists working in Guatemala during the early decades of the twentieth century to describe the body of locally prescribed religious belief, ritual, dress, language, and life ways (including daily activities such as weaving, cooking, etc.) that formed what John Watanabe has called "the way of being" in Mayan communities. Robert S. Carlsen and Martin Prechtel have defined costumbre more recently as "old religion," in "The Flowering of the Dead: An Interpretation of Highland Maya Culture," *Man* 26 (March 1991): 25. As Garry Sparks notes, "Costumbre is considered by many to be the remnant of a pre-Hispanic belief system. . . . Its treatment by Ladinos . . . ranged from viewing costumbre as nothing more than quaint practices to perceiving it as equivalent to ignorant superstition to condemning it as paganism and witchcraft. Garry Sparks, "A Proposed Framework for Inter-religious Interaction by Christians toward Native American Spiritualities," paper, University of Chicago School of Theology, 2002, 2.

27. "Entrevista a Demetrio Cojtí," *Voces del Tiempo* 1 (1992): 59.

28. Jesus Gómez, "Cuando el cañaveral retoña: el movimiento de las organizaciones mayas," *Voces del Tiempo* 22 (1997):15.

29. I am deeply indebted here to the work and insights of Garry Sparks, "A Proposed Framework for Inter-religious Interaction." See also Gómez, "Cuando el cañaveral retoña," 15.

30. Victor Montejo, "The Multiplicity of Mayan Voices," in Warren and Jackson, *Indigenous Movements,* 145.

31. Victor Perera, *Unfinished Conquest: The Guatemalan Tragedy* (Berkeley: University of California Press, 1993), 323.

32. Eric Hobsbawm, as cited by Victor Montejo in "The Multiplicity of Mayan Voices," in *Indigenous Movements,* ed. Warren and Jackson, 129.

33. Kay B. Warren, *Indigenous Movements and Their Critics: Pan-Mayan Activism in Guatemala* (Princeton: Princeton University Press, 1998).

34. See, for example, a scene in the forthcoming documentary, *Perilous Peace: God and Government in Guatemala,* in which Maya-Mayan "spiritual guides" conduct a fire ceremony, which has no Christian analog, at the ancient Kakchikel city of Iximché, which in recent years has become a restored sacred site for Mayan rituals. In the film at least four of the participants in the ceremony—three Protestant and one Catholic—are ordained Christian clergy.

35. I am using the word *evangélico* here in the sense it is used in Guatemalan Spanish, to refer to all non-Catholic Christians, regardless of denomination or sect.

36. Montejo, "The Multiplicity of Mayan Voices," 129.

37. Juan Hernández Pico, S.J., "Iglesia en cambio y cambios en la Iglesia: análisis," *Voces del Tiempo* 40 (October–December 2001): 21.

38. *Ad Gentes* 11 and *Lumen Gentium* 17, cited in Teodoro Nieto, "Biblia, palabra de Dios y espiritualidad maya," *Voces del Tiempo* 27 (1998): 34.

39. *Redemptoris Missio,* cited in Conferencia Episcopal de Guatemala, *Al servicio de la vida, la justicia y la paz: documentos de la Conferencia Episcopal de Guatemala, 1956– 1997* (Guatemala: CEG, 1997), 602. See also Luis Miguel Otero, *La inculturación de los documentos de la Iglesia* (Cobán: Textos Ak'Kutan, 1996).

40. Between Medellín and Santo Domingo, inculturation theology received some attention at a series of "Encuentros Misioneros Indigenistas de America Latina." These convened in Melgar, Colombia (1968), Asunción, Paraguay (1972), Goiania, Brazil (1975), Manaus, Brazil (1977), Puebla, Mexico (prior to the III CELAM meeting, 1977–1978), Manaus (1980), Brasilia, Brazil (1983), and Quito, Ecuador (1986). See Jesus de la Torre Arranz, *Evangelización inculturada y liberadora: la praxis misionera a partir de los encuentros latinoamericanos del postconcilio* (Quito: Abya-Yala, 1993), 12.

41. Edward L. Cleary, "Birth of Indigenous Theology," in *Crosscurrents in Indigenous Spirituality: Interface of Maya, Catholic, and Protestant Worldviews,* ed. Guillermo Cook (New York: E. J. Brill, 1997), 119. This chapter provides a much more nuanced explanation of the role that the bishops of largely indigenous churches (Bolivia, Guatemala, Mexico, and Ecuador) played in the reemphasis of indigenous theology in the universal church before, during, and after the Santo Domingo conference. See Cleary, "Birth of Indigenous Theology," 171–188.

42. Casariego's negative view may account at least in part for why, unlike in neighboring El Salvador and Nicaragua, the phrase "liberation theology" was never used widely in Guatemala, despite the fact that clergy and lay people were involved in social justice issues, particularly in the indigenous rural areas. Anthropologist Matt Samson has noted, "By the time I began regular field work in Guatemala in the mid 1990s, the term liberation theology was rarely, if ever used in public by Guatemalans. Even one Mayan evangelical told me on several occasions, 'They accuse us of liberation theology, but we didn't even know what it was.'" C. Matthew Samson, "The Martyrdom of Manuel Saquic," 9, fn. 12.

43. "II Encuentro Regional de Pastoral Indígena, Quetzaltenango, 1–3 September 1997," 3–4, photocopy, Centro Ak'Kutan, Cobán, Alta Verapaz.

44. In Guatemala, Fr. Jaime Curtin spearheaded efforts to promote inculturation theology by setting up a series of meetings and workshops between religious, clergy, and indigenous lay leaders. When the Guatemalan church became preoccupied by the exigencies of *la violencia* in the late 1970s and early 1980s, the center of gravity for

inculturation theology moved to Chiapas, where the diocese of San Cristobal de Las Casas actively encouraged the development of "Indian theology" (*teologia india*) by promoting dialogue between Mayan spiritual guides, *cofradias*, and clergy, and by integrating "indigenous" aspects into the liturgy and church life, such as moving Mayan elders into parish offices and including readings from the *Popol Vuh* during the celebration of the mass. See Sparks, "A Proposed Framework for Inter-religious Interaction," 17; for more detailed information on the Mexican approach, see Sylvia Marcos, "Teología India: La presencia de Dios en las culturas. Entrevista con Don Samuel Ruiz," in *Chiapas: El Factor Religioso: Un estudio multidisciplinario de las guerras santas de fin de milenio,* ed. Elio Masferrer et al. (Mexico: Revista Académica para el Estudio de las Religiones, 1998), 33–65.

45. Centro Ak'Kutan, *Evangelio y culturas en Verapaz* (Cobán: Centro Ak'Kutan, 1994), 47.

46. From the election of the corrupt general Romeo Lucas Garcia in 1978 until the end of the Ríos Montt administration, the war of counterinsurgency—characterized by political assassinations, murder of teachers, church people, and health promoters—and the kidnapping and torture of ordinary campesinos thought to be allied in some way with the guerrillas ravaged the country. Ríos Montt's scorched-earth campaign was known as *fusiles y frijoles*, roughly, "beans and bullets."

47. For more information about the state of the Catholic Church in Guatemala during *la violencia,* see Phillip Berryman, *Stubborn Hope: Religion, Politics, and Revolution in Central America* (Maryknoll, N.Y.: Orbis Press, 1994); Diocesis del Quiché, *El Quiché: El pueblo y su Iglesia* (Santa Cruz del Quiché: privately published, July 1984); Conferencia Episcopal de Guatemala, *Al servicio de la vida, la justicia y las paz* (Guatemala: CEG, 1997); Ricardo Falla, *Massacres in the Jungle: Ixcán, Guatemala, 1975–1982* (Boulder: Westview Press, 1994); Ricardo Falla, *Historia de un gran amor: Recuperación autobiográfica de la experiencia con las Comunidades de Población en Resistencia, Ixcán, Guatemala* (privately published, May 1993); Julio Cabrera Ovalle, *Consuela a mi pueblo: Selección de homilías* (Guatemala: Voces del Tiempo, 1997); (no single author), *Evangelio y culturas en Verapaz* (Cobán: Centro Ak'Kutan, 1994); as well as the REHMI report.

48. Julio Cabrera Ovalle, *Consuela a mi pueblo: Selección de homilías* (Guatemala: Voces del Tiempo, 1997), 11.

49. "Declaración de Pastoral Indígena de Guatemala. Chichicastenango," October 1990, photocopy, archives of Central Ak"Kutan.

50. The spelling of Mayan nouns corresponds to the orthography developed by the Academia de las Lenguas Mayas de Guatemala in the early 1990s, but I have retained the older spellings when they are written that way in quotations: hence, Quiché for K'iche', Cakchiquel for Kakchikel, Kek'chí for Q'eqchi', etc.

51. Julio Cabrera Ovalle, "Hacia una Iglesia inculturada," sermon for the 5th Sunday of Easter, May 17, 1992, *Consuela a mi pueblo: selección de homilías,* 138.

52. This is an unofficial organization, in that it did not have Episcopal support.

53. "Carta pastoral colectiva de los obispos de Guatemala, 500 Años sembrando el Evangelio, 15 August 1992," Conferencia Episcopal de Guatemala, *Al servicio de la vida, la justicia y la paz,* 572–630.

54. Cleary, "Birth of Indigenous Theology," 173.

55. For a more substantial discussion of these groups, see Sparks, "A Proposed Framework for Inter-religious Interaction," 17.

56. Personal conversation, Ven de la Cruz, October 2000.

57. "II Encuentro Regional de Pastoral Indígena, Quetzaltenango 1–3, September 1997," photocopy, archives, Centro Ak' Kutan.

58. For a powerful discussion of the intersection of social justice, theology, and Mayan political concerns, see C. Matthew Samson, "The Martyrdom of Manuel Saquic."

59. It bears note that the Presbyterian Church was the first missionary group to cede full control of the denomination to local leadership (1961). In the mid-1960s, the church carved out two Mayan (Kakchikel and Mam) synods (administrative districts) to reflect the denomination's long-standing respect for indigenous cosmovision and theological autonomy, although ladino-indigenous and theological conflicts seriously preoccupied the Guatemalan Presbyterians during the late 1990s. See Heinrich Schäfer, *Entre dos fuegos: una historia socio-política de la iglesia evangélica nacional presbiteriana de Guatemala* (Guatemala: CEDEPCA, 2002). Although the Presbyterians are a relatively small group in Guatemala and are greatly outnumbered by Pentecostal Protestants, they have a political and social presence in the country that belies their numbers, and the majority of Presbyterians in Guatemala are now Mayan.

60. See also Antonio Otzoy, "Traditional Values and Christian Ethics: A Mayan Protestant Spirituality," in *Crosscurrents in Indigenous Spirituality,* ed. Cook.

61. Sparks notes that in 1999, Similox and a non-Mayan *chuchqajaw* (Mayan spiritual specialist, such as healer, day-keeper, astrologer, midwife, etc.) ran as vice president and presidential running mates for the ANN party, which shared an overlapping membership with the URNG. This, says Sparks, "further blur[red] conventional distinctions between Mayan and Ladino culture and with Mayan and Christian religion." Sparks, "A Proposed Framework for Inter-religious Interaction," 18. Matt Samson, on the other hand, notes that Similox's political stance is primarily "informed by his political contacts as an indigenous activist and by his religious involvement with the IENPG. C. Matthew Samson, "From War to Reconciliation: Guatemalan Evangelicals and the Transition to Democracy, 1982–2001," draft for Pew Evangelicals and Democracy in the Third World Project, 20.

62. Having said this, the stereotype of evangelicals as political conservatives is not in the least borne out by the data. See Timothy J. Steigenga, *The Politics of the Spirit: The Political Implications of Pentecostalized Religion in Costa Rica and Guatemala* (Lantham: Lexington Books, 2001).

63. See: CIEDEG, *La Misión de la Iglesia Evangélica de Guatemala en la Etapa Post-Conflict* (Guatemala City: Ediciones Alternatives, 1998), 5.

64. It is important to note that there is no uniform, monolithic "Mayan comovision" or absolute agreement as to what constitutes "Mayan beliefs," which may vary significantly from one region to another or even from one person to the next. Nevertheless, there is a pervasive Mayan religious discourse that informs Mayan people's view of the temporal and metaphysical world; this is the "cosmovision" referred to in this work. For more on this subject, see Gary Gossens, ed., *Symbol and Meaning beyond the Closed Community: Essays in Mesoamerican Ideas* (Albany, N.Y.: Institute for Mesoamerican Studies, 1986); Robert S. Carlsen and Martin Prechtel, "Walking on Two Legs: Shamanism in Santiago Atitlán, Guatemala," in *Ancient Traditions: Shamanism in Central Asia and the Americas,* ed. Gary Seaman and Jane Day (Denver: Denver Museum of Natural History and University Press of Colorado, 1994).

65. Cadorette, as quoted by Cleary, "Indigenous Theology," 180.

66. Frank Saloman, "Chronicles of the Impossible: Notes on Three Peruvian Indigenous Historians," in *From Oral to Written Expression: Native Andean Chronicles of the Early Colonial Period,* ed. Rolena Adorno (Syracuse, N.Y.: Maxwell School of Citizenship and Public Affairs, 1982), 9–39, cited in Cleary, "Indigenous Theology," 180.

67. See David Scotchmer, "Life in the Heart: A Maya Protestant Spirituality," in *South and Mesoamerican Native Spirituality,* ed. Garry H. Gossens and León Portilla (New York: Crossroad Publishing Company, 1993), 507.

68. Sparks, "A Proposed Framework for Inter-religious Interaction," 19.

69. Cleary, "Indigenous Theology," 178.

70. For a very perceptive insight into the daily function of the Tzuultuq'a, see Abigail

Adams, "Making One Our Word: Protestant Q'eqchi' Mayas in Highland Guatemala," in *Holy Saints and Fiery Preachers: The Anthropology of Protestantism in Mexico and Central America,* ed. James Dow and Alan Sandstrom (Westport, Conn.: Praeger, 2001), 205–233.

71. Centro Ak'Kutan, *Evangelio y cultura,* 66.

72. Duncan Earle has noted that among some K'iche' Maya there is a belief that the soul splits in half at the moment of death; half goes to the Christian heaven (or hell, as the case may be) while the other half resides in Xibalba to await its reentry into the life force of the family (Earle, personal communication, 1995). By contrast, Sparks relates that an elderly Mayan chuchqajaw told him that a person was reborn seven times, "each time living a more moral life until finally becoming a star in the night sky after his or her seventh life." Sparks, "A Proposed Framework for Inter-religious Interaction," 26, fn. 90.

73. Duncan Earle, "The Metaphor of Quiché," in *Symbolism and Meaning beyond the Closed Community,* ed. Gossens, 161.

74. See Sparks, "A Proposed Framework for Inter-religious Interaction," 20.

75. Adams, "Making One Our Word," 212.

76. See Victoria Reifler Bricker, *The Indian Christ, the Indian King: The Historical Substrate of Mayan Myth and Ritual* (Austin: University of Texas Press, 1981).

77. Earle, "The Metaphor of Quiché," 163. John Watanabe notes that for Mam-speaking Chimaltecos, "space extends conceptually in concentric circles of decreasing familiarity from the pueblo to the most distant volcanoes. They distinguish four broad categories of space: *jaa,* 'the house;' *tnam,* 'the town;' *kjo'n,* 'corn fields;' and *chk'uul,* 'the wilds,' or 'the forest.'" See John M. Watanabe, *Maya Saints and Souls in a Changing World* (Austin: University of Texas Press, 1992), 62.

78. I am deeply indebted to Sparks for sharing his analysis of this material with me. See especially, Sparks, "A Proposed Framework for Inter-religious Interaction," 18–24.

79. Vitalino Similox Salazar, *Religión Maya: Fuente de Resistencia Milenaria* (Guatemala: CIEDEG, 1998), 146–147.

80. Vitalino Similox Salazar, *Algunos propuestas de la religiosidad Maya hacia un pluralismo religioso, en el marco de los Acuerdos de Paz* (CIEDEG: Guatemala City, 1997), pamphlet.

81. Cleary, "Indigenous Theology," 179.

82. Ernestina López Bac, "Principios de teología india," *Voces del Tiempo* 22 (1997): 22. The imagery of "heart" is more than poetic rhetoric in this context, as for many Maya the heart forms the "central pivot" of both the body and a person's social relations, which extend in the four cardinal directions, and is responsible for coordinating reciprocity with the temporal world and the cosmos. See Adams, "Making One Our Word," 212–213.

83. Vitalino Similox Salazar, "Evangelismo protestante y espiritualidad Maya en el Marco de los Acuerdos de Paz," CIEDEG, originally published in *Prensa Libre,* May 8, 1997.

84. C. Matthew Samson, "Interpretando la Identidad Religiosa: La Cultura Maya y La Religion Evangélica Bajo Una Perspectiva Etnográfica," paper presented at the Segundo Conferencia Sobre El Pop Wuj, Quetzaltenango, Guatemala, May 30–June 4, 1999, 9.

85. Similox Salazar, *Religión Maya.*

86. Ibid., 128.

87. Samson, "Interpretando la Identidad Religiosa," 10.

88. Similox Salazar, *Religión Maya,* 124–125.

89. Ibid., 139.

90. The orthography of the title, as with many Mayan words, is not always uniform; hence, it is sometimes written *Popol Wuj, Popul Vuh, Popool Wuuj, Pop Wuj,* etc.

91. Barbara Tedlock, *Time and the Highland Maya* (Albuquerque: University of New Mexico Press, 1982), 48. For a more thorough history and synopsis of the *Popol Vuh*, see Munro Edmundson, *The Book of Counsel: The Popol Vuh and the Quiché Maya of Guatemala* (New Orleans, Tulane University, MARI, 1971), publication #35; and Dennis Tedlock, *Popol Vuh: The Definitive Edition of the Mayan Book of the Dawn of Life and the Glories of Gods and Kings* (New York: Simon and Schuster, 1985).

92. *The Annals of the Kakchikels* was written down in 1524, at the time of the Guatemalan Mayas' first contact with the Spaniards. The *Books of Chilam Balam* date from the early seventeenth century. See Kay Warren, "Reading History as Resistance: Maya Public Intellectuals in Guatemala," in *Maya Cultural Activism,* ed. Fischer and Brown, 89–106.

93. Sparks, "A Proposed Framework for Inter-religious Interaction," 5.

94. Ibid., 17.

95. Pedro Us S., "La idea de Dios en el Pop Wuj, ensayo interpretativo," *Voces del Tiempo* 1 (1992): 21–28. Us is affiliated with the Instituto Federico Crowe, a Protestant institution of higher learning that conducts biblical immersion courses for rural pastors.

96. This is a paraphrase and translation of a much longer text that is printed in full in Samson, "Interpretando la Identidad Religiosa," 11–12.

97. Centro Ak' Kutan, *Evangelio y culturas,* 84.

98. Antonio Otzoy, "Hermandad de Presbiterios Maya," in his *Primera Consulta, La Misión de la Iglesia Evangélica de Guatemala en la Etapa Post Conflict* (Guatemala: Ediciones Alternativas, 1998), 38–39.

99. Ibid., 38

100. Similox Salazar, *Religión Maya,* 142–143.

101. See, for example, Harold Caballeros, *Victorious Warfare: Discovering Your Rightful Place in God's Kingdom* (Nashville: Thomas Nelson, Publishers, 2001), originally published in Guatemala as *De victoria en victoria.*

102. Email exchange with author, October 2002, anonymous by request.

103. Virginia Garrard-Burnett, *Protestantism in Guatemala: Living in the New Jerusalem* (Austin: University of Texas Press, 1998), 54.

104. David L. Parkyn, "Religious Folk Art of Guatemala: Catholic and Protestant Voices," paper presented at LASA meeting, Washington, D.C., September 6–8, 2001, p. 10.

CHAPTER 7

"Knowing Where We Enter"

INDIGENOUS THEOLOGY AND THE POPULAR CHURCH IN OAXACA, MEXICO

Kristin Norget

The reality has changed hugely in Oaxaca in the area of indigenous peoples; that fact implies giving a new face to the *pastoral indígena*. This resurgence of consciousness, of indigenous identity, of all the indigenous movements, including that of Chiapas, from the religious perspective of the *teología india,* also implies knowing how, where we enter. This is a challenge that has yet to be confronted.

—Padre Francisco Reyes, Coordinator of CEDIPIO
(Ecclesial Diocesanal Center of the
Indigenous Pastoral of Oaxaca)[1]

IN THE above quote, Father Reyes, a young priest working in the southern Mexican state of Oaxaca reflected on the role of the Catholic Church in a politically effervescent setting of indigenous mobilization and organizing. In the 1980s and early 1990s, the Oaxacan Catholic Church, with CEDIPIO, the Diocesanal Center of the Indigenous Pastoral, as its driving force, was a hotbed of liberation theological teachings and practice. Then, two well-known bishops, Bartolomé Carrasco in the Oaxacan Archdiocese of Antequera and Arturo Lona in the neighboring Diocese of Tehuantepec, were strong supporters of the teachings of Vatican II and the creation of a Popular Church rallying for social justice and for clergy's direct insertion in the realities of the poor. Along with Bishop Samuel Ruiz in the neighboring southern state of Chiapas, the bishops adopted a mode of pastoral praxis known as the *pastoral indígena,* or indigenous pastoral. This pastoral program was the unique stamp of Oaxacan and some Chiapan dioceses in particular, and a practical orientation directed explicitly at the special needs of working with the most marginalized social sectors, the indigenous communities, which in this region made up roughly a fifth of the country's total indigenous population.[2]

While liberation theology was alive and well in Oaxaca for almost a couple of decades, since then its influence has become strongly diluted in tandem with a neo-liberalization of the Mexican political and social landscape and concomitant reforms which have seen an end to the separation of church and state existing since the revolution.[3]

Nevertheless, wherever priests are working in rural areas throughout Oaxaca's ethnically diverse and rugged terrain, they are dealing with indigenous communities. And many of them trained in Latin American liberation theology continue their practices, fanning the flames of the original spirit of the pastoral indígena. Despite a backlash within the Catholic Church to liberationist theology which emerged in the late 1980s, and sharpened through the 1990s, the indigenous pastoral remains a thematic centerpiece of pastoral planning in Oaxaca. This fact says much about the engagement the ecclesial hierarchy is currently trying to renegotiate with indigenous peoples, who are among the most faithful of their flock, and, more indirectly, with the Mexican government.

This chapter examines the development of the indigenous pastoral in Oaxaca in relation to that region's religious field,[4] and in relation to the broader, significant changes that have taken place in Mexican and Oaxacan society and political life. I have borrowed this concept from Bourdieu's (1971) concept of the *champ réligieux,* referring to all the representatives of organized or institutional religion interacting in a given setting. Such a perspective draws attention to the changing and conflictual nature of the religious field, where religious agents are engaged with each other and with practitioners in a continuous dialogue and struggle over the dominance of certain practices and meanings. As we will see, in the broad picture, the momentous change of consciousness introduced within the church institution by Vatican II reforms and liberation theology represented a challenge to the *doxa,* in Bourdieu's (1977) terms, of church doctrine and practice—in other words, the tacit, taken-for-granted, undisputed aspects of Roman Catholic identity.[5] Liberationists have contested the Catholic Church's role and raison d'etre in the modern world and have called the institutional church to redefine its relationship with the people whose interests it purports to serve. Nevertheless, this "progressive" theology in Oaxaca is limited by the verticalism of this very religious field, a hierarchical order that moves very efficiently to muffle any dissent within its ranks and impede the entrenchment of alternative pastoral praxes.

The context I discuss in Oaxaca has included a blossoming of grassroots and indigenous organizing which has shaken up the existing political order and has necessarily led to a revision of the character of relations between official institutions and civil society more broadly. It is difficult to generalize about the role of church representatives in this context, for they are hardly a homogenous body: differences in age, experience, personal backgrounds, and kinds of theological training mean that a wide diversity of viewpoints and pastoral styles are found within their ranks. Yet from at least the 1960s, it was especially to Oaxaca and other dioceses in southern Mexico that clergy of a more progressive current gravitated, or else here found an ideological home.

Much scholarship on Latin American indigenous theology discerns in the fusion of progressive Catholicism and indigenous belief systems and practices a powerful transformative catalyst for a profound political conscienticization and empowerment of indigenous peoples.[6] Often written from the perspective of theologians sympathetic to liberation theology, these accounts are inclined to assume a fairly transparent relationship between theology and practice, seeing the church and its representatives as largely autonomous, with the capacity to act as free agents in interpreting and actualizing the will of God.

This chapter advocates the need for a more nuanced approach, underlining the reality of the church as a global institution, with an internal organizational structure that is still strongly hierarchical and authoritarian. In the spirit of post-structural emphasis on the inextricable intertwining of power and knowledge, I examine the discursive logic of the popular church's indigenist pastoral agenda as a program for action that, despite certain efforts and achievements toward bettering the lives of the poorest of the poor, remains mired in problems given by the historical position of the Mexican church as agent of official knowledge vis-à-vis indigenous peoples—a situation that has existed since colonization. This is especially so today, given the emergence of an even tighter rapprochement between the Mexican church and state at the national level, in which the ecclesial hierarchy's cooperation in an intransigent stance toward indigenous peoples represents a neo-colonial turn.

My examination of the Catholic Church is based on several periods of research over the past seven years in both rural and urban areas of Oaxaca State, including participant observation in several different kinds of church-directed settings and activities and extensive interviews with clergy and laypersons on their views of transformations within the church. With ample opportunity to observe the articulation of official and popular religiosities in various contexts, I have become particularly interested in the ways that religion has come to inform peoples' identities and shape their political affiliations. Important questions remain to be answered with regard to the direction of popular religious movements in contemporary Mexico in terms of whether they can pose a real challenge to the social order, and how religion may be informing people's senses of themselves and even attaching onto other kinds of social differentiation. Rather than investigating the ideological substance of indigenous theology, my aim is to elucidate the dynamics of a particular context wherein a Roman Catholic liberation theological version of indigenous theology was put into practice, with the implicit goal of instilling in people a more critical consciousness and fortified indigenous identity. By doing so, we can better see the limitations of indigenous theology and explore their implications for the church's progressivist wing.

THE INDIGENOUS MOVEMENT IN OAXACA

The current social field in Mexico in which the church is struggling to (re)affirm its social and moral role and status is a complex one. It has been produced in part by the crisis of the Mexican nation-state concurrent with a burgeoning civil society. In Oaxaca and other areas with a high indigenous population, since the 1970s several organizations have appeared that explicitly use their indigenous ethnicity to identify themselves according to historic, linguistic, and other cultural commonalities, as a means of legitimating their mobilization. Especially since the EZLN (Zapatista Army of National Liberation) uprising in Chiapas in January 1994, this is the platform these groups are using to forward their demands for incorporation into Mexican society on revised terms.[7] While attempting to forge a place within the national political culture, indigenous peoples are transforming the nature of their identity from fragmented, ethnically distinct communities to multicultural coexistence in regional and national political arenas. Through this process, notions of ethnicity and identity are being reconfigured within broader parameters.

The wide array of organizations that exist in Oaxaca illustrates the dynamic and plural character of the indigenous movement. The Coalición Obrero-Campesino-Estudiantil del Istmo de Tehuantepec (Worker-Peasant-Student Coalition of the Isthmus of Tehuantepec or COCEI), the Movimiento Unido para la Lucha Trique (Trique Unified Movement for Struggle or MULT), the Asamblea de Autoridades Mixes (Assembly of Authorities from the Mixe Region or ASAM), and the Unión de Comunidades Indígenas de la Zona Norte del Istmo (Union of Indigenous Communities of the North Zone of the Isthmus or UCIZONI) are among the best known of several groups to have emerged over the last thirty years, heralding their ethnic identity to lobby for improved rights for Oaxaca's indigenous peoples and, now, for political autonomy.[8] The specific agendas and modes of working of these groups are varied. Yet the overall demands of the indigenous movement involve the recognition and respect for indigenous culture, including traditional modes of self-government and subsistence and an end to state repression.

Together, such regional grassroots groups represent an ethnic movement as they rally for material goals characterized as being specific to "traditional" indigenous culture: communal territory, communal government, traditional technologies, traditional medicine, traditional economic systems of distribution and exchange, traditional value systems and language, and so on.[9] The multi-faceted character and far-reaching implications of this movement cannot be over-emphasized. Organizations in the movement have in common a struggle for democratization not just of the political system, but of many economic, social, and cultural practices. The struggle has been fertile ground for the blossoming of new conceptions of democratic citizenship, rights, nation, and community, conceptions that challenge rigid hierarchies and the customary authoritarian culture of paternalist and clientelist politics.

The many decades of indigenous mobilization especially in Mexico's southern states encouraged the formation of the pastoral indígena. Because many priests had necessarily become involved with local struggles within their communities, and due to the natural role of clergy as interlocutors, who (like teachers) often function as a prominent link between the community and the external world, in Oaxaca several priests had become conscienticized and politically engaged. The indigenous pastoral was a byproduct of this process, but also of an opening of the Mexican Catholic Church more generally.

I now turn to look at the concrete development of the indigenous pastoral in Oaxaca. This will provide a clearer picture of the dialogue between Catholic doctrine and political context, underlining the church's status as an institution whose actions cannot be understood apart from global political changes, and the interests of the church to retain its relative monopoly over the religious marketplace.

LIBERATION THEOLOGY AND THE PASTORAL INDÍGENA IN OAXACA

Since it emerged into popular (and academic) consciousness in the 1970s, liberation theology has been an over-generalized concept of limited value unless it is recognized as a discourse whose enunciation in a given context reflects the particularities of that setting. There are significant differences in the individual visions and modus operandi of so-called liberationist priests and in the pastoral programs they are able to implement in their communities. Resistance from powerful members of the local population, the relative strength of other churches or religions in the community, personal qualities of priests, ideological coherence of their pastoral team, and the extent of the material resources available to them in their work are all significant factors shaping the outcome of local pastoral plans.

In other words, we cannot take liberation theology at face value, or as meaning the same pastoral agenda wherever it is implemented as general praxis. But in addition, one tends to forget the broader interests of those who direct the institutional church, which has the capacity to control clergy's practice and discipline them if they engage in activities of which members of the hierarchy do not approve. Indigenous theology and the indigenous pastoral were born of a particular historical moment in the church in both local, national, and, indeed, international arenas, and these within a larger social climate that perhaps favored these ideas. As I explain, the path of its subsequent evolution has likewise been shaped by institutional and, arguably, sociopolitical factors.

In Oaxaca, interest in something explicitly named an "indigenous pastoral" began in the early 1970s, when the archdiocese was under the direction of Archbishop Ernesto Corripio Ahumada (1967–1976). The CEI (Comision Episcopal para Indígenas or Bishops Commission on the Indigenous) had been created in Mexico in 1965 before the end of Vatican II, in an attempt to transform the nature of the church's engagement with indigenous communities all over the country. While Ahumada was of a conservative theological background (in fact, he served as president of the Conference of Mexican Bishops [CEM] in three different periods and was made cardinal in 1979), he had been an active participant in Vatican II; at this point in his career he was at least nominally supportive of a more concerted effort to attune the pastoral plan in the archdiocese more directly to the reality of the state's poor and indigenous majority population.

The 1970s saw spaces opened throughout the Oaxacan diocese for clergy to meet and discuss the difficulties they confronted in "evangelizing" (which amounted to sustaining Catholic doctrine) in the indigenous communities where they worked. Many of these communities had a high number of non-Spanish speaking inhabitants and high rates of illiteracy. Following exhortations for self-reflection and self-critique issuing from Vatican II, the priests' acknowledged that their ignorance of indigenous culture and of the daily reality of their parishioners was perhaps the greatest obstacle to both religious participation and the maintenance of Catholic affiliation.

Out of these discussions, church representatives began to develop a holistic and integrated pastoral program aimed at, according to one official church document, "promoting, coordinating, and planning all the pastoral resources of liberating incarnation that brings with it the Christian integral development of persons and indigenous communities in the context of intercultural situations."[10] Such official church rhetoric, heavily flavored by the lexicon of Vatican II and the second conference of Latin American bishops at Medellín, Colombia, in 1968 (e.g., "liberation," "integral development," "intercultural situations"), underlined the reforming character of the Oaxacan church, signaling a milestone transformation in its attitude and vision. Notions of conscientization, empowerment, and liberation formed part of a powerful campaign for integral evangelization,[11] a "contextual theology" encouraging the assimilation of the message of the gospel through the reality of everyday experience. Throughout Latin America at this time, Catholic liberationists called the church to become the "church of the poor" in the sense that its overall mission was to empower them to become the agents of their own liberation, to create new change "from below" and also the "new society."

But, in fact, as early as 1959, Mexican bishops had formed the Commission on Indigenous Affairs and, in 1961, just before the Second Vatican Council, an advisory center—the National Center for Aid to Indigenous Missions, or CENAMI. It was this organization, and another working under the aegis of the CEM, namely CENAPI (National Center for Aid to the Indigenous Pastoral), that provided the Oaxacan diocese with financial and technical support. With this critical aid, the Oaxacan church prepared itself to promote the integral development of indigenous peoples through, in ideal terms, the knowledge of their cultures and the active involvement of people themselves.

Avowed liberationist bishop Arturo Lona Reyes joined Tehuantepec, Oaxaca's neighboring diocese, in 1971. At this point the renovation efforts in the church began to take on more momentum. Lona introduced a more radical critique of the social situation prevailing in the Isthmus region of Oaxaca, a critique which became integrated into the pastoral philosophy of the diocese.[12]

By the end of 1972, the Centro Ecclesial Diocesana del Pastoral indígena de Oaxaca (Indigenous Pastoral Center or CEDIPIO) was established in Oaxaca City. The center had two principal aims: first, the promotion and coordination of the pastoral indigenista and, second, the offering of a more rigorous and holistic training to the priests and nuns charged with carrying out this pastoral plan. CEDIPIO effectively functioned as the directive organ of the diocese offices charged with helping missionary teams in rural zones through financial support and with guidance in coordinating pastoral projects. CEDIPIO trained priests, nuns, and missionaries, who had as their principal tasks evangelization, "human promotion" (promoción humana), and the programming of what was referred to as a Pastoral de Conjunto; that is, a pastoral program that was to be both formulated implemented by all pastoral agents— priests, nuns, and even lay catequists—working together as a team.

As a way of compensating for the chronic shortage of priests especially in rural areas of Oaxaca, CEDIPIO also adopted the strategy of establishing casas-misión (mission houses) of nuns in various highly indigenous, widely dispersed sites in the state, so as to better attend "to the needs of our indigenous brothers."[13] To prepare themselves for this task, clergy, nuns, and lay workers in indigenous areas were given courses in pastoral anthropology (antropología pastoral) and were encouraged to study indigenous myths and traditions. They began working among Zapotec populations of the Northern Sierra and among Zapotecs and Mixtecs in the Oaxacan Valley, offering a varied pastoral program that included directing workshops in natural medicine, Protestantism and "popular religiosity" (meaning, for the church, indigenous religiosity), and the Mexican economic crisis in general. The significance of the new concerted *cultural* slant to pastoral programs, a new orientation for the church, will be addressed later.

Another crucial support for liberationist church agents in their efforts was the Seminario Regional del Sureste (Regional Seminary of the Southeast, or SERESURE), which had been founded in the wake of Vatican II, in 1969, in Tehuacán, Puebla, to forward the liberationist imperative of "integral evangelization" (or "integral development").[14] In the words of Bishop Lona, SERESURE marked a "critical point in the history of the Region of the Pacífico Sur."[15] The eight bishops of the Region del Pacífico Sur, led by Monsignor Rafael Ayala y Ayala (then bishop of Tehuacán), initiated the creation of this very unique institution, the students of which originated from nine dioceses in the southeast of the country.[16] While other seminaries already existed elsewhere in Mexico with an orientation expressly committed to the poor (such as in Tula, Hidalgo, and Papantla, Veracruz), SERESURE was the only one to offer a coherent alternative program of education: priests-in-training had the valuable opportunity to combine their more academic theological preparation with hands-on practical pastoral experience in rural indigenous communities, allowing them to witness firsthand the hardships faced by those who lived there. The seminary's program was especially suited to the needs of the region, which (as is typically the case in Latin America) had suffered a severe shortage of priests in rural zones since at least the onset of the Reform movement and drive toward national independence in the early part of the nineteenth century.[17]

SERESURE represented a tremendous catalyst and font of inspiration and a sense of continuity for clergy sympathetic to the tenets of liberation theology and the teachings of Vatican II and gave a huge impetus to the pastoral indígena. According to one former seminarian, "There were intense months of study and then other months in equal number of intense work with the people. It was fantastic. Most of the students at SERESURE were from indigenous communities: Chiapas, Oaxaca, Puebla, and from other places like Guerrero."[18]

The creation of SERESURE was inspired by the desire to form priests who could promote "autochthonous churches" which would, ideally, be inserted into indigenous communities and function to accompany indigenous peoples in their process of integral evangelization. Directed by the philosophy of the pastoral indígena, pastoral agents directed their efforts not only at attending to indigenous peoples in religious terms, but also at involving themselves in their struggles, anguishes, and hopes and, from the inside (*desde dentro*) at promoting a liberating evangelization "in which the same indigenous peoples are, ideally, active subjects of their own evangelization, expressed and lived according to the mentalities, traditions and customs of their peoples."[19] This reflected a typical liberation theological emphasis on praxis: the new society should be a *participatory* one in which people are the "subjects of their own development" (a catchphrase from Medellín).[20]

In 1976, Bartolomé Carrasco, another liberation theology sympathizer, assumed the helm of Oaxaca's archdiocese from Corripio Ahumada. The archbishop implemented a pastoral program which, though not politically confrontational, was directly oriented to the needs of socially and economically marginalized indigenous communities. Carrasco was one of the main proponents of the proposal to develop the indigeous pastoral, and of making the option for the poor more explicit in the Oaxacan diocese. The archbishop made attention to indigenous communities the priority of the Oaxacan church and granted to CEDIPIO better facilities for their work.[21]

Also facilitating the development of the indigenous pastoral was the official creation, in 1977, of the Región del Pacifico Sur. The "Pacifico Sur" quickly became known as one of the most radical of the eighteen official pastoral regions in the country. The bishops of the Pacifico Sur, including Bishops Lona and Ruiz,[22] formed a coherent force in support of liberation theology and an explicit "option for the poor." The Región del Pacifico Sur quickly began to develop its distinct voice. With a critical public missive in 1977, *Nuestro compromiso cristiano con los indígenas y campesinos,* the bishops of the Pacifico Sur declared themselves in favor of a "structural transformation" of the lives of indigenous peoples.[23] Their position was further elaborated in several official collective pastoral statements in which the bishops denounced the destitute material conditions suffered by the region's indigenous and peasant communities (characterized by, among other problems, environmental degradation, landlessness, chronic malnutrition and hunger, alcoholism, unemployment, repression and exploitation by the government and local political strongmen or *caciques*) and stated their resolve to work to transform this situation for a "more just, humane, divine, fraternal, and freer society"[24]

With the aim of identifying the causes that kept indigenous people poor, following the liberation theological credo (*ver, pensar, actuar,* or observe, think, act) so critical to the process of conscienticization, in collaboration with lay Catholic groups, CEDIPIO representatives encouraged people to critically assess the "diocesanal reality" and social situation in which they were immersed, in the light of the Gospel. Such a process was to lead people to identify the causes of poverty and marginalization; in actuality, the entailing discourse gradually solidified as a stance overtly critical of the government.

CEDIPIO promoters organized meetings, workshops, study groups, and other forums surrounding practical, yet pressing, issues, including the illegal or over-exploitation of the forests and disputes over land boundaries, with the aim of empowering people to defend their rights. Some clergy even began to involve themselves in the assemblies of authorities (*asambleas*), which function in rural communities as the sites of collective governance.[25] Others obtained legal training or took special courses in human rights training. A number of Oaxacan priests thus became prominent mobilizers in Oaxacan indigenous communities, often attracting the resentment of caciques.

Thus it was at the end of the 1970s and beginning of the 1980s, coinciding with the emerging dynamism of the indigenous movement in Oaxaca, that the practical application of liberation theology in the form of the indigenous pastoral was well underway. If all members of the Conference of Mexican Bishops (CEM) did not approve of all aspects of their work, at least protagonists of the pastoral plan in Oaxaca enjoyed the blessing of their leader at the time, Archbishop Bartolomé Carrasco.

Moving into the Indigenous Campaign

By 1990, CEDIPIO had divided its work into four principal areas: first, "culture" (the promotion of indigenous languages and "popular religiosity"); second, Communal Organized Work (Trabajo Común Organizado or TCO), involving various initiatives for the coordination of collective labor projects; third, commercialization (oriented mostly toward small-scale peasant coffee producers); and, finally, what was referred to as *formación* (training), which included initiatives aimed at improving health services, agricultural practices, and community organization.[26]

The 1992 proposals to reform Article 27 of the Mexican Constitution gave an edge of urgency to indigenous meetings all over the state, and church agents involved in the indigenous pastoral began to study other aspects of the Mexican Constitution. CENAMI aided the Oaxacan diocese with its training workshops, paying for the hiring of lawyers, health practitioners, and specialists in indigenous rights to direct them. But it was after the 1994 Zapatista uprising especially, when I first began concentrated research on the church in Oaxaca's two dioceses, that church agents intensified their efforts in promoting a more multifaceted conscienticization by holding workshops throughout the state on such topics as human rights, the economy, the Mexican Constitution, Agreement 169 of the International Labor Organization, the study of electoral and other constitutional reforms, indigenous rights, women's rights, and civic participation.

By this time, then, the needs of the (mostly indigenous) inhabitants of their parishes and the indigenous pastoral had motivated liberationist clergy to establish a wide variety of organizations and other social spaces from which to defend people's rights within the larger political and social sphere. Significantly, all of these projects, whether in urban or rural locales, referred to traditional indigenous social structure and attendant customs of communal labor as their models for organization and as identity referents for the purposes of mobilization.

Culture and Mobilization

The Oaxacan liberationist campaign has been guided by an *inclusive* discourse of democratic ideals, but also by one of an implicit class self-identification: in this, the highly resonant term *popular* has connotations of both class-based and indigenous identity. The equation of class and ethnicity mirrors the reality that most Indians are peasants and poor, but it has also allowed the campaign to articulate the needs of a broad base of social sectors. This mode of identification has been critical to the mobilizing dynamic of the work of liberationist clergy. It has shaped the character of the movement in both rural and urban settings by producing a discourse that presents social, political, and economic demands as part of an integrated campaign for *cultural* survival. In conflating Catholic identity with traditional, rural-derived culture, and by pressing forth an agenda of social justice wherein the church's "new social project" and the aims of the indigenous cause closely resemble one another, church agents inserted themselves in the wider popular and indigenous struggle. The implications of this cultural slant to the campaign will be addressed more directly later.

Thus, progressivist Oaxacan clergy declared themselves to be working toward the same basic goals as indigenous leaders: improving civil rights and living conditions for indigenous peoples, creating a better "new society" from the grassroots, engendering recognition and respect for indigenous identity and culture, and, ultimately, attaining formally recognized political autonomy. All over Oaxaca, this multifaceted, integral, popular conscienticization has been fostered, especially through Bible reflection groups and regular regional workshops on themes related to human rights and civic education. Priests also helped to establish officially registered human rights groups, production cooperatives, education programs, community-run savings programs (or *cajas populares*), and forums for the promotion of traditional health care.

Oaxaca's sister Diocese of Tehuantepec, led from 1971 until 2000 by Bishop Arturo Lona, offers further examples of the holistic pastoral scheme of the Pacific South Pastoral Region. Many of these initiatives are still in operation: A health clinic located just outside of the town of Tehuantepec services the area with basic hospital facilities and with programs for the promotion of natural medicine, the dissemination of information on nutrition, and the training of local healers or *curanderos*. An ecological center on the same site develops projects of recycling and the creation of organic fertilizer for distribution in the area. These projects demonstrate the alternative content of the Oaxacan liberationist campaign, which has its sources in indigenous as well as in wider grassroots culture.

The internationally known peasant-indigenous coffee cooperative UCIRI (Union de Comunidades Indígenas de la Región del Istmo) is another creation within the Isthmus Diocese impelled by clergy; it is a carefully con-structed attempt to uphold and protect the indigenous way of life. Formed in the early 1980s, UCIRI is today still one of the strongest and best-known in-digenous organizations in southeastern Mexico. Besides running an indepen-dent transportation service, a community savings programs, a life insurance program, and a hardware store, in its day-to-day operations UCIRI makes use of indigenous communitarian modes of administration and consensual deci-sion-making and depends on traditional assemblies as the main forums for the conveying of information to members and discussion of policy changes.[27]

In addition to the alternative character of health care, and environmental and subsistence programs, all facets of the pastoral projects in both Oaxacan dioceses are directed by cooperative principles; various kinds of church-organized peasant production cooperatives (e.g., coffee cooperatives, artisan cooperatives, or sheep- or chicken-raising farms), whether large or small, are structured around ancestral customs of labor based on communalism, mutual aid, and reciprocity (embodied by the custom of *tequio,* or community labor, often associated with the local Catholic Church).[28] This is part of a concerted effort to revive indigenous communal practices, a theme of particular interest in the campaign toward autonomy within the national political system.[29]

The special pastoral initiatives of Oaxaca's Popular Church all share a common mandate or agenda of implicit protest of the Mexican state: the aim of the diverse programs is the creation of a social and cultural model that stands in direct contrast with the market-based and individualistic neo-liberal culture of today's Mexico, in both structural and ideological terms. The in-digenous thrust of this pastoral campaign has meant that culture itself is seen as at stake in a larger struggle for a new social order. In the indigenous pastoral agenda, however, culture is both the raison d'etre of the movement and the banner behind which lurk some complex issues particularly troublesome for the church.

The Priest as Anthropologist?
Inculturation and the
"Autochthonous Church"

My first experience was with the Icots brothers, in a culture different from our own Zapotec culture—it was with the Huaves, close to the sea. I was there with other priest friends a year and a half. And with them we had an experience of initiation that definitely told us that the path is through here. That is, I learned also to follow a slower rhythm, not to throw out all the knowledge that they have and to go grounding oneself in existence in the daily contact with the people. With them I learned the work of fishing, because they are fishermen. But not large-scale fishing—just for daily needs. It's a hard life, with a lot of suffering . . . that of living day-to-day, with what is necessary for that day. And I learned that one can't say let's come together to pray, instead you have to go to where they are, so that also our language and what we want to share can be understood. And for me it was a real wake up.

—G. M., Catholic priest and Zapotec from Juchitán, Oaxaca, 1995

In general theological terms, the indigenous pastoral represents an attempt by the church to address cultural specificity and relativism in its practice. This was part of the Oaxacan church's efforts at democratization, a transformation of its top-down modus operandi and paternalistic stance toward its flock. One of the concerns of SERESURE, for example, was to prepare clergy precisely for dealing with indigenous communities in a manner that would enhance the relationship between priest and community. The words above of a priest of Zapotec background from the Tehuantepec diocese reflect the possibility for a special kind of mutually enriching exchange implied by the indigenous pastoral. The testimonies of him and other Oaxacan priests and nuns with whom I spoke, especially those of indigenous background, expressed clearly the profound change of consciousness wrought through their long-term work within indigenous communities. The pastoral indígena advocates the possibility for the same kind of existential transformation for indigenous persons, a critical process of conscienticization that could lead to a new kind of strengthening of indigenous identity, especially in confrontation with the larger national society and the state.

Ideally, this dialogic process between church agents and the indigenous would be what Johannes Fabian has termed *coevalness:* a context allowing for open intercultural communication and exchange, as free as possible of the taint of asymmetric social relations, especially the resonances of the relationship between church and indigenous people in the colonial period.[30] The ethos of the pastoral indígena rejects the concept of acculturation that underlay early Mexican state models for development. Instead, it follows a different hermeneutic principle, one premised on the equality of priests and indigenous persons and the accommodation of the institutional church to the social and historical realities of the *pueblos indígenas.*

The idea of inculturation is fundamental to this process. This concept, derived from Vatican II, has been a crucial tenet of the progressivist church philosophy in Oaxaca since its beginnings.[31] Documents of Vatican II speak of the doctrine of *seminae Verbi* (seeds of the Word), which explains that non-Christian religions were seen as "historical-cultural facts, social and institutional expressions of people's religious consciousness that have in them seeds which can germinate when exposed to the christian message."[32] The concept involves a shaking off of the negative resonances of the term *syncretism* and, along with the notion of indigenization (couching the Christian message in indigenous cultural forms), is part of a contextualization of the Christian message.

In theological terms, inculturation denotes a process wherein the priest or church agent evangelizes through the norms of the local community, using them as a sieve of interpretation, producing a kind of hybrid indigenous theology (*teología indígena*). Padre Chano, a young priest working in the Zapotec southern sierra of Oaxaca State, provided this explanation: "Indigenous theology involves trying to syncretize popular indigenous religion with Christianity. . . . Now it's really neither purely indigenous religion as it was, nor is it purely Christian religion. Instead it becomes a religious syncretism manifest in a very particular reflection of faith."[33]

As conceived by the church, the concept of inculturation hence refers to encounters wherein, theoretically, syncretism (regarded as the benign interaction of two cultural systems) does not involve a usurping of either of the cultures from which it arose. Anthropologist Michael Angrosino offers a critical view of the church perception: "Both parties to the intercultural exchange undergo internal transformation, but neither loses its autonomous identity. . . . [I]nculturation occurs when a dominant culture attempts to make itself accessible to a subdominant one without losing its own particular character."[34]

In keeping with this idealistic paternalism, and underlining the perceived great coincidences in indigenous and Catholic belief systems, this church-defined indigenous theology reflects the liberationist ideal of an equal dialogue or exchange between indigenous (popular) and official religiosity. In Latin America in particular, the concept has also come to denote a radical revision of church structure in line with alternative political and economic realities, that is, horizontal relations, including shared space, reciprocal learning, and exchange, as opposed to the customary vertical, authoritarian dynamic of imposition.[35]

Following the logic of inculturation and indigenous theology, Bishop Lona told me in 1995 that the goal of his diocese was to be an "autochthonous church" (*iglesia autóctona*). Like other clergy who support the idea of a distinctly popular church, the bishop believes that communities will apprehend the Christian message better if they do so "from their own [sociocultural] reality [*desde su propria realidad*]": "Indigenous theology is a theology very distinct from Western forms. Among the indigenous peoples there is that which is called the 'seed of the word' [*semilla de la palabra*] of God, and from there we try to inculturate the gospel and create a Zapotec theology, a Huave one, a Zoque one, from their own cultural richness. . . . It's a theology that can bring about change. For that reason an indigenous theology is always living, and demanding that it always begins from the people's own practical reality."[36]

Bishop Lona here implies that indigenous theology, guided by liberationist interpretations of the Gospel (*el evangelio*), results in the progressivist prototype of Catholic faith—an enlightened Christianity that is organic to people's way of life and that empowers them to work for social justice for

themselves and for others in their community. At the same time as it advocates
a relativist approach to pastoral practice, the underlying idea is that the message of the Gospel is a transcendent truth, not bound to a particular cultural
context. From the liberationist perspective, the "seeds of the Word"—an inchoate Christian spirituality—exist in any cultural setting. In the words of
Padre Chano, "Jesus is at the center of all cultures and from there, from his
own [Jewish] culture, with great respect, he is accompanying their rites, their
ceremonies, their dances, all their religious practices."

Protagonists of contemporary indigenous theology claim to be deferent
to the independence and autonomy of indigenous peoples. Following the example of Jesus, the priest's role in integral evangelization is to accompany
(*acompañar*) the community in their own quest for liberation—to act as guide,
but not to intervene or impose a foreign ideology. "We aren't trying to evangelize Indians," the director of the ecology center in the Tehuantepec Diocese
explained to me, "but instead, this is an inculturation of the Gospel. The Indian has his own rites, his own way of seeing life, of invoking God, of seeing
nature, which isn't that distinct from the Gospel, in its general form." The director's words reflect liberation theology's ecumenical tolerance and acceptance of religious pluralism: the Word of God, the message of the Gospel,
invoked by the liberationist movement refers not so much to a transcendent
Catholic theology, but to a Christian faith of a more generic or ecumenical
character, harking back to Catholicism in its original definition of a single,
monadic, transcendental, true religion.[37] The theological stance of the progressive or Popular Church is that the Gospel should be completely incarnated
in those other cultures while perfecting the human values already present
therein. The ethos of integral evangelization begins with addressing the material needs and problems of the people. Religious faith is depicted as an essential, implicit aspect of everyday existence, and spiritual understanding is
thought to develop in conjunction with, and to enrich, the awakening of social and political consciousness. Yet it is in relation to culture especially that the
agents of the pastoral indígena have focused much of their efforts at salvaging
indigenous ways of life.

Cultural "Recuperation"

Over the past thirty years, the increasing numbers of indigenous priests,
deacons, and catechists in Oaxaca symbolize the partial realization of the goals
of inculturation. In addition, the Oaxacan church has also undertaken programs of cultural "recuperation" as part of its pastoral mission. For example, although these activities have been watered down in recent years owing to a
severe reduction of funding from the archdiocese, CEDIPIO still devotes
much of its activities to reinforcing indigenous cultural identity through active translations of Catholic rituals, sacraments, and celebrations into indige-

nous languages; organizing workshops on popular religiosity (led by clergy), on traditional medicine, and on indigenous social memory; and encouraging activities like the transcription of local myths, songs, and folktales. In addition, autonomous intercultural schools (*escuelas interculturales*) have been established in a few parishes. In Centers of Peasant Education in the Tehuantepec Diocese, for example, especially those associated with UCIRI, children are instructed in agricultural skills and traditional knowledge, stories, and songs. In similar schools in other Oaxacan parishes, indigenous children and adults are taught to read and write in their own language (which survives almost exclusively in oral form) as well as in *castellano,* or Spanish. Such schools form part of the shared objectives of the progressive church's and the indigenous movement's campaign—the "rescue" of customs of collaboration and mutual aid, regarded as essential elements of rural indigenous (and *campesino*) life.

In sum, in the view of the liberationist church in Oaxaca, the essence of the faith is equated to local Catholic rites and customs which may continue to evolve, but which are also regarded as timelessly natural and autochthonous. The logic of the discourse of progressivist clergy therefore asserts that part of authentic indigenous—or popular—identity is being Catholic. Cultural practices that define or sustain indigenous identities are associated with the festival calendar and other communitarian rites and customs related to the civil-religious hierarchy or *cargo* system (traditionally the backbone of rural community social organization) and other Catholic rituals. Embodying a complex exchange of religious and political services, the cargo system—though originally imposed in large part by Spanish colonizers—has always represented the basis of a certain measure of self-sufficiency and political autonomy of indigenous communities.[38]

The pastoral indígena implies an important shift in the church view of the relationship between religiosity and culture: within liberationist practice, Catholic identity is no longer a part of national, mestizo culture at the center, but instead is rooted in indigenous culture, customarily relegated by the dominant cultural ideology to the sociopolitical periphery.

The Protestant Challenge

In the Oaxacan Popular Church campaign, a more inclusive, open, liberationist version of the faith, has been reworked to identify itself as part of local, morally resonant ethnic tradition and identity. Clergy's affiliation with the campaign for indigenous rights and autonomy aids the church in combating one of the banes of its existence, the incursion of Protestant evangelical sects into, especially, Oaxaca's rural zones.[39]

While Protestants have been in Oaxaca since the late nineteenth century, the two decades from 1950 to 1970 saw a rising tide of neo-evangelical churches in Oaxacan indigenous communities, including Pentecostal churches,

Adventists, Baptists, Jehovah's Witnesses, and Mormons, many of these of U.S. origin. Next to Chiapas, Oaxaca has the highest number of non-Catholics in the country, or approximately 10 percent of the total population.[40] Seasonal or permanent migration to the United States has been an additional factor in the increase of Protestants. Often conversion becomes just another layer on divisions already existing among families within indigenous communities. The Protestant presence then can cause significant tensions since many (though not all) evangelicals refuse to participate in *tequio* or other aspects of the civil-religious cargo system—the *vida comunitaria* that is so fundamental to the discourse of the indigenous movement and indigenous identity.

In the ecumenical spirit of liberation theology, Protestants are welcomed in Catholic church-led organizations such as UCIRI, as long as they demonstrate commitment to the rules and goals of the overall project. As Padre Chano emphasized regarding the difficulties faced in his sierra parish, "these aren't problems just of Catholics or of Protestants, they are problems we *all* share."

Nevertheless, proselytizers of Protestant denominations are accused by both indigenous leaders and the Catholic Church of exacerbating the loss of traditional culture and the ethnic identity of the indigenous population. For example, I have heard progressive clergy and others frequently speak of Protestants as threatening "natural and authentic" local Catholic rites and customs surrounding the cargo system and associated with indigenous communitarian identity. Leaders of many indigenous organizations include, in fact, among their first demands for autonomy the expulsion of Protestant promoters, or whole families, from their communities "for not respecting the customs."[41]

The Popular Church's more extreme discourse opposes certain evangelical fixes on their American origins. *Las sectas,* priests argue, are foreign, originating from an imperious, capitalist, and individualist political and economic system which is part of the social order which is being opposed. A valorization of indigenous culture, then, is intended as a means to combat the assumedly malevolent Protestant incursion.

At the same time, conflict between Protestants and Catholics is one of the most serious social problems faced by Oaxacan indigenous communities, a situation which the liberal church project is concerned with ameliorating. In certain parts of the state, for example, Protestants have also seen their homes and other property destroyed and have been obligated to contribute to Catholic festivals. Significantly, one of the clergy leaders of the coffee cooperative UCIRI claimed that for many communities, involvement in the organization has helped to mitigate such confrontations since non-Catholics (Protestants) now participate in tequio as a result of working with Catholics for a shared goal and UCIRI's engendering of common ethnic "conscience collective."[42]

The absolutism of the indigenous movement sits at odds with the new mood of religious tolerance now constitutionally guaranteed and the growing demands within indigenous communities for respect for human rights of all members of the community, not only Catholics. How the Oaxacan church—or at least the clergy who represent it—will reconcile their defensive posture vis-à-vis Protestant religions with their avowed goals of intra-community harmony and tolerance remains a key question.

Liberated Women?

A likewise tricky area for the pastoral indígena is the situation of indigenous women. Recognizing the prominent religious role of women in indigenous communities in Chiapas, the diocesan project of former Bishop Samuel Ruiz made a concerted effort to incorporate women into its organizational structure in active leadership roles. On this basis, some scholars have argued that indigenous women in Chiapas have used the space that the liberationist church provided to formulate a new kind of theology, a new political consciousness heavily inflected with religious overtones.[43]

However, indigenous women's experience in Oaxaca has been somewhat less sanguine. In many liberationist pastoral plans I have observed in Oaxaca, indigenous women are exalted for their central part in the reproduction of the community as wives and mothers, the safe-keepers of traditional cultural values and customs. At the same time, they are also encouraged to participate on equal terms with men in community projects, from UCIRI to those of human rights. In some parishes, and in some organizations such as UCIRI, special women's projects have been organized, such as literacy programs and artesian and agricultural production cooperatives. Yet the unique problems and issues of women (e.g., domestic violence and abuse, the lack of equal access to public political space) are rarely dealt with within the larger social program. In addition, according to the personal testimony of priests and of participants in such projects, many women experience violent reactions from their husbands for their non-domestic public involvement outside the home.

The female coordinator of the Centro de Promoción Comunitariá (Center for Communitarian Promotion or CEPROCUM) in the Diocese of Tehuantepec justified the church's approach in this manner: "In the indigenous communities the family is always one entity, the children, the father, the communitarian form of organization. Yes we have projects for women, but always looking at women from the indigenous cultural context. We don't have specific projects in which we say—these women are going to a meeting of women in the capital. We don't want to take them out of their molds, out of their cultural schemes, but rather we try as far as possible not to affect the culture... nor the values within it." The problem is that in this hermetic, egalitarian, corporate indigenous community—their cultural "mold"—women have few ensured sources of structural power, and the traditional normative system places severe constraints on their socially sanctioned public social activity.

Recent work on Mexican women's involvement in popular movements has drawn attention to aspects of women's social and political activism as sources of renewed concepts of democracy, critical in the long-term constitution of a democratized political culture in Mexico and Latin America as a whole.[44] Some of the new demands of women are those related to issues critical especially for indigenous women: demands for control over such things as their reproduction and whom they marry, but also demands for increased political participation.

It may be too early to judge the long-term impact of the conscienticization efforts of the Oaxacan church on indigenous women. While I saw women actively participating in forums such as human rights groups, traditional medicine workshops, and sewing and weaving cooperatives (these often organized by nuns, in my experience the true "worker bees" of the Catholic Church), indigenous women are still dealing with dominant ambient patriarchal cultural values from which not even the progressivist church has shown itself to be immune.

TRANSITION: THE INDIGENOUS PASTORAL TODAY

Liberationist practices and the pastoral indígena agenda in Oaxaca were dependent upon clergy with human and technical resources and support to carry these out. While such circumstances certainly existed in the region for over two decades, gaining momentum under Bishop Bartolomé Carrasco, they could not last after an eventual realignment of the balance of ideological power in the ecclesiastic hierarchy.

While the pastoral indigena was gaining momentum in Oaxaca in the 1970s and 1980s, critical changes were afoot in the church hierarchy both nationally, within Mexico, and at an international level. The gradual diminishment of church support for liberation theology coincided with sharpening divisions among the clergy in the late 1970s. In 1979 Pope John Paul II expressed his objections to the conception of Christ as a political revolutionary at the Third CELAM Assembly of Latin American Bishops, held in the Mexican city of Puebla. Also reversing the trends of Medellín, and CELAM's progressivist social doctrine, was the naming of Bishop Alfonso Lopez Trujillo of Colombia, a vociferous opponent of liberation theology, as secretary general in 1972.

The increasingly doctrinaire and authoritarian approach of the Vatican was directly felt in Mexico beginning in 1978 when Girolamo Prigione, the Vatican's envoy (nuncio apostólico) in Mexico, began his eighteen-year tenure as nuncio. Prigione pursued a very active liaison between the Holy Office and the Mexican bishopric and made recommendations on new bishops to be named by the Vatican.[45] Throughout the 1980s and 1990s the Vatican maintained its opposition to Latin American theology while promoting what the pope saw as "authentic" liberation (which revolved around individual conversion). Combined with Prigione's clout (and that of subsequent nuncios) was the apparent cosying up of church-state relations in Mexico, a trend that began in the mid-1980s and was formalized with the Salinas-initiated constitutional reforms in 1992.[46]

An ostracizing of progressive elements in the church was seen in Oaxaca, where at the beginning of the 1990s (1989–1991) two bishops shared the supervision of the Oaxacan archdiocese. In 1988, Prigione had pressured for a more conservative bishop, Hector González Martínez, to take up the role as diocese coadjutor. The official reason given for the need for two bishops was to aid the aging Carrasco in carrying out his duties in the extensive (47,000 km²) and difficult geography of the Oaxacan diocese. It was rumored that Carrasco had requested an auxiliary bishop to help him also with the problem of priests' violation of the vow of celibacy, a problem for which the archdiocese had earned infamy within the church nationally.[47]

Upon his arrival, González quickly intervened in realms of diocese activity in a manner many priests saw as inappropriate. More light was cast on the ulterior motives of Prigione's selection in November 1989, when it was announced publicly that Rome had given the coadjutor the ultimate word in any decisions passed regarding official diocese policy and local clergy. In a letter to a plenary meeting in the archdiocese in August 1990, Carrasco declared that the granting to González of these special powers was tantamount to the "deauthorization of the pastoral program that had been shaping the pastoral orientation [of the diocese]. . . . He [González] had no previous experience of the indigenous pastoral. He has not assumed it completely. . . . It is a completely new world for him."[48]

The announcement of González' authority over Carrasco raised the hackles of many Oaxacan clergy, who demanded that the nuncio appear in Oaxaca to defend his actions. He did so the following March, 1990, after public opposition to the matter had calmed down, and was effectively successful in reinforcing the authority of the new coadjutor González.[49]

Still, the worst was yet to come. SERESURE, the seminary so critical to the coherence and consistency of the distinct progressivist pastoral agenda of the pastoral region of the Pacifico Sur for almost twenty years, came to an end. In December 1989, nuncio Prigione paid a brief visit to the seminary. At the end of that same year, the Holy Office commissioned a more intense official review of the seminary and its program of study, sending two bishops to do the job, Emilio Berlié Belaunzarán of Tijuana and Alberto Suárez Inda of Tacámbaro. Afterwards, Inda and Berlié sent their evaluations to Rome.

Finally, the following year, August 9, 1990, Pio Laghi, prefect of the Sacred Congregation for Catholic Education, sent a letter to Norberto Rivera, archbishop of Mexico, commenting on the bishops' report. The bishops had claimed that the seminary conveyed a teaching "impregnated with a Marxist cosmovision" that harmonized with the line "of the theology of liberation that is used in Latin America."[50] It did not take long for the Holy Office to respond to the bishops' report, which it did by displacing the bishops directing the seminary, turning the reins over to Archbishop Rivera. In turn, the archbishop, renowned for his arch-conservative doctrinal and political positions, expelled all the professors at SERESURE and radically revised the programs and methods of study.[51] When it re-opened two years later, in 1992, it was no longer a regional seminary but a diocesan one and now promoted a clearly conservative pastoral line. With SERESURE's closure, a serious blow had been dealt to progressive Catholicism and the original incarnation of the pastoral indígena in Mexico's southeast.[52]

Prigione (or PRI-gione, as he came to be known in the media due to his bold courting of government officials of the ruling People's Revolutionary Party or PRI) was seen as the main figure behind the downfall of SERESURE. In the case of Oaxaca, Prigione's efforts had their intended effect. The closure of SERESURE in 1990, followed by the highly contentious replacement of Carrasco by González in 1992, had the effect of neutralizing the liberationist tone prevailing in the Oaxacan diocese.[53] In Oaxaca, this meant that the diocese of Tehuantepec in the Isthmus region of the state, led since 1971 by the renowned liberationist Bishop Lona, now clashed sharply with the pastoral orientation of the Oaxacan archdiocese headed by conservative theologian Bishop González. (In 1998 the CEM sent a staunchly Vatican-line coadjutor, Felipe Padilla, to Tehuantepec to replace Lona.) The situation divided the diocese for most of the 1990s as González repeatedly provoked the ire of Oaxacan clergy due to his actions and public statements, which clearly harmonized with the dominant conservative line of the CEM. He also closed the mission houses, run by nuns, that had been so crucial to carrying out the pastoral indígena program in indigenous communities. Gonzalez also replaced the coordinator of CEDIPIO and drastically curtailed the expansion of the center's working area of culture.

This important milestone marked a return of the diocese's main focus from a rural, indigenous orientation to an urban, mestizo one. In the Oaxacan Archdiocese, for example, González began to back enthusiastically the national movement of Charismatic Renewal in the Oaxacan diocese. The prelate's support of charismatic Catholicism is significant in that this form of Catholicism bears a strong resemblance to Pentecostalism in its emotional, mystical orientation, its involvement in faith healing, and—most importantly—its apolitical social outlook.

Thus, the pastoral indígena, the heartbeat of the Oaxacan diocese for over thirty years, was severely weakened, its survival and growth so reliant on the coherent ambient support, knowledge, and commitment of the directors of the Oaxacan Archdiocese. Although the indigenous pastoral remains the object of much debate within the church hierarchy generally, and Archbishop González claims it remains a primary focus of the pastoral plan of his archdiocesis, those who continue to promote a pastoral agenda as a legacy of Bartolomé Carrasco's original pastoral program, while many in number (approximately 50 percent of clergy in the Oaxacan Archdiocese)[54], are marginal to the reigning status quo.

Aside from the threat of ostracization from the ecclesial hierarchy, especially today, fulfilling the goals of the indigenous pastoral represents an ominous challenge, requiring considerable tenacity and patience. In zones of Oaxaca that are particularly internally conflictive, it also demands courage, since the priest, in a natural mediatory position, may sometimes find himself the object of hatred, or even of violence, from more powerful members of the community.[55]

Oaxacan clergy (and nuns) have had to deal with threats by local caciques and government representatives alike. Throughout the 1980s especially, the Diocese of Tehuantepec (and that of Chiapas) was subject to continual attack by regional power-holders. During the final years of his tenure as bishop, Lona suffered two serious assassination attempts, and elsewhere in the Tehuantepec diocese UCIRI members, including one of the organization's founders, have been murdered. Throughout Oaxaca, one priest has also been killed and other priests have had their lives threatened and their parishes have been more closely observed through an increasing militarization of rural areas in the context of government suppression of independent rural organizing of a political nature, in their efforts to nip in the bud any potential formation of autonomous indigenous peasant insurgent groups akin to the Zapatistas.[56]

AUTHENTIC PERFORMANCES OF INDIGENOUSNESS

The indigenous eruption demands profound changes in the schemes for understanding this phenomenon and for arriving at a solution. Today it's no longer possible to look at indigenous people with the same eyes as before, that is, as objects of study and integrationist actions, but instead as travelling companions, as protagonist subjects of our own development and evangelization. Indigenous cultures can today reformulate and recreate themselves in dialogue with other cultures in order to sustain themselves not just alive, but even more dynamic in the future.

—Eleazar López Hernández, Zapotec priest and coordinator of CENAMI[57]

Since the revolution at the beginning of the century, the relationship of indigenous groups with the larger Mexican society has been directed by indigenist models of development representing varieties of assimilationist and integrationist ideologies. In the original *indigenista* ideology, indigenous culture and folklore were appropriated and compartmentalized in the larger national Mexican body as a way of legitimating a distinct and independent post-revolutionary national society and culture.[58]

More recently, a "new *indigenismo*" insists on the need for the maintenance of cultural distinctiveness of Mexico's indigenous peoples.[59] A primary justification of the movement for indigenous autonomy is for Mexico's first peoples to wrest control of the social, economic, and cultural path of the development of their communities from the hands of the government and other external mediators, whose paternalistic, indigenist attitudes and oppressive practices are argued to have had deleterious effects on indigenous society and to have impeded the emergence of any pan-community ethnic identity or political consciousness.

The indigenous struggle for autonomy therefore represents on many levels a quest for true self-determination—liberation from the visions of modernization advanced by government policies (these influenced by European liberalist ideology) since before the revolution. This struggle also involves complex negotiations among leaders and participants of various ideologies vying for control over the movement of the right to define and shape its path.

Today various social actors, technically from outside traditional indigenous society—liberationist clergy, anthropologists, and a new generation of indigenous intellectuals who have appeared over the last couple of decades—fight on behalf of the most marginalized sectors of the indigenous masses in their encounter with the array of forces seen to threaten the viability of their communities and traditional ways of life. Yet in this specific area of the highly contested field of today's Mexican popular movements, the politics of ethnicity in some ways represent again a contest over power not drastically different from that found in the clientelist and authoritarian culture which indigenous organizations claim to oppose.

In recognizing the extent of the commitment and sacrifice many church agents have made, and the compromised conditions in which they often live, it is sometimes difficult to regard them as implicated in a system of power and self-interest—or even, sometimes, as representatives of the institutional church. In fact, some priests, especially those in isolated rural communities, have distanced themselves considerably from the central ecclesiastic institution in terms of their contact with other church representatives, especially those working in the present Oaxacan diocese administration. Many liberationist clergy with whom I have spoken (especially in the conservative-led archdiocese) are frustrated with the perceived backlash to liberation theology begun at Medellín and especially apparent in both Oaxacan dioceses today. This progressivist sector campaigns avidly for an opening of the institutional church, which for many even includes a relaxing of the rules of celibacy and a protection of clergy's "human rights" within the hierarchy.[60]

We must remind ourselves, however, that the ideological cleavage between conservatives and liberationists within the church is not part of a break from the institution: clergy still maintain official links with the institutional church and are to some extent subject to the hierarchy's control and reprimand. Priests know that their assignment to a certain parish is decided by the archdiocese central administration (which in turn is strongly influenced by the heads of the conservative Mexican *episcopado,* now with a renewed relationship with the government).[61] If their activities are disliked by the hierarchy, they may be abruptly moved, often ending or at least seriously damaging a progressive pastoral program they worked hard to put in place. The Vatican's appointment of adjunct bishops (*coadjutores*) to "aid" renowned progressive archbishops Carrasco in 1989, Ruiz in Chiapas in 1995, and Lona in 1998, for example, is a patent exercise of such control. Such measures are part of the symbolic violence or "conservation strategies" by which the upper echelons of the church hierarchy construct and underline their authority and the imperative of obedience, in an attempt to quash dissent and silence alternative theological or pastoral discourses.[62]

Yet further difficulties stem from the ambivalent and in some ways contradictory status of many clergy. The particularistic ethnic character of the popular church's formulation of a language of mobilization within the pastoral indígena mandate has led a few progressivist clergy to uphold agendas which are similarly exclusionary and purist in nature and, like some contemporary conservative clergy, to see their "true Christianity" as part of an enlightened vanguard in the larger struggle. This fact places them in a difficult position as being outsiders to indigenous culture yet, in various ways, staunch defenders of it.[63]

In this highly charged political climate, the church participates in legitimating a dominant paradigm of culture as a homogenous, bounded, integrated whole. This paradigm acts as the interpretive lens for any statements about the ontology of indigenous culture, the way it changes through time, and the relationship that indigenous people have to "their culture."[64] Today this tendency toward essentializing indigenous culture has not changed from past state-sponsored indigenist projects, but has taken on a slightly different premise. For example, in Oaxaca and throughout Mexico, leaders and participants in the indigenous movement are actively constructing ideologies that make reference to indigenous society as an egalitarian community embedded in a distinct moral economy.

Not surprisingly, most representatives of the progressivist church I have known in Oaxaca share in this tendency. However, for them, this communitarian indigenous society is fundamentally *religious* (in relation to corporate civil-religious identity) and collective (in opposition to the individualistic, alienating, competitive life-way of the wider Mexican society).

While proclaiming the imperative of the autonomy and independence of indigenous society, this view tends toward a homogenizing romanticism and idealism, seeing the indigenous world as an endangered society of primeval harmony and tradition, whose independent development since the conquest has been repeatedly violated by foreigners ignorant of its distinct cosmology and ways of being.

The inclusivist, pluralist theology implied by the liberationist concept of inculturation presents a potential problem for the popular church in terms of the coherence of its democratizing, grassroots political stance. First, syncretism is never a process free of the resonances of political confrontation and control. Such "indigenizing" projects are often efforts from above to control the orientation of religious synthesis:[65] in the case of Oaxaca, indigenous theology represents an attempt to define the interface of indigenous, folk religion with official Catholic religiosity, which was previously the territory of a more self-determined, autonomous popular faith.[66]

A central goal of the indigenous pastoral is inculturation or evangelization through indigenous languages. However, while the church promoted the learning of indigenous languages among clergy as early as the 1970s, this was one aspect of CEDIPIO's work that never had much success. The reality is that if they are not native speakers already, few priests master the language of the communities of their parishes. This problem alone is a significant impediment to communication and throws some doubt on the seriousness of the Oaxacan church's commitment to follow through with the full agenda of inculturation.

In the Oaxacan liberationist project of integral evangelization, the material conditions of social life are contrived to form the basis of the symbolic construction of a distinct cultural (and religious) identity. Essentialized, rural-derived values and customs of collective welfare and a moral rootedness are elaborated and embellished, then held up in contrast to the dominant (mestizo) society and the state. Through this evangelist process, priests may be viewed by the people, and may view themselves, as natural leaders of the popular or the indigenous cause.

For David Lehmann, adherents of the "People's Church" movement within the Catholic Church, or the practitioners of the indigenous theology of inculturation, are examples of what he calls *basista* tendencies, due to their faith in the faith of the poor or the grassroots: "They develop their theory about the proper place of indigenous practices at second remove, in order to set them up as an authentic performance of something 'other.'"[67] Along a similar vein, Homi Bhabha writes that "colonial discourse is an apparatus of power that turns on the recognition and disavowal of racial, cultural and historical differences."[68] In the case of the Catholic Church in Oaxaca, the church constructs these differences in a certain fashion to justify its continued mediatory role in indigenous communities as beneficent "accompanier." It represents Catholicism as being authentically traditional to the history and identity of indigenous peoples.

Innumerable millenarian and other religious resistance movements in Oaxaca and in Mexico attest to the fact that it is precisely popular religion's relatively autonomous social status which allows it to act potentially as an effective oppositional force.[69] We should also not forget that the Catholic Church, even in its liberationist guise, by virtue of the vast personal, financial, and institutional resources, retains a significant concentration of political and economic power, and not just of moral authority. For example, the links priests already have within the larger society (social, political, economic) are often crucial in obtaining key benefits for their pastoral projects, such as funding or other forms of aid from foreign or other outside sources (e.g., philanthropic organizations, foreign non-governmental organizations), as is the case with the priest/founder of UCIRI.[70] Thus, although the key goal of liberationist praxis is to empower indigenous people so that they might eventually lead themselves, giving priority to the enabling of power "from below" is not always the practice.

CONCLUSION

Since the Zapatista rebellion, the revindication of indigenousness has gained ground in Mexico. Nevertheless, in Oaxaca for several years indigenous organizations have emerged that are struggling for better participation in the political and free determination of their communities within a more democratic national political landscape.

Inspired by the opening of the Catholic Church emerging from Vatican II and Medellín, and concomitant calls for a greater social commitment with the poor and oppressed, with its pastoral program of the pastoral indígena, a liberation theological wing of the Catholic Church in Oaxaca also assumed the mantle of the indigenous cause, defending indigenous culture in the struggle against various forces seen to threaten it. The efforts of progressivist clergy encountered a reinvigorated and more politicized terrain of struggle in the wake of the emergence of the EZLN and the explosion of popular organizing that has arisen in its path. Following the ideal of inculturation, a program for incarnating the Gospel in the community as well as democratizing relations between church agents and indigenous peoples, the indigenous pastoral was seen by progressives to be the source of the emergence of a new, utopian social order and a strengthening of indigenous communities.

Despite the progressive church's efforts to valorize indigenous cultural forms and to defer to indigenous peoples in determining their own path toward liberation, I have suggested that the fundamental implications of the indigenous pastoral campaign cannot be understood outside of a consideration of power relations that have colored the engagement of the church and indigenous peoples since colonization.

My discussion of the background and evolution of the liberationist indigenous pastoral in Oaxaca has highlighted the rift between theology and
practice. For one, what clergy are able to put into practice in their given
parishes is contingent on factors specific to a given local context as well as a
priest's own personal resources. At the same time, I have pointed to the necessity of not losing sight of the larger institutional church in which priests of any
political stripe must operate, a church that has seen critical changes take place
to its own internal political culture at international and national levels. These
have involved a backlash against liberation theology and attempts to deepen
the church's political commitment, especially in developing areas of the world
such as Latin America. For many years there existed in Oaxaca a theological
climate supportive of liberationist practices. Yet since the end of the 1970s,
with a strengthening of the church's constitutional position and its relation to
the Mexican state, the Oaxacan church was gradually no longer a sanctioned
space for protest or for mobilization.

The apparent openness to modern ideas of democracy promoted by progressives has not been paralleled by an attempt to integrate modern values of
equality into the church's own internal organization. The church remains
very closed: autocratic leadership styles persist and so-perceived "radical"
activity is constrained by the ultimate decision-making power of the central
hierarchy.

The pastoral indígena provided a praxis for mobilization and an organizational and ideological basis for a reinvention of ethnic identity. The ethnic
basis of the discourse of the indigenous pastoral allowed the Oaxacan church
to combine an ability to be identified as a rallying cause for diverse social
problems with a capacity to invoke social and cultural particularisms, derived
from a sacred and idealized (transcendental) past, depicted as being opposed to
dominant Mexican society and forces aligned with the state.

Yet I have suggested that this discourse and its key concept of inculturation are also based on a view of indigenous culture that is patronizing and
utopian, wishing to preserve it according to conceptions of indigenous culture
as a homogenous, egalitarian whole, to which (Catholic) religiosity is both
central and authentic.

Precisely due to its insistence on the immanence of the Christian message
in any cultural context and its continued allegiance to the Catholic Church,
liberation theology's discourse is also underlain by a logic of universalism that
is premised on Catholicism's supposedly generic, non-culturally specific character. In this way, the apparently alternative ("heterodox," in Bourdieu's terms)
discourse of liberation theology does not represent, in fundamental terms, a
challenge to that aspect of church *doxa* which defines the church as an integral and implicitly necessary institution in Mexican society. As Angrosino
points out, "the rhetoric of sensitivity to cultural variation exists in a state of

some tension with a fundamental belief in the rightness of the beliefs or be-haviours that are the substance of the program of directed change."[71]

This contradictory logic is at the root of what is perhaps the greatest chal-lenge for the church to retain its relevance in indigenous communities. In today's context, where indigenous people in Oaxaca are increasingly aware of their right to shape and define the terms of their identities and cultures and are gaining political strength within the national society, where the church en-ters into this struggle will also be determined by indigenous peoples them-selves, according to their own ideas regarding what autonomy means.

Notes

I would like to thank Fonds de Recherche sui la Societé et la Culture (FCAR) and the Social Sciences and Humanities Research Council of Canada (SSHRC) for generous fi-nancial assistance that made this research possible. My sincere gratitude also goes to Pierre Beaucage, Enrique Marroquín, Nemesio Rodriguez, Jesús Lizama, and Jorge Hernández Díaz, who over the years have shared generously their knowledge and insight on the church in Mexico and Oaxaca. Mauricio Delfín, Ezequiel Toledo, Miranda Ortiz, and Stephanie Pommez provided invaluable research assistance in Oaxaca. This paper would also not have been possible without the generosity and *confianza* of members of the Oaxacan clergy, especially Msgr. Arturo Lona, Padre Juan Ortiz Carreño, Padre Wilfrido Mayrén Pelaez, and Madre Guadalupe Cortes. Finally, Edward Cleary, Tim Steigenga, and an anonymous reviewer of an earlier draft of this essay encouraged me to sharpen some of my central arguments. Some sections of this essay have appeared previ-ously in *Latin American Perspectives* 96, no. 5 (September 1997): 96–127.

1. In Jorge Hernández Díaz, *Reclamos de la identidad: La formación de las organizaciones indígenas en Oaxaca* (México, D.F.:Porrua, 2001), my translation.

2. 18.3 percent of the Oaxaca's state population is indigenous, from Jonathan Fox, "Mexico's Indigenous Population," Indigenous Rights and Determination in Mex-ico, *Cultural Survival Quarterly* 23, no. 1 (spring 1999): 26.

3. Since the end of the twentieth century, the Mexican state had traditionally been Ja-cobinist, anticlerical, though had not enforced constitutional articles which severely curtailed the church's power and influence in Mexican society. In 1992, the church's official status changed, ushering in a period of rapprochement between church and state. President Salinas initiated an amendment to five articles of the Constitution (Articles 3, 4, 24, 27, and 130): these momentous reforms recognized the church's juridical status, allowed it a broader role in education, permitted clergy to vote, le-galized the presence of foreign priests in their country, and allowed religious enti-ties to use the mass media to convey their views.

4. As used by Enrique Marroquín, *El Botín Sagrado: La dinámica religiosa en Oaxaca* (Oaxaca: IISUABJO-Comunicación Sociál, 1992).

5. Pierre Bourdieu, *Outline of a Theory of Practice* (Cambridge: Cambridge University Press, 1977); Pierre Bourdieu, "Genèse et structure du champ religieux," *Revue Française de sociologie* 12, no, 3 (July–September): 294–334.

6. For example, Eleazar López Hernández, *Teología india: antología* (Cochabamba, Bo-livia: Editorial Verbo Divino, 2000); Diego Irarrázaval, *Inculturation: New Dawn of the Church in Latin America* (Maryknoll: Orbis, 2000); Bartolomé Carrasco, "Incultura-tion del Evangelio," *Voces* 4 (1994):11–31.

7. Hernández Díaz, *Reclamos de la identidad*. Legislative changes achieved by the in-digenous movement have included the official ratification (on July 11, 1990) of new international norms for relations between states and indigenous peoples, contained

in the International Labour Organization's (ILO) Convention 169 (converted to a Supreme Law, Article 133 of the Constitution, stating that indigenous peoples should have the right to conserve their own customs and institutions), and changes to Article 4 and 27 of the Constitution dealing with indigenous rights. In-depth discussion of the indigenous movement in Mexico and in Oaxaca, which cannot be provided here, may be found in M. C. Pineros Mejia and Sergio Sarmiento Silva, *La lucha indigena: Un reto a la ortodoxia* (Mexico D.F.: Siglo XXI, 1991); Hernández Díaz, *Reclamos de la identidad*; and Lynn Stephen, *¡Zapata Lives! Histories and Cultural Politics in Southern Mexico* (Berkeley: University of California Press, 2002).

8. For example, Hernández Díaz, *Reclamos de la identidad*.

9. J. Rendón Monzón, *Rescate de la dignidad indígena* (Oaxaca: Cultura para el Tercer Milenio, 1994).

10. *Objetivo provisorio de la pastoral indigenista*, as cited in Hernández Diaz, *Reclamos de la identidad*, 127

11. Conscienticization or consciousness raising (*conscientización*) is a term borrowed from the hallmark pedagogical method of great Brazilian popular educator Paulo Freire. Conscientización refers to the development of a critical mind through the use of locally salient and politically charged images of conflict from everyday life.

12. Victor G. Muro González, *Iglesia y movimientos sociales en México, 1972–1987: Los casos de Ciudad Juárez y el Istmo de Tehuantepec* (Zamora: Colegio de Michoacán, 1994).

13. Hernández Díaz, *Reclamos de la identidad*, 128. *Casas-mision* were founded in the indigenous towns of Yalalag, Camotlan, Apaola, Tlaxiaco (in the Mixteca), and Panixtlahuaca and Zenzontepec in the southern Sierra.

14. See Philip Berryman, *Liberation Theology* (London: Pantheon, 1987), 94.

15. Interview with Msgr. Arturo Lona, Tehuantepec, Oaxaca, 1995.

16. Other clergy of the Pacific South considered as founders of SERESURE are the bishops of the dioceses of Oaxaca (Ernesto Corripio Ahumada, Bartolomé Carrasco), Tehuantepec (Lona), Tuxtla Gutiérrez, Tapachula, and San Cristobal (Ruiz).

17. In 1989, the number of Mexican Catholics per priest (7,116) was below average for Latin America (7,348). In 1945, there were only 5,380 Mexican Catholics per priest. George W. Grayson, *The Church in Contemporary Mexico*, Significant Issues Series XIV, no. 5 (Washington, DC: Center for Strategic Studies, 1992), 41.

18. Interview with Padre C. B., December 1995.

19. SERESURE, 1989, in Hernández Díaz, *Reclamos de la identidad*, 130.

20. Berryman, *Liberation Theology*.

21. In 1980, in recognition of his commitment to indigenous peoples, Bartolomé Carrasco was named president of the Bishops' Commission for Indigenous Peoples (Comision Episcopal para Indígenas or CEI) that formed part of the larger structure of the Mexican Bishop's Conference (CEM).

22. Ruiz sponsored the landmark Indigenous Congress of 1974, which marked the beginning of the resurgence of the Mexican indigenous movement.

23. See also Marroquín, *El Botín Sagrado*; Miguel Concha Malo, *La Participación de los Cristianos en el proceso popular de liberación en México* (México, D.F.: Siglo XXI Editores, 1986); Victor De la Cruz, "Reflexiones acercade los movimientos etnopolíticos contemporáneous en Oaraca," in *Etuicidad y Pluralismo Cultural*, ed. Alicia Barabas and Miguel Bartolome (México, D.F.: Dir. General, 1990), 423–446; CENAMI, *El Magisterio Pastoral de la Región Pacífico Sur* (México, D.F.: CENAMI, 1991).

24. "Tehuantepec, 1891–1991: Un Siglo de Fe," in CENAMI, *El Magisterio Pastoral de la Region Pacifico Sur,* 53–94; and see also other collective documents of bishops of the Pacific South region until the end of the 1980s. The eight bishops were Samuel Ruiz of San Cristobal de las Casas, Arturo Lona of Tehuantepec, Ernesto Corripio

Ahumada and Bartolomé Carrasco of Oaxaca, Braulio Sanchez Fuentes of the Prelature of the Mixes, Hermenegildo Ramirez of Huautla, Jesús Castillo Rentería of Tuxtepec, and Rafael Ayala Ayala of Tehuacán.

25. Hernández Díaz, *Reclamos de la identidad,* 131–132.

26. The organization that undertook the commercialization of coffee was named MICHIZA. The expectation was that promoters trained in either health or agroecology would then share this information with their communities. In 1991, MICHIZA became independent of the church. Hernández Díaz, *Reclamos de la identidad.*

27. See Jorge Hernández Díaz, "UCIRI: Viejas identidades, nuevos referentes culturales y politicos," *Cuadernos del Sur* 3, no. 8–9 (1995): 125–144.

28. *Tequio* is an ancient form of collective labor that today is expressed as social service owed periodically by a community's members to the community as physical labor or religious tasks.

29. On August 30, 1995, the Oaxacan State Congress approved the election law by *usos y costumbres* (law and customs), applied for the first time on November 12. The law allowed indigenous communities to elect municipal authorities on the basis of the civil-religious cargo system and the name of authorities within a general assembly, without having to register with a political party.

30. Johannes Fabian, *Time and the Other* (Cambridge, U.K.: Cambridge University Press, 1983).

31. See, for example, Carrasco, "Inculturation del Evangelio," 11–31.

32. Josué A. Nascimiento Sathler and Amós Sathler, "Black Masks on White Faces: Liberation Theology and the Quest for Syncretism in the Brazilian Context," in *Liberation Theologies, Post-modernity, and the Americas,* ed. David Bastone, Eduardo Mendieta, Lois Ann Lorentzen, and Dwight N. Hopkins (London: Routledge, 1997), 109–110.

33. Interview with Padre W. M., Oaxaca, 1995.

34. Michael V. Angrosino, "The Culture Concept and the Mission of the Catholic Church," *American Anthropology* 96 (1994): 825.

35. Ibid., 826.

36. Interview with Archbishop Arturo Lona, Tehuantepec, 1995.

37. As a document from SERESURE (1989) explains, "the idea of the pastoral indígena is that the priest no longer assists indigenous people, but instead involves himself with them in their path [*caminar*], their anxieties, their hopes and from the inside [*desde dentro*], to promote a liberating evangelization in which the same indigenous may be subjects of their own evangelization, expressed and lived according to their own mentalities, traditions and histories of the pueblos" (in Hernández Díaz, *Reclamos de la identidad,* 130).

38. See, for example, Miguel Bartolome and Alicia Barabas, *Etnicidad y pluralismo cultural: La dinamica etnicas en Oaxaca* (Mexico: Dir. General, 1990).

39. In Mexico, the category "Protestants" includes the historical Protestant churches such as the Anglicans, Presbyterians, and Baptists, but also evangelical sects such as Pentecostals, the Jehovah's Witnesses, and Mormons (Church of Jesus Christ of Latter-Day Saints).

40. Daniela Pastrana, "Religión y pueblos indios: De la intolerancia a la convivencia," *La Jornada,* April 8, 2001.

41. See Wim Gisjbers, *Usos y Costumbres, Caciquismo e Intolerancia Religiosa* (Oaxaca, Oax.: Centro de Apoyo al Movimiento Popular Oaxaqueño, 1996).

42. Personal interview, Padre C. B., Tehuantepec Diocese.

43. For example, Aída Hernández Castillo, "Women and the Pastoral Indígena in Chiapas," paper given at the Scientific Society for the Study of Religion, Montreal, November 1998.

44. C. Ramos Escandón, "Women's Movements, Feminism, and Mexican Politics," in *The Women's Movement in Latin America*, ed. J. Jacquette (San Francisco: Westview, 1994); Lynn Stephen, "Democracy for Whom? Women's Grassroots Political Activism in the 90s, Mexico City and Chiapas," in *Neoliberalism Revisited: Economic Restructuring and Mexico's Political Future,* ed. Gerardo Otero (San Francisco: Westview, 1996), 167–186.

45. According to Grayson, several factors explain the influence of the Vatican in Mexico. First, the Mexican church feels a debt to the Holy See for its support during the revolution, during the period of anticlerical practices following it, and during the Cristero Movement. Second, Mexico's political culture emphasizes discipline and obedience to authority. Bishops are extremely deferent toward the pope. Third, recent CEM presidents have offered relatively weak leadership, and the Vatican has filled the void. Fourth, since 1978, Pope John Paul II has selected conservative bishops who tow Rome's theological and political line. Finally, apostolic delegate Girolamo Prigione is a shrewd, manipulative, and influential figure. Over one-third of the country's ninety-three active bishops have been appointed with his imprimatur. Grayson, *The Church in Contemporary Mexico*, 33, 35.

46. Salinas courted influential bishops during his electoral campaign, invited church leaders to his inauguration, appointed a personal envoy to the Vatican in 1990 (Agustín Téllez Cruces), and was particularly attentive during Pope John Paul's visits to Mexico in 1990. Then in 1992, when he gained office, arguing for a need to "modernize" the relations with the church, he amended five articles of the Constitution that gave the church legal recognition and extended its public role.

47. Rodrigo Vera and Isodoro Yescas, "Con Pretexto de Abandono del celibato, el Vaticano reprime a sacerdotes que optan por los pobres," *Proceso*, March 12, 1990. Prigione was succeeded in 1997 by Justo Mullor, who in turn was replaced by Leonardo Sandri, who then was replaced after a couple of months by Guiseppe Bertello.

48. Quoted in Manuel Esparza, *Opción Preferencial* (Periodismo Crítico: Carteles Editores, 2001), 27 (my translation).

49. Marroquín, *El Botín Sagrado,* 39.

50. The students organized a pilgrimage in protest. Outraged by the march, Rivera expelled the seminary's 130 students and closed the doors of SERESURE, later saying they could return only on the condition they accepted the seminary's "new order." Only five students, all from the Tehuacan diocese, did so. The other students had long gone. Yet with so few students left, the seminary could no longer function, and so closed its doors for good.

51. All dioceses and regions formally united in SERESURE now have their own seminaries; these now exist in Oaxaca City, Tapachula, Tehuantepec, Huautla de Jiménez (all in Oaxaca), San Cristobal de las Casas (Chiapas), Acapulco (Guerrero), and Tehuacán (Puebla).

52. To add insult to injury, on June 29, following the final closure of SERESURE, in the Vatican Pope John Paul II made Rivera Carrera ("Prigione's man" as he was being popularly called) archbishop of Mexico; Berlié Belaunzarán became bishop of Yucatan; and Suárez Inda, bishop of Morelia.

53. In an ironic turn lamented by many progressivist clergy, González was made president of the Commission for Indigenous of the CEM. In the presidential elections of 2000, the archbishop made no secret of his delight at the victory of the oppositional, church-supporting National Action Party (PAN): "Never again a Mexico without Christ and his Gospel," he declared at the end of that year. In February of 2003, González was named archbishop of Durango, leaving the Archdiocese of Oaxaca temporarily without a leader.

54. Pedro Matías, "Celibato y Pederastía en Oaxaca," *Proceso Sur*, May 11, 2002, 19

55. Such was the case with the murder, in 1997, of Padre Mauro Ortiz Carreno, priest in the Oaxacan southern sierra town of San Juan Ozololtepec. The killing remains unsolved, but is believed by members of the church that he was the victim of caciques who objected to the priest's vocal denunciations of the illegal burning of local forests to grow opium.

56. Pedro Matías, "Sacerdotes Amenazados," *ProcesoSur*, November 10, 2001, 16–17. See also Amy Frumin and Kristin Ramírez, *The Untold Story of the Low Intensity War in Loxicha* (San Francisco: Global Exchange, 1998).

57. Quoted at the Latin American Meeting of Bishops that took place in April 2002 in Oaxaca City, "The Indigenous Emergence: A Challenge for the Indigenous Pastoral," presented in the forum Socio-Political and Cultural Realities of Indigenous Peoples in Mexico (in "Irrupción indígena: Enorme desafío para la Iglesia y para la sociedad," *Noticias*, April 28, 2002).

58. See Alan Knight, "Racism, Revolution, and Indigenismo: Mexico, 1910–1940," in *The Idea of Race in Latin America, 1870–1940*, ed. Richard Graham (Austin: University of Texas, 1990).

59. Judith Friedlander, "The National Indigenist Institute of Mexico Reinvents the Indian: The Pame Example," *American Ethnologist* 13, no. 2 (1986): 363–367; Hernández Díaz, "UCIRI"; Carol Nagengast and Michael Kearney, "Mixtec Ethnicity: Social Identity, Political Consciousness, and Political Activism," *Latin American Research Review* 25, no. 2 (1990): 61–91. See also Knight, "Racism, Revolution, and Indigenismo," for extensive discussion of these themes.

60. Pedro Matías, "Celibato y Pederastía en Oaxaca," *ProcesoSur*, May 11, 2002, 19.

61. A close relationship between church and government leaders in Mexico was formally reinstated by the constitutional reforms approved in 1992 and the reestablishment of diplomatic relations between the Mexican state and the Vatican. The constitutional amendments involved a reformulation of Article 130, granting the clergy more guaranteed rights. At the local level, this law signifies a tighter vigilance of a priest's activities through legal rights for the government to review his administrative and financial records.

62. Bourdieu, *Outline of a Theory of Practice*.

63. This was so even for indigenous clergy who, by virtue of their education and seminary training and affiliation with the church, are still culturally "other" to the communities in which they work.

64. Indeed, Mexican anthropologists have traditionally colluded with the state in informing and perpetuating essentialized conceptions of culture, especially as related to notions of ethnicity. See Judith Friedlander, *Being Indian in Hueyapan: A Study of Forced Identity in Contemporary Mexico* (New York: St. Martin's Press, 1975); Quetzil E. Castañeda, *In the Museum of Maya Culture* (Minneapolis: University of Minnesota, 1996); Cynthia Hewitt de Alcántara, *Anthropological Perspectives on Rural Mexico* (London: Routledge, 1984). "México Profundo" (deep Mexico), in the words of well-known Mexican anthropologist Guillermo Bonfil Batalla, was the Other Mexico, the primordial substratum of indigenous culture upon which the syncretic modern Mexican society, the fusion of the races into *la raza cósmica*, was built.

65. Charles Stewart and Rosalind Shaw, "Introduction: Problematizing Syncretism," in *Syncretism / Anti-Syncretism: The Politics of Religious Synthesis*, ed. C. Stewart and R. Shaw (New York: Routledge, 1994), 1–26.

66. See Kristin Norget, "Popular Religiosity and Progressive Theology in Oaxaca, Mexico," *Ethnology* 19 (1997): 1–17.

67. David Lehmann, "Fundamentalism and Globalism," *Third World Quarterly* 12, no. 4 (1998): 613.

68. Homi Bhabha, *The Location of Culture* (New York: Routledge, 1994), 66.

69. Alicia Barabas, *Utopias Indias: Movimientos socio-religiosos en México* (Mexico D.F.: Grijalbo, 1997).

70. UCIRI's funding comes from diverse sources: official programs of the INI, private banks, the Inter-American Foundation (IAF), the International Foundation of Organic Agricultural Movements of Germany (IFOAM). Significant donations have come for the purchase of equipment, infrastructure, and the promotion of the cultivation of organic coffee (Hernández Díaz, *Reclamos de la identidad*, 113).

71. Angrosino, "The Culture Concept and the Mission of the Catholic Church," 829.

CHAPTER 8

Mayan Catholics in Chiapas, Mexico

PRACTICING FAITH ON THEIR OWN TERMS

Christine Kovic

We are all equal, men and women, rich and poor, indigenous
and mestizo. We are all united because we are children of God.

—Juan, Mayan catechist of highland Chiapas

I was like the fish that sleep with their eyes open. For a long
time, I didn't see. I passed through communities where people
were being beaten because they didn't want to work more than
eight hours [a day]. But I saw old churches and a popular religiosity in process, and I said, "what good people." I didn't see
the tremendous oppression of which they were victims.

—Bishop Ruiz García[1]

JUAN, THE Mayan catechist, and Bishop Samuel Ruiz are two
resurgent voices that have transformed one another; they are two new voices
of the Catholic Church. During his forty years as bishop of the Diocese of San
Cristóbal de Las Casas, Chiapas, Samuel Ruiz underwent a radical transformation. He arrived in Chiapas in 1960 like a sleeping fish that neither saw nor
understood the oppression of residents of rural communities. Instead, Ruiz set
out to Christianize them, without challenging or even acknowledging the exploitation they experienced. Church leaders and government officials before
him had a five-hundred-year history of failing to listen to the voices of indigenous people. Yet Bishop Ruiz did listen to their voices and was transformed by this act. In time he and the pastoral workers of the diocese
committed themselves to working with and for "the poor."[2] They hoped to
walk with the poor in their path to liberation, in the bishop's words, to encourage the poor to become subjects of their own history.

Juan, a Tzotzil Catholic and catechist for over thirty years, speaks of the rightful equality of all—men and women, rich and poor, mestizo and indigenous—as

children of God. Like thousands of indigenous catechists throughout the diocese, he is a spiritual leader in his community. He is respected for his knowledge and experience and is regularly consulted about religious matters, community conflicts, and personal problems. Catholic residents of his community gather in a chapel several times a week to read and discuss the Bible. They share their own understandings of the word of God, which are formed by their everyday experience. These indigenous Catholics, like thousands of others in Chiapas, have affiliated with the pastoral project of the Diocese of San Cristóbal. They refer to themselves as followers of the "word of God" and differentiate themselves from Protestants and Traditionalists.

To label indigenous Catholics victims of Westernization is far too simplistic; it denies indigenous people agency. In his study of globalization and religion among Q'eqchi' Maya of Guatemala, Hans Siebers notes that Q'eqchis' do not uncritically accept religious beliefs of Catholic or Protestant churches. Instead, a religious creolization occurs in which Q'eqchis' selectively adopt and adapt their own and external religious traditions to "create their own blend of religion."[3]

In Chiapas, Word of God Catholics understand and practice their faith on their own terms. They are not "simple victims of a one-sided flow of religious beliefs and practices from other parts of the world," but agents who are actively transforming the church.[4] Mayan Catholics made the decision to form an alliance with the Diocese of San Cristóbal. The diocese became a new interlocutor, albeit a Western one, that approached indigenous people to dialogue with them and also supported them in their struggle to affirm their dignity. In this alliance, indigenous people gained concrete skills (from literacy to organizing skills), a language that justified their ongoing struggle for liberation, and a base for the development of regional networks. Through an evaluation of the development of the diocesan project under the leadership of Bishop Ruiz (1960–2000), this chapter explores the ways indigenous people and the Catholic Church in Chiapas have impacted one another and created a transformed church.[5]

The church's commitment to work with and for the indigenous poor raises a number of questions: If the poor are to be subjects of their own history, can the church as an institution act to promote indigenous rights? Is the church speaking for the poor or listening to them? Liberationist terminology often refers to the church as "the voice of the voiceless." Yet, people, no matter how marginalized, already have a voice and certainly do not need someone to speak for them. Daniel Levine notes that "being a voice for the voiceless is less difficult and demanding for institutions like the churches than is listening to what the hitherto voiceless have to say and giving them space and tools with which to act."[6] The metaphor voice of the voiceless fails to recognize the agency of indigenous people. A better metaphor for the ideal role of the church in its relationship to indigenous people is the ear of the earless. Throughout history, members of the Catholic Church and the Mexican government have ignored the voices of indigenous peoples. Both are earless while Mayan Catholics and other groups are speaking and demanding that their voices be heard. The metaphor ear of the earless allows for the recognition that indigenous people speak with their own voices. Listening to and walking with indigenous people is significantly different from the paternalism of pretending to speak for others. At times, the Church of San Cristóbal listened to and was transformed by indigenous voices; at times, the church attempted to speak for the voiceless.[7]

ENCOUNTERS: BISHOP RUIZ GARCÍA AND INDIGENOUS CATHOLICS OF CHIAPAS

One achievement of the diocesan work is that indigenous and campesino communities have taken the step to stop being the objects of the decisions of others to start to be subjects of their own history. It is worth pointing out that indigenes and campesinos' awareness of their dignity has grown, fed by the values of the gospel. They have begun to occupy the space that belongs to them in the church, and due to this, also in history. Gradually, they feel and live their own responsibility in the Church to which they belong and which belongs to them.

—Samuel Ruiz[8]

In January 1960 Samuel Ruiz was consecrated bishop of the Diocese of San Cristóbal de Las Casas in Mexico's southeastern state of Chiapas. Ruiz was an ardent anti-communist who followed the development and modernization theories of his time and planned to modernize and Westernize the peasant and indigenous inhabitants of Chiapas. Early on Bishop Ruiz elaborated a preliminary pastoral plan with three fundamental goals: first, to teach the indigenous peoples Spanish; second, to give them shoes since the majority were barefoot or wore sandals; and third, to teach them catechism. Rather than evangelize in native indigenous languages, Ruiz thought that indigenous peoples should learn Spanish since they were Mexican. In short, he believed the situation of indigenous peoples could be improved by making them more like mestizos. Decades later, after becoming known as one of the most progressive bishops of Latin American, Ruiz criticized his early goals, joking that perhaps he had desired to see people wear shoes because he was from the state of Guanajuato, a region dedicated to the production of shoes.[9]

As he spent time in rural communities, witnessing the poverty and humiliation of daily life along with the faith and hope evident in struggles for survival, Bishop Ruiz's view began to change, and he saw a need for a different type of pastoral work. The reality of political repression, poverty, racism, land scarcity, and the lack of social services demanded a pastoral line that supported indigenous people's struggles for a dignified life.

Chiapas is one of the poorest states in Mexico, and within Chiapas indigenous communities are poorest. More than half of the population of the
diocese was indigenous people who belong to a number of ethnic groups, primarily Tzotzil, Tzeltal, Ch'ol, and Tojolabal. Electricity, potable water, sewage
systems, and basic social services were seldom available in indigenous communities. Malnutrition, tuberculosis, and death from gastrointestinal and respira-
tory infections were (and still are) common.

At the same time that Bishop Ruiz began to witness exploitation in Chiapas, he was profoundly influenced by the historic meetings of the Second
Vatican Council (1962–1965) and the Latin American bishops' meeting in
Medellín, Columbia (1968). Bishop Ruiz was one of the youngest of the bishops from throughout the world to attend the meetings of Vatican II. A critical
theme of these meetings was "the opening of the church to the world," or the
recognition that the church must be involved in the realities and problems
faced by people, particularly by the oppressed.

Pope John XXIII, who convened the meetings, urged the church to read
the "signs of the times" by examining and responding to the political, economic, and social context in which the church worked. For many Latin American participants poverty and political repression were glaring "signs" of
concern. Gaudium et Spes (Pastoral Constitution on the Church in the Modern World) denounces poverty as it affirms the right of all people to have what
is necessary to live and the church's responsibility to take action in support of
the poor.

At the Medellín meetings Latin American bishops considered Vatican II's
relevance in their own context. The bishops strongly denounced the oppression and social injustice of Latin America, affirmed the church's responsibility
to work in solidarity with the poor, and called for the *concientización,* or the
promotion of political awareness and empowerment, of popular sectors.

Bishop Ruiz attended both of the meetings and in their wake was eager
to make changes in his pastoral work. He was also influenced by liberation
theology, one of several pastoral lines that emerged from the meetings of Vatican II and Medellín. First developed in Latin America, liberation theology
emphasizes that the church should work in solidarity with the poor, who are
the preferred subjects for the revelation of the word of God. It involves a re-
reading of the Bible from the perspective of the oppressed and offers hope for
change. The Kingdom of God is defined as liberation from all forms of oppression, and humans should work with God to build this kingdom on earth.[10]

At its best, the diocesan work under Ruiz's leadership was based on the
liberationist concept of *acompañamiento* (accompaniment) of the poor, that is,
the pastoral workers walked *with* the poor, not in front of them, learned from
the poor, and joined their struggle for justice.[11] Yet, as Daniel Levine writes,
"even with the best intentions, liberationist activists have had problems shed-

ding directive and paternalistic roles."[12] The bishop's conversion to the poor and the diocesan commitment to walk with the poor were not without contradictions. Although Bishop Ruiz and pastoral workers emphasized the importance of indigenous peoples being the "subjects of their own history," at times it seemed that diocesan workers saw themselves in the directive role of making indigenous subjects or in the paternalistic role of making people aware of their own dignity.

Juan's Story: A Tzotzil Catechist in Highland Chiapas

I turn to the story of Juan, a Word of God Catholic born in the highland township of San Juan Chamula. Juan now lives in a *colonia* inhabited by indigenous peoples on the outskirts of the city of San Cristóbal de Las Casas.[13] His faith and his work as a catechist can only be understood in relation to the political and economic context of his life. As Robert Orsi asserts, "Religion comes into being in an ongoing, dynamic relationship with the realities of everyday life."[14] Juan's faith and affiliation with the San Cristóbal Diocese is linked at once to his identity as a Tzotzil Maya and to the structural violence (poverty, racism, and political repression) that he resists in daily life. As noted in the introduction to this chapter, Juan affirms that the inequality present in Chiapas goes against God's will. The seemingly simple statement that all are equal in the eyes of God has great importance. It challenges the status quo in Chiapas, where a small group of mestizos have held political and economic power for decades. In his link to the church as institution, Juan recognizes an ally in resisting poverty and racism. In his work as a catechist, Juan has gained numerous skills as well as connections with Catholics throughout the diocese.

As Juan tells the story, a simple event, a literal knock on his door, unleashed a series of changes in his life. In the late 1960s Father Leopoldo Hernández, a diocesan priest, arrived at his home in Chamula to invite him to attend a catechist course in San Cristóbal de Las Casas. Juan, along with his two brothers, decided to attend the class. They would remain in the *internado*, a sort of boarding school for catechists, for four full months, studying day and night.

Why did Juan decide to leave his home in Chamula to participate in the class? He was an orphan—his mother had died when he was ten months old and his father died soon after. Like many other residents of Chamula, Juan did not own any land and had few prospects for earning a living. Perhaps in his alliance with Father Hernández and the Catholic diocese he saw the possibility, however small, of an alternative to a life that seemed to offer only poverty.

In 1994, Juan told me about his first catechist course some twenty-five years earlier. It was at the course that he learned to read and write and speak Spanish. He studied from a book with Tzotzil and Spanish on facing pages and, "with the help of God," learned to read. He was among thousands of campesinos who learned to read and write in these schools. Literacy was taught not only because it was a necessary skill for catechists (who had to be able to read the Bible and religious lessons), but also because it was a practical skill that would help the catechists in their negotiations with merchants and government officials. In addition to literacy, geography, biology, and other subjects, vocational skills were taught at these schools. Juan recalls studying long hours, "even when [they] were tired." In these months he received the sacraments of first communion and confirmation. Upon completion of the course, he received a credential formally recognizing his role as a catechist. He has saved his credential for over thirty years, guarding it among his most-valued documents.

A memorable aspect of the catechism class was meeting indigenous peoples of a variety of ethnic groups including Tzeltales, Tzotziles, Cho'les, Tojolabales, Mames, and Zoques. Juan recalls that there were more than sixty students in his group, and he made contacts and friendships with people from many regions of the diocese. In spite of the many differences among the ethnic groups—language among the most important—Juan told me that they helped one another in lessons and recognized their shared poverty and experiences of racism and political repression at the hands of the state.

Due to political conflict in Chamula in the 1980s, Juan and his family were forced to leave. They moved to the highland township of San Pedro Chenalhó, and then to the colonia in San Cristóbal, where they now reside. Juan works as a peon, or day laborer, in the city, constructing homes, roads, and buildings. The work is difficult and wages are low. Employment is intermittent, so he has no regular income.

He views his work as a catechist as a *cargo,* a duty or responsibility that he carries out for the benefit of his community. He receives no monetary compensation for his work. Juan carries out the traditional tasks of catechists: helping people prepare for the sacraments of weddings, first communions, and the baptisms of their children. He is one of several catechists in his community, but as the oldest, he is highly respected. In the community's local chapel, Juan reads from the Bible at religious celebrations held several times a week. A priest arrives to celebrate mass every few months, so responsibility for worship and daily spiritual concerns remains in the hands of indigenous lay Catholics. This is similar to other indigenous communities in Chiapas, although in more isolated rural communities, priests visit less frequently.

Juan considers one of his most important tasks as a catechist to be the building a community in which people share their faith, spiritual support, material goods, and, in many cases, create political alliances to resist poverty and oppression. One song that Juan learned in his 1969 catechist course begins like this:

Community, Community,
How much joy I find in you . . .
So I want to commit myself to the creation
Of a great community,
Full of faith, full of love,
To reach happiness.

Within the colonia where he lives, Juan works to build community by visiting the ill, mediating in local disputes, and sharing his scarce resources with those in need, among other tasks. Yet his work to build community extends to the highland townships of Teopisca and Chenalhó, where Juan travels to preach and visit with indigenous Catholics. For example, one week in the winter of 1995 Juan and another man from his colonia spent four full days fasting along with twenty-five men and women to give moral support to the lone catechist of a community in Teopisca. The Teopisca catechist was recently widowed, left with six young children. Afraid that the catechist would loose his faith during the crisis, community members organized a fast to show him their support and to pray for strength. The presence of two men from another community served as a visible reminder of the network of Catholics, who were willing to give their time (of course, Juan and others gave up four days' pay as well) to make a physical sacrifice by participating in the fast and to offer material support.

In addition to these visits, Juan meets monthly with Tzotzil catechists of his region to share information, discuss biblical readings, and make decisions about pastoral work and participation in regional or diocesan-wide events. At an annual catechist course, participants share news of community achievements, attempt to work through difficulties, and discuss changes or innovations in liturgy. In all of these events, the Tzotzil catechists recognize their commonalities and strengthen the networks they can count on for support. In other events, such as Juan's 1969 catechist course and the 1974 Indigenous Congress described below, campesinos from a number of ethnic groups recognize their shared oppression and shared struggles for liberation.

Within his community, Juan and other Catholics reject the use of alcohol, asserting that it goes against the will of God. This is not a strict moralism, but a rejection of the suffering caused by drinking. Juan's father drank excessively, which eventually led to his death. Drinking is criticized because for those living in extreme poverty, purchasing alcohol consumes precious cash. Drinking is also criticized because it is linked to domestic violence. In rejecting alcohol, Catholics reassert some control over their own lives and demand self-respect. They contrast drinking to thinking and emphasize the importance of keeping one's thoughts with God.

This rejection of alcohol is one of the many ways that indigenous peoples appropriate Catholicism and make it relevant to their own lives. Catholic doctrine does not prohibit the use of alcohol, although some priests in the diocese criticized excessive drinking, especially that associated with festivals. Yet, the priests' criticism of drinking was based on a moral critique, one often associated with an attempt to "civilize" indigenous peoples. In contrast, indigenous Catholics have organized themselves in recent years to limit problem drinking in their communities as a way of liberating themselves from economic and social control. They note that mestizo merchants profit from alcohol sales. (Many Zapatista supporters similarly reject the use of alcohol and have set up checkpoints to block its entrance into their communities.) In many cases it is women who have led this temperance movement, citing the link between alcohol abuse and domestic violence and criticizing the "waste" of money that should support the household.[15]

In his alliance with the Catholic Church, Juan has gained a number of skills, from literacy to organizing skills. In practicing his faith, Juan shares spiritual support with others and on a local level fights for a dignified life in his rejection of alcohol. He is part of an extensive network of indigenous Catholics who are united in their common vision of working toward the establishment of the Kingdom of God, a world with justice and equality for all. From this story of one catechist's work, I turn to a number of important transformations in the diocesan process.

FORMING CATECHISTS: GATHERING AND SPREADING THE WORD

In the early 1960s the diocese opened a number of schools for catechists, and in the ten years that followed, seven hundred catechists passed through, many walking long distances to attend. The Diocese of San Cristóbal covers more than thirty-six thousand square kilometers and contains hundreds of rural communities, many of which were accessible only by foot.[16] Like many other Latin American bishops, Ruiz recognized the necessity of training catechists who would assist in carrying out pastoral work. Initially, this was a pragmatic decision, but in time, indigenous catechists would play a critical role in transforming the church.

In 1962 two catechist schools were established in San Cristóbal, one by religious women of the Divine Shepard congregation and another by the Marist order. The Jesuit order established a third school in Bachajón (northeastern Chiapas). Initially, the schools followed a vertical or top-down model in which pastoral agents and other teachers imparted their knowledge in Spanish. These schools provided courses in Bible instruction and skills such as baking, sewing, and agriculture. Students like Juan were selected by pastoral agents and attended courses for three to six months.

The teachers treated students as if they were passive receptors of evangelization and failed to address the socio-cultural context of their peasant and indigenous students. Rather than dialogue, the schools followed a "banking model" of education with the expectation that catechists would receive information in class and repeat it in communities. This was the style of class that Juan attended. In spite of the shortcomings of the method, he was nonetheless impressed with the class.

It is not surprising that many catechists were frustrated by the top-down approach. In a 1968 meeting in the Tzeltal zone several indigenous catechists expressed their discontent: "The Church and the Word of God have said things to save our souls, but we don't know how to save our bodies. While we work for our own and others' salvation, we suffer hunger, illness, poverty, and death. Now we know the Bible, its authors, the names of its books, . . . we sing and pray every Sunday. . . . [T]here are catechists, choirs and leaders, but hunger and illness and poverty continue without end."[17] The catechists' concern that the church be relevant to the structural conditions of everyday life resonated with the conclusions of Vatican II and the Medellín meetings and the concerns of liberation theology.

In response to the "signs of the times," Bishop Ruiz and pastoral workers sought a new model for catechesis in the 1970s. Rather than planning the meetings themselves, pastoral workers began to consult with indigenous catechists to plan meetings around themes relevant to their lived experiences. In a 1971 catechist meeting in the township of Ocosingo (a primarily Tzeltal region), participants redefined the function of catechists, naming their method *Tiwanej* (Tzeltal for the one who gathers and spreads the word in community) rather than as *nopteswanej* (Tzeltal for teacher).[18] The new catechism classes were to be participatory, with community members playing an active role in selecting themes for group discussion. Recognizing that catechists had to be responsible to the people they served, communities rather than priests were to select catechists.

In the early 1970s in Ocosingo, Dominican missionaries along with Marist brother Javier Vargas recognized the similarity between the peasants' search for land and the Bible's second book, "Exodus." The misery and oppression of the Catholics and their search for a "promised land," dignity, and liberty was described as an exodus, and the book became a central theme of catechesis.[19] In a process that began in the 1930s but continued throughout the 1970s, peasants who had worked on plantations near Ocosingo, Altamirano, Comitán, Las Margaritas, and other towns colonized the Lancandón rain forest in order to cultivate their own land.[20] Peasants encountered tremendous hardships—disease and a lack of potable water, social services, and schools—but also the hope of freedom from the oppressive conditions of working for others. Inspired to respond to this reality, Javier Vargas and other pastoral agents worked with Tzeltal Catholics to develop a new catechism that addressed the peasants' struggle for a dignified life.

One lesson was based on Exodus 3:7–12, in which God promises to liberate the sufferings of the Israelites in Egypt and to lead them to a land "flowing with milk and honey." To facilitate group discussion, the lesson gives an example of catechists' reflection on this reading: "God wants us to stop everything that crushes us. The Word of God tells us that as a community we must get out to look for freedom. God says that if we are looking to make our lives better and for freedom, He will be accompanying us. We have already said that we are crushed because there is no accord among us, because we are divided."[21] In another lesson, catechists reflect on cultural oppression: "The Second Commandment of God's Law says this: Love your brother as you love yourself. . . . We Indians are made by God and therefore we are of value and have a force of growth in our heart. Brothers, let us not crush ourselves. Let us recognize the force that there is in our Indian heart and let us make it grow."[22]

In the new model of catechesis, community members met in local chapels once or more a week to reflect on and analyze biblical readings in the context of their everyday lives.[23] In this process indigenous Catholics became the agents of inculturation as they appropriated and interpreted texts that were meaningful to their way of life. The new methodology for catechism took seriously "the notion that ordinary Catholics are protagonists of their own evangelization rather than mere recipients."[24]

INDIGENOUS CONGRESS OF 1974:
UNITY AND EQUALITY

The First Indigenous Congress, held in San Cristóbal de Las Casas in October 1974, marked a watershed in the political mobilization of peasants in Chiapas as well as in the diocese's commitment to working with the poor. The importance of this congress cannot be overemphasized; it was the first opportunity in five hundred years for the four ethnic groups to unite and speak about their situation in public spaces that had been dominated by mestizos. Dr. Manuel Velasco Suárez, then governor of Chiapas, conceived the congress in order to commemorate the five hundredth anniversary of the birth of Fray Bartolomé de Las Casas, remembered as "Defender of the Indigenous."[25] Recognizing the weakness of the government's networks in indigenous communities, the governor asked Bishop Ruiz to assist in convening the congress. The bishop agreed to assist on the condition that it would not be a tourist or folkloric event, but rather that the indigenous would be permitted to give their word in public after living in silence for so many years.

Preparations for the congress began a year prior to the event and lay the groundwork for much of the organizing that would follow. Between October of 1973 and September of 1974 local, regional, and municipal meetings were held in indigenous communities to discuss the upcoming event. Initially, people met to "know our reality," that is, to talk about the situation of indigenous communities, and to discuss Fray Bartolomé de Las Casas's work in relation to indigenous rights.

Hopes, desires, and future goals were also addressed, and each of the four major ethnic groups of the diocese—Tzeltales, Tzotziles, Ch'oles, and Tojolabales—prepared their presentation on the themes of the congress: land, commerce, education, and health. In the course of these meetings, representatives were democratically selected to attend the congress. The social conditions of the early 1970s favored the beginning of an organizational process. At this time, there were no institutional political structures representing the indigenous people of the state. Day laborers who worked on plantations were challenging their oppression and taking over land; and people were calling for an end to commercial exploitation.[26]

Over 1,230 indigenous delegates from 327 communities from the state of Chiapas attended the meetings and reached agreements on each of the four themes discussed. Land distribution was of special importance given the existence of large estates and plantations (many of them holding land in a way that was illegal under the Mexican Constitution) in Chiapas.

The indigenous participants recognized that they shared similar problems and could unite in their political struggles. For example, this was expressed in the final agreements on land: "We all want to resolve the problems of land, but we are divided, each one on his own. Because of this we do not have strength. We are looking for the organization of each group in order to have strength because unity gives us strength."[27]

The importance of the event in uniting indigenous peoples from various regions, and in initiating organization beyond local communities, is worth comment. Juan attended the conference and was most impressed by the presence of so many indigenous peoples from throughout the diocese. In 1994, twenty years after the congress, he proudly recalled the large number of Tzotziles, Tzeltales, Cho'les, and Tojolabales who united to exchange ideas, reach agreements, and even dance and play traditional music.

But the notion of "unity" described in the Indigenous Congress was, in 1974, a goal to strive for rather than the reality. There was not, and is not, unity within or between indigenous communities, and different groups within communities chose distinct political options. Some affiliated with the Partido Revolucionario Institucional (Institutional Revolutionary Party or PRI, Mexico's ruling party from 1929 to 2000) in order to receive benefits (however small) in the form of land or credit. Beginning in the 1970s, increasing numbers of indigenous peoples joined one of several Protestant churches. According to government census data, the state's Protestant population was less than 5 percent in 1970 and over 21 percent in 2000.

In writing about the current crisis of the progressive Latin American Catholic Church, John Burdick urges scholars to listen to a wide range of voices. Burdick warns that listening to only clergy, pastoral agents, and a small group of the most enthusiastic Catholics will not reveal contradictions in and discontent with the progressive church.[28] Pastoral agents in Chiapas certainly would have benefited from carefully listening to diverse voices, including those of PRI-supporters, Protestants, among others. Understanding the reasons for dissent would have allowed the diocese to critically assess its project. Nonetheless, in the context of political repression and the polarization between the Mexican state and the Diocese of San Cristóbal, possibilities for dialogue between these two actors and between the diocese and other actors were limited.

Father Pablo Iribarren, a Dominican priest who carefully recorded much of the diocese's history in published and unpublished manuscripts, remarked on the importance of the congress, noting that one of its key achievements for the poor was "the discovery that the plan of God was not their actual situation of misery and marginalization. God had other more just and kind projects for them. But in their action, the projects were impeded by the ambition of the powerful and the lack of adequate channels for their voices to be heard."[29]

Here it is worth pointing out that the poor did not suddenly wake up to "discover" their oppression, it was obvious enough. Perhaps they realized that their suffering contradicted the will of God, perhaps they were already aware of this. What I would argue was the most important outcome of the congress is that the indigenous peoples recognized the Catholic Church as a new interlocutor (albeit a mestizo institution) that was willing to engage in a dialogue with them and support their struggle for dignity. In this sense, rather than a "voice of the voiceless," the church served as an "ear," listening to the voices of the marginalized. It is not that the church spoke *for* the poor; they could already speak for themselves. The church listened to them and, as Pablo Iribarren stated, provided a channel for their voices to be heard.

The congress was also important in establishing logistic and symbolic ties between the four ethnic groups. Indigenous representatives—*hombres de buena palabra* (men of good word) or those who were consistent in what they said and what they did—were elected to take the proposals of the congress to their communities. It provided the space for the formation of independent peasant organizations. In fact, an organization named after Fray Bartolomé de Las Casas was formed to continue the congress's work. A Marist brother from the Tojolabal zone was named president and other pastoral agents served as its advisors. In 1977, one of the advisors to this group asked, "Who will be the new Fray Bartolomé de Las Casas?" The Indians answered, "We will. We are Bartolomé. We needed one before because everything was decided in Spain, where we couldn't go and where we didn't have a voice; then they spoke for us. Now we are beginning to speak for ourselves."[30]

At the same time, the congress also had an important impact on the consciousness of the pastoral workers of the Diocese of San Cristóbal. They recognized the Indians' ability to organize, the values that can come from evangelization, and the evidence of a liberating process supported by the Gospel. Furthermore, they decided that it was necessary to revise all pastoral work.[31] Bishop Ruiz later reflected on the importance of the 1974 congress: "When the pastoral agents of the Diocese saw and heard what the indigenous people were saying about their own situation, it was very clear that our Pastoral Plan had been elaborated without taking into account the aspirations, necessities, and hopes of the communities. In response to this appeal we made a Plan that tried to respond in some way from the faith of the necessities described."[32]

In a November 1975 meeting (which later became known as the first Diocesan Assembly) priests, nuns, and lay workers began to plan the new direction of their pastoral work.[33] In this historic meeting, two key lines of work emerged: first, a commitment to "work with and for the poor" and, second, support for the formation of an autochthonous church.[34] Linking their work to the meetings of Vatican II and Medellín as well as to liberation theology, the diocese chose at this 1975 meeting "the preferential option for the poor" as the path of all future work.

The second line was more fully developed in the 1980s and 1990s and would involve a series of changes in the diocese. A central element of this process involved an attempt to "inculturate" pastoral practices by recognizing and respecting the connection between faith and culture and by taking culture into account in evangelization. In supporting the formation of an autochthonous church, Bishop Ruiz and the pastoral workers began to educate themselves about indigenous customs and beliefs. "Traditional" Mayan customs were incorporated in liturgy; ancient stories, symbols, and myths were reexamined; and some pastoral workers learned indigenous languages.

Another element of the project of building an autochthonous church was an attempt to change the very structures of the church to make it more relevant to the indigenous and rural communities. Over time, this led to the ordination of indigenous deacons who, along with catechists, would be responsible for religious matters on a local level. Their voices would lead the church in new and unanticipated directions.

REPRESSION AND RESISTANCE IN THE 1980S

The decade of the 1980s began with soldiers and police killing twelve peasants in Wolochán in the northern township of Sitalá. This event, referred to as the massacre of Wolochán, foreshadowed the violence that would come as well as the difficulties of defining the role of pastoral workers in relation to indigenous peoples and campesinos. During this decade, campesino organizations independent of the government began to form in several regions of Chiapas at the same time that government repression against them increased.[35]

The conflict in Wolochán began decades before 1980 when a group of campesinos petitioned the government office of agrarian reform to gain legal rights to the land once occupied by the plantation of Wolochán.[36] Following the Indigenous Congress a peasant organization of the same name developed in the region. In 1980 pastoral workers realized that they could not offer a viable political solution to the problem and stopped advising the organization. The Socialist Worker's Party (PST, a left-of-center organization that was co-opted to be a satellite group of the PRI) stepped in. The group was pushing for land invasions at a national level and proposed an invasion at Wolochán. The invasion took place, and soon after, the police arrived accompanied by large landowners of the area. Father Mardonio Morales—a Jesuit priest of the diocese—met with the state governor on June 2, 1980, and the next day the governor went to visit the plantation. Nonetheless, on June 15, 1980, police and soldiers arrived and began firing at the families who occupied the land. The firing lasted two and a half hours, leaving at least twelve people dead and countless others wounded. The government later offered to purchase the land for the peasants, but only under the condition that the peasants would pay the government back within ten years and affiliate with the PRI. The peasants refused.

The case of Wolochán exemplifies the tensions implicit in the church's work to accompany the poor in their struggles for land and liberation. Ideally, the pastoral workers walk *beside* the poor, but this position is difficult given the privilege of pastoral workers in comparison to peasants. The vast majority of the pastoral workers are mestizos, and, although many live modestly (having voluntarily renounced some of their economic privilege in order to walk with the poor), they have the backing of religious orders or other institutions. This is not to deny that pastoral workers sacrificed a great deal; because of their political commitments, some received threats and several were jailed in the 1990s. Even in accompanying the poor, a dramatic social and economic distance divided pastoral workers and those they accompanied; pastoral agents are aware of and struggle with this distance. Yet increasing government repression against campesino groups and the diocese strengthened the alliance between the later two.

Beginning in 1981, thousands of Guatemalan refugees fleeing the repressive regimes of Lucas García, Ríos Mott, and Mejía Víctores began to arrive in Chiapas. In the township of Ocosingo, which shares a border with Guatemala, pastoral workers together with the Christian Solidarity Committee attended to some fifteen thousand Guatemalan refugees in the Lacandón rain forest, providing material assistance in the form of food, clothing, and housing. When the Mexican government "relocated" a number of refugee camps (in some cases violently), the diocese responded by firmly denouncing these human rights abuses. The government responded in turn by criticizing the diocese's work.

In the midst of this oppression, pastoral workers elaborated a 1986 pastoral plan that would guide their future work. The doctrinal framework begins, "We believe in God our Father who wills the lives of his children and a life of abundance," and contains objectives in the areas of evangelization, concientización, accompaniment, culture, communications, and coordination. The plan asserts that the church will commit itself "to serve the people, inserting itself, as Jesus, in the process of the liberation of the oppressed in which they are the agents of their own history, and together we will build a new society in anticipation of the Kingdom."[37]

Of particular interest is recognition of the importance of culture in the process of evangelization. Actions related to this area include learning indigenous language and history as well as promoting cultural expression. One of the pastoral goals is "to insert ourselves (as a Church) into the culture of our people and to take on the social utopia hidden there, accompanying them on their historic path and accepting the sacramental signs of the Indians and their ministries."[38] In their recognition of its "social utopia," pastoral workers challenge development strategies that attempt to modernize and Westernize the supposedly backward peasants. Yet the idea of a social utopia also represents a romantic construction of indigenous and campesino life.

"LET MEXICO SPEAK!" SOCIAL MOVEMENTS OF THE 1990S

In 1988 Carlos Salinas de Gortari won the presidency in an election clouded by charges that his party, the PRI, had committed massive electoral fraud. "Let Mexico Speak!" was Salinas's campaign slogan. His invitation for Mexico to speak certainly did not include indigenous Mexico. Salinas followed his predecessor Miguel de la Madrid in implementing structural adjustment policies set forth by the International Monetary Fund and World Bank. For rural producers, these policies meant dramatic cuts in public spending and the privatization of the once inalienable *ejidal* lands. In response to these reforms, numerous organizations of indigenous people carried out local, regional, and national protests to draw attention to their demands. Even as the state and national government repressed these groups the protests intensified.

On January 1, 1994, during the last year of Salinas's presidency, thousands of members of the Ejército Zapatista de Liberación Nacional (Zapatista Army of National Liberation, EZLN) took over seven towns in Chiapas and demanded basic human rights—land, housing, jobs, food, health care, democracy, and justice—with much emphasis on the rights of peasants and indigenous peoples. While several Zapatista leaders had participated in the pastoral process of the diocese before joining the EZLN, the diocese did not condone armed violence. Yet, the Mexican government and other sectors attempted to discredit the Zapatistas and their demands by claiming that outsiders—Bishop Ruiz, priests and nuns of the diocese, and the mestizo Subcomandante Marcos—had manipulated them. Attributing the struggles in Chiapas to "outside" actors fails to grant any agency to the indigenous and peasant poor; it assumes that indigenous Catholics are passive victims of the church and other institutions.

Within the much publicized polemic on whether Bishop Ruiz contributed to the formation of the EZLN, the many nonviolent movements supported by the diocese, movements which preceded the public appearance of the Zapatistas, are rarely mentioned, let alone examined with any seriousness. Yet, in the early 1990s, several indigenous organizations whose members were motivated by their faith and supported by the diocese engaged in acts of nonviolent resistance to demand that their voices be heard. Two such groups are Xi' Nich' (The Ant) and Las Abejas (The Bees)—their names reflecting the collective base of their organizations.[39] These groups grew out of local concern about injustices; in a sense, this same repression and resistance began with the arrival of the Spanish and has persisted for hundreds of years. The historic context of the 1980s—the work of the economic crisis, the growing campesino mobilization throughout the state, and government repression that accompanied this mobilization—created the conditions for the formation of these groups. Specific human rights violations or community crises pushed people to establish formal organizations of resistance. A third group, CODIMUJ, or the Diocesan Coordination of Women, brings together Catholic women from throughout the diocese to participate in local discussion groups, regional workshops, cooperatives, and other activities.

The foundation for Xi'Nich' was built in December of 1991 when members of three indigenous organizations began a peaceful demonstration in the central plaza of the city of Palenque. Some two hundred campesinos participated in the protest, demanding public works and services for their communities (potable water, roads), the regularization of land and a solution to agrarian conflicts, support for agricultural production, interpreters in government offices, the democratic election of municipal officials, and participation in local radio, among other things. Once the campesinos began their protest in the central plaza, they stayed there for days, insisting that the government see them and hear them and that it respond to their demands. In the context of racism in Mexico, their demand to be heard was a powerful statement.

On the third day of the protest a large group of police stormed the plaza, hitting and handcuffing the protesters, pushing them into trucks, and arresting 103 people.[40] After being held in the state attorney general's office for two days, 93 of the prisoners were released. (The remaining protesters were released a month later.) Since the state government had refused to respond to their demands, the protesters decided to go to the federal authorities to try to make them listen. On March 7, 1992, 700 Indians from over one hundred communities began the Xi'Nich' March for Peace and Human Rights of the

Indigenous Peoples. (The name Xi'Nich' signifies "ant" in the Ch'ol language.) Ch'ol, Tzeltal, and Zoque Indians marched for fifty days from Palenque to Mexico City.

The march was a strategic attempt to broaden support for their demands. As the Ants passed through villages on their way to Mexico City, people provided food, clothing, and lodging to the marchers, and the campesinos saw that their struggle had much in common with that of campesinos in other regions. Representatives of the federal government met with Xi'Nich' marchers just outside Mexico City, in a sort of "damage control," wanting to keep the indigenous invisible, to prevent them from entering the city. The officials agreed to comply with their demands, although, in many cases, these were empty promises. Then the marchers convened at the Basilica in Mexico City to give thanks to the Virgin of Guadalupe. In an attempt to discredit the march, the newspaper *El Excelsior* wrote on April 20, 1992, that the marchers were "recruited" by the pastoral workers for political motives and did not even know why they had gone to Mexico City.

In the highland Tzotzil township of Chenalhó, Las Abejas came together during a violent agrarian conflict in 1992.[41] As members of one community were urged to join one of two opposing factions and to take up arms to defend themselves, a group of Catholics decided to take a third path. This group, which became the civil organization Las Abejas, opted for nonviolence and insisted on the necessity of dialogue to resolve the crisis. Following arrests and assassinations in their communities, members of Las Abejas joined together in fasting and prayer in a chapel to decide what to actions to take. They marched forty-one kilometers from Chenalhó to San Cristóbal and held a sit-in in front of the cathedral. After a second march and additional protests, the prisoners were released. Las Abejas's struggle expanded beyond the immediate conflict to include the defense of a broad range of political and economic rights. Members fought for the right to work the land, formed cooperatives for the production of coffee and honey, and protested electoral fraud, impunity, and corruption. At the same time, Las Abejas members struggle for reconciliation, that is, they work to restore their own dignity while rejecting violence, vengeance, and hatred.

In December of 1997 Las Abejas attracted international attention when forty-five of its members were killed while praying in a local chapel in Acteal, Chenalhó. Dozens of men belonging to the paramilitary group La Mascara Roja (The Red Mask) carried out the massacre. Although Mexico's attorney general declared that the massacre was caused by a family feud, investigations revealed that high-ranking military officers were complicit in the massacre.

The Diocese of San Cristóbal also played an important role in the formation of women's groups. Women religious (nuns) have supported local women's groups since the 1970s. The commitment to women's rights was formalized in 1992 with the creation of CODIMUJ, the Diocesan Coordination of Women.[42] Thousands of indigenous and mestiza women (primarily members of impoverished communities) take part in CODIMUJ. At the local level, women meet in community discussion groups to read the Bible "with the eyes, mind, and heart of a woman." At regional meetings and workshops, women share their experiences and recognize their common problems. Many CODIMUJ participants also take part in political organizations such as Xi'Nich'. They have joined state, national, and international events such as marches for International Women's Day and the World March of Women 2000.

Through its evangelization process, human rights courses, and other types of institutional support, the Diocese of San Cristóbal contributed to the formation of Xi' Nich', Las Abejas, and CODIMUJ. Pastoral workers literally accompanied campesinos in their struggles, walking with them in marches and pilgrimages, helping to find legal assistance, and facilitating connections with regional and international organizations. Clergy provided resources, strategic support, and even theological validation to the groups.[43] This support does not mean, as the state and federal government have claimed, that the members of Las Abejas and Xi'Nich' were controlled or manipulated by pastoral workers. Such claims erase indigenous agency, assuming that indigenous people cannot make decisions or engage in political actions on their own. At the same time, these claims attempt to silence indigenous protesters by discrediting their demands. To the contrary, indigenous people critically assess ideas and forms of support emanating from diverse "external" actors and decide when and under what conditions to form alliances with diverse groups. In the religious arena, some indigenous people identify as Word of God Catholics, while others identify themselves as Traditionalists or Protestants. In the political arena, some affiliate with the PRI, others with the EZLN, and others with independent organizations of nonviolent resistance.

As indigenous peoples in Chiapas engage in political protest to demand their rights, they challenge the status quo and the "violent peace,"[44] or pseudo-peace, that Spanish and mestizos have tried to preserve for hundreds of years. This violent peace failed to address the just demands of the impoverished peasants and indigenous peoples. In response to attacks by the Mexican media following the EZLN uprising, Bishop Ruiz repeatedly stated that the Diocese of San Cristóbal did not condone the use of arms. Yet he added that if a popular movement for social justice had not arisen in his decades as bishop, then he would consider his own work a failure.

CONCLUSION

As stated at the beginning of this chapter, listening to and taking seriously the voices of indigenous peoples transformed the Diocese of San Cristóbal. At their best, pastoral agents served as an ear of an earless church and engaged in a dialogue of mutual exchange rather than assuming a position of superiority in disseminating knowledge. Indigenous Catholics found in the church an ally in their struggles against cultural domination, extreme poverty, and political repression. These Catholics "indigenized" beliefs and practices, making them relevant to their lives.[45] Two important examples of this are the creation of a new role for catechists and the critique of alcohol.

The process of listening to the poor, being an ear of the earless, in the Diocese of San Cristóbal is not without contradictions and tensions. Clergy denounce injustice in Chiapas and challenge the Mexican state and the Catholic Church, two groups with a long history of ignoring indigenous voices. Yet, clergy can lose sight of their own class, race, and gender privilege and the ways this privilege distances clergy from Mayan Catholics. This privilege can also limit clergy's ability to understand indigenous people on their own terms. The diocesan process advanced in spite of these contradictions because pastoral agents spent time in rural communities listening to Mayan Catholics. Serving as an ear of the earless, pastoral agents could transcend, at least partially, the paternalistic role of being voice of the voiceless.

In spite of the many accusations lodged against the diocese by the state and federal government, Bishop Ruiz was asked to be the official mediator in the peace talks between the two parties in conflict, the EZLN and the federal government. The first round of peace talks began on February 21, 1994, in San Cristóbal's cathedral. In a country that spent a great part of the nineteenth century fighting over the separation of church and state, the political role of a religious figure appeared alarming and difficult for many Mexican politicians and intellectuals to accept. With the dramatic events of the Zapatista uprising and Ruiz's role as mediator, the Catholic Diocese of San Cristóbal received much national and international attention. But the long-term view of the diocesan process was neglected as the public came to know the diocese out of context, as if the Zapatistas themselves had brought it into existence. In May of 1998, Bishop Ruiz renounced his role as official mediator, citing a lack of commitment on the part of the government. The negotiations have been at a standstill since then.

The political scenario at the national and state level is changing as a result of the 2000 elections. President Vicente Fox of the National Action Party (PAN) breaks the PRI's seventy-one years of control, and Pablo Salazar Mendiguchía, of a multi-party coalition, is the first non-PRI governor of Chiapas. At the federal level, Fox's victory opened the possibility that the thousands of federal troops stationed in Chiapas would be removed and that Congress would approve the San Andrés Accords on Indigenous Rights and Culture.[46] At the state level, these changes opened the possibility that the government would punish the intellectual authors of the Acteal massacre and dismantle the paramilitary groups. Yet a few years into their terms, the situation seems less hopeful. A strong military presence continues in many regions of Chiapas. In April 2001 Congress passed a watered-down version of the San Andrés Accords that fails to support the indigenous demand for autonomy. In many ways, the state and federal government are managing conflict without addressing the underlying poverty, historical racism, and political repression that gave rise to the numerous popular movements in past decades and led to the Zapatista rebellion.

In this context, the Diocese of San Cristóbal could continue to accompany poor campesinos in their struggles for a dignified life. The reasons behind the diocesan commitment to work with and for the poor continue to exist. On March 31, 2000, Felipe Arizmendi, former bishop of Tapachula (Chiapas), was named Ruiz's successor. There is much concern that that the new bishop might try to dismantle Ruiz's work, as many bishops replacing progressives have done in Latin America. The new bishop could separate faith and politics, withdraw to exclusively administering sacraments, and accommodate those in power to avoid conflict. There is also hope that the new bishop can be transformed by his experience in Chiapas as Bishop Ruiz was. While it is too soon to assess the work of Bishop Arizmendi, it is clear that the thousands of Mayan Catholics who are building a new church will play a central role in defining the direction of the diocese's work. It is precisely because indigenous Catholics have the power to practice their faith in their communities that their work continues. What remains to be seen is whether the church hierarchy (from Bishop Arizmendi to the Vatican) will have the capacity to listen to these new voices.

NOTES

Some sections of this paper will appear in *Walking with One Heart: The Catholic Church and Human Rights in Highland Chiapas*, (Austin: University of Texas Press, forthcoming).

1. Quoted in Carlos Fazio, *Samuel Ruiz, El Caminante* (Mexico City: Espasa Calpe, 1994), 106.
2. In numerous diocesan documents and meetings of the 1970s, the term "the poor" (*los pobres* in Spanish) was used to describe an undifferentiated group of people suffering similarly from structures of inequality. This designation reifies a heterogeneous group of people. In time, the pastoral workers recognized the specific role of ethnicity in structuring the marginality and poverty of indigenous peoples of Chiapas. That is, they recognized the necessity of seeing the intersection of class and ethnicity. Nonetheless, the labeling of all oppressed peoples in the diocese as the poor (or at times *los hermanos,* the brothers) would continue.
3. Hans Siebers, "Globalization and Religious Creolization among the Q'eqchi'es of Guatemala," in *Latin American Religion in Motion*, ed. Christian Smith and Joshua Prokopy (New York: Routledge, 1999), 267–268.
4. Ibid., 272.
5. Samuel Ruiz formally retired as bishop at age seventy-five in 1999 in accordance with canonical law. On March 31, 2000, the Vatican named Felipe Arizmendi as his successor. Enrique Díaz Díaz was consecrated auxiliary bishop in July of 2003.

6. Daniel Levine, *Popular Voices in Latin American Catholicism* (Princeton: Princeton University Press, 1992), 6.

7. Data for this paper is drawn from interviews, participant observation, and archival research conducted in San Cristóbal from 1993 to 2002.

8. Samuel Ruiz García, *"En Esta Hora de Gracia,"* Pastoral Letter (Mexico City: Dabar, 1993), 33.

9. José Álvarez Icaza, "Don Samuel Ruiz García: Un acercamiento," in *Chiapas: El Factor Religioso. Revista Académica para el estudio de las Religiones*, vol. 2 (Bosques de Echegaray: Estudio Científico de las Religiones, 1998).

10. Bishop Ruiz has publicly distanced himself from liberation theology, most likely to avoid his work being de-legitimized in the context of Vatican accusations of it being Marxist. Ruiz has referred to the work of his diocese as *teología india* (indigenous theology), or indigenous reflection on their faith. He argues that all theology is liberation: "If some think that there is or was a theology of slavery, then they do not understand what theology is. . . . All theology has to express the mystery of Christ who came to save humanity and not to defend slavery." Sylvia Marcos, "Si no hay opción por el pobre no hay Iglesia de Cristo" (Interview with Samuel Ruiz), *Memoria* 115 (July 1999): 11.

11. For a discussion of the role of accompaniment in liberation theology, especially in Latin America, see Phillip Berryman, *Stubborn Hope: Religion, Politics, and Revolution in Central America* (New York and Maryknoll: The New Press—Orbis Books, 1994).

12. Daniel Levine, "On Premature Reports of the Death of Liberation Theology," *The Review of Politics* 57 (winter 1995): 105–131.

13. Juan is one of many Catholic converts who have been violently exiled from their native homes in the highland township of San Juan Chamula. When a family is exiled (or expelled), they may be jailed, beaten, or threatened; their home may be robbed or burned; and their crops may be destroyed. Then they are told that they must leave the community or suffer further violence. Those responsible for expulsion are *caciques*, or locally entrenched indigenous leaders, yet state and federal government officials play a critical role in expulsion by their failure to address the issue in spite of hundreds of complaints over decades. Complex political, economic, and religious factors underlie expulsion. For a detailed analysis of expelled Catholics see Christine Kovic, "Walking with One Heart: Human Rights and the Catholic among the Maya of Highland Chiapas" (Ph.D. diss., City University of New York, 1997).

14. Robert Orsi, "Everyday Miracles: The Study of Lived Religion," in *Lived Religion in America: Toward a History of Practice*, ed. David Hall (Princeton: Princeton University Press 1997), 7.

15. On the movement against alcohol in indigenous communities, see Christine Eber, "'Take My Water': Liberation through Prohibition in San Pedro Chenalhó, Chiapas," *Social Science and Medicine* 53 (2001): 251–262; and Christine Eber and Christine Kovic, *Women in Chiapas: Making History in Times of Struggle and Hope* (New York: Routledge, 2003).

16. The entire state of Chiapas comprised a single diocese until 1964, when the church at Bishop Ruiz's suggestion divided it into three separate dioceses. He decided to work in eastern Chiapas, the area with the highest concentration of peasants and indigenous peoples. This diocese was named San Cristóbal de Las Casas.

17. Quoted in Reyna Matilde Coello Castro, "Proceso Catequistico en la Zona Tzeltal y Desarrollo Social" (thesis, Universidad Autonoma de Tlaxcala, 1991), 61.

18. Ibid.

19. Ibid. On Tzeltal catechists, see also Xóchitl Leyva Solano, "Catequistas, Misioneros y Tradiciones en las Cañadas," in *Chiapas: Los Rumbos de otra historia*, ed. Juan Pedro Viqueira and Mario Humberto Ruz (Mexico City: UNAM, CIESAS, CEMCA,

UG, 1995), 375–405; and Jan De Vos, *Una tierra para sembrar sueños: Historia reciente de la Selva Lacandona, 1950–2000* (Mexico City: CIESAS, 2002), 215–243. For a detailed account of catechists of the Diocese of San Cristóbal and democratization, see J. Charlene Floyd, "The Government Shall Be upon Their Shoulders: The Catholic Church and Democratization in Chiapas, Mexico" (Ph.D. diss., City University of New York, 1997).

20. For a detailed discussion of this process, see Ascencio Franco, Gabriel Solano, and Xóchitl Leyva Solano, "Los municipios de la Selva Chiapaneca. Colonización y dinámica agropecuaria," in *Anuario 1991 del Instituto Chiapaneco de Cultura* (Tuxtla Gutiérrez: Instituto Chiapaneco de Cultura, 1992).

21. Misión de Ocosingo-Altamirano, 1972–1974, quoted in John Womack Jr., *Rebellion in Chiapas: An Historical Reader* (New York: The New Press, 1999), 140.

22. Ibid., 137.

23. Local meetings in rural chapels are similar to meetings of members of Christian Base Communities (CEB's). In these chapels Catholics meet regularly to read the Bible and have established broad social networks based on connections through the church. Yet these are not CEBs in the formal sense. In the 1980s members of the Diocese of San Cristóbal attempted to establish Christian Base Communities in rural and urban areas following the model of other Latin American countries. Although the base communities grew in urban areas, particularly among mestizos, pastoral workers realized that rural indigenous communities were in many ways de facto base communities.

24. Thomas Bamat and Jean-Paul Wiest, "The Many Faces of Popular Catholicism," in *Popular Catholicism in a World Church: Seven Case Studies in Inculturation*, ed. Thomas Bamat and Jean-Paul Wiest (Maryknoll: Orbis Books, 1999), 15.

25. Las Casas played a critical role in securing the passage of two laws to protect indigenous people from exploitation at the hands of colonizers. Although Las Casas criticized the Spaniards' brutal treatment of indigenous people, he did not criticize the enslavement of Africans in the New World.

26. Jesús Morales Bermúdez, "El Congreso Indígena de Chiapas: Un Testimonio," in *Anuario 1991 del Instituto Chiapaneco de Cultura* (Tuxtla Gutiérrez: Instituto Chiapaneco de Cultura, 1992), 248.

27. Ibid., 349.

28. John Burdick, "The Progressive Catholic Church in Latin America: Giving Voice or Listening to Voices," *Latin American Research Review* 29 no. 1 (1994): 184–197.

29. Pablo Iribarren, "Experiencia: Proceso de la Diocesis de San Cristóbal de Las Casas, Mexico," mimeo, 1985.

30. Cited in Samuel Ruiz García, *En Búsqueda de la libertad* (San Cristóbal de Las Casas: Editorial Fray Bartolomé de Las Casas, 1999).

31. Iribarren, "Experiencia: Proceso de la Diocesis de San Cristóbal de Las Casas, México."

32. Samuel Ruiz García, *"En Esta Hora de Gracia," Pastoral Letter* (Mexico City: Dabar, 1993), 26.

33. After this important meeting of all pastoral workers, a Diocesan Assembly was called each year in order to examine and revise the pastoral work. Occasionally, Extraordinary Assemblies are called for special events.

34. Iribarren, "Experiencia: Proceso de la Diocesis de San Cristóbal de Las Casas, Mexico," 7.

35. On independent campesino organizations, see Neil Harvey, *The Chiapas Rebellion: The Struggle for Land and Democracy* (Durham: Duke University Press, 1998).

36. *El Caminante*, Internal Bolletin of the Diocese of San Cristóbal de Las Casas, June/July 1985; and Iribarren, "Experiencia: Proceso de la Diocesis de San Cristóbal de Las Casas, Mexico."

37. Quoted in Reyna Matilde Coello Castro, "Proceso Catequístico en la Zona Tzeltal y Desarrollo Social" (thesis, Universidad Autonoma de Tlaxcala, 1991), 95.

38. Quoted in Pablo Iribarren, *Los Dominicos en la pastoral indígena* (Mexico City: Imprentei, 1991), 32.

39. Xi' Nich' and Las Abejas are two of many organizations in Chiapas which have been influenced by the Catholic Church. Quiptic Ta Lecubtesel (Tzeltal for Our Strength Is Our Unity for Progress), a productive cooperative run by catechists and predeacons in the region of Ocosingo, was established in the aftermath of the Indigenous Congress of 1974. In the 1980s in the township Amatán, a number of local groups such as the Flor de Amatán and Frente Cívico grew out of a struggle to get rid of a corrupt municipal president. Catholic identity played an important role in these groups. In time, these organizations became involved in the struggle for land, and, in 1988, with women at the front of the struggle, one group took over the town's government building. *Pueblo Creyente* (People of Faith) is a diocesan-wide group formed in 1991. It is composed of Word of God Catholics who work though their faith to build unity and resist poverty and political repression.

40. Among the detained was Gerónimo Hernández, a Jesuit priest working in Palenque and judicial advisor to one of the groups that had organized the march.

41. For an analysis of the formation of Las Abejas, see Christine Kovic, "The Struggle for Liberation and Reconciliation in Chiapas, Mexico: Las Abejas and the Path of Nonviolent Resistance," *Latin American Perspectives* 30 (2003): 58–79. See also Heidi Moksnes, "Mayan Suffering, Mayan Rights: Faith and Citizenship among Catholic Tzotziles in Highland Chiapas, Mexico" (Ph.D. diss., Goteborg University, 2003).

42. On CODIMUJ, see Christine Kovic, "Demanding Their Dignity as Daughters of God: Catholic Women and Human Rights," in *Women in Chiapas,* ed. Eber and Kovic, 131–146. For a life history of one CODIMUJ participant, see Pilar Gil Tébar, "Irene, A Catholic Woman in Oxchuc," in *Women in Chiapas,* ed. Eber and Kovic, 149–154.

43. For discussion of the role of he Catholic Church in other regions of Latin America, see Daniel Levine, *Popular Voices in Latin American Catholicism* (Princeton: Princeton University Press, 1992); and Susan Eckstein, introduction to *Power and Popular Protest: Latin American Social Movements,* ed. Susan Eckstein (Berkeley: University of California Press, 1989).

44. Rosa Rojas, *Chiapas: La paz violenta* (Mexico City: La Jornada Ediciones, 1995).

45. Hans Siebers, "Globalization and Religious Creolization among the Q'eqchi'es of Guatemala," in *Latin American Religion in Motion,* ed. Christian Smith and Joshua Prokopy (New York: Routledge, 1999), 272.

46. The San Andrés Accords support the demand for autonomy by expanding specific cultural, territorial, and political rights for indigenous peoples. The EZLN and government representatives signed the San Andrés Accords during the 1996 peace talks.

CHAPTER 9

The Indigenous Theology Movement in Latin America

ENCOUNTERS OF MEMORY, RESISTANCE, AND HOPE AT THE CROSSROADS

Stephen P. Judd

OVER THE past several years there has been a revival of an old Andean myth that periodically undergoes revision and lends itself to new interpretations in changing social and cultural contexts. The myth "Two Brothers" tells a timeless story of reciprocity in human relationships and has enduring and defining value for the peoples of the Andes.[1] In the retelling of the myth the younger brother of an Indian family is forced by conditions of poverty to leave his ancestral home to go in search of sustenance for his family in a far off place. For the journey all he takes is a handful of green vegetables. Along the way he reaches a well-known crossroads called an *apacheta*. There he meets up with a stranger who is obviously much better off economically. The ensuing conversation goes like this:

"Friend, where are you headed," says the stranger.

"Sir, I am very poor so I am traveling to find work to help my family

"Don't go my son, because in those places there is no work."

"Then, sir, let's stop to rest awhile."

They both sit down to rest a bit and the poor Indian lays out his poncho so that they can sit down. And after resting awhile, the Indian takes out the only thing he has to eat, which is the bundle of greens.

"Help yourself, sir!" he says.

The man serves himself and then says, "Don't go my son; you will not find anything. It's better for you to return."

"Yes, sir, then I am going to return home."

"I am going to give you this flower."

And so he gives him a bouquet of carnations with a single native flower.

"Take it, bring it back home with you, and don't look back!"

After this experience the young Indian man returned to his cultural home newly aware and appreciative of the wealth and beauty of his ancestral homeland and cultural heritage.

An Intercultural Encounter
at a Latin American Crossroads

In the context of several recent theological gatherings of indigenous people in Latin America, this story takes on enhanced meaning. In what has come to be known as the movement to elaborate a new theological expression among Latin America's indigenous peoples, called *teología india,* the story represents the point where two distinct worlds meet. For many, it signifies one of the emerging paradigms for intercultural dialogue, where different cultures share the richness and wisdom of their respective ancestral heritage, the gift they are to each other above and beyond whatever material wealth might ordinarily separate them.[2]

It might be said that apachetas mark the turning points in the journeys of a people to greater self-understanding and awareness of their place in history according to cyclical patterns. Unlike the people in the West, who continue to be dominated by a linear vision of history, indigenous peoples follow a different pattern. Yet at this real or imaginary crossroads they enter into relationships with the "other" who is different. Today, whenever indigenous people meet to reflect on their identity and role in the world, stories like "Two Brothers" stand out as examples of intercultural communication. In the religious world of Latin America the telling of this story marks another turning point in the search for inter-religious dialogue whereby indigenous people both reclaim their native identity and affirm a place of respect in the worldwide Christian movement.

Witness People, Insurgencies,
and New Encounters

The revival of this myth represents merely one among many manifestations of a resurgence of indigenous identity throughout the Americas during the past decade. Latin America's formerly invisible people have suddenly become visible actors on the world stage. Alongside and with deep respect for the indigenous worldview, an emerging social movement took shape. From a church standpoint this grew out of the process of renewal brought about by the Second Vatican Council (1962–1965). Later the Conference of Latin American Catholic Bishops that took place in Medellín, Colombia, in 1968 marked the first definitive shift in the church's relationship with indigenous people with its celebrated option for the poor and a distancing of its long identification with powerful elites.

Visionary bishops and high-profile leaders—like the charismatic, now retired bishop of Chiapas, Samuel Ruiz, and the late bishop of Riobamba,

Ecuador, Leonidas Proaño—in the 1970s and 1980s prepared the ground for the formation of indigenous leaders for roles in civil society. They began by opening up spaces for lay participation in ministries within the church long before their entrance into public life. Long-condemned rituals of pre-Columbian origin, many practiced clandestinely, were reintroduced into official ceremonies of the institutional church and celebrated in the indigenous languages. Long-condemned indigenous ministries suddenly became recognized and officially sanctioned. The influence of the emerging theology of liberation that spread throughout the Latin American continent played an equally important role in raising awareness of indigenous identity and the peoples' right to self-determination. Throughout the hemisphere and region, emboldened indigenous peoples are reinventing democracy according to a worldview that does not make distinctions between the realms of the sacred and the social.

Unbeknownst to world leaders and the Western world at large has been a slow process of building an identity that is not simply based on a clarion call to return to an idyllic past before the European discovery of America, but reflects an ability to confront modernity and post-modernity with an alternative worldview based on indigenous values of respect for the earth and bio-diversity, human relationships that are inclusive and reciprocal, and a sense of sacred time and place.

The worldwide protest against globalization, as it touches on land and natural resources, notions of sacred territory, and communal organizations, resonates with developments in the religious worldview of indigenous peoples. According to the Chilean sociologist of religion Christian Parker, "religion is a part of the process of recovery of ethnic identity, even though it is under threat from globalization."[3] Similarly, this movement finds common cause with those who propose a different kind of globalization "from below" that builds international networks of solidarity and self-determination. It is not just the religious expression of the lament of a downtrodden remnant living clandestinely, but a vital force for historical transformation in Latin American countries with high percentages of indigenous populations, countries like Mexico, Guatemala, Ecuador, Bolivia, Peru, and Chile. The awakening of the nearly sixty million indigenous peoples of the Americas—the ones that the Brazilian historian Darcy Ribeiro calls "witness peoples"—represents a new social force to be reckoned with now more than ever, when disenchantment with the false promises of the globalization project appear. However, it remains to be seen whether these social developments will translate into a sweeping redesign of the apparatus of the national government structures in places like Bolivia and Ecuador.

The explanations for this global shift are complex and diverse, but developments in the contemporary Latin American Catholic Church over the past forty years warrant greater attention and treatment as one of the variables and interpretative keys for understanding a unique historical and cultural phenomenon at the beginning of the third millennium. Interestingly, all of these developments transpired during the decade designated by the United Nations as the Decade of Indigenous Peoples (1993–2003).

During the build up to 1992 many indigenous peoples began to give voice to a phrase that has helped in their own self-understanding: they are peoples of "memory, resistance, and hope." The various forms of protest are part of this resistance that has its counterpart in the religious recovery of memory and the promise of raising hope for wide-sweeping transformations on every level within and beyond the borders of Latin America. At certain moments we have heard echoes of the dialogue between the young brother and the rich stranger at the crossroads, apacheta.

RELIGIOUS VARIABLES WITH TRANSFORMING SOCIAL IMPLICATIONS

In underscoring this social development we can point to several variables and trace their convergence in leading to the emergence of a new and unique theological movement in the Catholic Church, and to a lesser extent in other Christian churches in Latin America, called *teología india*.[4] We trace the integral role of a religious dimension to indigenous identity that has grown into a full-fledged theological movement, one that is ecumenical and pluralistic and whose leaders have received education in pastoral programs organized by Catholic communities and religious orders in the last half of the twentieth century.

First of all, events and developments leading up to the five-hundred-year commemoration of the European arrival in the Americas in 1992 played a key role in raising awareness of the role of religion and the religious worldview of indigenous peoples within broader social movements. Language that spoke of the continent's indigenous peoples as endowed with "memory, resistance, and hope" was used by progressive church sectors and elites committed to recovering the tradition of figures like the sixteenth-century Dominican friar and missionary Bartolomé de Las Casas (1484–1566). The recovery of the Las Casas style of prophetic and peaceful evangelization based on the encounter with the "other" had inspired others like the Jesuits in their utopian social projects and experiments of the Reductions that prospered in the seventeenth and eighteenth centuries in the areas of what are now eastern Bolivia, Paraguay, Brazil, and Argentina. Over against the Inquisition and the campaigns to extirpate indigenous religious symbols and practices, this prophetic current gained advocates and continues to guide and inspire many who see the latest flowering of the Las Casas vision in the theological movement of indigenous theology.[5]

In an interesting historical twist, it was the abandonment of the evangelization process, due in no small part to the expulsion of the Jesuits in the eighteenth century and a waning of the first missionary fervor of the other orders, that helped many indigenous people become freer to preserve their religious worldview and practices. When left to their own devices, and with the mechanisms used to punish idolatrous practices no longer in place, there was a certain revival among indigenous peoples whereby they began the practice of a creative syncretism or what Eleazar López calls "popular indigenous religiosity."[6] In many areas of Indian Latin America this continues but with several variations and a plurality of ritual expressions.

The importance of the revival of interest in the Las Casas legacy cannot be underestimated as an antidote to official campaigns to glorify the Spanish Conquest and its spiritual dimensions that surfaced around the commemorative events and celebrations of 1992. Nothing demonstrates the two opposing views of Spain's five hundred years than the scene in the harbor of Santo Domingo. At one end visitors are overwhelmed by the outsized triumphalistic monument to Christopher Columbus. On the other side stands the profoundly moving statue dedicated to the Dominican Friar Montesino, who preached the sermon of the "voice crying in the desert" that led to Las Casas's conversion in 1511.

Las Casas continues to fascinate and baffle scholars and provoke contrasting and sometimes erroneous images in the popular imagination. As such, he remains a controversial, enigmatic figure, both praised and maligned. For some, especially in Spain, he is still identified as the cause of the infamous Black Legend. To others, he represents an unwitting advocate for black slavery, despite his avowed and passionate defense of the Indian peoples. Still, for many in the progressive sector of the Latin America church, he is the precursor of liberation theology and a forerunner of the indigenous social and theological movements.

Along with the development of liberation theology in the post–Vatican II and Medellín eras, the first appearance of a new contextual theology movement began to be felt. The Peruvian theologian considered as the father of liberation theology, Gustavo Gutiérrez, pays tribute to Las Casas as one of the inspirations behind his own original theological production that takes as its starting point the option for the poor. One of his best-known works based on the Las Casas perspective is entitled *Bartolomé de Las Casas: In Search of the Poor of Jesus Christ*.[7]

Although born of an indigenous family and heritage, Gutiérrez was schooled in European Christian movements like Catholic Action and deeply influenced by social scientific theories in vogue in urban Latin American intellectual circles and social movements. While the Las Casas influence is unmistakable, his theology takes its lead from his presence and experience among the urban poor migrants newly arrived in Peru's coastal cities. But Gutiérrez went to great lengths to differentiate his new theology from the first writings of indigenous theology in the early 1990s. While sympathetic to this new current of theological reflection and thought, the Peruvian offered some cautionary notes in a little-known lecture given at one of the first theological conferences that treated this new current of theological reflection, organized in 1990 in Puno, Peru.[8]

For Gutiérrez and others of his school of thought, the main focus remains physical poverty and the current exclusion of millions of people as a result of the implementation of neo-liberal economic policies. His European social-scientific outlook did not initially give much priority to factors like cultural identity or creation-based worldviews. Scandalous levels of oppression were and are for him the primary starting point for theological reflection captured most recently in the question in the subtitle of his latest and forthcoming work, "Where will the poor sleep tonight?" For Gutiérrez and others identified with liberation theology, Las Casas's words—the poor of Latin America are a "people who die before their time of an unjust death"—still ring true in the present context.

At the same time, religious communities and orders that were identified more directly with the legacy of Bartolomé de Las Casas began to organize international meetings to critically re-examine their own past perspectives and styles of evangelization vis-à-vis their relationship with indigenous peoples. Aware of experiences in places like Chiapas, Mexico, Las Casas's own Dominican Order was one of the first to organize a symposium along these lines in 1988 in Cobán, Guatemala, for the purpose of re-ordering its pastoral priorities to reflect advocacy for incipient indigenous social movements.[9]

A missionary society of North American origins, Maryknoll, soon followed suit by organizing its own conferences and workshops around the topic of its evangelizing role. Maryknoll's long experience in preparing indigenous leaders since the early 1940s in the Mapuche lands of southern Chile, in Bolivia and Peru among the highland Quechua and Aymara people, as well as in Mexico and Guatemala began to receive a more systematic treatment. A commitment to listen to and live more closely with the people, as well as efforts to change and adapt church structures, set the stage for a later emergence of this new theological current. Through a periodic series of workshops since 1989 and a dialogue with indigenous peoples and leaders, this particular religious community has promoted and facilitated its ongoing development. Significantly, indigenous leaders and representatives participate in these workshops alongside Maryknollers.[10]

Maryknoll's social location on the periphery of the Latin American countryside contributed to changes within these groups that were the forerunners of a large-scale missionary movement from North America and Europe in the

1960s, whereby many like-minded missionaries were assigned to remote areas with high indigenous populations. Most of these groups introduced modern training and education programs, mostly for indigenous lay leaders, that awakened a newly discovered identity. Some courses began with a catechetical purpose or for biblical instruction but later evolved into workshops of a more political nature and orientation and led directly or indirectly to the creation of popular autonomous *campesino* organizations that pressed claims for human rights and a recovery of lands that were expropriated by haciendas and government officials.

Advocacy for indigenous rights and organizations was compatible with the affirmation of indigenous identity, or, in more theological language, the merger between inculturation and liberation. Inculturation is the process whereby the Gospel takes root in a determined cultural context without doing violence to that culture and its symbols, myths, and rituals. Many missionaries became imbued with the values of the indigenous cultural worldview. This led to labeling them as *culturalistas,* as opposed to those inside and outside the church who adopted a more class-based analysis of social conflicts.

In the midst of land struggles and the environment of political violence, the Church of the South Andes in 1986 issued a pastoral reflection, entitled "La tierra: Don de Dios, derecho del pueblo," that recognizes the symbolic value of land within the Andean worldview as much as its value as an economic commodity.[11] The giftedness of land is captured in the title of Hans Van den Berg's provocative book, *La tierra no da así no más: Los ritos agrícolas en la religión de los aymara-cristianos* (that is, the repetitious cycle is marked by ritual and prayer along with the tasks of planting, cultivating, and harvesting).[12] These themes run through documents and pastoral letters from bishops and church leaders from Guatemala to Brazil.[13]

Likewise, experiences under the leadership of charismatic and pastorally oriented bishops like Leonidas Proaño, Samuel Ruiz, and lesser known figures spurred the formation of regional organizations in the Pacífico Sur area of Mexico, around the Isthmus of Tehuantepec, Riobamba, in Ecuador, and the Sur Andino, in Peru. Pastoral research and education centers like the Instituto de Pastoral Andina (IPA) in Cusco, Peru, the Centro Nacional de Ayuda a Misiones Indígenas (CENAMI) in southern Mexico, and many others supplied the theological and anthropological reflection to guide the experience of a new encounter. These were first created out of the post–Vatican II renewal and the Medellín Conference of Latin American bishops in 1968. But in places like Guatemala, the relationship was solidified during the thirty-year civil war and in the historical memory process that the Catholic Church helped to mobilize and organize, the "Recovery of Historical Memory Project Report" (REMHI), after the adoption of the Peace Accords.[14] Two days after its publication in 1998, one of its prominent leaders and an outspoken advocate for indigenous rights, Bishop Julio Gerardi, was assassinated in Guatemala City.

There has been an organic growth process and evolution in showing the theological uniqueness and content of the movement. Slowly but surely the indigenous religious worldview has worked itself into diverse church documents and pronouncements, culminating in 1992 when the Latin American bishops met in Santo Domingo. During that conference one of the most stirring moments occurred with the announcement that Rigoberta Menchú, herself a product of formation in church movements, was awarded the Nobel Peace Prize. But by 1992 the movement had already achieved recognition and a status as part of the process for inter-religious dialogue within Latin America, signaled by the bishops assembled in Santo Domingo who stated, "We want to draw closer to the indigenous and Afro-American peoples so that Gospel already incarnated in their cultures [will] manifest all of its vitality and that they enter into a dialogue of communion with the rest of Christian communities for the mutual enrichment of everyone."[15]

Increasingly, legitimacy was given to indigenous theology on Pope John Paul II's several visits and dialogues with indigenous peoples over the course of his pontificate. What started out as rather timid overtures blossomed into sincere and warm ceremonies. In 1985 in Cusco, Peru, an indigenous religious leader boldly thrust a Bible into the pope's hands as a sign of returning the Bible, saying that indigenous peoples were never consulted whether they wanted the Bible in the first place. From that awkward moment subsequent visits showed a deeper appreciation, as in a large meeting with the pope in Xoclán, Mexico, in 1993. On the occasion of the canonization of Juan Diego, the fifteenth-century Indian leader who witnessed the Marian apparitions in December 2002 at the Basilica of Our Lady of Guadalupe, indigenous men and women performed a ritual dance with incense to purify the Holy Father prior to the canonization ceremony.

Public manifestations of pardon by church officials have gone a long way toward repairing the breach between the official church and indigenous peoples. Symbolic actions like this indicate the progress made by the indigenous theological movement in gaining acceptance within the official Catholic Church. While actions not always enthusiastic, great strides have been made. The grounds for further dialogue have been established at different apachetas and in international theological dialogues.

OUT OF THE CAVE AND INTO THE LIMELIGHT

However, this theology was given fuller shape at the four international conferences that started in 1990. A number of diverse regional and ecumenical gatherings and conferences have consolidated the movement, generated momentum, and created networks for continuous interchange across the continent. Frequent pronouncements and church documents are likewise a guide to its development. One collection in particular, prepared by Samuel Ruiz, *Carta Pastoral: En esta hora de gracia* (1993), stands out for its non-apologetic approach.[16] Several issues and articles of the thirty-plus-year-old journal *Allpanchis,* published by the Instituto de Pastoral Andina (IPA) in Peru, document well the various stages in this development.[17] The results of anthropological research, complemented by grassroots experience of church pastoral workers, are found in journals of this nature throughout Latin America.

These international gatherings held in Mexico (1990), Ecuador (1993), Bolivia (1997), and Paraguay (2002) highlight the main developments and organic growth of the movement and give shape to its content. While the survival of what were often clandestinely celebrated rituals was central to the early reflections, this emphasis on ritual does not spell a nostalgic return to the past but a reinterpretation of beliefs, rituals, and symbolic systems in light of the confrontation with modernity and post-modernity and its manifestations in a more globalized context. Participants at these conferences came from a range of religious backgrounds. While the majority was Catholic, a significant number were drawn from mainline Protestant denominations. There have always been religious practitioners, roughly akin to local shamans, at nearly every conference, whether local or international.

Indigenous theology, for the most part, taps into the mythical and ritual worlds of the people, whether they reside in urban or rural areas. It does not lend itself to dogma or conceptual academic notions in the discipline, but rather takes shape in narrative forms or through proverbs, ritual actions, and native sources of the culture's wisdom traditions. Despite efforts made to document the richness of its content, much remains to be done to collect and make a compendium of what is a diverse array of local practices. The use of a methodology and a commonly accepted working vocabulary by the participants at these gatherings will help to discover the universality of themes whose richness can be enhanced by local experiences. Eventually, this will help in giving this theology more of a standing in international and interfaith dialogues.

The first international encounters were largely characterized by a recovery of the memory of the existent practices, many of which were the fruits of the silent process of inculturation or syncretism of the past five centuries, especially ritual actions associated with the agricultural cycle and the surviving oral traditions. Even at these early meetings and conferences there was an urgency to identify the historically liberating elements in the fragments of localized rites and celebrations. Still, there was a sense of the need to preserve the clandestine nature of many of the rites for lingering fears of being condemned, especially by those theologians who were and are part of the official church establishment. The memory of past condemnations, persecution, and campaigns to extirpate idols was, and is, a very present danger and suspicion among some.

The two most recent ecumenical encounters outside Cochabamba, Bolivia, in August 1997 and near Asunción, Paraguay, in May 2002 were significant for advancing and consolidating the development of the movement as well as for broaching themes of larger global significance.[18] At Cochabamba, for example, one could see the passage from a posture of clandestine practices and lament to one of a full-fledged movement in its final message that, besides the perfunctory recapitulation of the ever-present wounds of the past, calls for change in the prevalent global economic model with its disregard for the sacredness of the Earth.[19]

Moreover, the final message points to signs of hope in the growing reaffirmation of indigenous identity, recognition by church authorities, and the contributions of teología india to the humanization process by its contemplative appreciation of the unity of all creation. It takes note of the acceptance of this theology found in indigenous organizations as an integral part of the structure and functioning within civil society. In other words, this theology begins to view itself and its empowering role as an integral part of a wider network of organizations working in solidarity to create a different kind of global social movement.

The concluding statements and reflections of the most recent encounter in Paraguay offer an even more nuanced understanding of this theological movement's expanded role within and beyond the borders of Latin America. Certainly there are continuities with the previous reflections, but new ground was broken at the Fourth International Encounter, judging by recently published commentaries. But unlike past occasions, this time the participants went to greater lengths to distinguish the indigenous worldview from that of the dominant modern and neo-liberal capitalistic societies.

Using a metaphor from the creation myth of the Guaraní people of Paraguay and Brazil of an idyllic *tierra sin mal,* one of the participants, Paulo Suess, set the grounds for a dialogue between the emergent teología india and Western Christian models.[20] In his interpretation, only a Western theology that is ready to make a critique of Western societies is capable of entering equally into a dialogue with the theologians who author works in indigenous societies. Only then, as fellow pilgrims on the road, can the two dialogue partners ever approximate the search for meaning and truth, knowing beforehand that neither one possesses all of human wisdom. Underneath every theology lie the deep reservoirs of vulnerability and hope, the points of semiotic density, which characterize each culture in the human family.

In the utopian tierra sin mal, something akin to the Christian notion of the Kingdom of God, the conditions exist for societies based on inclusiveness and pluralism, societies that admit of a diversity of approaches to absolute truth. This myth does not promise an earthly paradise without pain and suffering but marks a return to reciprocal human relationships and a radical acceptance of alterity. Unlike the false, alluring, and all-encompassing promises that underpin Western-style capitalism, this myth paints a more humble portrait of the quest for truth and meaning.

According to Suess, the myth explains the constant movement of the Guaraní people in migratory patterns, always in search of the abundance of the *fiesta* where reciprocal and complementary relationships are discovered and celebrated. Under the power of this myth, borders and boundaries become blurred. When there were attempts to usurp Guaraní lands throughout this past century and to restrict the people to reservations, the culture entered into a decline. Consequently, a large number of young people committed suicide.

Although the myth of the tierra sin mal and the Kingdom of God are not so easily accessible in the present reality, their persistence leads people to create notions of time and space in which equality and peace among peoples, reciprocal relationships, cultural diversity, religious pluralism, and harmony in the environment reign. Such compatible notions make possible an authentic dialogue founded on these values and an ethic of life. They allow people like the Guaraní to be protagonists in the formation of a historical project based on self-determination. Moreover, within the scope of this cosmovision there is room to create the common ground to build new forms and networks of solidarity with other peoples and cultures.

At the Asunción encounter the link between this theological reflection and the larger indigenous struggle was made explicit. Myths, rituals, and the wisdom of the elders are not something extraneous to the claims for recognition of each people's fundamental human dignity. Throughout the entire encounter the refrain was sounded that it is in the witness of the continent's indigenous people that the destiny of the these people lies. Together with this realization comes the commitment to the ideal that indigenous peoples have been placed on the Earth for a purpose and are called to contribute to the Earth's process of healing. From their own brokenness and pain they argue convincingly for the new vision for humanity of greater planetary unity.

One of the strong features of teología india is that it has been able to grow and develop irrespective of national borders and has brought people together on the basis of natural affinities, people who otherwise would not have the opportunity to be so closely connected. Herein lies its chief challenge, to move from the unfinished and incomplete project of inculturation to intercultural communication in a more globalized world. The indigenous theological movement is one of the elements in a growing awareness of the need to dialogue with diverse cultural and social movements. It does not merely constitute a "restoration of the ancient rituals and beliefs of Indian America" but makes a bridge to greater communication across borders and hemispheres for mutual enrichment. One of the signs of its maturity is its potential to generate these people-to-people networks of solidarity across national borders.

ARTISANS OF THE CREATION
OF THE VITAL SYNTHESIS

Initially, many of the key figures in the creation of a vital synthesis were clerics and missionaries from outside Latin America who acted as interlocutors in articulating the various dimensions of the movement. Church elites with academic credentials and a long-standing presence as missionaries, like Suess in Brazil, the Spanish Jesuit Xavier Albó in Bolivia, and Diego Irarrázaval, a Chilean Holy Cross priest with a long history in the altiplano of Peru, served as important links between liberation theology and the movement of teología india, facilitating contacts in a wide international network. Even while they cease to be its chief protagonists, their contributions are quite extensive and significant in paving the way for a new generation of indigenous theologians who maintain close ties to their communities of origin but have academic preparation and specialized studies. In the best of cases, Albó and Irarrázaval serve as interpreters of the phenomenon for those outside Latin America, while they act as the mentors for the chief exponents and protagonists of the movement.

Albó co-authored a book with four other Jesuits who have played key roles in promoting this movement entitled *Los rostros indios de Dios* on the occasion of the 1992 commemoration.[21] For all of its considerable merits in bringing together experiences in Mexico, Peru, Paraguay, and Bolivia, the book lacks the voice of the indigenous theologians themselves. However, anyone with knowledge of the history of popular indigenous social movements in Bolivia since the 1952 revolution recognizes the committed scholarship and leadership of Xavier Albó, whose knowledge of these movements is encyclopedic and highly credible.

Irarrazával, whose writings and research originate in his commitments among the Aymara people in the Peruvian altiplano at the Instituto de Estudios Aymaras (IDEA), provides a link between liberation theology and the nascent movement and other currents of theology around the world. He views their development as growing out of the original breakthroughs made by liberation theology over forty years ago. As such, the new theology is "polifaceted and multidimensional," highlighting features of the ongoing process of God's revelation in ever newer contexts.[22] For Irarrázaval it is a question not of indigenous theology supplanting liberation theology, but of it continuing its original insights in a changing global context.

One of the first authentic indigenous voices in the movement and a forerunner of a younger generation is the Aymara Catholic priest Domingo

Lllanque from Puno, Peru, who began to document the religious manifestations and symbolic universe of his people in the 1970s. Coming out of the
rural areas of Puno, where there is a history of a strong Seventh-Day Adventist presence that stressed indigenous rights through a vast educational system,
Llanque approaches his world as one familiar with the mythical-ritual world
of his people. He is particularly adept at applying the tools of the social sciences to his research and writing.[23] Llanque plays a critical role as a bridge figure and interpreter between the younger generation and those from outside
Andean culture.

One individual in particular stands out as a voice for the movement. The
Zapotec Indian theologian and Catholic priest from Mexico, Eleazar López, is
the most articulate spokesperson, leader, and advocate for indigenous theology. His long association with the Centro Nacional de Ayuda a Misiones
Indígenas (CENAMI) and close collaboration and advisory role with the bishops and leaders of the regional organization of dioceses in southern Mexico
have given him a great deal of experience and credibility. Among those leaders are Samuel Ruíz and the late archbishop of Oaxaca, Bartolomé Carrasco.
López epitomizes the internal struggle to arrive at a synthesis between his self-
discovery of indigenous identity and his official status as an ordained priest
cleric within the official church structure.[24] Others of his generation who
passed through the Roman Catholic priestly education process long ago have
rejected the values and ways of their people in favor of social and economic
ascendancy that comes with insertion into the ecclesiastical power structure.
López and his cohorts who span the geography of Indian Latin America have
begun to do the slow, patient work of systematizing the theological expressions lived out in daily life throughout the continent.

In his writings López comes to a fuller understanding of the historical
roots of the movement, its present situation, and its future prospects; he shows
an appreciation for a more systematic theological approach to arrive at this
vital synthesis. Indigenous social movements within the larger civil society, according to López, have served to provide a more favorable context for "coming out of the caves without fear of being labeled heretics, diabolical or
idolatrous." He quotes a statement from one of the many meetings and encounters that have taken place prior to and after 1992. This time, from a public forum in Tiahuanaco, Bolivia, representatives from all over the continent
stated, "We are not romantics nor much less filled with nostalgia and neither
are we motivated by revenge and trying to make our spirituality and cultures
relevant, because we deeply believe that the wisdom of our nations is the pre-
ponderant factor for the salvation of the entire planet and for all humanity.
Our original spirituality is founded on balance, complementarity, identity and
consensus."[25]

Throughout his work, López insists on the newness of teología india that builds on both indigenous identity and the richness of the Catholic Christian tradition, taking heart from reflections since Vatican II on the notion of "seeds of the Word," a notion that points to God's action and Christ's saving word already present in cultures before the arrival of the Spanish conquerors and the first evangelizers. Others would say that there are fully grown sprouts and not just seeds. At the same time, López recognizes the difficulty of such a new vital synthesis because of the wounds of the past and the persistence of doubts and suspicions on both sides. Still, he has an unwavering commitment to his role to facilitate the reconciliation, building on what his precursors have already achieved under less favorable conditions. Out of what was once a religious battleground, he believes, new expressions of both Christian witness and community and indigenous self-understanding and wisdom will blossom.

The younger generation is typified by the Peruvian Aymara priest Narciso Valencia and the Peruvian Oblate missionary Nicanor Sarmiento, who have participated in important shifts and ongoing developments.[26] So, too, is the pioneering work of the Bolivian Efraín Lazo worthy of closer examination.[27] They bridge the distance between the everyday experiences of the people and church officials who are open to dialogue with the indigenous experience and reality. But as all these high-profile exponents insist, the originality of this theology is found in the daily practices, devotions, and rituals outside of and often parallel to official ceremonies. In fact, the place of *lo cotidiano,* or the quotidian factor, more accurately defines the movement, and not any great systematic theological treatise that has yet to be produced. Valencia traces in his work the role played by the Pachamama in the daily life of the people, not as some overlay on the cult to the Blessed Virgin Mary, but as one of the embodiments of the divinity in the Aymara religiously charged worldview.

Sarmiento attempts to trace the contours of one of the first systematic treatments of this nascent theology from the missiological perspective in which he was trained as a member of the Catholic Oblates of Mary Order, a group with a long history of evangelization among indigenous peoples in Bolivia and Canada. Presently, Sarmiento belongs to a missionary team in Labrador that gives him a cross-cultural experience in which he can recover the deeper meanings of his own religious and cultural roots. His starting point is that teología india is a reflection that "gives the reason for the hope of indigenous peoples." Moreover, a theologian like Sarmiento tries to point out how such a theology has a missionary dimension inasmuch as it opens up a dialogue with other theologies from the particular to the universal.

From an immersion into the mythic-ritual world of his Aymara people, Valencia probes new meanings of the concept of the Pachamama, not, as so often is believed, as a manifestation of the Mother Earth, but as the central point of his people's understanding of their revelation of the Creator God. All of the Aymara cosmovision and the ritual offerings surrounding it are representative of humanity's search for meaning, harmonious human relationships, and a sense of unity and place in a world that is so badly fragmented and divided. Belief in the Pachamama allows Andean peoples to appreciate their role as co-creators with God and their responsibility to care for and nurture the earth. Like Sarmiento's experience, Valencia's experience outside his own culture during his years of study in Brazil allows him the opportunity to place his heritage in dialogue with other traditions.

The Bolivian Efraín Lazo develops new understandings of the role of ritual practitioners and specialists, those who are often described as shamans, within the Andean world of the Aymara and Quechua peoples. A Christian interpretation of ministerial roles helps him to shed more light on the multifaceted roles of the *yatiri* (literally, in Aymara, one who knows) as healers, religious intermediaries, and people of wisdom who carry on and transmit the oral and ritual traditions of the people. In Lazo's view they represent more than religious functionaries. Rather, they are examples of the blossoming of "seeds of the Word" so prevalent in the theological language of Vatican II. They interpret and define the religious worldview of Andean peoples, and their role is not in competition with the priestly functions of ordained Christian ministers. For him they play a complementary role to the Catholic priest in Andean communities, although to this day their role has not been fully understood or appreciated.

An important Protestant figure of the same generation who has played a role in the international indigenous theological conferences is a young Aymara Methodist theologian, Vicenta Mamani Bernabé. In one of her first works, *Ritos espirituales y practices comunitarias del aymara,* Mamani brings, in addition to her immersion in the indigenous worldview, a feminist perspective and critique.[28] She also stands out as one who moves quite comfortably between the rural and urban realities of the Bolivian altiplano. As such, she is a representative figure of the indigenous theological movement and straddles both worlds to play a bridge-building role.

This younger generation of Catholic and Protestant indigenous theologians with roots in native communities, complemented by an exposure to classical European and North American styles of theological education, go to great lengths to emphasize the ecclesial character of the movement. At the same time, they are highly critical of church leaders and structures that may impede or try to co-opt this new theological movement. In both official and unofficial circles they continue to press claims for a place for theological reflection inside the church and a pastoral practice and church structures more attuned to the indigenous perspective and worldview.

López, Lazo, Sarmiento, Mamani, and Valencia are people of a "second naiveté experience," to borrow from the interpretation theory espoused by the French philosopher Paul Ricouer.[29] In their journeys they have taken that road of critical distancing from their native cultures only to return and reclaim the richness and wisdom of their traditions, as if to discover them for the first time. While they claim a privileged place for the religious experience of their people, they often borrow from the wisdom of the Western philosophical tradition but not from the traditional sources. Rather, they find resonance and commonality with the Lithuanian philosopher Emmanuel Levinas and his notions of alterity, or the ethical demands of the "other," that loom very large as an influence in their thought and writings.[30] In the words of Gustavo Gutiérrez, they drink freely from the "wellsprings" of their own culture. Clearly, they are scholars with their ears to the ground, but with gifts to articulate and interpret the worldviews of their people. They have sojourned to the apachetas of Indo-America and have lingered there long enough to produce other theological works of a more universal appeal.

A New Horizon of Hope

The teología india movement has found mixed receptivity within and outside the churches. Through the interventions of church leaders with experience in Indian areas of the continent, it merited a place and a somewhat elevated status alongside other theological currents in the conclusions of the Santo Domingo Conference in 1992. Those sections that call for interreligious dialogue with the indigenous religious worldview represent an important innovation in the ongoing process first initiated at Medellín in 1968 and continued at the following conference in Puebla, Mexico, in 1979. In the different visits and discourses of Pope John Paul II, down to the recent canonization of the humble Indian Juan Diego, who witnessed the Guadalupe apparitions, we have evidence that this movement is more than a quaintly interesting localized feature on the broader theological landscape for the universal church.

Notwithstanding signs of recognition, these encounters have often been part of the five-hundred-year history of *desencuentros,* or missed opportunities. The emergence of teología india has been met by Vatican officials with guarded and cautious openness; at times they prefer to call it a source of indigenous wisdom and not give it its due as a new theological expression worthy of systematic study and inclusion in the theological academy. Often church authorities place it over against liberation theology as a more benign expression of theological thought. At times it rates only a description as Indian wisdom, and not as theology in its own right. More open and consistent encouragement has come through the continent-wide Latin American Bishops' Conference (CELAM) in Bogóta, Colombia, and its Department of Missions (DEMIS). In the past few years DEMIS has actively convened several gatherings of theologians and bishops in a fruitful dialogue about issues of doctrinal import, most recently in Quito, Ecuador, in 2002. As a result of these formal and informal gatherings, several Latin American bishops and missiologists have taken a more favorable and activist stance toward promoting a spirit of inter-religious dialogue with indigenous theologians, a stance that was called for by the Santo Domingo conference in 1992. In this way, the institutional church legitimizes what began as a grassroots movement.

The scholarly research, writings, and lectures of Maryknoll missionary priest and missiologist John Gorski have attempted to bridge differences and open the door to more dialogue. Interpreters like Gorski are no mere apologists for either the guardians of dogmatism or the indigenous theological movement. In their brokering role they make possible the expansion of understanding that there are many different ways of being a church of the people of God and that God's revelation in history is an ongoing development.[31] They afford a privileged place for the indigenous theological movement in theological discussions in contemporary Latin America.[32]

Outsiders without an in-depth understanding of the complexity of teología india or links to social movements can embrace indigenous theology rather superficially because of their postmodern sensibilities and enchantment with its more exotic and folkloric features. This may block them from grasping the close relationship that this movement has with the social movements for transformation. Within liberationist circles, teología india enjoys a newly earned status despite some early misgivings expressed by Gutiérrez back in 1990. There is a close connection with feminist and ecologically based theologies that see themselves as sympathetic dialogue partners and voices from the margins often excluded from official circles.

The dramatic growth of Protestantism in Latin America, especially Pentecostalism, can make for an uneasy relationship and mutual suspicions, despite the ecumenical and pluralistic nature so characteristic of the movement. For example, in one of the most highly indigenous countries of all, Guatemala, there has been a phenomenal growth of highly diverse Protestant churches of a more evangelical and Pentecostal bent, alongside a consistent accompaniment of the people by Catholic Church leaders and workers during the thirty-year civil war. The Pentecostal tradition of resistance to world-transforming language can be detrimental to expressions such as teología india, and poses a threat of confusing it with a return to idolatry and a rejection of modernity, social mobility, and progress.

The REMHI historical memory process was an initiative organized by Guatemalan church leaders and human rights groups that did not, for the most part, engage members of the more fundamentalist Protestant churches, despite the fact that members of these churches were not always immune from the genocide of the thirty-year civil war. Yet, in stressing its ecumenical, religiously pluralistic identity, teología india gives witness to yet another way of being openly inclusive and all-embracing of religious diversity. Protestant theologians like Vicenta Mamani are not exceptions to the rule. Once their writings become better known, Protestant voices, whether conciliar, evangelical, or Pentecostal, will take their places alongside their Catholic counterparts.

Within the Catholic tradition, practitioners of teología india go to great lengths to stress their ecclesial identities, even while they pursue and promote new currents of thought and break new ground in creating this vital synthesis. The resurgent neo-conservative climate in the church today can militate against such new expressions that fall outside the scope of those who insist with renewed energy on sanctions for theologians, whether from Europe, North America, or, increasingly, from Asia. Recent Vatican documents like *Iesus Dominus* (2000) send off mixed messages to those who seek greater interreligious dialogue, casting a cloud of suspicion over initiatives like this one. Worse yet, this can lead to self-censorship that can stifle the necessary creativity needed to stretch the limits of theological understanding that goes beyond Western academic theology as the norm. The cautious legitimacy afforded to teología india by influential church authorities can always be taken away with little or no forewarning.

We can view the emergence of teología india as a contribution from the indigenous religious world to the calls for greater intercultural dialogue and communication. The perspective and thought of a pioneer thinker in this area, Raúl Fornet-Betancourt, is especially illuminating in that he sees in the "dialogue of cultures a challenge of an alternative horizon of hope."[33] In the face of the cultural bombardment of the message of uniformity behind globalization, it is only through a dialogue of cultures that true universality can be achieved. Each dialogue partner goes beyond the specificity and particularity of his or her own cultural to enter another level of communication.

Through the process of *interculturalidad,* one sees the limitless possibilities for a culture to not only reproduce its cultural forms and patterns but to expand those horizons to embrace new symbolic universes. In a world wracked by new manifestations of religious fundamentalism, teología india comes as a welcome insight and hopeful development for the ongoing conversation. In Fornet-Betancourt's view, the intercultural dialogue is one where the values of reception, reciprocity, and hospitality take root as in the myth "Two Brothers," mentioned earlier.[34] Increasingly, the Latin American teología india movement has brought indigenous peoples together to find common ground and to build new networks of communication on all the continents through international forums.

To summarize the main features of the indigenous theological movement, we need go no further than the words of Eleazar López, quoted earlier. This theology from the underside of history looks at "balance, complementarity, identity, and consensus" as alternative ways of understanding peoples' relationship with the transcendent and with each other respecting the quality of difference. The originality in this movement derives from its departure from more standard and traditional methods in theology based on European and classical models. New currents of theological thought, often described as examples of contextual theologies, attempt to underscore the ways that indigenous peoples throughout the Americas have resisted the imposition of a dominant religious worldview from outside. They do this by stubbornly holding on to their symbolic and mythic-ritual worldviews, popular devotions, stories, and wisdom traditions, where they find a sense of the meaning of life in the midst of their daily struggles to achieve dignity and recognition of their "otherness."

At the same time, representatives of this movement go to great lengths to show their adherence to Catholic and Christian identities in an ever-changing global context. Teología india points to the fact that there has been an interreligious dialogue taking place for five hundred years, albeit often in an asymmetrical and disjointed fashion, and often undetected. What has emerged, however, is a creative integration of Christian and indigenous belief systems in which we witness a distinct way of being Christian. This theology is a reflection of how indigenous peoples express their relationship to God and each other in varying historical circumstances.

By and large, indigenous peoples throughout the hemisphere attempt to profess their Christian identity without dispossessing themselves of their cultural roots and traditions. Teología india in its reflections enhances our understanding of such important Christian traditions as the Communion of Saints, Marian devotion, community life, ministerial roles, and the Paschal Mystery as it is lived out in the suffering and resurrection of a people that Las Casas and Gutiérrez proclaim "die before their time of an early and unjust death."

On purely theological grounds, teología india transcends the customary categories for introducing new content and language through its symbols, rituals, and alternative worldview. David Tracy, a prominent North American theologian, sees in peoples of "memory, resistance, and hope" the convergence of pre-modern, modern, and post-modern currents of thought which, through the witness of their survival and the flourishing of their cultures, surpass each of these currents.[35] In Tracy's view, new theological expressions that have surfaced from the margins constitute one of the forms of a mystical-prophetic expression that can enrich theologies from the Western world. Elsewhere, Tracy speaks of what constitutes a classic text, the work of art as "a journey of intensification into particularity."[36] Only by an immersion into particularity can we possibly have a disclosure of the deeper meanings of the universal. In what has been traced here we have the making of new classic texts in which original dimensions and interpretations of the universal emerge. Certainly this new movement has stretched the imagination and limits of theological discourse in the Christian world, showing that no single expression of the Christian message exhausts its full meaning.

Eleazar López sums up the place of indigenous theology within this new configuration: "Our emerging theologies are more difficult to pursue than liberation theologies. Nevertheless we believe we are witnessing an important historic moment, a *kairos* of grace, indicating God's passage through our midst."[37] Every meeting at one of the apachetas that dot the landscape of the indigenous world in Latin America bears the potential of a mutually fruitful and enriching encounter between peoples of "memory, resistance, and hope" and the rest of the human family.

NOTES

1. In the Aymara language, spoken in the highlands of Bolivia and Peru near Lake Titicaca, it is called "Iskay Hermanontinmanta."
2. The mythical tale "Two Brothers" was presented by a group of indigenous theologians from Peru at the Fourth Latin American Ecumenical Workshop for Indigenous Theology that took place in Asunción, Paraguay, May 5–11, 2002.
3. Christian Parker, "Religión and the Awakening of Indigenous People in Latin America," *Social Compass* 49, no. 1 (2002): 67–81.
4. Eleazar López Hernández, "Indigenous Theologies," in *Dictionary of Third World Theologies*, ed. Virginia Fabella and R. S. Sugirtharajah (Maryknoll, New York: Orbis Books, 2000), 108–109.
5. Brian Pierce, "Seeing with the Eyes of God: Bartolomé de Las Casas," *Spirituality* 9, no. 46 (January–February 2003). The revival in Las Casas studies was spurred by the research and writings of Helen Rand Parish. See the work by Parish and Harold E. Weidman, *Las Casas en México: Historia y obra desconocidas* (Mexico: Fondo de Cultura Económica, 1992).
6. Eleazar López, "Insurgencia teológica de los pueblos indios," *CHRISTUS*, September 1993.
7. Gustavo Gutiérrez, *Bartolomé de Las Casas: In Search of the Poor of Jesús Christ* (Maryknoll, New York: Orbis Books, 1996).
8. Gustavo Gutiérrez, "Nueva evangelización con rostro andino quechua y aymara," lecture, August 1990, Chucuito (Puno), Peru.
9. Latin American Dominican meeting, October 1988, in Cobán, Guatemala, organized by the Latin American Center of the Dominican Order, CIDAL.
10. There are several documented accounts, called "memorias," of the seven workshops sponsored by the Maryknoll Missioners from 1989 through 2003; they can be found in the library of the Maryknoll Instituto de Idiomas in Cochabamba, Bolivia.
11. Church of the South Andes, "La tierra: Don de Dios, derecho del pueblo," in *La señal de cada momento: Documentos de los obispos del Sur Andino, 1969–1994,* ed. Andrés Gallego (Lima, Peru: Centro de Estudios y Publicaciones [CEP], 1994).
12. Hans Van den Berg, *La tierra no da así no más: Los ritos agrícolas en la religión de los aymara-cristianos* (Amsterdam: Centre for Latin American Research and Documentation [CEDLA], 1989).
13. *500 años sembrando el Evangelio* (Guatemala City: Carta pastoral colectiva de los obispos de Guatemala, 1992).
14. Human Rights Office, Archdiocese of Guatemala, *Guatemala, Never Again! REMHI Recovery of Historical Memory Project* (Maryknoll, N.Y.: Orbis Books, 1999).
15. Alfred T. Hennelly, S.J., ed., *Santo Domingo and Beyond: Documents and Commentaries of the Fourth General Conference of Latin American Bishops* (Maryknoll, N.Y.: Orbis Books, 1993), 153. In the same volume see Stephen P. Judd, M.M., "From Lamentation to Project: The Emergence of an Indigenous Theological Movement in Latin America," 226–235.
16. Samuel Ruiz García, *Carta Pastoral: En esta hora de gracia* (Mexico: Ediciones Dabar, 1993).
17. *Allpanchis* is a scholarly journal published by the Instituto de Pastoral Andina (IPA)

located in Cusco, Peru. From 1969 until the present there have been fifty-nine issues of this journal that treat of many themes of the sociocultural and religious reality of Southern Peru.

18. Paulo Suess, "Encuentros y desencuentros en la búsqueda de 'la tierra sin mal,'" Cuatro Encuentro Ecuménico Latinoamericano de Teología India, Ykua Sati, Asunción, Paraguay, May 10, 2002.

19. III Encuentro-Taller Latinoamericano, *Sabiduría indígena: Fuente de esperanza,
Teología india, memoria* (Cusco, Peru: Instituto de Pastoral Andina, 1997).

20. Suess, "Encuentros y desencuentros."

21. Xavier Albó, *Rostros indios de Dios* (La Paz, Bolivia: CIPCA, HISBOL, UCB, 1992).
For the English translation see Xavier Albo, Manuel Marzal, Eugenio Maurer, and
Bartomeu Melià, *The Indian Face of God in Latin America* (Maryknoll, N.Y.: Orbis
Books, 1996).

22. Diego Irarrázaval, "¿A dónde va la teología latinoamericana?" *Pastoral Popular* 4
(2002):19 –22. Irarrázaval has published extensively on the religious and theological worldview of the Aymara people of southern Peru. See his work translated into
English: *Inculturation: New Dawn of the Church in Latin America* (Maryknoll, N.Y.:
Orbis Books, 2000).

23. Domingo Llanque, *La cultura aymara: Desestructuración o afirmación de identidad* (Lima,
Peru: Tarea e IDEA, 1990).

24. López, "Insurgencia teológica," 12.

25. Ibid., 11.

26. Nicanor Sarmiento, *Caminos de la teología india* (Cochabamba, Bolivia: UCB, Editorial Guadalupe, Verbo Divino, 2000); Narciso Valencia Parisaca, *Revelación del Dios
Creador* (Quito, Ecuador: ABYA-YALA, 1998).

27. Efraín Lazo, *El yatiri: ¿ministro del tercer milenio?* (Cochabamba, Bolivia: Verbo Divino,
1999).

28. Vicenta Mamani, *Ritos espirituales y prácticas comunitarias del aymara* (La Paz, Bolivia:
Creatart Impresiores, 2002).

29. This notion first appeared in Paul Ricouer's seminal work *The Symbolism of Evil*
(Boston: Beacon Press, 1969).

30. Jhonny Montero, "Las culturas indígenas desde una perspectiva multidisciplinaria"
(Master's thesis, Universidad Católica Boliviana, Cochabamba, Bolivia, 2003), cites
the influence of Emmanuel Levinas as a reference point for *teología india*. For a good
summary of Levinas's philosophical thought, see *The Levinas Reader*, ed. Sean Hand
(Oxford, Great Britain: Blackwell, 1992).

31. John Gorski, "El contenido y las grandes líneas de la así llamada 'teología india,' po-
nencia en el Encuentro sobre la Emergencia Indígena en América Latina," Oaxaca,
Mexico, April 24, 2002. In addition to this latest presentation, Gorski for many years
has collected and chronicled all of the major documents and commentaries produced by the indigenous theological movement.

32. See the issue of the Spanish journal *Misiones extranjeras*, "La mission de los pueblos
indígenas" vol. 165 (May–June 1998), with articles by Diego Irarrázaval, Simón
Pedro Arnold, and Esteban Judd Zanon.

33. Raúl Fornet-Betancourt, "Aprender a filosofar desde el contexto del diálogo de las
culturas," *Revista de Filosofía* (México) 90 (1997): 365–382.

34. Raúl Fornet-Betancourt, "Interculturalidad e immigración," in *10 palabras claves
sobre globalización*, ed. J. J. Tamayo Acosta (Navarra, España: Editorial Verbo Divino,
2002), 220.

35. David Tracy, "On Naming the Present," *Concilium* 1 (1990): 80–82.

36. David Tracy, *The Analogical Imagination: Christian Theology and the Culturé of Pluralism*
(New York: Crossroad Publishing Co., 1986), 105.

37. López, "Indigenous Theologies," 109.

CHAPTER 10

Conclusion

LISTENING TO RESURGENT VOICES

Timothy J. Steigenga

FORTY YEARS ago modernization theorists predicted that the salience of religion and ethnicity would fade as culture, ideas, and economic practices were transported from "modern" to "traditional" societies.[1] In 1992, as the Americas prepared for the Columbian quincentenary, even the most casual observer was aware that these predictions could not have been more wrong. From Ecuador to Mexico, indigenous political movements made their presence known through marches, uprisings, and political statements. Religion played a critical role in laying the groundwork for this indigenous resurgence. While ideas and practices were transported between societies, the effects were precisely the opposite of that predicted by the modernization theorists. New religious ideas and movements supported and celebrated indigenous rights and culture, while shifts to liberal political and economic doctrines provided the political openings for indigenous mobilization.

The contributions to this volume highlight the complex and sometimes contradictory relationships between religion and indigenous mobilization in Latin America. As always, the intersection between religion and politics raises issues of agency and constraints, hierarchy and liberation, community and conflict.[2] The role of religion is shaped by the various political, economic, and social contexts in which the interactions take place. While the contexts of Bolivia, Peru, Guatemala, Mexico, Ecuador, and Paraguay differ significantly, the case studies presented in this book yield important thematic generalizations and raise further research questions about the connections between religion, identity, and indigenous social movements in Latin America. We have consciously approached these questions from an interdisciplinary perspective, combining insights and methods from historians, political scientists, anthropologists, and sociologists.

Four primary themes emerged in the preceding chapters. The first theme involves the controversial topic of syncretism, including questions of "creole" or "hybrid" identity, as well as inculturation theology. How has indigenous activism and participation changed the practice and institutions of religion? How can religious institutions balance the desire for universal truth claims in the face of cultural relativity? As inculturation theology gives way to what Stephen Judd describes as *teología india* in Latin America, what does it mean for relationships of power and identity among religious participants and social activists?

The second theme relates to the connections between religion and social movements. What resources, motivations, and ideological legitimacy has religion provided indigenous social movements? How do religious differences impact identity and collective action? Can religious actors claim to speak on behalf of the indigenous and what issues does this raise in terms of potential conflict and cooptation?

A third set of questions has to do with evaluating outcomes. How effective are religiously based or identity-based social movements in achieving their goals? What are the obstacles to and achievements of indigenous movements in Latin America?

Finally, the chapters in this volume provide ample evidence of the complexity and fluidity of both the religious marketplace and religious politics in Latin America. As we evaluate the outcomes of indigenous social movements in the region, we must pay attention to critical changes at the level of personal empowerment and collective identity. These changes often defy simple labels and run counter to conventional wisdom. The flexibility within religious practice and politics should not come as a great surprise, yet we seem to rediscover it each time we hear the testimony of a charismatic Catholic who still practices some elements of *costumbre*,[3] or read the liberationist statements of a Mayan evangelical pastor. The fact is that these religious practices and beliefs are not mutually exclusive in the minds of those who take part in them, even if they remain so in the minds of those who study them. If religious practices and beliefs are malleable across time and context, we should expect the social and political trajectories of religious mobilization to be as well.

RELIGIOUS AND CULTURAL MIXING: SYNCRETISM, CREOLIZATION, AND HYBRIDIZATION

Any analysis of indigenous movements and religion must be prefaced with a discussion of terminology and definitions. An entire literature has emerged around the project of defining and redefining syncretism, hybridism, and creolization.[4] This book does not replicate these debates or the potentially confusing language through which they often take place. Rather, we asked the authors in this volume to begin by adopting the most general definitions of these terms for purposes of clarity and foundation-building.

Creolization and hybridization both refer to the process of cultural mixing. As used by cultural and literary theorists, these terms generally refer to a positive process that allows colonized societies to both critique and appropriate elements of more dominant cultures.[5] Similarly, syncretism may be understood as, "the combination of elements from two or more different religious traditions within a specific time frame."[6] Such an elemental definition purposely allows for an exploration of the ambiguity and power relations inherent in defining and interpreting orthodoxy. Syncretism may be used by the powerful to define and impose orthodoxy or by the powerless to subvert such definitions.[7] We have focused, therefore, on the process rather than the definition of syncretism, exploring the practices and beliefs that affect and are affected by religious exchanges.[8]

This is not to negate or diminish the ongoing debate within anthropology and cultural studies over historical, pejorative, and evolving understandings of cultural syncretism and hybridization. Three critical insights arise from this debate and inform our analysis. First, the use of each of these terms (syncretism, creolization, and hybridism) comes with significant historical baggage. In *Reinventing Religions: Syncretism and Transformation in Africa and the Americas* Sidney Greenfield and André Droogers carefully outline the differing trends in European and American anthropological approaches to syncretism, noting the evolution of the concept from a pejorative theological term, to an assumed stage in the process of acculturation, to a platform for power struggles over the most "pure" or "authentic" form of cultural identity.[9] The evolution of the terms "creolization" and "hybridism" are no less contentious. As Charles Stewart explains, "*Creole* draws attention to the inequities of power that allowed European colonizers to discursively legislate the importance of 'race,' culture, and environment in determining where one fit along a chain of being that placed the Old World homeland and its subjects at the pinnacle."[10] Hybridism, a potential synonym for creolization, suffers from equally problematic connections with nineteenth-century biological racism.[11]

Second, as these definitional issues make clear, the process of religious and cultural mixing always entails questions of power. Who defines what is authentic, pure, or orthodox? While the answer in the Latin American case most often has been the Catholic Church, we should note that essentialism (used here as the notion that identities or beliefs have certain a priori core elements that define them) is not the sole property of powerful religious institutions. Questions about who represents the "true" or "authentic" indigenous perspective are equally contentious. As Lois Ann Lorentzen eloquently points out in the case of Chiapas, to ask "who is an Indian" is to elicit a broad set of conflicting replies.[12] In some cases, academics, activists, and religious actors appear to be so engrossed in the debate over *quién es más Maya* that they lose sight of their own role in cultural and religious mixing.[13]

Kristin Norget's chapter on Oaxaca is particularly revealing in this respect. According to Norget, the notion that Catholic priests in Oaxaca serve as Gramcian "organic intellectuals" for the indigenous community is problematic because the majority of the priests are not from the community, and serve the community most effectively precisely because of that fact. In other words, the very individuals who serve as leaders of the indigenous community and who promote a powerful, identity-based critique of the existing social structure are best able to serve their adopted community due to their strong connections to powerful actors within the social structure (through the institutional church, philanthropic organizations, and non-governmental organizations). Norget cautions us about accepting religiously based intermediaries for indigenous communities with an uncritical eye.

Norget's warning raises one of the basic challenges involved in the study of identity politics in Latin America: the problematic question of who speaks for whom?[14] She also raises the question of whether or not the larger strategic purpose of challenging powerful structures justifies some "essentialization" of the indigenous community by actors who seek to represent that community. While we can imagine that most individuals would choose essentialization over subjugation, the question remains as to whether or not this is simply trading one form of social control for another, perhaps more subtle, form.[15] Either way, researchers and activists should carefully reflect on whether or not their arguments tend to deny agency to the very groups and individuals they seek to study or support.[16]

Even though syncretism is often characterized by asymmetrical power relationships, it can also be used by subaltern groups to subvert existing power structures. The interpretations, symbols, rituals, and practices of the more dominant or orthodox religion may be used in ways that go well beyond the intent of those who originally framed or defined orthodoxy. René Harder Horst makes this argument in the case of Paraguay, noting that the choices of indigenous groups to adopt different religious elements may have to do with social or economic advantage or simply with the resources necessary for survival. In either case, the meaning of religious symbols and practices holds the potential to be transformed into a subversive act or protest against more powerful actors (government authorities, Protestant missionaries, or the Catholic Church).[17]

Virginia Garrard-Burnett's chapter explicitly takes this approach, arguing that the authors of Mayanized theology in Guatemala appropriate and invert the powerful messages and symbols of Christianity for their own purposes. This is not to say that their project is a singularly political one, but rather to note that religious syncretism provides a milieu for multiple political, social, and theological agendas. Indigenous activists and the Catholic Church may each have a stake in the elaboration of a *teología maya,* but the process and results of creating such a theology are unlikely to match perfectly with either party's agenda.

A final insight arising from this debate pits one hybrid identity against another. The identity categories of both evangelical Indians and secular indigenous movements can act as challenges to the "established" hybrid form of social organization that has buttressed the assimilationist projects of most Latin American states. In other words, indigenous and evangelical identities, though perhaps themselves hybrid forms, make claims to cultural and religious truths that allow them to break out of the system of racial hierarchy that has dominated Latin American society.[18] New claims of identity as "indigenous" or as "Pentecostal" can serve as strategic weapons in the battle for collective recognition or individual survival and mobility. Though very different in their tactics and political agendas, these two movements are both indigenous responses to the same objective conditions and opportunity structure.

To review, the debate over religious and cultural mixing provides us with three important insights for the study of religion and indigenous social movements in Latin America. First, the terms used to describe religious mixing have evolved across time and academic disciplines (particularly in the fields of religious studies and cultural studies) and raise normative questions about power dynamics. To avoid choosing a definition of syncretism that answers these questions a priori, we adopt an elemental approach that allows us to explore the multiplicity of power relations and agendas involved in cultural and religious mixing. Our second insight results from this approach, as we discover that syncretism can be utilized by groups with less power to subvert the agendas of more powerful groups or by the powerful to define and impose orthodoxy, often at the same time. Finally, the identities that indigenous people adopt (evangelical, Catholic, or Indian activist) can be utilized to undermine or transcend hierarchical social structures in Latin America or to reinforce existing ethnic and religious divisions. Each of these themes is illustrated, in part, through the movement in Latin America from Catholic inculturation theology to a new and evolving *teología india*.

FROM INCULTURATION THEOLOGY
TO INDIGENOUS THEOLOGY

The *teología maya* in Guatemala, *pastoral indígena* in Oaxaca and Chiapas, and *teología india* in the Andes all have their roots in Catholic inculturation theology. Inculturation theology emerged out of Vatican II documents, including *Gaudium et spes,* which specified an openness of the church and theology to the world, and *Ad Gentes,* which pointed to the "seeds of the Word" said to be contained in the world's variant cultures. These messages were reaffirmed in 1968 at Medellín, again with *Redemptoris Missio* in 1979, and expanded in the 1992 CELAM (Consejo Episcopal Latinoamericano) conference in Santo Domingo.[19]

As several of our contributors note, those involved in doing inculturation theology would not choose to label their work as a form of syncretism.

Rather, they view their endeavor as an attempt to recognize and valorize pre-existing expressions of the divine within indigenous practices and beliefs, and to contextualize Christian theology so that it can be made more relevant to people of various cultures. As the evangelical pastor interviewed by Virginia Garrard-Burnett explained, they seek to prove that "God was already here when Columbus arrived."

Despite this careful distinction, most of the examples of inculturation theology included in this volume meet the minimal standard of the elemental and procedural definition of syncretism outlined above. This is significant not because it allows us to define certain results of inculturation theology as syncretism, but because it allows us to acknowledge and explore the fact that all parties involved in the process have agency and strategic agendas.

For Kristin Norget, the construction of an authentic indigenous identity politics allows the church to both justify an intermediary role and control the process of religious synthesis, a process that has previously been out of its reach in the realm of "popular religion." Norget argues that, in crude terms, some liberationists adopt indigenous identity politics because it promotes their liberationist social and political agenda. The institutional church is tolerant of this process only insofar as it allows a blurring of the lines between indigenous culture and Catholic culture and thus provides a strategy for competing with religious challengers such as Pentecostalism.[20]

Christine Kovic takes a different approach, arguing for a more positive interpretation of the church's role as interlocutor in Chiapas. While recognizing the privileged position of mestizo pastoral workers relative to indigenous peasants in Chiapas, Kovic emphasizes the unity and solidarity that bridged these differences in the face of shared repression. While Norget warns us that the institutional church and different tendencies within it have their own agendas, Kovic reminds us that attributing outcomes purely to those motives denies agency to indigenous groups themselves.

Garrard-Burnett, too, points to the fact that indigenous practitioners of inculturation theology have their own strategic agendas. In the tradition of opportunistic social movements, Mayan theologians can make use of religious resources and protection to explore, valorize, and interpret their own culture. It should come as no surprise that some Mayan activists sought to abandon Christianity all together as part of the revindication of Mayan culture. The popularity of this movement, however, remains unclear. Garrard-Burnett suggests that it may be more popular among Mayan elites and intellectuals than it is among the general Mayan population.

Stephen Judd's chapter provides us with an outline of the emerging indigenous theology that has grown out of and alongside inculturation theology. Judd traces the evolution of a teología india from early encounters calling for the simple recovery of existent indigenous practices to the more recent formulation of the utopian concept of *tierra sin mal,* characterized by inclusiveness, reciprocal and complementary relationships, pluralism, and harmony with the environment. Judd argues that indigenous theology is more than a restorationist movement, because it generates solidarity across religious and national borders. As with liberation theology, indigenous theology takes multiple forms and emphasizes the critical role of praxis for generating and understanding theological reflection.

RELIGION AND INDIGENOUS SOCIAL MOVEMENTS

Though not explicitly, all of the chapters in this volume adopt some version of what Christian Smith has called the "insurgent consciousness" role of religion in "framing" ideological or motivational resources to social movements.[21] Activists (in this case religious workers and indigenous leaders) "frame" their identity (often in opposition to other identities, Indian versus ladino, peasant versus patron) through certain religious resources, beliefs, practices, rituals, and cultures that make adherents more prone to be engaged and mobilized for collective action.[22] Inculturation theology, liberation theology, and indigenous theology play this role in the cases we have examined in this volume.

In his discussion of the indigenous–missionary dialogues in Peru and Bolivia, Edward Cleary notes that a theological basis for community solidarity and national liberation for the Amyara nation emerged. As missionaries trained catechists and catechists spread this theological message, the groundwork for an insurgent consciousness was laid.

Kovic also points to the role of religious beliefs in justifying certain ideological stances in the case of Chiapas. As she recounts the story of the indigenous catechist Juan, Kovic returns to a critical biblical theme that crosses denominational lines in Latin America: the notion that all people are equal in the eyes of God. This powerful notion of equality within both liberationist Catholic and Pentecostal Protestant discourses has important implications for inequalities relating to gender as well as class.[23] For Juan, this religious concept framed his struggle for social and economic equality in Chiapas.

In the case of Oaxaca, Kristin Norget describes an indigenous development model, with emphasis on collectives and ecological goals, that contains an inherent critique of neo-liberalism. Alison Brysk notes that many of the recent waves of Indian mobilization in Ecuador have also been aimed at government economic programs. In these cases, the insurgent consciousness behind the movements appears to have emerged from a convergence of traditional forms of indigenous practice and belief and liberationist elements of Catholicism. Stephen Judd echoes this finding, arguing that indigenous theology represents both a protest against globalization from above and a support network for globalization from below.

Simply put, the interactions between Christianity and indigenous religion in the past forty years gave rise to the basis for an insurgent consciousness framed within an identity as both Christian and Indian. Indigenous peoples and the religious workers who interacted with them became more receptive to the potential for mobilization as they developed religiously based critiques of existing structures of power and authority.

Explaining the Rise of Indigenous Identity Politics: Levels of Analysis

While it is beyond the scope of this chapter to provide a comprehensive review of the literature on social movements and identity politics in Latin America, our cases do provide insights into some of the pivotal questions arising in that literature.[24] Charles Hale's definition of identity politics as "collective sensibilities and actions that come from a particular location within society, in direct defiance of universal categories that tend to subsume, erase, or suppress this particularity," provides a useful starting point for analyzing these questions.[25] Most observers are in agreement that social movements in Latin America have taken a turn toward the sort of identity politics Hale defines, but the causes for, attractions to, and results of such politics remain contentious issues.

At the individual level of analysis, we have already addressed the precipitating factor of insurgent consciousness in the formation of social movements. Born in liberation theology, contextualized through inculturation theology, and reinforced through indigenous theology, this insurgent consciousness formed the ideological basis for an indigenous agenda of self-determination, political reform, and cultural, land, and citizenship rights. Activists in the indigenous rights movements in Latin America have consistently framed their identities either as indigenous or as religiously motivated advocates who accompany the indigenous in their struggle.

Moving beyond the individual level of analysis, we must also examine the contextual and institutional causes for the growth of social movements. As we have already noted, a particular moment in the history of the institutional Catholic Church (Vatican II) provided the context for the growth of liberation theology and inculturation theology. How this played out on the ground was determined by national and local structures and individuals.

In the case of Mexico, Kristin Norget explains both the growth of Oaxaca's pastoral indígena and its eventual retreat in terms of changes in the direction of the institutional Catholic Church over time. She argues that ideological shifts in the Vatican combined with altered church-state relations in Mexico have effectively undermined the religious support for indigenous movements in Oaxaca through the appointment of more conservative local bishops and the closing of key seminaries.

Local leadership also played a key role in Guatemala and Chiapas. The conservative Guatemalan archbishop Mario Casariego (1968–1983) severely limited the impact of inculturation theology during his tenure, while his successor, Próspero Penados del Barrio, encouraged it. Bishop Julio Cabrera accelerated the impact of inculturation theology after he was ordained as bishop of El Quiché in 1987. In Chiapas, Kovic points to the evolution of Bishop Samuel Ruiz's career as a critical leader in promoting indigenous theology.

The differing role of social Catholicism across time and national contexts also illustrates the need to condition generalizations about the impact of religious actors across cases. Bruce Calder notes that in Guatemala in the 1940s and 1950s, Catholic Action represented an attempt by the church to revitalize and restore orthodoxy to rural Catholicism while also combating the spread of socialist ideas. Edward Cleary notes that "reform Catholicism" was prevalent in Peru and Bolivia as well. According to Cleary, some liberationist missionaries went so far as to portray traditional indigenous practices as part of the ongoing mestizo dominance of Indians in the region.

In Chiapas, by contrast, the local church representatives were more open to, and in many cases encouraged, traditional indigenous expressions.[26] According to Kay Warren, even in the Guatemalan case, catechists trained through Catholic Action in the 1950s and 1960s have more recently attempted to revitalize elements of traditionalism, primarily as an attempt to reach a younger generation of indigenous practitioners.[27]

At another level of analysis, transnational and national economic structures and policies provide both the incentives for indigenous mobilization and a context that permits it. In many of our cases, state actors attempted to incorporate indigenous groups into national society through corporatist and populist forms of interest mediation. However, these projects lost economic, institutional, and ideological support with the onset of the debt crisis, eventual structural adjustment, privatization, decentralization, and other neo-liberal reforms.[28] Left without traditional sources of access to the state, indigenous groups made use of the resources available to them: religious institutions and resources, the increasing role of NGO's in previously state-led development projects, and a devolution of state power to local and municipal levels. Not surprisingly, they framed their demands in terms of the very language of political liberalization that had recently come into vogue in the region, complete with reference to constitutional rights and inclusiveness.

Out of these transnational connections, a transnational advocacy network developed around indigenous movements in Latin America.[29] Transnational advocacy networks include NGOs, scholarly networks, local social movements, and some international and national governmental organization and actors. According to Margaret E. Keck and Kathryn Sikkink, such networks tend to arise when local social movements find their access to the state or policy makers blocked. Local actors may then turn to the international realm to create and maintain pressure on their governments.[30]

In the case of indigenous movements we have examined, the transnational network includes the United Nations and the Organization of American States (through the declaration of 1993 to be the year of indigenous peoples, the International Labor Organization's Convention 169, and the United Nations and Organization of American States draft Declarations on Indigenous Rights), the Catholic Church (through regularly held bishops meetings, Catholic universities and seminaries, and the training of catechists), and scholarly networks (as evidenced in the role of the Barbados I and Barbados II meetings). As Keck and Sikkink point out, social movements that involve a vulnerable population and raise issues of legal equality and opportunity have been most successful in organizing effective transnational networks.[31] The movement for indigenous rights in Latin America meets both of these criteria.

An analysis of our cases suggests that the international "leverage politics" that transnational advocacy networks employ are most effective when regimes base their legitimacy in appeals to liberal ideals.[32] This schema allows us to understand why Peru's indigenous movement remained relatively underdeveloped under the Alberto Fujimori regime, despite the strong presence of the same precipitating factors that led to larger and more effective indigenous mobilization in other cases.[33]

One final catalyzing factor for indigenous mobilization is repression of religious leaders or church representatives. As John Booth has argued, religious organizations play a key role in rebellions because they generate grievances both through their ideology and through the victimization of their members.[34] In the cases of Guatemala, Paraguay, Chiapas, Peru, and Bolivia, we have seen this process repeated over time. As church leaders become the target of government repression and intimidation, local and transnational movements become energized to take up their cause.

Religion, Resource Mobilization, and Mediation

Across the cases covered in this volume, the common factors linking religion and indigenous mobilization are community building, resource mobilization, and a role for religious institutions and leaders as interlocutors in indigenous-state relationships. These are familiar themes for social movement theory and echo earlier findings from studies of the role of religion in the civil rights movement in the United States.[35] Our case studies provide ample evidence that many insights arising from this literature still ring true.

In numerous social movement studies, religious organizations have been found to provide the networks, skills, discretionary resources (time and effort of members), free spaces (free from the physical or ideological control of other powerful actors), and collective identity (shared sense of community) necessary to begin and maintain social movements.[36] We found evidence of each of these factors in the relations between religious actors and indigenous social movements.

In Ecuador, Alison Brysk notes that the Italy-based Salesian order worked closely with the Shuar, while Monseñor Leonidas Proaño (the "Bishop of the Indians") developed agricultural cooperatives in the highlands, began an Indian seminary, and lobbied to return church lands to indigenous groups. Kristin Norget and Christine Kovic point to similar processes in Mexico, with the promotion of mission houses, seminaries, workshops, as well as collective labor projects, health promotion programs, language programs, educational opportunities, peasant cooperatives, and community saving programs. In the case of Mexico, these church-based programs were often organized around indigenous customs of communalism. The Worker-Peasant-Student Coalition of the Isthmus of Tehuantepec (COCEI), the Truique Unified Movement for Struggle (MULT), and the Union for Indigenous Communities of the North Zone of the Isthmus (UCIZONI) in Oaxaca all owe some debt to the training and resources that came to the region through the pastoral indígena.[37] In Chiapas, Kovic outlines the religious ties in the emergence of indigenous organizations such as Xi' Nich' (The Ant) and Las Abejas (The Bees).

Edward Cleary's chapter on Bolivia and Peru illustrates the role that religious intellectual and cultural centers and indigenous catechists have played in developing the intellectual basis for indigenous political activism in those countries. As Cleary explains, indigenous catechists have become community leaders, in many cases nudging traditionally reticent indigenous communities into the more contentious public sphere. At the same time, a number of Catholic religious studies centers conducted field work in the region, producing high-quality research and a network of religious scholars and practitioners who began to weave calls for cultural liberation into their perspectives on liberation theology. Out of this movement for consciousness-raising emerged such social movements and organizations as the Katarists and the Confederation of Peasant Workers.

Key to all of the cases presented in this volume is the role of religious education. Cleary notes the role of the Adventist schools around Lake Titicaca in producing graduates who would go on to fill local and national leadership roles. In Ecuador, Mexico, Bolivia, and Peru, Catholic seminaries trained indigenous and non-indigenous priests who, in turn, trained catechists who would later go on to become community leaders and key organizers in indigenous social movements. In Guatemala the individuals trained under Catholic Action came to represent a new generation of leadership in indigenous communities. Some Protestant pastors (particularly Mayan Presbyterians) have also emerged as local and national indigenous leaders of the Mayan movement. Religious leaders also played a key role in the National Reconciliation Commission (CRN) and 1996 peace agreements in Guatemala.

One of the most controversial roles played by religious institutions in social movements is the role of mediator or interlocutor. In the Diocese of San

Cristóbal in Chiapas, Bishop Samuel Ruiz served as negotiator, mediator, and advocate for indigenous people. In Ecuador, church human rights and development agencies have pursued indigenous causes and served as intermediaries with the government in times of crisis. During the national protests of 1994, the church provided sanctuary to indigenous leaders and ultimately brokered the agreement that settled the protests. In Bolivia and Peru, Cleary argues that catechists formed critical networks and served as buffers between indigenous communities and state authorities. In each of these cases, the role of religious individuals and institutions as mediators also raises issues of conflict and co-optation.

Problems of Conflict and Co-optation

Any time significant resources are at stake in social movements or one group seeks to speak for another, the potential for both conflict and co-optation becomes greater.[38] As several of our chapters demonstrate, religiously based resources do not always translate into community building. Bruce Calder's evaluation of Catholic Action, the Christian Democratic Party, and the Maryknolls in Guatemala suggests that these actors were critical in providing the necessary resources to develop a new set of indigenous leaders in Guatemala. However, this process also bred conflict within the community, as it both challenged the traditional *cofradia* system and threatened local ladino interests.

The influx of evangelical missionaries into indigenous areas and the growth of Pentecostal Protestantism among indigenous peoples has also led to conflicts, many times over the very traditional religious practices that inculturation theology has reinvigorated.[39] Alison Brysk describes how Protestant missionaries in Ecuador have undermined indigenous "social capital" due to the fact that converts refuse to participate in the *minga* because the communal work is done on Sundays. Kristin Norget outlines similar lines of confrontation in Oaxaca, Mexico. The issues that arise from these conflicts present serious challenges for state and local authorities in terms of defining and protecting communal and individual citizenship rights.[40]

However, even this apparently clear line of conflict does not hold across all of our cases. René Harder Horst argues that in Paraguay, the Nivaklé and Ehlhit were able to maintain their traditional religious cosmologies after joining the Mennonite Colonies in the Chaco. The Mennonite and Anglican focus on translating the scriptures into native languages served as an impetus for later movements based in indigenous identity. In Guatemala, Garrard-Burnett documents the key role of Mayan Presbyterian leaders in the wider Pan-Mayan movement. Even in the case of Mexico, Norget confirms Christine Eber's findings that some evangelicals and traditionalists have negotiated mutually acceptable solutions to the issue of community service demanded by costumbre.[41]

While the conflicts initiated by outside religious involvement in indigenous communities can be potentially mediated, the question of co-optation is a much thornier issue. One perspective on the identity-based social movements that have proliferated in Latin America is that states encourage them because they are easily co-opted and represent a much less powerful challenge than class-based or popular movements.[42] Our contributions suggest that such broad characterizations may be overstated. State actors who actively seek alliances with religious organizations should be careful what they wish for.

The Paraguayan and Ecuadorian cases demonstrate the dilemmas faced by state actors who wish to use religious organizations to pursue their own agendas. In Paraguay, the Stroessner regime was frustrated as its traditional ally, the Catholic Church, began to turn against the regime and advocate indigenous rights. In the final analysis, Pope John Paul II's 1988 meeting with indigenous leaders at the Santa Teresita Mission in the Chaco played a key role in galvanizing international and internal opposition to Stroessner's regime. The Paraguayan case is not an exception.

In Ecuador, Alison Brysk raises the issue of Evangelical missionaries acting as delegated authorities of the state (a parallel with the case of Guatemala).[43] Brysk outlines the roles of the Summer Institute of Linguistics (SIL) and World Vision and concludes that the effect of these organizations is firmly ambiguous. On one hand, SIL's missions clearly aided the state in resource extraction and acculturation of indigenous groups. On the other hand, the missionaries provided their converts with social services and many of the basic skills that would later be used to promote their cause. World Vision, through contracts related to its humanitarian missions, initially fomented a series divisions and conflicts within some indigenous communities. However, the eventual results of the World Vision projects included greater indigenous input and representation in the development programs and greater cooperation with the Catholic Church and other NGOs. Some indigenous evangelicals involved in World Vision went on to become activists in Ecuador's indigenous rights movement.

Cleary's analysis of Peru and Bolivia confirms the image of religious missions as a double-edged sword for states seeking social control over their indigenous populations. In these countries, the short-range radio stations used in missionary work came to serve as key elements in the movement for the revindication of indigenous culture and the eventual political mobilization of Amayra and Guaraní people. Again, religious actors may relieve the state of costs by providing infrastructure (this time in terms of communications), but that infrastructure is used by indigenous groups to spread the news of their own rebellion against the state.

While it may be that governmental and elite actors in Latin America continue to perceive religious movements and identity-based indigenous movements as less threatening than traditional class alliances, an analysis of our cases suggests that they may wish to revise their opinions. As Amalia Pallares has recently argued in the context of Ecuador, the shift toward identity politics has strengthened indigenous movements, allowing them to effectively incorporate rather than reject many of the material concerns of earlier class-based movements.[44] Indigenous groups have made major strides in gaining official recognition and in increasing their political capacity. Religious actors, for their part, frequently act on their own agendas and impact the process of indigenous mobilization in unexpected ways.

MILESTONES AND CHALLENGES
TO THE INDIGENOUS RESURGENCE

What are the goals of the indigenous movements we have examined in this volume? The primary goals that cross cases include conservation and respect for indigenous cultures and value systems, self-determination, and political reform (generally defined in terms of land rights, communal labor, and traditional modes of government and law). The obstacles that stand between Latin America's indigenous movements and these goals are formidable. Despite legal and institutional support from international organizations and nongovernmental organizations, indigenous demands for the recognition of communal rights remain at odds with the dominant neo-liberal agenda in Latin America. As Rodolfo Stavenhagen and Rachel Sieder have pointed out, the primary demands of indigenous movements in Latin America regarding cultural autonomy, customary law, land rights, and alternative development policies cut to the core of long-standing assimilationist development projects, widely held notions of national identity, and neo-liberal policy prescriptions.[45] What Sieder calls the indigenous "politics of difference" demands nothing less than a redefinition of citizenship in the region, an extremely ambitious agenda given the complexities of legal pluralism, the potential for inter-ethnic conflict, and the long-standing challenges to equitable development in Latin America.[46]

The indigenous agenda represents a double threat to traditional notions of state sovereignty in Latin America because it challenges both the norm of non-intervention (through claims to universal human and cultural rights) and the notion of the existing nation-state (through claims to national sovereignty for Indian peoples). This may be one of the most serious and understudied dilemmas facing all nation-states with significant indigenous populations.[47] The fact that the "indigenous question" is on the national agenda at all in many Latin American countries can be interpreted as a victory in itself.

Given the clear challenges to the status quo involved in Latin America's indigenous movements, the degree to which they have recently succeeding in meeting some goals is extraordinary. Significant advances have been made in terms of gaining international recognition and constitutional protection of indigenous rights through the International Labor Organization's Convention 169, the United Nations and Organization of American States draft Declarations on Indigenous Rights, and changes during the 1990s in the constitutional language of Bolivia, Colombia, Ecuador, Mexico, Nicaragua, Paraguay, Peru, and Venezuela to recognize indigenous rights.[48] For the local and transnational indigenous groups working to pursue autonomy, cultural rights, and reform, translating legal recognition into effective legislation and policy is the challenge that lies ahead.

As we noted earlier, the process of globalization and some of the policy prescriptions of neo-liberalism have opened certain opportunities for indigenous movements in Latin America. First, as Kristin Norget has demonstrated, administrative decentralization and devolution of power to the departmental or municipal level has created the possibility for greater ethnic and territorial autonomy for indigenous groups in Latin America.[49] In particular, the cases of Bolivia, Columbia, and Ecuador suggest that a political opportunity structure that combines a severe governmental legitimacy crisis with elite-driven movements for reform may provide an opening for indigenous groups to effectively insert their agenda into national and constitutional dialogue.[50] In the comparative section of his chapter, Cleary uses a similar argument based on opportunity structure to explain the strength and achievements of Bolivia's indigenous rights movement relative to Peru. While the church played a key role in aiding indigenous rights movements in both countries, the context of civil war and authoritarian politics under the Fujimori regime in Peru limited openings for effective national organizing. Cleary is quick to note, however, that local indigenous organizing has also taken place in Peru in the form of the *rondas campesinas* in the northern Andes and through other groups in the Amazon.

Second, as state programs such as Mexico's National Indigenista Institute (INI) lose funding due to government downsizing and budget shortfalls, international and local NGOs play a larger role in providing resources in indigenous areas.[51] In many cases, the NGOs have years of experience working with indigenous communities and have ideological positions that coincide with indigenous agendas (or at least are less overtly assimilationist than state-directed projects).[52]

Finally, the process of globalization has opened opportunities for NGOs and indigenous organizations to expand their networks and ties across borders.[53] Alison Brysk, Kay Warren, and others have documented the transnational networks that increasingly link national and local movements for indigenous rights.[54] This is a fertile ground for further research, as it crosses the traditional boundaries separating comparative and international politics and raises questions that can breathe new life into international relations theory.

Despite these openings, the concrete effects of neo-liberalism on indigenous communities in Latin America has been far from positive, as states have cut social services, eliminated agricultural subsidies, privatized land markets, and ended support for the peasant federations that had previously connected indigenous groups to the state.[55] These changes have challenged traditional indigenous survival strategies and brought widespread suffering and discontent. From an extremely pessimistic perspective, we could conclude that the shift toward identity politics represents an "atomization" of society, making it more individualized and amenable to market initiatives.[56] Our findings suggest, however, that to draw such a determinist conclusion would seriously underestimate the fluidity and adaptability of religious and indigenous identity-based social movements in Latin America.

THE OUTCOME IS IN THE IDENTITY: FLEXIBLE IDENTITIES AND FLUID MARKETS

As social scientists, our biases in evaluating the outcomes of social movements tend toward measurable and comparable structural and macro-social effects. Both the structural accomplishments of and the structural impediments to indigenous movements in Latin America are formidable. However, if we are to heed Kay Warren's call to drop the "unified social movement paradigm," we must also reconsider the tools we use to evaluate the outcomes of social movements. As Warren explains, "There will be no demonstrations to count because this is not a mass movement that generates protest. But there will be new generations of students, leaders, teachers, development workers, and community elders who have been touched in one way or another by the Pan-Mayan movement and its cultural production."[57] The existence of this "cultural production" may be considered one of the most important outcomes of the interface between religion and indigenous groups in Latin America.

While many of Latin America's indigenous movements *have* generated effective demonstrations as part of their political strategy (Ecuador, Bolivia, and Mexico are prime examples), Warren's point about education is the deeper issue. All of our cases provide evidence to support the notion that indigenous "cultural production" has been facilitated through the proliferation of pastoral training, catechists, research centers, and other forms of religious education among the indigenous population. The indigenous may choose to take their training out into the streets in protest or into their churches, jobs, and homes.

And this is where we must expand our level of analysis when we evaluate the role of religion in identity-based social movements to include the realm of personal and individual empowerment. As Anna Peterson, Manual Vasquez, and Philip Williams explain, "Everyday forms of citizenship fostered by religion, such as local, national, and transnational social movements, respond creatively to larger processes, helping individuals and their families and neighborhoods resist or accommodate."[58] Religion infuses social movements with symbols, narratives, and other shared meanings that form a basis for common identity. To gain a sense of common identity and the empowerment that accompanies it may be considered an achievement in itself, given the social, political, and economic forces at work fracturing traditional ways of life in Latin America.[59]

Daniel Levine and Scott Mainwaring have also emphasized this point, arguing, "People learn about politics and religion, not only through explicit messages, but also through the implicit models of good societies and proper behavior that they encounter in the contexts of daily routine. As these contexts change, legitimations of power and authority are reworked."[60] Critical values such as social trust and community solidarity emerge out of such activities on a day-to-day basis.[61] In other words, shared identity has something to do with a shared way of living and acting in the world. Religion, in all of its plural forms in Latin America, offers the resources necessary to maintain such identities.

Learning to Listen to Multiple Resurgent Voices

This brings us full circle to our discussion of syncretism and hybridism, now in the context of religious pluralism in Latin America. The fluidity of the Latin American religious market means that "being Indian" can have multiple religious meanings. René Harder Horst's chapter on Paraguay provides a useful illustration of this fluidity. As Horst explains, the Nivaklé people were more than willing to move between Mennonite and Catholic missions, depending on the resources available to them. The Enlhit, too, converted en masse from Anglicanism to the New Tribes Mission, only to return to the Anglican Church when access to resources changed. Throughout the process, Horst argues, the Enlhit quietly maintained elements of their traditional spirituality.

The scenario Horst describes has played out at the individual and group level throughout Latin America. It is partly for this reason that Manuel Vasquez warns us not to fall into a reductive understanding of religious movements in Latin America, attempting to boil them down into their class or ethnic elements so that we can produce broad generalizations about their political effects.[62] The cross-fertilization between religions and the increasing Pentecostalization of religious practice in Latin America render such generalizations increasingly useless. Rather, as David Smilde has recently argued, we must accept that "there is no single Latin American Evangelicalism or Catholicism when it comes to politics (or any other issue for that matter). There are only Evangelicalisms and Catholicisms. Different Evangelical and Catholic actors pursue different, even contradictory political (as well as religious) goals."[63] We could add that there is no single "Indian" in Latin America either. Rather, there are many "Indians," who are, as Lois Ann Lorentzen explains, "again transforming religious traditions and indigenous beliefs, making them their own."[64]

As we listen to the "resurgent voices" of indigenous peoples in the Americas, we must also avoid the temptation to romanticize their struggle or to imbue it with our own goals and aspirations. While indigenous worldviews may promote communitarian values and more sustainable agricultural practices, to charge them with the task of using these views to alter the national political landscape is far too heavy a burden. Like all forms of political organization and authority, indigenous communities and indigenous movements struggle with their own issues of power. A number of investigators have noted that increasing local autonomy in indigenous communities may also reinforce existing clientalist networks, increase discrimination against perceived outgroups, and hinder progress in terms of gender equality.[65] As Jeffrey Rubin argues, ambiguous and contradictory positions on these issues may even be a prime source of the strength of some indigenous social movements.[66]

Acknowledging the complexity of the subject in no way implies that we cannot apply the methods of social science to understand the relationships between religion and social movements or that there are not important comparisons to be drawn and generalizations to be made. From the level of family, gender, and local politics to the level of transnational networks, understanding the connections between religion and indigenous politics requires careful attention to the details of contexts, networks, time frames, beliefs, religious organizations, religious practices, and political and social relationships. In the words of Daniel Levine, "The key point for analysis is to avoid reifying a particular unit or orientation, freezing it in time and treating it as once and forever the same."[67]

In sum, understanding the impetus for the resurgent voice of indigenous mobilization requires a multi-layered analysis that accounts for ideological framing, resource mobilization, variance in institutional and other religious factors over time, and local, national, and international opportunity structure. Indigenous movements are now among the most important new political actors in Latin America. They have achieved this status by taking advantage of a unique convergence of political openings, economic and social changes, and ideological and material resources available through religious organizations. This process unfolded over nearly forty years, and the effects will continue to shape the face of Latin American politics for many years to come.

We conclude on a cautionary, yet hopeful note. Latin America's forty million Indians have recently made major strides in gaining official recognition and rights. Religious institutions, resources, and communities have played a major role and have been changed, themselves, by the process. But the story does not end here. Severe inequality, grinding poverty, and institutionalized racism continue to characterize Latin America's political and social landscape. As indigenous peoples struggle to translate their gains into concrete political and economic changes, religion will continue to play a critical role. The increasingly fluid forms of practice and beliefs that make up Latin America's religious geography will have their greatest impact where they always have, at the level of lived reality of Latin America's poor and indigenous populations.

NOTES

1. See Walt Rostow, *The Stages of Economic Growth: A Non-Communist Manifesto* (Cambridge: Cambridge University Press, 1960); and N. J. Smelser, *Social Change in the Industrial Revolution* (London: Routledge, 1958).

2. See Daniel Levine, *Popular Voices in Latin American Catholicism* (Princeton: Princeton University Press, 1992).

3. As Virginia Garrard-Burnett explains in this volume, *costumbre* describes "the body of locally prescribed religious belief, ritual, dress, language, and lifeways" of being Mayan.

4. See Charles Stewart, "Syncretism and Its Synonyms: Reflections on Cultural Mixture," *Diacritics* 29 (fall 1999): 40–62; Nederveen Pieterse, "Globalization as Hybridization," *International Sociology* 9 (1994): 161–184; Ulf Hannerz, "The World in Creolization," *Africa* 57 (1987); Aylward Shorter, *Toward a Theology of Inculturation* (New York: Maryknoll, 1988); André Droogers, "Recovering and Reconstructing Syncretism," in *Reinventing Religions: Syncretism and Transformation in Africa and the Americas*, ed. Sidney M. Greenfield and André Droogers (Maryland: Lanham, Rowman and Littlefield Publishers, 2001); Stephen L. Selka Jr., "Religious Synthesis and Change in the New World: Syncretism, Revitalization, and Conversion" (Florida Atlantic University, Boca Raton, Masters thesis, 1997).

5. Stewart, "Syncretism," 41.

6. Ibid., 58.

7. See Charles Stewart and Rosalind Shaw, eds., *Syncretism / Anti-Syncretism: The Politics of Religious Synthesis* (London: Routledge, 1994), 7–21. Also see Selka, "Religious Synthesis," 14.

8. André Droogers, "Syncretism: The Problem of Definition, the Definition of the Problem," in *Dialogue and Syncretism: An Interdisciplinary Approach,* ed. J. Gort, H. Vroom, R. Fernhout, and A. Vessels (Grand Rapids: Eerdmans, 1989) 13–14. For examples of practical treatments of this issue, see Jean Comaroff, *Body of Power, Spirit of Resistance : The Culture and History of a South African People* (Chicago: University of Chicago Press, 1985). Also see Sabine MacCormack, *Religion in the Andes: Vision and Imagination in Early Colonial Peru* (Princeton: Princeton University Press, 1991).

9. André Droogers and Sidney M. Greenfield, "Recovering and Reconstructing Syncretism," in *Reinventing Religions*, ed. Greenfield and Droogers, 21–42.

10. Stewart, "Syncretism," 44.

11. Underlying these concepts is a separate problematic assumption that there exists some prior cultural or religious form that was not hybrid or Creole. Since most analysts accept the notion that all religious and cultural forms engage in some degree of cross-cultural borrowing, this debate can, at times, appear impossibly self-referential and self-defeating. See Stewart, "Syncretism," 45. Also see Ulf Hannarz, "American Culture: Creolized, Creolizing," in *American Culture: Creolized, Creolizing*, ed. Erik Asared (Uppsala: Swedish Institute of North American Studies, University of Uppsala, 1988), 7–30.

12. Lois Ann Lorentzen, "Who Is an Indian? Religion, Globalization, and Chiapas," in *Religions / Globalizations: Theories and Cases,* ed. Dwight N. Hopkins, Lois Ann Lorentzen, Eduardo Mendieta, and David Batstone (Durham and London: Duke University Press, 2001) 84–102. Also see Kay B. Warren and Jeanne E. Jackson, *Indigenous Movements, Self-Representation, and the State in Latin America* (Austin: University of Texas Press, 2003).

13. See David Lehmann, "Fundamentalism and Globalism," *Third World Quarterly* 12, no. 4 (1998): 611–613 for a critique of this kind of essentialism. Also see Nina Laurie, Robert Andolina, and Sarah Radcliffe, "The Excluded 'Indigenous'? The Implications of Multi-Ethnic Policies for Water Reform in Bolivia," in *Multiculturalism in Latin America: Indigenous Rights, Diversity, and Democracy*, ed. Rachel Sieder (New York: Palgrave Macmillan, 2002), 252–276.

14. This is one of the key questions informing the David Stoll and Rigoberta Mechú controversy. See David Stoll, *Rigoberta Menchu and the Story of All Poor Guatemalans* (New York: Westview, 2001). It was also a key issue at the Barbados II conference in 1979, when indigenous leaders criticized anthropologists for presuming to speak for them. See Charles Hale, "Cultural Politics of Identity in Latin America," *Annual Review of Anthropology* 26, no. 6 (1997): 567–590.

15. Bruce Calder's chapter reminds us that this dilemma is far from new, as foreign missionaries in Guatemala in the 1950s allowed anti-ladino prejudice to impact their work among the Maya.

16. For an example of the more critical approach, see Hans Siebers, "Globalization and Religious Creolization among the Q'eqchi'es of Guatemala," in *Latin American Religion in Motion*, ed. Christian Smith and Joshua Prokopy (New York: Routledge, 1999).

17. See Selka, "Religious Synthesis," 14.

18. See Andrew Canessa, "Contesting Hybridity: Evangelistas and Kataristas in Highland Bolivia," *Journal of Latin American Studies* 32, no. 1 (2000): 115.

19. See David Batstone, Eduardo Mendieta, Lous Ann Lorentzen, and Dwight N. Hopins, eds., *Liberation Theologies, Post-modernity, and the Americas* (London and New York: Routledge, 1997).

20. This argument has been articulated most completely by Anthony Gill. See Anthony Gill, *Rendering unto Caesar: The Catholic Church and the State in Latin America* (Chicago and London: University of Chicago Press, 1998).

21. Christian Smith, *The Emergence of Liberation Theology: Radical Religion and Social Movement Theory* (Chicago: University of Chicago Press, 1991). Smith borrows the concept of insurgent consciousness from earlier work on social movements conducted by Doug McAdam, *Political Process and the Development of Black Insurgency, 1930–1970* (Chicago: University of Chicago Press, 1982). Also see Charles Tilly, *From Mobilization to Revolution* (Reading, Mass.: Addison-Wesley, 1978).

22. See David A. Snow, "Frame Alignment Processes, Micromobilization, and Movement Participation," *American Sociological Review* 51 (1986): 464–481; and David A. Snow and Robert D. Benford, "Ideology, Frame Resonance, and Participant Mobilization," in *International Social Movements Research*, vol. 1 (Greenwich: JAI Press, 1988), 197–217. Also see Christian Smith, *Disruptive Religion: The Force of Faith in Social Movement Activism* (New York: Routledge, 1996). For an example of frame theory applied to evangelicals in Latin America, see David Smilde, "El Clamor por Venezuela: Latin American Evangelicalism as a Collective Action Frame," in *Latin American Religion in Motion: Tracking Innovation, Unexpected Change, and Complexity*, ed. Christian Smith and Joshua Prokopy (New York and London: Routledge Press, 1999), 125–145.

23. See Timothy J. Steigenga and David Smilde, "Wrapped in the Holy Shawl: The Strange Case of Conservative Christians and Gender Equality in Latin America," in *Latin American Religion in Motion: Tracking Innovation, Unexpected Change, and Complexity*, ed. Christian Smith and Joshua Prokopy (New York and London: Routledge Press, 1999), 173–186.

24. For an example of such an overview, see Charles Hale, "Cultural Politics of Identity in Latin America," *Annual Review of Anthropology* 26, no. 6 (1997): 567–590.

25. Ibid., 567.

26. Christine Eber, *Women and Alcohol in a Highland Maya Town: Water of Hope, Water of Sorrow* (Austin: University of Texas Press, 1995), 223.

27. Kay B. Warren, *Indigenous Movements and Their Critics: Pan-Maya Activism in Guatemala* (Princeton: Princeton University Press, 1998), 180–191.

28. Deborah J. Yashar, "Contesting Citizenship: Indigenous Movements and Democracy in Latin America," *Comparative Politics* 31 (October 1998): 23–42. Also see Deborah J. Yashar, "Democracy, Indigenous Movements, and the Postliberal Challenge in Latin America," *World Politics* 52 (1999): 76–104; and Deborah J. Yashar, "Indigenous Protest and Democracy in Latin America," in *Constructing Democratic Governance: Latin America and the Caribbean in the 1990s,* ed. Jorge Dominguez and Abraham Lowenthal (Baltimore: Johns Hopkins University Press, 1996), 87–122.

29. Margaret E. Keck and Kathryn Sikkink, *Activists beyond Borders: Advocacy Networks in International Politics* (Ithaca and London: Cornell University Press, 1998).

30. Ibid., 9–12.

31. Ibid., 27.

32. Ibid., 23, 205.

33. See Edward Cleary's comparison of Peru and Bolivia, contained in this volume.

34. John A. Booth, "Theories of Religion and Rebellion: The Central American Experience," paper presented at the Midwestern Political Science Association Meeting, Chicago, 1991, 5.

35. McAdam, *Political Process.* Also see Mayer N. Zald, "Theological Crucibles: Social Movements in and of Religion," *Review of Religious Research* 23, no. 4 (1982), for a review of some of this literature.

36. On resource mobilization see John D. McCarthy and Mayer N. Zald, "Resources Mobilization and Social Movements: A Partial Theory," *American Journal of Sociology* 82 (May 1977): 1212–1239; Anthony Oberschall, *Social Conflict and Social Movements* (New York: Prentice Hall, 1973); Charles Tilly, *From Mobilization to Revolution* (Reading, Mass.: Addison Wesley, 1978). For arguments relating to "social capital" see Andrew Greely, "The Other Civic America: Religion and Social Capital," *The American Prospect* 32 (1997): 68–73. For comprehensive reviews of identity-based social movements, see Francesca Polletta and James M. Jasper, "Collective Identity and Social Movements," *American Review of Sociology* 27 (August 2001): 283. Also see Darren E. Sherkat and Christopher G. Ellison, "Recent Developments and Current Controversies in the Sociology of Religion," *Annual Review of Sociology* 25 (1999): 363–394.

37. For an overview of COCEI, see Jeffrey Rubin, "Ambiguity and Contradiction in a Radical Popular Movement," in *Cultures of Politics / Politics of Cultures*, ed. Sonia E. Alvarez, Evelina Dagnino, and Arturo Escobar (Boulder: Westview, 1997), 141–163.

38. Gary H. Gossen's self-reflective study of the Maya in Mexico suggests that the role of non-indigenous interlocutors may actually be a part of indigenous culture. Gossens distills three themes that he sees as characterizing the deep roots of Mayan ways of thinking and acting. First, the Mayan view of the world is fundamentally opaque, and thus there is a constant need for individuals who can interpret it. Second, the Mayan conception of co-essences or co-spirits that are apart from the individual but to which one's destiny is linked invokes a degree of fatalism in the Mayan worldview. Third, the concept of the non-Mayan "other" playing a role in the community may be a central element of Mayan identity. Extrapolating from these themes, Gossens argues that Mayan social movements (such as the Zapatistas) may seek non-Mayans as public representatives precisely because of their identity as Mayans. See Gary H. Gossen, *Telling Maya Tales: Tzotzíl Identities in Modern Mexico* (New York and London: Routledge, 1999), 253–263.

39. Manuel A. Vasquez, "Toward a New Agenda for the Study of Religion in the Americas," *Journal of Interamerica Studies and World Affairs* 41, no. 4 (winter 1999): 1–20.

40. See Raquel Yrigoyen, *Pautas de coordinación entre el derecho indígena y el derecho estatal* (Guatemala: Fucanción Myrna Mack, 1999). Also see Guillermo de la Peña, "Social Citizenship, Ethnic Minority Demands, Human Rights, and Neoliberal Paradoxes: A Case Study in Western Mexico," in *Multiculturalism in Latin America*, ed. Rachel Sieder, 131–133, for a fascinating case study surrounding these issues in Jalisco, Mexico.

41. Christine Eber, "Buscando una nueva vida: Liberation through Autonomy in San Pedro Chenalhó, 1970–1998," *Latin American Perspectives* 28, no. 2 (2001): 45–72.

42. N. Larson, "Postmodernism and Imperialism: Theory and Politics in Latin America," in *The Postmodern Debate in Latin America,* ed. John Beverly, José Oviedo, and Michael Aronna (Durham: Duke University Press, 1995), 110–134.

43. See David Stoll, *Is Latin America Turning Protestant? The Politics of Evangelical Growth* (Berkely: University of California Press, 1990).

44. Amalia Pallares, *From Peasant Struggles to Indian Resistance: The Ecuadorian Andes in the Late Twentieth Century* (Norman: University of Oklahoma Press, 2002).

45. See Sieder, ed., *Multiculturalism in Latin America.*

46. Ibid., 4–13.

47. The Quebec issue in Canada and the role of indigenous actors in the sovereignty debate illustrate the complicated dilemmas associated with this question. See Kent R. Weaver, ed., *The Collapse of Canada?* (Washington, D.C.: Brookings Institution, 1992).

48. See Donna Lee Van Cott, *The Friendly Liquidation of the Past: The Politics of Diversity in Latin America* (Pittsburgh: University of Pittsburgh Press, 2000), for an analysis of this process.

49. Donna Lee Van Cott, "Constitutional Reform in the Andes: Redefining Indigenous-State Relations," in *Multiculturalism in Latin America,* ed. Sieder, 45–73. Also see Van Cott, *The Friendly Liquidation of the Past,* chapter 4.

50. Van Cott, "Constitutional Reform in the Andes," 45–46.

51. Guillermo de la Peña, "Social Citizenship, Ethnic Minority Demands, Human Rights, and Neoliberal Paradoxes: A Case Study in Western Mexico," in *Multiculturalism in Latin America*, ed. Sieder, 131–133.

52. Of course religious NGOs may have their own agendas, some of which correspond conveniently with the general state retreat from responsibility for social and economic welfare in the region.

53. Walter Mignolo, "Globalizations, Civilization Processes, and the Relocation of Languages and Cultures," in *The Cultures of Globalization,* ed. Fredric Jameson and Masao Miyoshi (Durham: Duke University Press, 1998), 44–51.

54. See Warren, *Indigenous Movements and Their Critics.* Also see Alison Brysk, *From Tribal Village to Global Village: Indian Rights and International Relations in Latin America* (Stanford: Stanford University Press, 2000).

55. Yashar, "Democracy, Indigenous Movements, and the Postliberal Challenge," 85.

56. Sonia E. Alvarez, Evelina Dagnino, and Arturo Escobar, "Introduction: The Cultural and the Political in Latin American Social Movements," in *Cultures of Politics, Politics of Cultures: Re-visioning Latin American Social Movements*, ed. Sonia E. Alvarez, Evelina Dagnino, Arturo Escobar (Boulder: Westview Press, 1998), 1–32.

57. Kay B. Warren, "Indigenous Movements as a Challenge to the Unified Social Movement Paradigm for Guatemala," in *Cultures of Politics*, ed. Alvarez, Dagnino, and Escobar, 165–195.

58. Anna Peterson, Manual Vasquez, Philip Williams, "The Global and the Local," in *Christianity, Social Change, and Globalization in the Americas*, ed. Anna L. Peterson, Manuel A. Vasquez, Philip J. Williams (New Brunswick: Rutgers University Press, 2001), 219.

59. See Daniel H. Levine and David Stoll, "Bridging the Gap between Empowerment

and Power," in *Transnational Religion: Fading States*, ed. Susanne Hoeber Rudolph and James Piscatori (Boulder, Colo.: Westview Press, 1997), 63–103, for a more complete statement of this argument.

60. Daniel H. Levine and Scott Mainwaring, "Religion and Popular Protest," in *Power and Popular Protest: Latin American Social Movements*, ed. Susan Eckstein (Berkeley: University of California Press, 2000), 203–240.

61. Robert Putnam terms these values as "social capital." See Robert Putnam, *Making Democracy Work: Civic Traditions in Modern Italy* (Princeton: Princeton University Press, 1993).

62. Vasquez, "Toward a New Agenda."

63. David Smilde, "Evangelicals and Politics in Latin America: Moving beyond Monolithic Portraits," *History of Religions* 42, no. 3 (2003): 245.

64. Lorentzen, "Who Is an Indian?" 99.

65. See Yashar "Democracy, Indigenous Movements, and the Postliberal Challenge," 96. Also see Rubin, "Ambiguity and Contradiction," 141–163.

66. Rubin, "Ambiguity and Contradiction," 160.

67. Levine, *Popular Voices*, 373.

CONTRIBUTORS

ALISON BRYSK revised her Stanford doctoral dissertation into *The Politics of Human Rights in Argentina*, a widely acclaimed book. Later she published *From Tribal Village to Global Village: Indian Rights and International Relations in Latin America* and an edited volume, *Globalization and Human Rights*. She is an associate professor of political science at the University of California, Irvine.

VIRGINIA GARRARD-BURNETT received her history doctorate at Tulane University and is lecturer in Latin American studies at the University of Texas, Austin. She authored *Protestantism in Guatemala: Living in the New Jerusalem* and numerous other works, especially dealing with Protestantism in Latin America.

BRUCE J. CALDER is professor of history at the University of Illinois, Chicago. His first research in Guatemala was conducted with Richard Adams and resulted in *Crecimiento y cambio de la Iglesia guatemalteca, 1944–1966*. He then published a highly acclaimed history of the effects of U.S. intervention in the Dominican Republic. He is currently working on a comprehensive history of the Catholic Church in Guatemala.

EDWARD L. CLEARY, O.P., is professor of political science and director of Latin American Studies at Providence College. He was president of the Bolivian Institute of Social Study and Action and edited *Estudios Andinos*. He is author of *The Struggle for Human Rights in Latin America, Crisis and Change,* and other works.

RENÉ HARDER HORST teaches history at Appalachian State University. He received his Ph.D. at Indiana University, writing his dissertation on religion in Paraguay. In 2003 he published "Consciousness and Contradiction: Indigenous Peoples and Paraguay's Transition to Democracy" in *Contemporary Indigenous Movements in Latin America,* edited by Erick Langer and Elena Muñoz.

STEPHEN P. JUDD, M.M., directs the Instituto de Idiomas, Cochabamba, Bolivia. He worked with indigenous peoples in Peru and Bolivia for a number of years, served on the General Council, Maryknoll, and obtained a Ph.D. at the Graduate Theological Union, Berkeley, writing on southern Peru.

CHRISTINE KOVIC, associate professor of anthropology at the University of Houston, Clear Lake, obtained her doctorate at the City University of New York. She has conducted extensive research in Chiapas, Mexico. She is co-editor and co-author of a forthcoming work on women and religion in Chiapas and other publications.

KRISTIN NORGET, associate professor of anthropology at McGill University, Montreal, has focused her work for several years on the Oaxacan region of Mexico. She has published on the impact of liberation theology in Oaxaca.

TIMOTHY J. STEIGENGA is an associate professor of political science and Latin American studies at the Wilkes Honors College of Florida Atlantic University. He received his Ph.D. from the University of North Carolina in Chapel Hill. He is author of *The Politics of the Spirit: The Political Implications of Pentecostalized Religion in Costa Rica and Guatemala* and numerous other works on religion and politics in Latin America.

INDEX

Las Leyes de las Indias, 6
liberation theology, 8–12, 45, 48–51, 59,
 93, 101–105, 126, 127, 154–156, 158–
 159, 161–162, 170, 172–174, 176, 179–
 180, 187, 189–190, 193, 195, 199–201,
 212, 214–216, 221, 225, 232, 237–238,
 241
liberals, Guatemala, 94, 117
Library of Congress, 49
Library of Ethnography, Bolivia, 51
Llanque, Domingo, 12, 221
Loaysa, Jerónimo de, 6
Lona Reyes, Arturo 154, 160–162, 164,
 167, 174–175, 177
López Bac, Ernestina, 140
López Hernández, Eleazar, 12, 175, 214,
 222–223, 227, 228
López, Carlos Antonio, 79
López Levy, Marcelo, 57
López Trujillo, Alfonso, 172
Lorentzen, Lois Ann, 75, 233, 247
Loyola University, 98
Lumen Gentium, 132

Macas, Luis, 30, 31
Madrid, Miguel de la, 201
Mahuad, Jamil, 17
Mainwairing, Scott, 247
Mak'a, 67
Mam, 139, 142
Mamani Barnabé, Vicenta, 224, 227
Mames, 192
Mapuche, 215
Marandú Project, 74–75
Marbury-Lewis, David, 16
Margaritas Las, 195
María Auxiliadora Mission, 82
Marist Congregation, 194–195
Marxist guerrillas, 58
Maryknoll Society, 1, 2, 48, 97, 105, 215–
 216, 226, 242
Marzal, Manuel, 48
Mascara Roja La, 203
Maskoy. *See* Toba-Maskoy
Mataco-Mataguayo, 67

Maya national movement (also called
 movimiento maya or Pan Maya Movement), 15, 93, 105, 125–146
Mayan: cosmovision, 136–139; cultural
 and political mobilization, 105–107;
 cultural survival, 94; Mayan Holocaust,
 127–128, 131; immigrant community,
 3; priests, 2; religion, 94, 125–146;
 revindication, 18, 102, 110, 130,
 236–243; students and seminary, 112;
 theology, 139–140. *See also* indigenous:
 theology
Mayanization, 102
Mburuvicha, 57
Mbyá, 66, 72, 81, 87
McGourn, Francis, 48, 51
McGrath-Andino, Lester, 60
Medellín Conference, 9, 68, 72, 102, 114,
 132–133, 159, 199, 211, 216, 225
mediation, religious, 240–242
Mejía Víctores, 200
Meliá, Bartomeu, 72–74
Menchú Tum, Rigoberta, 29, 129, 217
Mennonite, 66, 68–71, 74–78, 81, 85,
 242
Messiah mechanism, 60
mestizo, 8
Methodist, 224
Mexican Constitution: Article 27, 163
Mexican model for indigenous, 67
Mexican peasants, 76
Meyer, Brigit, 78
Míguez Bonino, José, 10
military coup, Ecuador, 31, 34
Miller, Elmer, 71
Milky Way, 138, 145
Ministry of Peasant Affairs, Bolivia, 53
Ministry of Social Welfare and Land
 Reform, Ecuador, 29
missionaries: Catholic and Protestant,
 twentieth century, 8, 10, 44–45, 47, 50,
 97–101
Mixtec, 5
mobilization: Mayan, 101–109
modernization theorists, 231

CPSIA information can be obtained
at www.ICGtesting.com
Printed in the USA
LVHW100608051122
732397LV00004B/34

9 780813 534619